KETO CHAFFLE
RECIPES COOKBOOK

Discover 800 Simple Mouth-Watering Waffle Ideas to
Definitively Forget Bread, Pizza and Sandwiches.
Stick with Low Carb Diets Won't Be a Pain Anymore

AMY DELAUER

Table Of Contents

CHAPTER 2: BREAKFAST AND BRUNCH 51

Introduction

Ketogenic diets are becoming increasingly popular, especially among people who want to lose weight. Keto diets are high-fat, low-carbohydrate dietary patterns that help the body burn fat as its primary source of fuel.

Keto chaffles are a delicious new product taking the keto community by storm. They are so popular with low-carb and keto ways of life because they taste like a waffle, crunch, and everything.

The basic ones are low-carb, sugar-free, and gluten-free waffles made with a batter mix of eggs and cheese, baked in a chaffle iron. This straightforward keto formula is fresh, brilliant dark-colored, sugar-free, low-carb, and exceptionally simple to make. Chaffles are turning into an extremely well-known keto/low-carb nibble.

They are currently the best low-carb bread substitute that's perfect for those who are following a keto program or any other low-carb diet. In fact, one of the most common difficulties when you want to lose weight with these kinds of diets, is just to eliminate foods such as sandwiches, hamburgers, and classic waffles that we love as much as they are rich in carbohydrates. The temptation to eat these foods is always there, ready to vanquish the efforts made to follow your diet. Chaffles are the winning weapon to defeat these temptations. They are simply as tasty as bread or waffles but without carbohydrates! That's why I consider them as game-changer. They are the element that will allow you to stick to your diet and make you forget the craving you had for fast foods.

What is Ketogenic Diet

The ketogenic diet is a low-carb, high-fat diet. This means that the macronutrient ratio of your diet should be made up of mostly fat and protein with only a small percentage of carbohydrates.

The idea behind the Ketogenic diet is that you can force your body into using fat rather than glucose as the main fuel source. When we are in ketosis, we can function off of almost any source of fuel.

A ketogenic diet induces the body to use fat instead of carbohydrates for nutrition, resulting in creating ketone bodies by the liver. Reduce your carbohydrate intake to a minimum, which may result in some reactions. It is not, however, a high-protein diet. It consists of a moderate-protein, low-carbohydrate, and high-fat diet. The exact percentage of macronutrients depends on your requirements. Fats account for 60% of the calories you consume, making them an essential part of your diet, while protein accounts for 30% and carbohydrates for 10%.

Proteins, carbohydrates, and fats are used by the body throughout certain cases. This diet removes carbohydrates, depleting the system's reserves and forcing the body to find another source of energy.

Ketone bodies are generated as a by-product of insufficient free fatty acid disintegration. Fat derived from non-carbohydrate sources is used by organs such as the brain to provide energy. Ketosis occurs as a result of the rapid production of ketone bodies, which causes them to accumulate in the blood. In addition, the amount of glucose produced and used in your system is decreased, as is the amount of protein used for energy.

Ketogenic diets affect glucagon and glucose levels. Insulin converts glucose to glycogen, which is then recycled as fat, while glucagon converts glycogen to glucose, which fuels the system. Removing carbohydrates from the diet raises glucagon levels and lowers insulin levels. This, in turn, causes a rise in FFA liberation and decomposition in the liver, resulting in the development of ketone bodies and the induction of ketosis.

The diet is similar to starvation in several ways, with the exception that food is consumed in one. The metabolic changes that occur and the modifications during malnutrition are similar to those that occur during a diet. The reaction to complete hunger has been extensively studied, perhaps more so than the diet on its own. As a result, most of the data presented come from fasting individuals' analyses. There are a few exceptions, but the metabolic effects of the diet, as a result of carb restriction, are close to those of starvation. Protein and fat content aren't as relevant in this case.

Given that carbs are not permitted on this diet, you might be wondering how much is needed for daily sustenance by your body. When carbohydrates are excluded from the diet, the body makes at least three major changes to conserve the little glucose and protein it has.

The most significant improvement is a switch from glucose to FFA as the primary energy source in most of your organs. This action conserves the small amount of glucose available to fuel the brain.

The second adaptation occurs in leukocytes, erythrocytes, and bone marrow that continue to use glucose. To prevent depletion of the available glucose reserve, these tissues break down glucose into lactate and pyruvate, which are transported to the liver and converted back to glucose. As a result, this problem does not result in a significant drop in blood glucose levels and can be overlooked in terms of the body's carbohydrate requirements.

The third and most significant transition occurs in your body, which, by the third week of continuous ketosis, has switched to using ketones for 75% of its energy needs rather than carbs. We just need to worry about the daily carbohydrate demands because the brain constantly depletes glucose in the body.

In normal circumstances, the brain uses around 100g of glucose every day. This means any diet containing less than 100g of carbs a day can induce ketosis, the severity of which is determined by the number of carbs ingested, i.e., the fewer carbs consumed, the greater the ketosis. Ketosis occurs when carbs are consumed in amounts less than 100g. When your brain adapts to using ketones as a source of energy and your system's glucose demands decrease, fewer carbs should be consumed to keep you in ketosis.

When it comes to how much of your total calorie requirement should come from carbohydrates, there is no one-size-fits-all solution. Some nutritionists advise people to keep it at the low end, about 5%, but this isn't always a safe idea because the exact amount depends on the system. Choose a percentage to see if it affects you; if you don't like the outcome, you can change it. There is no exact number for anyone when it comes to fats and protein, just as there is no exact amount for everyone when it comes to carbohydrates. It all depends on you, but a starting point of 75% is a good place to start.

There is no room here to "cheat" on your diet. You should stick to it to the letter, as even one meal that deviates from the plan will stall your progress for up to a week as your body adjusts to being out of ketosis. Always make sure you've eaten enough to avoid being tempted by a snack that might undo anything you've worked hard for.

All About Chaffles

The simplest definition of a chaffle is a low-carb waffle with a base ingredient of cheese and egg.

Chaffles use cheeses such as mozzarella, cheddar, and Colby Jack instead of flour to give the waffle its shape and texture. The fundamentals are a mix of egg and cheddar; however, from here, you can riff like wild-eyed. You can use an arrangement of cheeses, including cream cheddar, parmesan cheddar, etc. Some incorporate almond flour and flaxseed, and baking powder, and others don't. The major recipe for a chaffle contains cheddar and an egg.

You combine the ingredients in an instant and pour them into your waffle maker. Waffle makers are no doubt on the rising right now after this chaffle recipe exploded a while back. I was to some degree suspicious at the beginning that there was no way this would turn out with just mixing everything and pouring the batter over the waffle maker. I tried to sprinkle the waffle maker well. The waffle wound up exceptional, and it was firm on the outside and soft on the inside.

You can make a chaffle utilizing a waffle iron or mini waffle maker. The cooking time is just 4/5 minutes and, if you cook the chaffle properly, you end up with a fresh, gooey, flavorful bread/waffle alternative.

It's made with cheddar, get it? At the point when you work cheddar and waffle—you get chaffle (and you additionally get enchantment). Well, enough with the back story. Since you realize what this keto food is, how about, we make one and let you see with your own eyes how astounding this keto waffle is.

How to Make Basic Chaffles

Making chaffles requires a few steps and nothing more than a waffle maker for flat chaffles, a bowl to mix the batter, and less than 10 minutes of your time.

I love to use my 4" mini waffle maker because it's very handy and super easy to use and clean.

Ingredients:
You'll get two chaffles out of a large egg and about a half cup of cheddar or mozzarella cheese. These melt easily, making them the go-to for most recipes. Meanwhile, always ensure that your cheeses are finely grated or thinly sliced for use.

Directions:
Now, to make a normal chaffle:
1. First, preheat your waffle maker until hot enough.
2. Meanwhile, in a cup, mix the egg with cheese on hand until well mixed.
3. Open the iron, pour in half of the mixture, and close it.
4. Cook the chaffle for 5 to 7 minutes or until it is crispy.
5. Transfer the chaffle to a plate
6. Enjoy the crispy taste.

Basic Chaffles Nutrition Values

Depending on the cheddar you use, your calories and net carbs will change a tad. Yet, as a rule, expecting you to utilize genuine, complete milk cheddar (rather than cream cheddar or American cheddar), chaffles are almost completely carb-free. The normal serving size of two chaffles, 1 large egg, and a half cup of cheddar cheese contains generally:

- Calories: 300
- Carbs: 1g
- Protein: 20g
- Fat: 25g

As should be obvious, chaffles are about as keto as the formula can be: high-fat, high-protein, and zero-carb. They even work on the flesh-eater diet if you eat cheddar.

Alternative Tastes Ideas

1. If you find the taste too eggy, you can add a tbsp. of almond flour or any keto-friendly flour like coconut flour, psyllium husk flour, ground flaxseed, and the like. You can also top it with sugar-free syrup and make your taste buds happier. If you aren't comfortable with the smell of eggs in your chaffles, try using egg whites instead of egg yolks or whole eggs.
2. Would you choose to make your chaffles less cheesy? Then, use mozzarella cheese.
3. If you want it crunchier, you have to sprinkle shredded cheese on the waffle maker first and let it melt for half a minute before adding butter.
4. You can also try other kinds of cheese to see what will happen to the mixture.

This is just the classic chaffle, though. Remember that you can be creative with it, and possibilities are endless!

Chaffles can be used for a hamburger bun, hotdog bun, sandwich, and pizza crust.

Tips and Tricks

1. Preheat Well: Yes! It sounds obvious to preheat the waffle iron before use. However, preheating the iron moderately will not make your chaffles as crispy as you would like. The easiest way to preheat before cooking is to ensure that the iron is very hot.
2. Patience. That is the best tip. They don't take long, yet if you need a fresh keto waffle, you simply must be somewhat patient and let it take the 5-7 minutes it takes to clean up. Exactly when you believe it has finished, allow it one more moment or two. Try not to hurry.
3. To Shred or Slice: Many recipes call for shredded cheese when making chaffles, but I find sliced cheeses to offer crispier pieces. While I stick with mostly shredded cheese for convenience's sake, be at ease to use sliced cheese in the same quantity. When using sliced cheeses, arrange two to four pieces in the waffle iron, top with the beaten eggs and some cheese slices. Cover and cook until crispy.
4. Shallower Irons: For better crisps on your chaffles, use shallower waffle irons as they cook easier and faster.
5. Layering: Don't fill up the waffle iron with too much batter. Work between a quarter and a ½ cup of total ingredients per batch for correctly done chaffles. It is the firm cheddar on the base and top that will make them fresh.
6. Patience: It is a virtue even when making chaffles. For the best results, allow the chaffles to sit in the iron for 5 to 7 minutes before serving.
7. No overloading. Stuffed Chaffle producers know well; they flood, which makes tremendous wreckage! So, if all else fails, underfill as opposed to packing. Close to ¼ cup of total ingredients one after another.
8. No Peeking: 7 minutes isn't too much of a time to wait for the outcome of your chaffles, in my opinion. Opening the iron and checking on the chaffle before it is done stands you a worse chance of ruining it.
9. Squeeze it. I have known about others using press bottles so they can get only a little egg into the mini waffle maker.
10. No looking. I can let you know from lots of individual experience that opening the waffle iron at regular intervals "just to check" does not help the chaffle cook any quicker. Your most logical option is to not by any means open it for 4-5 minutes.
11. Crispy Cooling: For better crispiness, I find that allowing the chaffles to cool further after transferring to a plate aids a lot.

30-Day Meal Plan

Days	Breakfast	Lunch	Dinner	Dessert
1	Peanut Butter Chocolate Chips Chaffles	Pumpkin Spice Chaffles	Chicken Green Butter Chaffle	Pumpkin-Cinnamon Churro Sticks
2	Cinnamon Garlic Chaffles	Sausage and Chaffles	Artichoke and Spinach Chicken Chaffle	Peanut Butter Chaffles
3	Lemon-Poppy Seed Chaffles	BLT Chaffle Sandwich	Ricotta and Spinach Chaffles	Almond Butter Chaffles
4	Crispy Chaffles with Egg and Asparagus	Spinach Chaffles	Aromatic Chicken Chaffles	Cinnamon Chaffles
5	Monterrey Jack Chaffle	Swiss Cheese and Vegetables Chaffles	Ground Chicken Chaffles	Blueberry Cream Cheese Chaffles
6	Berries Syrup Chaffles	New Year Chaffle with Coconut Cream	Italian Chicken and Basil Chaffle	Strawberry and Cream Cheese Chaffles
7	Jalapeño Grilled Cheese Bacon Chaffle	Pumpkin Spice Chaffles	Turnip Hash Brown Chaffles	Raspberry Chaffles
8	Japanese Styled Breakfast Chaffle	Rosemary Cherry Tomatoes Chaffles	Garlicky Chicken Pepper Chaffles	Red Velvet Chaffles
9	Chocolate Chips Lemon Chaffle	Sausage and Pepperoni Sandwich Chaffle	Spicy Shrimps and Chaffles	Walnut Pumpkin Chaffles
10	Mini Breakfast Chaffles	Barbecue Chaffle	Spiced Chicken Chaffles with Special Sauce	Cream Mini-Chaffle
11	Minty Mini Chaffles	Grill Pork Chaffle Sandwich	Beef Taco Chaffle	Chocolate Cherry Chaffles
12	Blueberry Chaffles	Pumpkin Chaffles with Choco Chips	Bacon and Smoked Gouda	Sweet Vanilla Chocolate Chaffle
13	Mushroom Stuffed Chaffles	Walnuts Chaffles	Pecan Pumpkin Chaffle	Pecan Pie Cake Chaffle
14	Sausage Biscuits and Gravy Breakfast Chaffle	Holidays Chaffles	Gruyere and Chives Chaffles	Blueberry Shortcake Chaffle
15	Flaky Delight Chaffles	Fish and Chaffle	Swiss Bacon Chaffle	Banana Cake Pudding Chaffle
16	Breakfast Bowl with Chaffles	Bacon, Egg and Avocado Sandwich Chaffle	Bacon, Olives and Cheddar Chaffle	Peanut Butter Chaffles with Dark Chocolate
17	Cheddar Biscuit Chaffle	Avocado and Boiled Eggs Chaffles	Easy parmesan Garlic Chaffles	Brownie Chaffle
18	Garlic and Parsley Chaffles	Sloppy Joe Chaffles	Cheeseburger Chaffle	Raspberry and Cream Cheese Chaffles
19	Scrambled Eggs and Spring Onions Chaffle	Minutes Sandwich Chaffle	Minutes Sandwich Chaffle	Cream Coconut Cake Chaffle
20	Coffee Flavored Chaffle	Egg and Cheddar Cheese Chaffle	'Nduja Pesto Chaffles	Chocolate Melt Chaffles
21	Avocado Toast Chaffle	Chicken Bites with Chaffles	Garlicky Chicken Pepper Chaffles	Fruity Vegan Chaffles

Days	Breakfast	Lunch	Dinner	Dessert
22	Vanilla Chaffle	Ham and Green Bell Pepper Chaffle Sandwich	Halloumi and Boiled Chicken "Chaffle"	Blueberry Chaffles
23	Creamy Cinnamon Chaffles	Bacon and Chicken Ranch Chaffles	Pumpkin Chicken Chaffles	Italian Cream Sandwich-Cake Chaffle
24	Mushroom Chaffles with Salted Caramel Sauce	Mozzarella Peanut Chaffle	Zucchini Parmesan Chaffles	Chocolate Melt Chaffles
25	Hot Ham Chaffles	Mozzarella Panini Chaffle	Sliced Chicken and Chaffles	German Chocolate Chaffle Cake
26	Gingerbread Chaffle	Double Cheese Chaffles Plus	Broccoli Cheese Chaffles	Blueberry Cream Cheese Chaffles
27	Monte Cristo Chaffle	Sausage and Egg Sandwich Chaffle	Avocado Croque Madam Chaffle	Softened Chaffles with Sugar-Free Maple
28	Coconut Chaffles	Corndog Chaffles	Basil Pesto Chaffles	Chocolate Cannoli Chaffle
29	Zucchini Nut Bread Chaffle	Ham, Cheese and Tomato Sandwich Chaffle	Turkey Sandwich Chaffle	Butter and Cream Cheese Chaffles
30	Coconut Flour Chaffles	Pizza Flavored Chaffle	Black Olives and Cheddar Chaffles	Ice Cream Chaffles

CHAPTER 1:

Basic Chaffle Recipes

1. Plain Chaffles

Preparation time: 3 minutes
Cooking time: 6 minutes
Servings: 1
Ingredients:

- 1 egg
- ½ cup shredded cheddar cheese

Directions:
Preheat the mini waffle maker until hot.
Whisk the egg in a bowl, add cheese, and then mix well.
Stir in the remaining ingredients (except toppings, if any).
Grease the waffle maker and Scoop ½ of the batter onto the waffle maker spread across evenly.
Cook until a bit browned and crispy, about 4 minutes.
Gently remove it from the waffle maker and let it cool.
Repeat with the remaining batter.
Store in the fridge for 3-5 days.
Per serving: Calories: 280Kcal; Fat: 22g; Carbs: 1g; Protein: 18g

2. Vanilla Chaffle

Preparation time: 3 minutes
Cooking time: 4 minutes
Servings: 1
Ingredients:

- 1 egg
- ½ cup cheddar cheese, shredded
- ½ tsp. vanilla extract

Directions:
Switch on the waffle maker according to the manufacturer's directions.
Crack the egg and combine it with cheddar cheese in a small bowl.
Add vanilla extract and combine thoroughly.
Place half of the batter on the waffle maker and spread evenly.
Cook for 4 minutes or until as desired.
Gently remove from the waffle maker and set it aside for 2 minutes, so it cools down and becomes crispy.
Repeat for the remaining batter.
Per serving: Calories: 285Kcal; Fat: 22g; Carbs: 1g; Protein: 18g

3. Chia Chaffles

Preparation time: 3 minutes
Cooking time: 4 minutes
Servings: 1
Ingredients:

- 1 egg
- ½ cup cheddar cheese, shredded
- ½ tbsp. chia seeds

Directions:
Switch on the waffle maker according to the manufacturer's directions.
Crack the egg and combine it with cheddar cheese in a small bowl.
Place half of the batter on the waffle maker and spread evenly.
Sprinkle chia on top, cover, and cook it for 4 minutes or until as desired.

Gently remove from the waffle maker and set it aside for 2 minutes, so it cools down and becomes crispy
Repeat for the remaining batter.
Serve it with desired toppings.
Per serving: Calories: 280Kcal; Fat: 22g; Carbs: 1g Protein: 19g

4. Flaky Delight Chaffles

Preparation time: 3 minutes
Cooking time: 4 minutes
Servings: 1
Ingredients:

- 1 egg
- ½ cup cheddar cheese, shredded
- ½ cup coconut flakes

Directions:
Switch on the waffle maker according to the manufacturer's directions.
Crack the egg and combine it with cheddar cheese in a small bowl.
Place half of the batter on the waffle maker and spread evenly.
Sprinkle coconut flakes and cook for 4 minutes or until as desired.
Gently remove from the waffle maker and set it aside for 2 minutes, so it cools down and becomes crispy.
Repeat for the remaining batter.
Serve it with desired toppings.
Per serving: Calories: 320Kcal; Fat: 23g; Carbs: 7g; Protein: 20g

5. Minty Base Chaffles

Preparation time: 3 minutes
Cooking time: 4 minutes
Servings: 1
Ingredients:

- 1 egg
- ½ cup cheddar cheese, shredded
- 1 tbsp. mint extract (low carb)

Directions:
Using a mini waffle maker, preheat according to the maker's directions.
Combine the egg and cheddar cheese in a mixing bowl. Stir thoroughly.
Add mint extract and place half of the batter on the waffle maker; spread evenly.
Cook for 4 minutes or until as desired.
Gently remove from the waffle maker and set it aside for 2 minutes, so it cools down and becomes crispy.
Repeat for the remaining batter.
Garnish it with desired toppings.
Per serving: Calories: 320Kcal; Fat: 25g; Carbs: 1g; Protein: 22g

6. Blueberry Chaffles

Preparation time: 8 minutes
Cooking time: 15 minutes
Servings: 2
Ingredients:

- 2 eggs
- ½ cup blueberries
- ½ tsp. vanilla
- 1 cup mozzarella cheese, shredded

Directions:
Preheat your waffle maker.
In a medium bowl, mix the eggs, vanilla, and cheese.
Add blueberries and stir well.
Spray the waffle maker with cooking spray.
Pour ¼ of the batter in the hot waffle maker and cook for 8 minutes or until golden brown.
Repeat with the remaining batter.
Per serving: Calories: 396Kcal; Fat: 30g; Carbs: 2g; Protein: 26g

7. Jalapeño Cheddar Chaffles

Preparation time: 12 minutes
Cooking time: 5 minutes
Servings: 2
Ingredients:
- 2 eggs
- 16 slices deli jalapeño
- 1½ cup cheddar cheese

Directions:
Preheat and grease a waffle maker. Make a mixture containing ½ of cheddar with beaten eggs, then mix evenly.
Sprinkle some shredded cheese at the base of the waffle maker, and then pour the batter on the cheese and top again with more cheese with 4 slices of Jalapeño.
With the lid closed, cook for 5 minutes to a crunch.
Repeat the process for the remaining mixture.
Serve it and enjoy.
Per serving: Calories: 225Kcal; Fat: 13g; Carbs: 1g; Protein: 12g

8. Bacon Cheddar Chaffles

Preparation time: 12 minutes
Cooking time: 6 minutes
Servings: 2
Ingredients:
- 2 eggs
- Bacon bite, as per your taste
- 1½ cup cheddar cheese

Directions:
First, preheat and grease the waffle maker. Make a mix of all the ingredients in a bowl, and then pour into a waffle maker and heat for 4 minutes until it turns crispy.
Repeat the process for the remaining mixture. Serve the dish to enjoy.
Per serving: Calories: 373Kcal; Fat: 27g; Carbs: 1g; Protein: 22g

9. Crispy Chaffles

Preparation time: 12 minutes
Cooking time: 6 minutes
Servings: 1
Ingredients:
- 1/3 cup cheddar cheese
- ¼ tsp. baking powder
- 1 egg
- 1 tsp. (ground) flaxseed

Directions:
Mix the egg, baking powder, flaxseed, and cheddar cheese.
Preheat and grease the waffle maker.
Sprinkle the shredded cheddar cheese at the base of the waffle maker and pour the mixture into the waffle maker, then add some more shredded cheese at the top of the mixture.
Heat the mixture to cook to a crispy form. Repeat the process for the remaining mixture. Serve the dish to enjoy.
Per serving: Calories: 333Kcal; Fat: 22g; Carbs: 2g; Protein: 17g

10. Crispy Zucchini Chaffles

Preparation time: 18 minutes
Cooking time: 12 minutes
Servings: 1
Ingredients:
- 1 zucchini, small, finely grated
- 1 egg
- ½ cup shredded mozzarella
- 1 tbsp. parmesan
- pepper, as per your taste
- 1 tsp. basil

Directions:
Preheat and grease the waffle maker. Make a mix of all the ingredients in a mixing bowl.
Pour the mixture into a large-sized waffle maker and spread evenly.
Heat the mixtures to a crunchy form.
Repeat the process for the remaining mixture.
Serve it hot and enjoy the crispy taste.
Per serving: Calories: 230Kcal; Fat: 16g; Carbs: 5g; Protein: 21g

11. Rich and Creamy Mini Chaffles

Preparation time: 10 minutes
Cooking time: 8 minutes
Servings: 2
Ingredients:
- ¾ tbsp. baking powder
- 2 eggs
- 2 tbsp. cream cheese
- 2 tbsp. almond flour
- 2 tbsp. water (optional)
- 1 cup shredded mozzarella

Directions:
Preheat and grease the waffle maker. Make a mix of all the ingredients in a mixing bowl.
Pour the mixture into a large-sized waffle maker and spread evenly.
Heat the mixtures to a crunchy form for 5 minutes.
Repeat the process for the remaining mixture.
Serve it hot and enjoy the crispy taste
Per serving: Calories: 388Kcal; Fat: 29g; Carbs: 5g; Protein: 21g

12. Jalapeño Bacon Swiss Chaffles

Preparation time: 18 minutes
Cooking time: 12 minutes
Servings: 1
Ingredients:
- ½ cup shredded Swiss cheese
- 1 tbsp. fresh jalapeños (diced)
- 2 tbsp. bacon piece
- 1 egg

Directions:
First, preheat and grease the waffle maker.
Using a pan, cook the bacon pieces, put off the heat and shred the cheese and egg.
Add in the diced fresh jalapeños and mix evenly.
Heat the waffle makers to get the mixture into a crispy form.
Repeat the process for the remaining mixture.
Serve the dish to enjoy.
Per serving: Calories: 388Kcal; Fat: 28g; Carbs: 3; Protein: 21g

13. Easy Taco Chaffle

Preparation time: 5 minutes
Cooking time: 8 minutes
Servings: 1
Ingredients:

- 1 egg white
- ¼ cup Monterey Jack cheese, shredded (packed tightly)
- ¼ cup sharp cheddar cheese, shredded (packed tightly)
- ¾ tsp. water
- 1 tsp. coconut flour
- ¼ tsp. baking powder
- ⅛ tsp. chili powder
- a pinch of salt

Directions:
Plug in your waffle maker and, once it is hot, grease it lightly.
Mix all of the ingredients in a medium-sized bowl and whisk well until properly combined.
Spoon out ½ of the batter on the waffle maker and close the lid.
Cook it for about 4 minutes, and do not open the lid until the cooking time is up. If you do, it will seem like the taco chaffle shell is not correctly set up, but it is.
Set the taco chaffle shell aside after removing it from the waffle iron. Repeat the previous procedures with the remaining chaffle batter. Turn a muffin pan upside down and place the taco chaffle shells between the muffin cups. Allow setting for a few minutes.
You can enjoy this delicious crispy taco chaffle shell with your favorite toppings.
Per serving: Calories: 274Kcal; Fat: 25g; Carbs: 5g; Protein: 21g

14. Cheddar Biscuit Chaffle

Preparation time: 15 minutes
Cooking time: 5 minutes
Servings: 1
Ingredients:

- 1 egg
- ¼ cup sharp cheddar cheese
- 2 tbsp. almond flour
- ½ tsp. baking powder
- ½ tsp. garlic powder
- a pinch of salt

Directions:
Preheat the waffle maker to medium-high heat.
Whisk together the egg, cheddar cheese, almond flour, baking powder, garlic powder, and salt.
Pour the chaffle mixture into the center of the waffle iron. Close the lid of your maker and let cook for 3-5 minutes or until the waffle is golden brown and set.
Enjoy the chaffles with a black coffee or tea.
Per serving: Calories: 250Kcal; Fat: 24g; Carbs: 2g; Protein: 22g

15. Blueberry Almond Chaffles

Preparation time: 3 minutes
Cooking time: 15 minutes
Servings: 2
Ingredients:

- 1 cup mozzarella cheese
- 2 tbsp. almond flour
- 1 tsp. baking powder
- 2 eggs
- 1 tsp. cinnamon
- 2 tsp. Swerve
- 1 tbsp. blueberries

Directions:
Heat up your waffle maker.
In a medium-sized bowl, add eggs, mozzarella cheese, almond flour, baking powder, cinnamon, blueberries, and Swerve. Combine well all the ingredients to obtain a homogeneous mixture.
Use a non-stick cooking spray on your mini waffle maker to prevent the batter from sticking
Add in a little bit less than ¼ a cup of blueberry keto waffle batter.
Cook the chaffle for 3-5 minutes. At the 3-minute mark, check to see whether it is crispy and golden. If it isn't, or if it adheres to the top of the waffle maker, shut the cover and cook for another 1-2 minutes.
Serve the chaffles with a sprinkle of Swerve confectioners' sugar or sugar-free maple syrup.
Per serving: Calories: 523Kcal; Fat: 18g; Carbs: 7g; Protein: 3g

16. Pumpkin Chocolate Chips Chaffle

Preparation time: 4 minutes
Cooking time: 12 minutes
Servings: 1
Ingredients:

- ½ cup shredded mozzarella cheese
- pumpkin puree
- 1 egg
- 2 tbsp. granulated Swerve
- ¼ tsp. pumpkin pie spice
- 4 tsp. sugar-free chocolate chips
- 1 tbsp. almond flour

Directions:
Heat up your waffle maker.
In a medium-sized bowl, mix the pumpkin puree and egg. Make sure to properly combine the pumpkin and the egg.
Next, add in almond flour, mozzarella cheese, Swerve, and pumpkin spice and mix well.
Then add in your sugar-free chocolate chips.
Cook, for 4 minutes, half of the chaffle mix at a time in the waffle machine. Do not open it before the 4 minutes are up. It's essential not to open the waffle machine before the 4-minute mark. After that, you may open it to examine it and make sure it's fully cooked. Remember: keeping the lid closed the whole time is essential.
Enjoy with some Swerve confectioners' sugar or whipped cream on top.
Per serving: Calories: 380Kcal; Fat: 13g; Carbs: 11g; Protein: 22g

17. Peanut Butter Chocolate Chips Chaffles

Preparation time: 2 minutes
Cooking time: 8 minutes
Servings: 1
Ingredients:

- 1 egg
- ¼ cup shredded mozzarella cheese
- 2 tbsp. creamy peanut butter
- 1 tbsp. almond flour
- 1 tbsp. granulated Swerve

Directions:
Preheat your waffle maker.
In a small-sized bowl, mix the egg and the peanut butter, making sure to obtain a homogeneous batter.
Next, add to the batter the rest of the ingredients and whisk well.
Add half of the mix to the Dish Mini waffle maker at a time.
Cook, for 4 minutes, the chaffle batter in the waffle maker.
Top the chaffle with some sugar-free maple syrup or Swerve confectioners' sugar
Per serving: Calories: 296Kcal; Fat: 24g; Carbs: 3g; Protein: 16g

18. Broccoli Cheese Chaffles

Preparation time: 2 minutes
Cooking time: 8 minutes
Servings: 1
Ingredients:

- ½ cup cheddar cheese
- ¼ cup fresh chopped broccoli
- 1 egg
- ¼ tsp. garlic powder
- 1 tbsp. almond flour

Directions:

In a bowl, mix the cheddar cheese, almond flour, egg, and garlic powder. I find it easier to mix everything using a fork.

Add half of the broccoli and cheese chaffle batter to the waffle maker at a time.

In a waffle machine, cook the chaffle batter for 4 minutes.

Allow each chaffle to firm up for 1-2 minutes.

Enjoy alone or dipping in sour cream or ranch dressing.

Per serving: Calories: 502Kcal; Fat: 26g; Carbs: 13g; Protein: 27g

19. Cream Cheese Frosting Chaffles

Preparation time: 30 minutes
Cooking time: 15 minutes
Servings: 2
Ingredients:

- 2 tbsp. cream cheese or a mixture of 1 tbsp. cream cheese and 1½ tbsp. shredded mozzarella cheese
- ½ tbsp. unsalted butter, melted
- 1 tbsp. finely shredded and chopped carrot
- 1 tbsp. sweetener of your choice
- 1 tbsp. almond flour
- 1 tsp. pumpkin pie spice
- ½ tsp. keto-friendly flavor of choice
- ½ tsp. baking powder
- 1 a pinch of salt
- 2 eggs
  Cream Cheese Frosting:
- 1 tbsp. cream cheese
- 1 tbsp. unsalted butter
- 1 tsp. sweetener of choice

Directions:
Making the Cream Cheese Frosting:
Heat the butter and cream cheese for the frosting.
Mix until smooth and add the sweetener.
Making the Chaffles:
Heat up the waffle maker.
Melt the cream cheese, mozzarella, and butter for 15 seconds on low heat.
Mix the flour, sweetener, flavor, salt.
Mix the melted butter content with the dry ingredients.
Whisk the egg thoroughly.
Gently whisk the egg into the existing batter thoroughly.
Add the carrot and the pumpkin pie spice. Mix thoroughly.
Grease the waffle maker.
Add batter to waffle maker.
Repeat the baking procedures till the batter is finished.
Drizzle the frosting over the chaffles as desired.
Per serving: Calories: 236Kcal; Fat: 15g; Carbs: 7g; Protein: 18g

20. Berries Syrup Chaffles

Preparation time: 5 minutes
Cooking time: 15 minutes
Servings: 2

Ingredients:

- 2 cup almond/ coconut flour
- 1 tbsp. mozzarella cheese
- 2 tsp. baking powder
- a pinch of salt
- 2 oz. unsweetened chocolate, coarsely chopped
- ¾ cup Lakanto sugar-free maple syrup
- 2 large eggs
- 2 tbsp. unsalted butter, melted
- ½ pint fresh raspberries
  Berry Syrup:
- 3 fresh berries
- 1 tsp. grated lemon zest
- ½ cup sweetener
- Lemon juice

Directions:
Making the Berry Syrup:
Mix the berries and ½ cup of water in a large saucepan and boil over medium-high heat.
Crush the berries with the spoon or masher. Lower the heat and cook the mixture for 10 minutes.
Place a fine-mesh sieve over a bowl or cup.
Pour the berries into the sieve, pressing lightly to release the juices.
Pour the juice into a small-size saucepan and gently stir in the lemon zest, sugar, and lemon juice. Dissolve the sugar by bringing it to a boil over medium heat and stirring constantly. Leave to simmer for about 8-10 minutes until the syrup has thickened slightly.
Serve warm or refrigerate it for about 1 week.
Making the Chaffles:
Heat up your waffle iron.
In a bowl, preferably a large one, mix the flour, sweetener, baking powder, and salt.
Stir in the chocolate.
Whisk the cheese, eggs, and butter together in a separate medium bowl.
Gently mix the egg mixture into the dry ingredients.
Lightly grease the waffle iron.
Ladle the batter into the waffle iron.
Bake until crispy and golden brown, according to the manufacturer's directions.
Repeat the baking procedure until all the batter is baked.
Sprinkle with raspberries to serve.
Serve it with berry syrup.
Per serving: Calories: 168Kcal; Fat: 6g; Carbs: 3.5g; Protein: 1.3g

21. Yeast-Risen Overnight Chaffles

Preparation time: 10 minutes
Cooking time: 10 minutes
Servings: 2
Ingredients:

- 2 cup almond flour
- 1 tbsp. sweetener
- ½ tsp. salt
- ½ tsp. instant yeast
- 2 cup cheese, slightly warmed
- ½ cup unsalted butter, melted, room temperature
- 1 tsp. pure vanilla extract
- 2 large eggs, separated the next day

Directions:
Mix the flour, sweetener, salt, and yeast in a large bowl.
In a medium-size bowl, mix the cheese, butter, and vanilla together.
Gently mix the wet ingredients with the dry ingredients.
Stir the mixture thoroughly.
Close up the mix with plastic wrap or a tight-fitting lid and leave for an hour at room temperature before refrigerating overnight.
The next morning, the batter will bubble a bit.

Preheat the waffle iron on medium. Gently grease the waffle iron.
Preheat the oven on its lowest setting.
Stir the egg yolks into the batter.
In a medium-sized bowl, firmly beat the egg whites.
Gently mix the wet and dry ingredients until smooth.
Ladle the batter in the waffle iron and bake it for about 3 to 5 minutes until light golden brown.
Bake all the batter.
Serve them with butter and maple syrup.
Per serving: Calories: 169Kcal; Fat: 15g; Carbs: 6g; Protein: 3g

22. Cocoa Chaffles with Coffee Cream

Preparation time: 15 minutes
Cooking time: 15 minutes
Servings: 3
Ingredients:

- ½ cup heavy cream
- 1 tsp. espresso powder (or substitute 3 tbsp. espresso or strong brewed coffee)
- 2 tbsp. low carb sweetener of choice (Lakanto or monk fruit)
- 6 oz. mascarpone
- 2 cup almond flour
- 1 tbsp. baking powder
- 1 tsp. baking soda
- ¼ tsp. salt
- 1 tbsp. Dutch-process cocoa powder
- 3 large eggs
- 1¾ cup shredded mozzarella cheese
- 6 tbsp. unsalted butter, melted
- 1/3 cup cacao nibs
- Dark chocolate shavings for garnish (optional)

Directions:
Making coffee cream:
In a medium bowl, mix the cream, espresso powder, and 2 tbsp of low-carb sweetener of choice.
Whisk the cream thoroughly.
Fold in the mascarpone and set it aside.
Making the chaffles:
Preheat a waffle maker.
In a large bowl, mix the almond flour, baking powder, baking soda, salt, and cocoa powder together
In a bowl, preferably small size, whip the egg yolks till beaten, add the shredded cheese and melted butter together.
Create a hole in the dry ingredients, pour in the egg mixture, stir in the cacao nibs and mix to form a smooth batter.
Grease the waffle maker.
Ladle the batter into the waffle maker in ½ -¾ cup measures.
Bake for about 3-4 minutes till the chaffle is crispy and golden brown.
Take it out using a spatula and leave it to cool. Repeat the baking process till the whole batter is finished.
Serve it with coffee cream and sprinkle with chocolate shavings as desired.
Per serving: Calories: 152Kcal; Fat: 22g; Carbs: 1g; Protein: 22g

23. Mushroom Chaffles with Salted Caramel Sauce

Preparation time: 15 minutes
Cooking time: 15 minutes
Servings: 4
Ingredients:

- 4 white mushrooms (washed and shredded)
- ¾ cup whole cheese
- 3 large eggs
- 4 tbsp. unsalted butter, melted
- 2 cup almond flour
- 2 tbsp. sweetener
- 1½ tbsp. baking powder
- ½ tsp. salt

For 1 cup Salted Caramel Sauce:

- ¼ cup sweetener
- 4 tbsp. unsalted butter, melted
- 1 tsp. vanilla
- ¾ cup cheese cream
- 1 tsp. salt

Directions:
Heat a waffle iron beforehand according to the manufacturer's directions.
In a bowl (medium size), whisk the white mushroom, cheese, eggs, and butter.
In a bowl (large size), mix the flour, brown sweetener, baking powder, and salt together.
Gently mix the butter mixture into the dry ingredients until thoroughly mixed.
Lightly grease the waffle iron.
Ladle the batter in the preheated waffle iron.
Bake it until golden brown.
Repeat the baking procedure until all the batter is baked.
Drizzle with the warm salted caramel to serve.
Per serving: Calories: 241Kcal; Fat: 16g; Carbs: 13g; Protein: 9g

24. Lemon-Poppy Seed Chaffles

Preparation time: 10 minutes
Cooking time: 20 minutes
Servings: 4
Ingredients:

- 2 large eggs
- 1½ cup cream cheese
- ½ cup (4 oz./125 g) no salt butter, melted
- 2 tbsp. finely grated lemon zest
- 2 tbsp. fresh lemon juice
- 1 tsp. French vanilla flavor
- 1½ cup (7½ oz./235 g) almond flour
- 1/3 cup (3 oz./90 g) monk fruit or any keto-friendly sweetener of choice
- 1½ tsp. baking powder
- 1 tsp. baking soda
- ¼ tsp. salt
- 1 tbsp. poppy seeds

Directions:
Heat a waffle maker beforehand
In a bowl (medium), whisk together the eggs, cheese, butter, lemon zest, lemon juice, and vanilla.
In a bowl (large), combine the flour, sweetener, baking powder, baking soda, and salt. Stir in the poppy seeds.
Create a hole in the center of the bowl containing the dry ingredients. Pour in the egg mixture.
Whisk thoroughly until mostly smooth.
Grease the waffle maker
Ladle the batter in the waffle maker, using a ½-¾ cup of batter per batch.
Bake for about 3-4 minutes until the waffles are crisp and golden brown.
Remove the waffles from the waffle maker.
Either you serve them immediately or leave them to cool before serving.
Top with any keto-friendly sauce and dust with cheese.
Per serving: Calories: 144Kcal; Fat: 3g; Carbs: 5g; Protein: 1g

25. Softened Chaffles with Sugar-Free Maple Syrup

Preparation time: 15 minutes
Cooking time: 15 minutes
Servings: 6
Ingredients:

Maple Butter:
- 6 tbsp. (3 oz./90 g) unsalted butter softened
- 1½ tbsp. pure maple syrup
- a pinch of cinnamon
- a pinch of salt

Chaffles:
- 2 large eggs
- 1½ cup of any keto cheese
- ½ cup (4 oz./125 g) no salt butter, melted
- 1 tsp. keto-friendly flavor of choice
- 1½ cup (7½ oz./235 g) almond/coconut flour
- 3 tbsp. Lakanto sugar-free maple syrup
- 1 tbsp. baking powder
- 1½ tsp. ground ginger
- 1 tsp. cinnamon
- ¼ tsp. ground cloves
- sweetener

Directions:
Making maple butter:
To the maple butter, in a bowl (small size), whisk together the butter, maple syrup, cinnamon, and salt.
Scoop into a ramekin or other serving dish.
Place it in the freezer for 5 minutes or in the refrigerator for 15 minutes to firm up before serving.
Making coffee cream:
Preheat, a waffle maker
Whisk together the eggs, cheese, butter, and flavor in a medium bowl.
Mix the flour, sweetener, baking powder, ginger, cinnamon, cloves, and salt together in a large bowl.
Carefully pour the egg mixture into the dry ingredients.
Whisk thoroughly till smooth.
Grease the waffle maker and ladle the batter into the waffle maker.
Cooking for about 3-4 minutes till the chaffles are crisp and browned.
Remove the waffles from the waffle maker and serve right away, or allow cooling before serving.
Top with pats of maple butter and/or drizzle with maple syrup
Per serving: Calories: 402Kcal; Fat: 27g; Carbs: 8g; Protein: 23g

26. Peanut Butter and Jam Chaffles

Preparation time: 15 minutes
Cooking time: 15 minutes
Servings: 2
Ingredients:

- 1 cup jam of your choice (raspberry, strawberry, blackberry, etc.)
- 2 large eggs
- 1½ cup cheese of your choice
- ½ cup natural peanut butter
- ¼ cup unsalted butter, melted,
- 1½ cup (almond flour
- 3 tbsp. keto-friendly sweetener
- 1 tbsp. baking powder
- ½ tsp. salt

Directions:
Making the jam:
Place the jam in a small saucepan.
Heat for about 1 to 3 minutes until just gently warmed and loose enough to pour; stir continuously.

Stir and place in a serving bowl or pitcher.
Making Chaffles:
Preheat your waffle maker
Whip the eggs, cheese, ½ cup of peanut butter and butter on medium speed for about 2 minutes in the bowl until smooth.
In a bowl (medium), mix together the flour, sugar, baking powder, and salt.
To the peanut butter mixture, add the dry ingredients until well mixed.
Ladle the batter into the waffle maker.
Cook for about 3-4 minutes until the waffles are crisp and browned.
Remove the waffles from the waffle maker.
Repeat the cooking procedure until all the batter is finished.
Cut chaffles into half or quarters.
Place a waffle piece on a plate; spread some peanut butter on top.
Pour some of the warmed jam on top, then top with another piece of chaffle, or leave open-faced if desired.
Repeat with the remaining chaffles and serve them right away or allow them to cool.
Per serving: Calories: 387Kcal; Fat: 26g; Carbs: 5g; Protein: 22g

27. Cheddar Thyme Chaffles with Bacon Syrup

Preparation time: 15 minutes
Cooking time: 15 minutes
Servings: 4
Ingredients:

Cheddar:
- 2 cup almond/chocolate flour
- 2 tsp. baking powder
- 1 tsp. salt
- 2 large eggs
- 2 cup cream cheese
- unsalted butter, melted
- 2 cup shredded cheddar
- 1 tsp. chopped fresh thyme
- 1 cup Bacon Syrup
- 1 lb. bacon, cut crosswise into 1" pieces
- 2 tsp. unsalted butter
- 3 tbsp. finely chopped onion
- ¼ cup desired sweetener
- 1 cup sugar-free maple syrup
- 1 tsp. chopped fresh thyme
- ½ tsp. finely ground black pepper
- 1 tbsp. peanut oil

Directions:
Making the Chaffles:
Heat up the waffle iron beforehand according to the manufacturer's directions.
Mix the flour, baking powder, and salt in a large bowl.
Whip the eggs together in a separate medium bowl. Whisk in the cream cheese and melted butter until thoroughly mixed. Stir the butter mixture and cheddar cheese into the flour mixture until thoroughly mixed.
Grease the waffle maker.
Ladle the batter in the preheated waffle iron.
Bake until golden brown, according to the manufacturer's directions.
Repeat the baking procedure till the batter is finished.
Serve it with warm Bacon Syrup.
Making the Bacon Syrup:
Line a baking sheet with paper towels (2 layers) and set it aside.
Add the bacon to a large skillet and heat on low heat.
Cook the bacon for about 12-15 minutes, turn if needed until the fat is rendered, and the bacon is lightly browned all over
Transfer the bacon to drain. Allow it to cool slightly.
Finely chop the bacon till crumbled. Set it aside.

Pour off all but about 1 tbsp. of the bacon fat from the pan. Melt the butter and heat for about 1 minute, and add it to the bacon fat. Add the onion to the pan and cook it over medium heat. Stir continuously for about 7-10 minutes until translucent.

Add ½ cup of water, maple syrup, thyme, and black pepper and bring to a boil. Reduce to low heat and cook for 2 minutes, stirring and scraping up any browned bits. Add the bacon and mix well.

Cook uncovered for about 5-7 minutes, always stirring until the liquid is slightly reduced and thickened.

Remove from the heat and stir in a little peanut oil. Serve warm or refrigerate for up to 1 week.

Per serving: Calories: 410Kcal; Fat: 45g; Carbs: 8g; Protein: 24g

28. Chicken Breast Stuffed Chaffles with Spinach

Preparation time: 20 minutes
Cooking time: 15 minutes
Servings: 4
Ingredients:

- 1 cup finely chopped fresh baby spinach
- ¾ cup feta cheese, crumbled
- 2 tbsp. toasted pine nuts
- 2 cloves garlic, minced
- ½ tsp. dried thyme
- 4 boneless, skinless chicken breast halves
- ½ tsp. salt
- ½ tsp. freshly ground black pepper

Note: The use of baby spinach reduces the stress of picking through to remove large stems. The use of toasted pine nuts is to bring out the flavor.

Directions:
Toasting the Pine Nut:
Put the pine nuts inside a dry pan over medium heat.
Stir frequently till the nuts become fragrant and are barely turning brown.
Remove from the heat and pour them onto a plate to cool.
Making the Chaffles:
Preheat the waffle iron and oven on medium.
Put the spinach, cheese, nuts, garlic, and thyme in a small bowl.
Smash together until the filling becomes cohesive and easier to handle.
Lightly grease the waffle iron
Make a parallel cut into the thickest portion of each chicken breast half to form a pocket. But do not cut through.
Divide the combination into four equal parts and fill up each pocket in the chicken breasts, leaving a margin at the edge to close.
Season the chicken with salt and pepper.
Arrange the chicken into the waffle iron to allow the lid to press down on the chicken more evenly.
Close the lid.
Cook the chicken for 8 minutes. Check and rotate if need be and cook for about 3 minutes. The chicken should be golden brown.
Remove the chicken from the waffle iron
Repeat the baking procedure with any remaining chicken.
Keep the cooked chicken warm and serve it warm.
Per serving: Calories: 358Kcal; Fat: 34g; Carbs: 9g; Protein: 23g

29. Light and Crispy Bacon Cheddar Chaffles

Preparation time: 5 minutes
Cooking time: 5 minutes
Servings: 2
Ingredients:

- 2 eggs
- 1 cup cheddar
- ½ coconut/almond flour
- ½ tsp. baking powder

- bacon
- shredded parmesan cheese on top and bottom.

Directions:
Heat up the waffle iron on medium.
Mix the eggs, cheddar cheese in a small bowl.
Whisk the egg thoroughly
Mix the flour, baking powder, salt together in a large bowl
Gently whisk the egg mixture into the dry ingredients.
Whisk thoroughly until smooth
Add the bacon into the mixture and mix thoroughly
Lightly grease the waffle iron
Ladle the batter into the waffle maker
Bake it till crispy and golden brown.
Repeat the baking procedure till the batter is finished.
Serve them warm.
Per serving: Calories: 329Kcal; Fat: 33g; Carbs: 6g; Protein: 23g

30. Stuffed Chaffles

Preparation time: 15 minutes
Cooking time: 15 minutes
Servings: 4
Ingredients:

- 1 tbsp. extra-virgin olive oil
- ¾ tsp. salt
- ½ cup chopped onion
- ¼ cup chopped celery
- ½ tsp. poultry seasoning
- ½ tsp. freshly ground black pepper
- ¼ tsp. dried sage
- 6 cup low-carb dry bread cubes (about ½-inch square)
- ½ cup unsalted butter, melted
- 1 cup low-sodium chicken broth
- 1 cup cheese
- 4 eggs (separated)

Note: Cut any slightly stale pieces or ends into cubes and leave them at room temperature for an hour before using.
Directions:
Put the bread cubes in a bowl, preferably big size.
Mix the butter, cheese, egg white, and chicken broth together in a medium bowl.
In another bowl, mix all the vegetables together.
Pour the butter mixture over the bread.
Add the vegetable mixture and stir.
Leave the stuffing mixture to sit for 5 minutes to completely absorb the liquid, stir it once or twice.
Preheat the waffle iron on medium heat.
Lightly grease the waffle iron.
Drop half of the mixture into the waffle maker. Cook for about 3-4 minutes or until golden brown.
Repeat the baking procedure until all stuffing mixtures are baked.
Keep completed chaffles warm.
Serve them cool.
Per serving: Calories: 229Kcal; Fat: 29g; Carbs: 6g; Protein: 21g

31. Simple Broccoli Chaffles

Preparation time: 5 minutes
Cooking time: 8 minutes
Servings: 1
Ingredients:

- ¼ cup broccoli florets
- 1 egg, beaten
- 1 tbsp. almond flour
- ½ cup cheddar cheese

Directions:
Preheat your waffle maker.
Add the broccoli to the food processor.
Pulse until chopped.
Add to a bowl.
Stir in the egg and the rest of the ingredients.
Mix well.
Pour half of the batter into the waffle maker.
Cover and cook for 4 minutes.
Repeat the procedure to make the next chaffle.
Per serving: Calories: 307Kcal; Fat: 25g; Carbs: 10g; Protein: 21g

32. Sausage and Chaffles

Preparation time: 5 minutes
Cooking time: 15 minutes
Servings: 1
Ingredients:

- ¼ cup sausage, cooked
- 3 tbsp. chicken broth
- 2 tsp. cream cheese
- 2 tbsp. heavy whipping cream
- ¼ tsp. garlic powder
- pepper to taste
- 2 basic chaffles

Directions:
Add the sausage, broth, cream cheese, cream, garlic powder, and pepper to a pan over medium heat.
Bring to a boil and then reduce the heat.
Simmer for 10 minutes or until the sauce has thickened.
Pour the gravy on top of the basic chaffles
Serve them.
Per serving: Calories: 340Kcal; Fat: 37g; Carbs: 10g; Protein: 22g

33. Crispy Chaffle Bags

Preparation time: 30 minutes
Cooking time: 10 minutes
Servings: 10
Ingredients:

- 90g stevia erythritol (sweetness 1: 1 like sugar)
- pieces of sweetener tabs (sweetness per tab 6g sugar)
- 100g almond flour
- 250ml unsweetened almond milk (I use Alpro)
- 15g locust bean gum
- drops of vanilla flavor
- 70g butter, melted
- 5g coconut flour
- 40g protein powder vanilla
- 15g egg white powder

Directions:
Finely grind the stevia erythritol and sweetener tabs. Stir the sweet mix into the melted butter.
Stir in the almond milk with a whisk. Now mix in almond flour, coconut flour, egg white, and egg white powder, and vanilla flavor.
Finally, sift carob flour over it and quickly work into the mixture.
Let the chaffle batter rest for about 10 minutes. In the meantime, preheat the croissant machine at the highest level.
Now, reduce the temperature a little and place 1 to 1.5 tbsp. of the chaffle batter in the middle of the hot plate and spread lightly. Carefully close the lid and wait briefly (approx. 20 seconds) until the mass "bakes on" something.
Now push the lid all the way down so that the dough spreads even further. After about 1 to 1½ minutes, carefully remove the chaffle with a spatula from the croissant machine and place it on a worktop lined with baking paper.

Wait a moment - be careful, the chaffle is hot! After half a minute at the latest, place the chaffle over the chaffle cone and roll the cone gently back and forth and press the chaffle onto the overlapping ends. Let the chaffle cool down on the cone (it only takes so long until the next chaffle is baked, i.e., at the most 2 minutes).
Bake more chaffles with the rest of the dough and either form a croissant (with a cone) or chaffle cup by pouring the hot chaffle over an upturned coffee cup and pressing it down all around.
Let the chaffles cool and serve them either with ice cream or any other filling as desired.
If you like, you can refine the wafers with chocolate—either dip the top/bottom ends in chocolate and sprinkle with coconut flakes or grated nuts, or brush the chaffle cup with melted chocolate.
This brings an additional taste kick and prevents soaking.
Per serving: Calories: 495Kcal; Fat: 33g; Carbs: 13g; Protein: 27g

34. Mozzarella Chaffles

Preparation time: 40 minutes
Cooking time: 15 minutes
Servings: 1
Ingredients:

- 1 medium or large egg
- ½ cup of grated mozzarella cheese
- salt
- pepper

Directions:
While the chaffle iron is heating, whisk the egg and then fold in the fresh mozzarella.
Season with pepper and salt, and add a little butter to the iron. As soon as it is melted and well distributed, add the dough and bake the cheese chaffles until they are golden brown and crispy.
Salty chaffles of this type taste both warm and cold.
Per serving: Calories: 326Kcal; Fat: 16g; Carbs: 9g; Protein: 20g

35. Hearty Jalapeño Chaffles

Preparation time: 10 minutes
Cooking time: 5 minutes
Servings: 2
Ingredients:

- 2 large eggs
- 2 to 3 jalapeños, cored, one diced, the other cut into strips
- 4 slices of bacon
- 225g cream cheese
- 115g grated cheddar cheese
- 3 tbsp. coconut flour
- 1 tsp. baking powder
- ¼ tsp. Himalayan salt

Directions:
In a pan, fry the bacon until crispy. In the meantime, mix the dry ingredients together and beat the cream cheese in a separate bowl until creamy. Heat the chaffle iron and grease it. Whisk the eggs and fold in half of the cream cheese and cheese, then the dry ingredients. Finally, fold in the diced jalapeños.
Bake the cheese wafers by putting half of the dough in the iron, taking out the chaffle after about 5 minutes, and then baking the other half. Serve the chaffles with the rest of the cream cheese, the bacon, and the remaining jalapeños.
Per serving: Calories: 337Kcal; Fat: 28g; Carbs: 5g; Protein: 22g

36. Vanilla and Cinnamon Chaffles

Preparation time: 10 minutes
Cooking time: 5 minutes
Servings: 2

Ingredients:

- 2 eggs
- 2 cup grated mozzarella
- 1 tbsp. almond flour
- 1 tsp. baking powder
- 1 tsp. vanilla extract
- a pinch cinnamon
- fat for the chaffle maker

Directions:

Mix the egg with the vanilla extract.

Mix the dry ingredients in a separate bowl and add them to the egg.

Finally, fold in the cheese, grease the chaffle iron, and pour half of the dough into it.

Now bake the chaffle for about 5 minutes, checking periodically not to burn.

Repeat with the other half of the batter and serve the still-warm chaffles with a little butter and low-carb syrup as you like.

Per serving: Calories: 278Kcal; Fat: 28g; Carbs: 9g; Protein: 23g

37. Chocolate Twinkie Copycat Chaffles

Preparation time: 5 minutes
Cooking time: 12 minutes
Servings: 2
Ingredients:

- 2 tbsp. of butter (cooled)
- 2 oz. cream cheese softened
- 2 large egg room temperature
- ¼ cup sweetener
- ¼ cup almond flour
- 2 tbsp. coconut powder
- 2 tbsp. cocoa powder
- 1 tsp. baking powder

Directions:

Preheat the Corndog Maker:

Melt the butter for a minute and let it cool.

In the butter, whisk the eggs until smooth.

Remove the sugar, cinnamon, sweetener and blend well.

Add the almond flour, coconut flour, cacao powder, and baking powder.

Blend until well embedded.

Fill each well with ~2 tbsp. of batter and spread evenly.

Close the lid and let it cook for 4 minutes.

Lift from the rack and cool it down.

Per serving: Calories: 4202Kcal; Fat: 37g; Carbs: 3g; Protein: 29g

38. Corndog Chaffles

Preparation time: 10 minutes
Cooking time: 4 minutes
Servings: 2
Ingredients:

- 2 eggs
- 1 cup Mexican cheese blend
- 1 tbsp. almond flour
- ½ tsp. cornbread extract
- ¼ tsp. salt
- hot dogs with hot dog sticks

Directions:

Preheat the corndog waffle maker.

Whip the eggs in a small-sized bowl.

Add the remaining ingredients, except the hotdogs

Use a non-stick cooking spray to the corndog waffle maker.

Fill the corndog maker (halfway filled) with the batter.

Place a stick in the hot dog, and place it in the batter.

Slightly press down.

Spread a thin layer of batter on top of the hot dog, just enough to cover it.

Make about 4 to 5 chaffle corndogs repeating the process.

The corndog chaffles should be cooked for about 4 minutes or until golden brown.

With a pair of tongs, remove from the corndog waffle maker.

Serve with sugar-free ketchup, mustard, or mayo.

Per serving: Calories: 304Kcal; Fat: 28g; Carbs: 2g; Protein: 25g

39. Blackberry Jelly Donuts

Preparation time: 10 minutes
Cooking time: 3 minutes
Servings: 1
Ingredients:

- 1 egg
- ¼ cup mozzarella cheese shredded
- 2 tbsp. cream cheese softened
- 1 tbsp. sweetener
- 1 tbsp. coconut flour
- ½ tsp. baking powder
- 15 drops glazed donut flavoring

Raspberry Jelly Filling

- ¼ cup blackberries
- 1 tsp. chia seeds
- 1 tsp. sweetener

Directions:

Make the chaffles first by mixing everything together to make the batter.

Cook half quantity of the batter a time for about 2½-3 minutes.

Make the Raspberry Jelly Filling:

In a small pot, mix together the ingredients, and cook on medium heat.

Gently mash raspberries.

Let them cool.

Add between the layers of chaffles and enjoy!

Per serving: Calories: 386Kcal; Fat: 22g; Carbs: 11g; Protein: 27g

40. Cream Cheese and Marshmallow Frosting Chaffles

Preparation time: 15 minutes
Cooking time: 5 minutes
Servings: 2
Ingredients:

Chaffle Batter:

- 2 large egg room temperature
- 2 oz. cream cheese softened
- 2 tbsp. Lakanto sweetener
- 1 oz. pork rinds crushed
- 1 tsp. baking powder

Marshmallow Frosting:

- ¼ cup heavy whipping cream
- ¼ tsp. pure vanilla extract
- 1 tbsp. Lakanto confectioners' sugar
- ½ tsp. xanthan gum

Directions:

Plug in your mini waffle maker to preheat.

In a medium mixing bowl, add the egg, cream cheese, and vanilla.

Whisk until blended well.

Add the sweetener, crushed pork rinds, and baking powder.

Mix until well incorporated.

If you want, you can sprinkle extra crushed pork rinds onto the waffle maker.

Then, add about ¼ scoop of batter over, sprinkle a bit more pork rinds.

Cook for 3-4 minutes, then remove and cool it on a wire rack.

Repeat for the remaining batter.

Make the Marshmallow Frosting:

Whip the HWC, vanilla, and confectioners' sugar until thick and fluffy. Slowly sprinkle in the xanthan gum and fold in until completely combined.

Spread the icing over the chaffles and cut them as desired, then place them in the refrigerator until firm.

Enjoy it cold or warmed slightly in the microwave for 10 seconds.

Per serving: Calories: 203Kcal; Fat: 22g; Carbs: 6g; Protein: 24g

41. Biscuits Chaffle

Preparation time: 10 minutes
Cooking time: 5 minutes
Servings: 2
Ingredients:

- 2 tbsp. unsalted butter melted
- 2 large eggs
- 1 cup mozzarella cheese shredded
- 1 tbsp. garlic minced
- drops cornbread extract optional
- ½ tbsp. Lakanto confectioners' sugar (optional)
- 1 tbsp. almond flour
- ¼ tsp. granulated onion
- ¼ tsp. granulated garlic
- 1 tsp. dried parsley
- 1 tsp. baking powder
- 1 batch keto sausage biscuits and gravy recipe

Directions:

Preheat your Dash Mini Waffle Maker.

Melt the butter, let cool.

Whisk in the eggs, and then fold in the shredded cheese.

Add the rest of the ingredients and mix thoroughly.

Scoop ¼ of batter onto waffle maker and cook for 4 minutes.

Remove and let them cool on a wire rack.

Repeat for the remaining 3 chaffles.

Per serving: Calories: 270Kcal; Fat: 30g; Carbs: 6g; Protein: 26g

42. Classic Tuna Melt Chaffle

Preparation time: 15 minutes
Cooking time: 8 minutes
Servings: 1
Ingredients:

- 1 packet tuna 2.6 oz. with no water
- ½ cup mozzarella cheese
- 1 egg
- a pinch salt

Directions:

Preheat your waffle maker

Whip the egg in a small mixing bowl.

Mix in the tuna, cheese, and salt until completely combined.

Cook ½ of the mixture to the waffle maker and cook it for a minimum of 4 minutes.

Always check that the chaffle is golden before removing it from the maker.

Remove it and cook the remaining tuna chaffle for 4 minutes.

Optional: To obtain a crispier crust, you could melt, for about 30 seconds, 1 tsp. cheddar in the waffle maker before adding the mixed ingredients.

Once the tuna chaffle is done, the cheese will be so crispy.

Per serving: Calories: 283Kcal; Fat: 28g; Carbs: 2g; Protein: 25g

43. Blueberry and Brie Grilled Cheese Chaffle

Preparation time: 10 minutes
Cooking time: 10 minutes
Servings: 2
Ingredients:

- 1 tsp. blueberry compote
- 1 oz. Wisconsin brie sliced thin
- 1 tsp. Kerrygold butter

Chaffle:

- 1 egg, beaten
- ¼ cup mozzarella shredded
- 1 tsp. Swerve confectioners' sugar
- 1 tbsp. cream cheese softened
- ¼ tsp. baking powder
- ½ tsp. vanilla extract

Blueberry Compote:

- 1 cup blueberries washed
- zest of ½ lemon
- 1 tbsp. lemon juice freshly squeezed
- 1 tbsp. Swerve confectioners' sugar
- ⅛ tsp. xanthan gum
- 2 tbsp. water

Directions:

Chaffles:

Mix everything together.

Cook ½ of the batter for 2½-3 minutes in the mini waffle maker

Repeat and let the chaffles cool slightly on a cooling rack.

Blueberry Compote:

Add everything, except xanthan gum, to a small saucepan. Bring to a boil, and then turn the heat down and simmer for 5-10 minutes until it starts to thicken. Sprinkle with xanthan gum and stir well.

Remove from the heat and let it cool. Store it in the refrigerator until ready to use.

Grilled Cheese:

In a small pan, over medium heat, let the butter melt.

Place brie slices on a Chaffle and top with a generous scoop of the prepared blueberry compote.

Grill the sandwich in a pan for about 2 minutes per side, flipping once until the waffle is golden and cheese has melted.

Per serving: Calories: 373Kcal; Fat: 27g; Carbs: 4g; Protein: 22g

44. BBQ Chicken Chaffles

Preparation time: 3 minutes
Cooking time: 8 minutes
Servings: 1
Ingredients:

- 1/3 cup cooked chicken diced
- ½ cup shredded cheddar cheese
- 1 tbsp. sugar-free BBQ sauce
- 1 egg
- 1 tbsp. almond flour

Directions:

Heat up your waffle maker.

Mix the almond flour, egg, BBQ sauce, diced chicken, and cheddar cheese in a small-sized bowl.

Add ½ of the batter into your waffle maker and cook it for about 4 minutes. After this, check that the chaffles are cooked; otherwise, leave them to cook for another 2 minutes.

Create another chaffle with the rest of the batter and enjoy the chaffles with BBQ sauce.

Per serving: Calories: 350Kcal; Fat: 30g; Carbs: 5g; Protein: 25g

45. Cheddar Chicken and Broccoli Chaffles

Preparation time: 2 minutes
Cooking time: 8 minutes
Servings: 1
Ingredients:

- ¼ cup cooked diced chicken
- ¼ cup fresh broccoli chopped
- shredded cheddar cheese
- 1 egg
- ¼ tsp. garlic powder

Directions:
Heat up your waffle maker.
Mix the egg, cheddar cheese, and garlic powder in a small-sized bowl.
Add the chicken and broccoli and mix well.
Add ½ of the batter into your waffle maker and let it cook for 4 minutes. Cook for an extra couple of minutes if they are still not cooked.
Make a second chaffle with the rest of the batter.
After cooking each chaffle, remove it from the pan and let it sit for 2 minutes.
Dip in sour cream or enjoy it alone.
Per serving: Calories: 278Kcal; Fat: 25g; Carbs: 7g; Protein: 21g

46. Jamaican Jerk Chicken Chaffles

Preparation time: 5 minutes
Cooking time: 10 minutes
Servings: 4
Ingredients:
Jamaican Jerk Chicken Filling:

- 1 lb. organic ground chicken browned or roasted leftover chicken chopped finely
- 2 tbsp. Kerrygold butter
- ½ medium onion chopped
- 1 tsp. granulated garlic
- 1 tsp. dried thyme
- ⅛ tsp. black pepper
- 2 tsp. dried parsley
- 1 tsp. salt
- 2 tsp. Walkerswood traditional Jamaican jerk seasoning, hot and spicy
- ½ cup chicken broth

Chaffles:

- ½ cup mozzarella cheese
- 1 tbsp. butter melted
- 1 egg well beaten
- 2 tbsp. almond flour
- a pinch of garlic powder
- ¼ tsp. baking powder
- a pinch of xanthan gum
- a pinch of onion powder
- ¼ tsp. turmeric
- a pinch of salt

Directions:
Cook the onion in the butter using a medium saucepan.
Add all the spices and herbs. Sauté until fragrant.
Add the chicken.
Stir in the chicken broth.
Cook on low for 10 minutes.
Raise the temperature to medium-high and reduce the liquid until none is left in the bottom of the pan.
Per serving: Calories: 304Kcal; Fat: 34g; Carbs: 6g; Protein: 24g

47. Wasabi Chaffles

Preparation time: 15 minutes
Cooking time: 15 minutes
Servings: 1
Ingredients:

- 1 whole avocado, ripe
- 5 slices pickled ginger
- 1 tbsp. gluten-free soy sauce
- 1/3 cup edamame
- ¼ cup Japanese pickled vegetables
- ½ lb. sushi-grade salmon, sliced
- ¼ tsp. wasabi

Directions:
Cut the salmon and avocado into thin slices. Set them aside.
If the edamame is frozen, boil it in a pot of water until done. Set them aside.
Follow the Classic Chaffle recipe.
Once the chaffles are done, pour a tbsp. of soy sauce onto the chaffle and then layer the salmon, avocado, edamame, pickled ginger, pickled vegetables, and wasabi.
Per serving: Calories: 321Kcal; Fat: 25g; Carbs: 6g; Protein: 23g

48. Nachos Chaffle

Preparation time: 15 minutes
Cooking time: 15 minutes
Servings: 1
Ingredients:

- 2 classic chaffles
  Nachos:
- taco meat
- 1 whole avocado, ripe
- ½ cup sour cream
- ½ cup cheddar cheese, shredded
- ½ an onion
- 1 handful of coriander, chopped
- 1 lime, cut into wedges
- lettuce

Directions:
Dice the coriander, lettuce, onions, and limes.
Shred the cheese in a bowl. Melt if desired.
Follow the directions for the Taco Meat recipe.
Follow the Classic Chaffle recipe.
Once the chaffles are done, rip them into triangles.
Spread the chaffle triangles onto a plate and layer on the sour cream, meat, avocado, onions, cilantro, cheese, and lime.
Per serving: Calories: 393Kcal; Fat: 27g; Carbs: 5g; Protein: 21g

49. Mozzarella Panini Chaffle

Preparation time: 15 minutes
Cooking time: 15 minutes
Servings: 1
Ingredients:

- 2 classic chaffles
  Sandwich Filling:
- ½ cup mozzarella, thinly sliced
- 1 heirloom tomato, thinly sliced
- ¼ cup pesto

Directions:
Follow the Classic Chaffle recipe.
Once the chaffles are done, lay two side by side.
Spread the pesto on one, then layer the mozzarella cheese and tomatoes and sandwich together.
Per serving: Calories: 334Kcal; Fat: 35g; Carbs: 2g; Protein: 23g

50. Lox Bagel Chaffle

Preparation time: 15 minutes
Cooking time: 15 minutes
Servings: 1
Ingredients:

- 2 classic chaffles
- 2 tbsp. everything bagel seasoning

  Filling:
- 1 oz. cream cheese
- 1 beefsteak tomato, thinly sliced
- 4-6 oz. salmon gravlax
- 1 small shallot, thinly sliced
- capers
- 1 tbsp. fresh dill

Directions:
Slice the tomato and the shallots.
Follow the Classic Chaffle recipe and add everything bagel seasoning.
Once the chaffles are done, sprinkle more everything bagel seasoning onto the tops of both chaffles.
Lay two chaffles side by side and layer on the cream cheese, salmon, and shallots.
Sprinkle dill and capers and sandwich the two chaffles together.
Per serving: Calories: 369Kcal; Fat: 37g; Carbs: 9g; Protein: 21g

51. Cuban Sandwich Chaffle

Preparation time: 15 minutes
Cooking time: 15 minutes
Servings: 1
Ingredients:

- 2 classic chaffles
- ¼ lb. ham, cooked and sliced
- ¼ lb. pork, roasted and sliced
- ¼ lb. Swiss cheese, thinly sliced
- 3 dill pickles, sliced in half

Directions:
Follow the Classic Chaffle recipe.
Take two chaffles and lay side by side.
Lay on the meat, cheese, and pickles.
Sandwich the two chaffles together.
Put the sandwich in a toaster oven if you want it hot.
Heat for 5 minutes or until cheese is melted.
Per serving: Calories: 323Kcal; Fat: 32g; Carbs: 7g; Protein: 25g

52. Easy Parmesan Garlic Chaffles

Preparation time: 10 minutes
Cooking time: 5 minutes
Servings: 1
Ingredients:

- ½ cup shredded mozzarella cheese
- 1 whole egg, beaten
- ¼ cup grated parmesan cheese
- 1 tsp. Italian Seasoning
- ¼ tsp. garlic powder

Directions:
Preheat your waffle maker.
Mix all the ingredients in a medium-sized bowl, except for the mozzarella cheese, to prepare the batter.
Mix until well combined, and then add the mozzarella cheese.
Spray your waffle plates with non-stick spray and add half the batter to the center. Cook for 3-5 minutes, or maybe a little bit more depending on how crispy you want your Chaffles.
Enjoy them with a drizzle of olive oil, grated parmesan cheese, and fresh chopped parsley.
Per serving: Calories: 340Kcal; Fat: 30g; Carbs: 8g; Protein: 22g

53. Key Lime Chaffles

Preparation time: 10 minutes
Cooking time: 5 minutes
Servings: 2
Ingredients:

  Chaffles:
- 1 egg
- 2 tsp. cream cheese room temp
- 1 tsp. powdered sweetener Swerve or monk fruit
- ½ tsp. baking powder
- ½ tsp. lime zest
- ¼ cup almond flour
- ½ tsp. lime extract or 1 tsp. freshly squeezed lime juice
- a pinch of salt

  Cream Cheese Lime Frosting:
- 4 oz. cream cheese softened
- 4 tbsp. butter
- 2 tsp. powdered sweetener Swerve or monk fruit
- 1 tsp. lime extract
- ½ tsp. lime zest

Directions:
Preheat the waffle iron.
Put all the chaffles ingredients in a blender and blend on high until the mixture is smooth and creamy.
Cook each chaffle for about 3 to 4 minutes until it's golden brown.
Let's do the frosting while the chaffles are cooking.
Combine all the ingredients for the frosting in a bowl, and mix until smooth.
Allow the chaffles to cool before frosting them completely.
Per serving: Calories: 368Kcal; Fat: 26g; Carbs: 3g; Protein: 19g

54. Jicama Loaded Baked Potato Chaffle

Preparation time: 10 minutes
Cooking time: 15 minutes
Servings: 2
Ingredients:

- 1 cup cheese of choice
- 2 eggs, whisked
- 1 large jicama root
- ½ medium onion, minced
- salt and pepper
- 2 garlic cloves, pressed

Directions:
Peel the jicama and shred it in the food processor.
In a large colander, place the shredded jicama and sprinkle with 1-2 tsp. of salt. Mix well and allow draining.
Squeeze out as much liquid as possible.
Microwave for 5-8 minutes.
Mix all the ingredients together.
Sprinkle some cheese on the waffle iron, then add 1/3 of the mixture and put more cheese on top of the mixture.
Cook for 5 minutes. Flip and cook for 2 more minutes.
Top with some sour cream, cheese, bacon pieces, and chives.
Per serving: Calories: 321Kcal; Fat: 33g; Carbs: 5g; Protein: 28g

55. McGriddles Chaffle

Preparation time: 10 minutes
Cooking time: 5 minutes
Servings: 2
Ingredients:

- 1 egg
- ¾ cup shredded mozzarella
- 1 sausage patty
- 1 slice American cheese

- 1 tbsp. sugar-free flavored maple syrup
- 1 tbsp. Swerve or monk fruit (or any sugar replacement of choice)

Directions:

Preheat your Dash Mini Waffle Maker.

Beat the egg into a small mixing bowl.

Add shredded mozzarella, Swerve/monk fruit, and Maple Syrup. Mix until well combined.

Place ~2 tbsp. of the resulting egg mix onto the Dash Mini Waffle Maker, close the lid, and cook for 3-4 minutes. Repeat for the rest of the batter.

Meanwhile, follow the cook directions for the sausage patty and place cheese onto the patty while still warm to melt it.

Assemble McGriddles chaffle and enjoy!

Per serving: Calories: 321Kcal; Fat: 32g; Carbs: 1g; Protein: 26g

56. Light and Crispy Chaffles

Preparation time: 10 minutes
Cooking time: 5 minutes
Servings: 2
Ingredients:

- 1 egg
- 1/3 cup cheddar
- ¼ tsp. baking powder
- ½ tsp. ground flaxseed
- shredded parmesan cheese on top and bottom

Directions:

Mix the ingredients together and cook in a mini waffle iron for 4-5 minutes until crispy.

Once cool, enjoy your light and crisp Keto waffle.

You can experiment with seasonings to the initial mixture depending on the mood of your taste buds.

Per serving: Calories: 360Kcal; Fat: 8g; Carbs: 33g; Protein: 19g

57. Sandwich Chaffle with Bacon and Egg

Preparation time: 10 minutes
Cooking time: 5 minutes
Servings: 1
Ingredients:

- 1 large egg
- ½ cup of shredded cheddar cheese
- thick-cut bacon
- fried egg
- sliced cheese

Directions:

Preheat your waffle maker.

In a small mixing bowl, mix together the egg and shredded cheese. Stir until well combined.

Pour one-half of the mixture into the waffle maker. Let it cook for about 3-4 minutes or until golden brown. Repeat with the second half of the batter.

In a medium pan over medium heat, cook the bacon until crispy.

In the same skillet, in 1 tbsp. of reserved bacon drippings, fry the egg over medium heat. Cook until the desired doneness.

Assemble the sandwich and enjoy!

Per serving: Calories: 358Kcal; Fat: 29g; Carbs: 7g; Protein: 26g

58. Bacon and Smoked Gouda Cheese Chaffles

Preparation time: 5 minutes
Cooking time: 5 minutes
Servings: 2

Ingredients:

- ½ cup almond flour
- 3 bacon strips
- ¼ cup sour cream
- 1½ cup cheddar cheese
- ½ cup smoked Gouda cheese
- ½ tsp. onion powder
- ½ tsp. baking powder
- 1 egg
- 1½ tbsp. butter
- ¼ tsp. salt
- ½ tsp. parsley
- ¼ tsp. baking soda

Directions:

Heat the waffle maker.

Take a bowl, add the almond flour, baking powder, baking soda, onion powder, garlic salt, and mix well.

In another bowl, whisk the eggs, bacon, cream, parsley, butter, and cheese until well combined.

Now pour the mixture over the dry ingredients and mix well.

Pour the batter over the preheated waffle maker and cook for 5 to 6 minutes or until golden brown.

Serve hot and crispy chaffles.

Per serving: Calories: 233Kcal; Fat: 31g; Carbs: 1g; Protein: 24g

59. Jalapeño and Bacon Chaffles

Preparation time: 5 minutes
Cooking time: 5 minutes
Servings: 3
Ingredients:

- 3 tbsp. coconut flour
- 1 tsp. baking powder
- 3 eggs
- 8 oz. cream cheese
- ¼ tsp. salt
- 4 bacon slices
- 2 to 3 jalapeños
- 1 cup cheddar cheese

Directions:

Wash the jalapeño and slice them.

Take a pan and cook the jalapeño until golden brown or crispy.

Take a bowl, add flour, baking powder, and salt, and mix.

In a mixing bowl, add cream and beat well until fluffy.

Now, in another bowl, add the eggs and whisk them well.

Pour the cream, cheese and beat until well combined.

Add the mixture with the dry ingredients and make a smooth batter.

After that, fold the jalapeño in the mixture.

Heat the waffle maker and pour the batter into it.

Cook it for 5 minutes or until golden brown.

Top it with cheese, jalapeño, and crème and serve the hot chaffles.

Per serving: Calories: 310Kcal; Fat: 30g; Carbs: 3g; Protein: 20g

60. Light and Crispy Bagel "Chaffle" Chips

Preparation time: 5 minutes
Cooking time: 5 minutes
Servings: 2
Ingredients:

- 3 tbsp. parmesan cheese
- 1 tsp. bagel seasoning

Directions:

Preheat the waffle maker.

Add the parmesan cheese to the pan and melt it well.

Now, pour the melted parmesan cheese over the waffle maker and sprinkle bagel seasoning over the cheese.

Cook the mixture for about 2 to 3 minutes without closing the lid.

Let it settle or turn crispy for 2 minutes, then remove and serve the crispy chis crunch.

Per serving: Calories: 280Kcal; Fat: 25g; Carbs: 1g; Protein: 21g

61. Coconut Flour Chaffles

Preparation time: 5 minutes
Cooking time: 5 minutes
Servings: 4
Ingredients:

- 8 eggs
- ½ cup butter or coconut oil (melted)
- 1 tsp. vanilla extract
- ½ tsp. salt
- ½ cup coconut flour
- ½ tsp. cinnamon

Directions:
Preheat the mini waffle maker and whisk the eggs in a bowl.

Then, you add the melted butter or coconut oil, cinnamon, vanilla, and salt, mix properly, then add the coconut flour.

Ensure the batter is thick.

Add the mixture into the mini waffle maker and cook till it has a light brown appearance.

Serve them with butter or maple syrup.

Per serving: Calories: 357Kcal; Fat: 28g; Carbs: 7g; Protein: 25g

62. Agave and Cream Cheese Chaffles

Preparation time: 10 minutes
Cooking time: 5 minutes
Servings: 4
Ingredients:

- 2 cup flour
- 1 tsp. baking powder
- ⅛ tsp. salt
- 2 tsp. light brown sugar
- 4 oz. 1/3 less fat cream cheese
- 2 eggs
- ½ cup of milk
- 2 tbsp. canola oil
- ½ tbsp. pure vanilla extract
- 4 tbsp. agave syrup

Directions:
The first step is to preheat the mini waffle maker.

Then, you mix the flour, baking powder, salt, and light brown sugar; mix thoroughly to ensure uniformity.

In your bowl, add the cream cheese and egg yolks; mix until smooth.

Then, you add milk, oil, and vanilla; mix properly.

Add the flour mixture to the cream cheese mixture and stir until moist. Set it aside.

The next step is to put the egg whites in a bowl and beat them until it forms a stiff peak.

With a spatula, Gently incorporate the egg whites into the waffle batter.; fold just until thoroughly combined.

Pour 1/3 cup of the batter onto the preheated mini waffle iron.

Allow to cook for about 2 to 3 minutes, or until it has a light brown appearance.

To do the whipped cream, start pouring the heavy cream into a large mixing bowl and beat on until it becomes thick.

Continuing to beat, add honey until soft peaks form.

Serve the waffles topped with honey whipped cream and fresh berries (optional).

Per serving: Calories: 302Kcal; Fat: 34g; Carbs: 4g; Protein: 22g

63. Brownie Chaffle

Preparation time: 5 minutes
Cooking time: 3 minutes
Servings: 2
Ingredients:

- 1 egg whisked
- 1/3 cup mozzarella cheese shredded
- 1½ tbsp. cocoa powder, Dutch-processed
- 1 tbsp. almond flour
- 1 tbsp. monk fruit sweetener
- ¼ tsp. vanilla extract
- ¼ tsp. baking powder
- a pinch of salt
- 2 tsp. heavy cream

Directions:
As always, preheat your mini waffle iron before starting chaffles preparation.

Next, whisk the egg, add the dry ingredients, and add the cheese.

Mix well all the ingredients.

Pour 1/3 of the batter on the waffle iron. Allow it to cook for 3 minutes or until steam stops coming out of the waffle iron.

Serve with your favorite low-carb toppings.

Per serving: Calories: 473Kcal; Fat: 38g; Carbs: 10g; Protein: 30g

64. White Bread Keto Chaffle

Preparation time: 5 minutes
Cooking time: 4 minutes
Servings: 2
Ingredients:

- 2 egg whites
- cream cheese, melted
- 2 tsp. water
- ¼ tsp. baking powder
- ¼ cup almond flour
- a pinch of salt

Directions:
Preheat the mini waffle maker.

Whisk the eggs whites together with the cream cheese and water in a bowl.

The next step is to add the baking powder, almond flour, and salt and whisk until you have a smooth batter. Then, you pour half of the batter into the mini waffle maker.

Allow it to cook for roughly 4 minutes or until you no longer see steam coming from the waffle maker.

Remove and allow to cool.

Per serving: Calories: 393Kcal; Fat: 28g; Carbs: 7g; Protein: 22g

65. Cranberry and Brie Chaffle

Preparation time: 10 minutes
Cooking time: 20 minutes
Servings: 2
Ingredients:

- 4 tbsp. frozen cranberries
- 3 tbsp. Swerve sweetener
- 1 cup/115g shredded brie cheese
- 2 eggs, at room temperature

Directions:
Take a non-stick waffle iron, plug it in, select the medium or medium-high heat setting and let it preheat until ready to use; it could also be indicated with an indicator light changing its color.

Meanwhile, make the batter and for this, take a heatproof bowl, add cheese in it, and microwave at high heat setting for 15 seconds or until the cheese has softened.

Then, add sweetener, berries, and egg into the cheese and whisk with an electric mixer until smooth.

Use a ladle to pour one-fourth of the prepared batter into the heated waffle iron in a spiral direction, starting from the edges, then shut the lid and cook for 4 minutes or more until solid and nicely browned; the cooked waffle will look like a cake.

When done, transfer the chaffles to a plate with a silicone spatula and repeat with the remaining batter.

Let the chaffles stand for some time until crispy and serve them straight away.

Per serving: Calories: 320Kcal; Fat: 22g; Carbs: 7g; Protein: 21g

66. Banana Foster Chaffle

Preparation time: 10 minutes
Cooking time: 20 minutes
Servings: 4
Ingredients:
For Chaffles:
- ⅛ tsp. cinnamon
- ½ tsp. banana extract, unsweetened
- 4 tsp. Swerve sweetener
- 1 cup/225g cream cheese, softened
- ½ tsp. vanilla extract, unsweetened
- 8 eggs, at room temperature
For Syrup:
- 20 drops banana extract, unsweetened
- 8 tsp. Swerve sweetener
- 20 drops caramel extract, unsweetened
- drops rum extract, unsweetened
- 8 tbsp. unsalted butter
- ⅛ tsp. cinnamon

Directions:
Take a non-stick waffle iron, plug it in, select the medium or medium-high heat setting and let it preheat until ready to use; it could also be indicated with an indicator light changing its color.

Meanwhile, make the batter for the chaffle, and for this, take a large bowl, crack the eggs in it, add sweetener, cream cheese, and all the extracts and then mix with an electric mixer until smooth; let the batter stand for 5 minutes.

Use a ladle to pour one-fourth of the prepared batter into the heated waffle iron in a spiral direction, starting from the edges, then shut the lid and cook for 5 minutes or more until solid and nicely browned; the cooked waffle will look like a cake.

When done, transfer the chaffles to a plate with a silicone spatula, repeat with the remaining batter and let the chaffles stand for some time until crispy.

Meanwhile, make the syrup and for this, take a small heatproof bowl, add butter in it, and microwave at high heat setting for 15 seconds until it melts.

Then add the remaining ingredients for the syrup and mix until combined.

Drizzle syrup over the chaffles and then serve.

Per serving: Calories: 440Kcal; Fat: 326g; Carbs: 5g; Protein: 20g

67. Basil Pesto Chaffles

Preparation time: 5 minutes
Cooking time: 5 minutes
Servings: 1
Ingredients:
- 1 egg
- ½ cup shredded cheddar cheese

Directions:
Turn on the waffle maker to heat and oil it with cooking spray.
Whisk the egg in a bowl until well beaten.
Add cheese to the egg and stir well to combine.

Drop half of the mixture into the waffle maker and cook it for about 3-5 minutes.

Transfer the chaffle to a plate and set it aside for 2-3 minutes to crisp up.

Repeat for the remaining batter.

Per serving: Calories: 300Kcal; Fat: 20g; Carbs: 1g; Protein: 25g

68. Layered Parmesan Chaffles

Preparation time: 8 minutes
Cooking time: 5 minutes
Servings: 1
Ingredients:
- 1 organic egg, beaten
- 1/3 cup cheddar cheese, shredded
- ½ tsp. ground flaxseed
- ¼ tsp. organic baking powder
- 2 tbsp. parmesan cheese, shredded

Directions:
Preheat the mini waffle iron and then grease it.
In a bowl, place all the ingredients except parmesan and beat until well combined.
Place half the parmesan cheese in the bottom of the preheated waffle iron.
Place half of the egg mixture over THE cheese and top with the remaining parmesan cheese.
Cook for about 3-minutes or until golden brown.
Serve them warm.

Per serving: Calories: 380Kcal; Fat: 31g; Carbs: 3g; Protein: 233g

69. Ice Cream Chaffles

Preparation time: 10 minutes
Cooking time: 14 minutes
Servings: 1
Ingredients:
- 1 egg, beaten
- ½ cup finely grated mozzarella cheese
- ¼ cup almond flour
- 2 tbsp. Swerve confectioners' sugar
- ⅛ tsp. xanthan gum
- low-carb ice cream (flavor of your choice) for serving

Directions:
Preheat the waffle iron.
In a medium bowl, mix all the ingredients, except the ice cream.
Open the iron and add half of the mixture. Close and cook until crispy, 7 minutes.
Transfer the chaffle to a plate and make the second one with the remaining batter.
On each chaffle, add a scoop of low-carb ice cream, fold into half-moons and enjoy.

Per serving: Calories: 320Kcal; Fat: 27g; Carbs: 5g; Protein: 22g

70. Mozzarella Chaffles with Vanilla

Preparation time: 10 minutes
Cooking time: 12 minutes
Servings: 2
Ingredients:
- 1 organic egg, beaten
- 1 tsp. organic vanilla extract
- 1 tbsp. almond flour
- 1 tsp. organic baking powder
- a pinch of ground cinnamon
- 1 cup mozzarella cheese, shredded

Directions:
Preheat your mini waffle iron and then grease it.
In a bowl, combine the egg and vanilla extract. Stir until homogeneous.
Add the baking powder, cinnamon, flour and mix well.
In a small bowl, place the egg and mozzarella cheese and stir to combine.
Pour half of the mixture into the preheat waffle iron and cook for about 5 minutes or until golden brown.
Repeat with the remaining mixture.
Per serving: Calories: 321Kcal; Fat: 28g; Carbs: 4g; Protein: 23g

71. Bruschetta Chaffle

Preparation time: 10 minutes
Cooking time: 5 minutes
Servings: 1
Ingredients:
- 2 basic chaffles
- 2 tbsp. sugar-free marinara sauce
- 2 tbsp. mozzarella, shredded
- 1 tbsp. olives, sliced
- 1 tomato sliced
- 1 tbsp. keto-friendly pesto sauce
- basil leaves

Directions:
Spread marinara sauce on each chaffle.
Spoon pesto and spread on top of the marinara sauce.
Top with the tomato, olives, and mozzarella.
Bake in the oven for 3 minutes or until the cheese has melted.
Garnish with basil.
Per serving: Calories: 211Kcal; Fat: 12g; Carbs: 8g; Protein: 19g

72. Egg-Free Psyllium Husk Chaffles

Preparation time: 8 minutes
Cooking time: 4 minutes
Servings: 1
Ingredients:
- 1 ounce mozzarella cheese, shredded
- 1 tbsp. cream cheese softened
- 1 tbsp. psyllium husk powder

Directions:
Preheat your waffle iron and then grease it.
In a blender, place all the ingredients and pulse until the mixture becomes slightly crumbly.
Place the mixture into the preheated waffle iron and cook for about 4 minutes or until golden brown.
Serve them warm.
Per serving: Calories: 290Kcal; Fat: 25g; Carbs: 1g; Protein: 28g

73. Mozzarella and Almond Flour Chaffles

Preparation time: 10 minutes
Cooking time: 8 minutes
Servings: 1
Ingredients:
- ½ cup mozzarella cheese, shredded
- 1 large organic egg
- 2 tbsp. blanched almond flour
- ¼ tsp. organic baking powder

Directions:
Preheat the mini waffle iron and then grease it.
Place all the ingredients in a bowl and mix them until properly combined.
Drop half of the mixture into the preheated waffle iron and cook for about 4 minutes or until golden brown.
Repeat with the remaining mixture.
Per serving: Calories: 348Kcal; Fat: 28g; Carbs: 2g; Protein: 21g

74. Pulled Pork Sandwich Chaffle

Preparation time: 9 minutes
Cooking time: 28 minutes
Servings: 2
Ingredients:
- 2 eggs, beaten
- 1 cup finely grated cheddar cheese
- ¼ tsp. baking powder
- 2 cups cooked and shredded pork
- 1 tbsp. sugar-free BBQ sauce
- 2 cup shredded coleslaw mix
- 2 tbsp. apple cider vinegar
- ½ tsp. salt
- ¼ cup ranch dressing

Directions:
Preheat the waffle iron.
In a medium bowl, mix the eggs, cheddar cheese, and baking powder. Open the iron and add a quarter of the mixture. Close and cook until crispy, 7 minutes.
Transfer the chaffle to a plate and make 3 more chaffles in the same manner.
Meanwhile, in another medium bowl, mix the pulled pork with the BBQ sauce until well combined. Set it aside.
Also, mix the coleslaw mix, apple cider vinegar, salt, and ranch dressing in another medium bowl.
When the chaffles are ready, on two pieces, divide the pork and then top with the ranch coleslaw. Cover with the remaining chaffles and insert mini skewers to secure the sandwiches.
Per serving: Calories: 314Kcal; Fat: 31g; Carbs: 5g; Protein: 28g

75. Cheddar and Egg White Chaffles

Preparation time: 9 minutes
Cooking time: 12 minutes
Servings: 2
Ingredients:
- 2 egg whites
- 1 cup cheddar cheese, shredded

Directions:
Preheat your mini waffle iron and then grease it.
Place the egg whites in a small-sized bowl and cheese and stir to combine.
Place ¼ of the mixture into the preheated waffle iron and cook for about 4 minutes or until golden brown.
Repeat with the remaining mixture.
Per serving: Calories: 300Kcal; Fat: 25g; Carbs: 31g; Protein: 20g

76. Spicy Shrimps and Chaffles

Preparation time: 9 minutes
Cooking time: 31 minutes
Servings: 2

Ingredients:
Shrimps:
- 1 tbsp. olive oil
- 1 lb. jumbo shrimp, peeled and deveined
- 1 tbsp. Creole seasoning
- salt to taste
- 2 tbsp. hot sauce
- 3 tbsp. butter
- 2 tbsp. chopped fresh scallions to garnish

Chaffles:
- 2 eggs, beaten
- 1 cup finely grated Monterey Jack cheese

Directions:

Shrimps:

Heat the olive oil in a medium skillet over medium heat.

Season the shrimp with Creole seasoning and salt. Cook in the oil until pink and opaque on both sides, 2 minutes.

Pour in the hot sauce and butter. Mix well until the shrimp is adequately coated in the sauce, 1 minute.

Turn the heat off and set it aside.

Chaffles:

Preheat the waffle iron.

In a medium bowl, mix the eggs and Monterey Jack cheese.

Open the iron and add a quarter of the mixture. Close and cook until crispy, 7 minutes.

Transfer the chaffle to a plate and make 3 more chaffles in the same manner.

Cut the chaffles into quarters and place them on a plate.

Top with the shrimp and garnish with the scallions.

Per serving: Calories: 406Kcal; Fat: 35g; Carbs: 4g; Protein: 20g

77. Creamy Chicken Sandwich Chaffle

Preparation time: 10 minutes
Cooking time: 10 minutes
Servings: 2
Ingredients:

- cooking spray
- 1 cup chicken breast fillet, cubed
- salt and pepper to taste
- ¼ cup all-purpose cream
- 4 garlic chaffles
- parsley, chopped

Directions:

Spray your pan with oil.

Put it over medium heat.

Add the chicken fillet cubes.

Season with salt and pepper.

Reduce the heat and add the cream.

Spread the chicken mixture on top of the chaffle.

Garnish with parsley and top with another chaffle.

Per serving: Calories: 451Kcal; Fat: 26g; Carbs: 4g; Protein: 21g

78. Cannoli Chaffle

Preparation time: 9 minutes
Cooking time: 28 minutes
Servings: 2
Ingredients:
Chaffles:

- 1 large egg
- 1 egg yolk
- 3 tbsp. butter, melted
- 1 tbsp. Swerve confectioners' sugar
- 1 cup finely grated parmesan cheese
- 2 tbsp. finely grated mozzarella cheese

Filling:

- ½ cup ricotta cheese
- 2 tbsp. Swerve confectioners' sugar
- 1 tsp. vanilla extract
- 2 tbsp. unsweetened chocolate chips for garnishing

Directions:

Preheat the waffle iron.

Meanwhile, in a medium bowl, mix all the ingredients for the chaffles.

Open the iron, pour in a quarter of the mixture, cover and cook until crispy, 7 minutes.

Remove the chaffle onto a plate and make 3 more with the remaining batter.

Cannoli filling:

Beat the ricotta cheese and Swerve confectioners' sugar until smooth. Mix in the vanilla.

On each chaffle, spread some of the filling and wrap over.

Garnish the creamy ends with some chocolate chips.

Serve immediately.

Per serving: Calories: 446Kcal; Fat: 37g; Carbs: 9g; Protein: 27g

79. Strawberry Shortcake Chaffle Bowls

Preparation time: 15 minutes
Cooking time: 28 minutes
Servings: 1
Ingredients:

- 1 egg, beaten
- ½ cup finely grated mozzarella cheese
- 1 tbsp. almond flour
- ¼ tsp. baking powder
- 3 drops cake batter extract
- 1 cup cream cheese, softened
- 1 cup fresh strawberries, sliced
- 1 tbsp. sugar-free maple syrup

Directions:

Preheat a waffle bowl maker and grease lightly with cooking spray.

Meanwhile, in a medium bowl, whisk all the ingredients, except the cream cheese and strawberries.

Open the iron, pour in half of the mixture, cover and cook until crispy, 6 to 7 minutes.

Remove the chaffle bowl onto a plate and set it aside.

Make a second chaffle bowl with the remaining batter.

To serve, divide the cream cheese into the chaffle bowls and top with the strawberries.

Drizzle the filling with maple syrup and serve.

Per serving: Calories: 457Kcal; Fat: 39g; Carbs: 7g; Protein: 23g

80. Chocolate Melt Chaffles

Preparation time: 9 minutes
Cooking time: 36 minutes
Servings: 2
Ingredients:
For the Chaffles:

- 2 eggs, beaten
- ¼ cup finely grated gruyere cheese
- 2 tbsp. heavy cream
- 1 tbsp. coconut flour
- 2 tbsp. cream cheese softened
- 3 tbsp. unsweetened cocoa powder
- 2 tsp. vanilla extract
- a pinch of salt

For the Chocolate Sauce:

- 1/3 cup + 1 tbsp. Heavy cream
- 1½ oz. unsweetened baking chocolate, chopped
- 1½ tsp. sugar-free maple syrup
- 1½ tsp. vanilla extract

Directions:

Chaffles:

Preheat the waffle iron.

In a medium bowl, mix all the ingredients for the chaffles.

Open the iron and add a quarter of the mixture. Close and cook until crispy, 7 minutes.

Transfer the chaffle to a plate and make 3 more with the remaining batter.

Chocolate Sauce:

Pour the heavy cream into the saucepan and simmer over low heat, 3 minutes.

Turn the heat off and add the chocolate. Allow melting for a few minutes and stir until fully melted (5 minutes).

Mix in the maple syrup and vanilla extract.

Assemble the chaffles in layers with the chocolate sauce sandwiched between each layer.

Slice and serve immediately.

Per serving: Calories: 438Kcal; Fat: 34g; Carbs: 8g; Protein: 25g

81. Pumpkin and Pecan Chaffles

Preparation time: 10 minutes
Cooking time: 10 minutes
Servings: 1
Ingredients:

- 1 egg, beaten
- ½ cup mozzarella cheese, grated
- ½ tsp. pumpkin spice
- 1 tbsp. pureed pumpkin
- 2 tbsp. almond flour
- 1 tsp. sweetener
- 2 tbsp. pecans, chopped

Directions:
Turn on the waffle maker.
Beat the egg in a bowl.
Stir in the rest of the ingredients.
Pour half of the mixture into the device.
Seal the lid.
Cook for 5 minutes.
Remove the chaffle carefully.
Repeat the steps to make the second chaffle.
Per serving: Calories: 304Kcal; Fat: 26g; Carbs: 1g; Protein: 24g

82. Spicy Jalapeño and Bacon Chaffles

Preparation time: 10 minutes
Cooking time: 5 minutes
Servings: 1
Ingredients:

- 1 oz. cream cheese
- 1 large egg
- ½ cup cheddar cheese
- 2 tbsp. bacon bits
- ½ tbsp. jalapeños
- ¼ tsp. baking powder
- vanilla extract

Directions:
Switch on your waffle maker.
Plug in your waffle maker to preheat it and grease it.
Mix together the egg and vanilla extract in a bowl first.
Add baking powder, jalapeños, and bacon bites.
Add in the cheese last and mix together.
Pour the chaffles batter into the maker and cook the chaffles for about 2-3 minutes.
Once the chaffles are cooked, remove them from the maker.
Per serving: Calories: 311Kcal; Fat: 27g; Carbs: 2g; Protein: 21g

83. Zucchini Parmesan Chaffles

Preparation time: 10 minutes
Cooking time: 14 minutes
Servings: 1
Ingredients:

- 1 cup shredded zucchini
- 1 egg, beaten
- ½ cup finely grated parmesan cheese
- salt and freshly ground black pepper to taste

Directions:
Preheat the waffle iron.
Put all the ingredients in a medium bowl and mix well.
Open the iron and add half of the mixture. Close and cook until crispy, 7 minutes.
Remove the chaffle onto a plate and make another with the remaining mixture.
Cut each chaffle into wedges and serve afterward.
Per serving: Calories: 341Kcal; Fat: 3427g; Carbs: 4g; Protein: 21g

84. Cheddar and Almond Flour Chaffles

Preparation time: 10 minutes
Cooking time: 10 minutes
Servings: 1
Ingredients:

- 1 large organic egg, beaten
- ½ cup cheddar cheese, shredded
- 2 tbsp. almond flour

Directions:
Preheat the mini waffle iron and then grease it.
In a bowl, place the egg, cheddar cheese, and almond flour and beat until they are properly combined.
Pour half of the mixture into the preheated waffle iron and cook for about 5 minutes or until golden brown.
Repeat with the remaining mixture.
Serve warm.
Per serving: Calories: 310Kcal; Fat: 27g; Carbs: 3g; Protein: 23g

85. Asian Cauliflower Chaffles

Preparation time: 9 minutes
Cooking time: 28 minutes
Servings: 1
Ingredients:

Chaffles:
- 1 cup cauliflower rice, steamed
- 1 large egg, beaten
- salt to your taste
- freshly ground black pepper to your taste
- 1 cup finely grated parmesan cheese
- 1 tsp. sesame seeds
- ¼ cup chopped fresh scallions

Dipping Sauce:
- 3 tbsp. coconut aminos
- 1½ tbsp. plain vinegar
- 1 tsp. fresh ginger puree
- 1 tsp. fresh garlic paste
- 3 tbsp. sesame oil
- 1 tsp. fish sauce
- 1 tsp. red chili flakes

Directions:
Preheat the waffle iron.
In a medium bowl, mix the cauliflower rice, egg, salt, black pepper, and parmesan cheese.
Open the iron and add a quarter of the mixture. Close and cook until crispy, 7 minutes.
Transfer the chaffle to a plate and make 3 more chaffles in the same manner.
Meanwhile, make the dipping sauce.
In a medium bowl, mix all the ingredients for the dipping sauce.
Plate the chaffles, garnish with the sesame seeds and scallions and serve with the dipping sauce.
Per serving: Calories: 327Kcal; Fat: 28g; Carbs: 6g; Protein: 22g

86. Flaxseed Chaffles

Preparation time: 10 minutes
Cooking time: 20 minutes
Servings: 4
Ingredients:

- 2 cup ground flaxseed
- 2 tsp. ground cinnamon
- 1 tsp. sea salt
- 1 tbsp. baking powder
- 1/3 cup/80 ml avocado oil
- 5 eggs, at room temperature
- ½ cup/120 ml water
- whipped cream as needed for topping

Directions:

Take a non-stick waffle iron, plug it in, select the medium or medium-high heat setting and let it preheat until ready to use; it could also be indicated with an indicator light changing its color.

Meanwhile, make the batter and for this, take a large bowl and then stir in flaxseed, salt, and baking powder until combined.

Crack the eggs in a jug, pour in oil and water, whisk these ingredients until blended and then stir this mixture into the flour with the spatula until incorporated and fluffy mixture comes together.

Allow the batter to rest for 5 minutes, and then stir in cinnamon until mixed.

Use a ladle to pour one-fourth of the prepared batter into the heated waffle iron in a spiral direction, starting from the edges. Then shut the lid and cook for 5 minutes or more until solid and nicely browned; the cooked waffle will look like a cake.

When done, transfer the chaffle to a plate with a silicone spatula and repeat with the remaining batter.

Top the waffles with whipped cream and then serve them straight away.

Per serving: Calories: 379Kcal; Fat: 29g; Carbs: 2g; Protein: 22g

87. Hazelnut Chaffles

Preparation time: 10 minutes
Cooking time: 30 minutes
Servings: 3
Ingredients:

- 1 cup/100g hazelnut flour
- ½ tsp. baking powder
- 2 tbsp. hazelnut oil
- 1 cup/245g almond milk, unsweetened
- 3 eggs, at room temperature

Directions:

Take a non-stick waffle iron, plug it in, select the medium or medium-high heat setting and let it preheat until ready to use; it could also be indicated with an indicator light changing its color.

Meanwhile, make the batter. For this, take a large bowl, add flour in it, stir in the baking powder until mixed, and then mix in oil, milk, and egg with an electric mixer until smooth.

Use a ladle to pour one-sixth of the prepared batter into the heated waffle iron in a spiral direction, starting from the edges. Then shut the lid and cook for 5 minutes or more until solid and nicely browned; the cooked waffle will look like a cake.

When done, transfer the chaffle to a plate with a silicone spatula and repeat with the remaining batter.

Let the chaffles stand for some time until crispy and serve them straight away.

Per serving: Calories: 343Kcal; Fat: 34g; Carbs: 3g; Protein: 25g

88. Maple Pumpkin Chaffles

Preparation time: 5 minutes
Cooking time: 4 minutes
Servings: 2

Ingredients:

- 2 eggs
- ¾ tsp. baking powder
- 2 tsp. 100% pumpkin puree
- ¾ tsp. pumpkin pie spice
- 4 tsp. heavy whipping cream
- 2 tsp. sugar-free maple syrup
- 1 tsp. coconut flour
- ½ cup mozzarella cheese, shredded
- ½ tsp. vanilla
- a pinch of salt

Directions:

Preheat the waffle maker.

Combine all the ingredients in a small mixing bowl.

If you're using a mini waffle maker, pour around ¼ of the batter. Allow it to cook for 3-4 minutes.

Repeat.

Per serving: Calories: 3280Kcal; Fat: 43g; Carbs: 3g; Protein: 23g

89. Nutty Chaffles

Preparation time: 5 minutes
Cooking time: 5 minutes
Servings: 1
Ingredients:

- 1 egg
- 1 tsp. coconut flour
- 1½ tbsp. unsweetened cocoa
- 2 tbsp. sugar-free sweetener
- 1 tbsp. heavy cream
- ½ tsp. baking powder
- ½ tsp. vanilla

Directions:

Preheat the mini waffle maker.

Combine all the ingredients in a small-sized bowl. Mix well.

Drop half of the mixture into the waffle maker and spread evenly.

Allow it to cook for 3-5 minutes until golden brown and crispy.

Carefully remove and add the remaining batter.

Per serving: Calories: 2348Kcal; Fat: 26g; Carbs: 8.4g; Protein: 24g

90. Chaffles with Everything But the Bagel Seasoning

Preparation time: 5 minutes
Cooking time: 5 minutes
Servings: 1
Ingredients:

- 1 egg
- ½ cup parmesan cheese
- 1 tsp. everything but the bagel seasoning
- ½ cup mozzarella cheese
- 2 tsp. almond flour

Directions:

Preheat the waffle maker.

Sprinkle the mozzarella cheese onto the waffle maker. Let it melt and cook for 30 seconds until crispy. Remove this from the waffle maker.

Using a whisk, combine the eggs, parmesan, almond flour, seasoning, and the toasted cheese in a small bowl.

Pour the batter into the waffle maker.

Allow 3-4 minutes for the batter to cook until crispy and golden brown in color.

Per serving: Calories: 327Kcal; Fat: 34g; Carbs: 4g; Protein: 22g

91. Strawberry and Cream Cheese Chaffles

Preparation time: 5 minutes
Cooking time: 5 minutes
Servings: 2
Ingredients:
- 2 tsp. coconut flour
- 4 tsp. monk fruit
- ¼ tsp. baking powder
- 2 eggs
- 1 oz. cream cheese, softened
- ½ tsp. vanilla extract
- ¼ cup strawberries

Directions:
Preheat the waffle maker.
In a bowl, put in the coconut flour, then add the baking powder and the monk fruit.
Add in the egg, cream cheese, and vanilla extract. Mix well with a whisk.
Cook the batter into the waffle maker for 3-4 minutes.
Repeat until the batter is finished.
Allow the chaffles to cool before topping with strawberries.
Per serving: Calories: 398Kcal; Fat: 33g; Carbs: 2g; Protein: 23g

92. Pumpkin Chaffle with Cream Cheese Glaze

Preparation time: 5 minutes
Cooking time: 5 minutes
Servings: 1
Ingredients:
- 1 egg
- ½ cup mozzarella cheese
- ½ tsp. pumpkin pie spice
- 1 tbsp. pumpkin

For the Cream Cheese Frosting:
- 2 tbsp. cream cheese, softened at room temperature
- 2 tbsp. monk fruit sweetener
- ½ tsp. vanilla extract

Directions:
Preheat the waffle maker.
Whip the egg in a small bowl.
Add the cheese, pumpkin, and pumpkin pie spice to the whipped egg and mix well.
Pour half of the batter into the waffle maker and cook it for 3-4 minutes.
While waiting for the chaffle to cook, combine all the ingredients for the frosting in another bowl. Continue mixing until a smooth and creamy consistency is reached. Feel free to add more butter if you prefer a buttery taste.
Allow the chaffle to cool before frosting the chaffles with cream cheese.
Per serving: Calories: 455Kcal; Fat: 48g; Carbs: 4g; Protein: 22g

93. Cream Cheese and Cereal Cake Chaffle

Preparation time: 10 minutes
Cooking time: 5 minutes
Servings: 1
Ingredients:
Chaffles:
- 1 egg
- 2 tbsp. almond flour
- ½ tsp. coconut flour
- 1 tbsp. butter, melted
- 1 tbsp. cream cheese, softened
- ¼ tsp. vanilla extract
- ¼ tsp. baking powder
- 1 tbsp. sweetener
- ⅛ tsp. xanthan gum

Toppings:
- 20 drops Captain Cereal flavoring
- Whipped cream

Directions:
Preheat the mini waffle maker.
Blend or mix all the chaffles ingredients until the consistency is creamy and smooth. Allow them to rest for a few minutes so that the flour absorbs the liquid ingredients.
Scoop out 2-3 tbsp. of batter and put it into the waffle maker. Allow it to cook for 2-3 minutes.
Top the cooked chaffles with freshly whipped cream.
Add syrup and drops of Captain Cereal flavoring for a great flavor.
Per serving: Calories: 335Kcal; Fat: 2g; Carbs: 8g; Protein: 10g

94. Pumpkin Chaffles with Maple Syrup

Preparation time: 10 minutes
Cooking time: 16 minutes
Servings: 2
Ingredients:
- 2 eggs, beaten
- ½ cup mozzarella cheese, shredded
- 1 tsp. coconut flour
- ¾ tsp. baking powder
- ¾ tsp. pumpkin pie spice
- 2 tsp. pureed pumpkin
- 4 tsp. heavy whipping cream ½ tsp. vanilla
- a pinch of salt
- 2 tsp. maple syrup (sugar-free)

Directions:
Turn your waffle maker on.
Combine well all the ingredients, except maple syrup, in a large bowl.
Pour half (or a quarter) of the batter into the waffle maker and cook for 8 minutes.
Transfer to a plate to cool for 2 minutes.
Repeat the steps with the remaining mixture.
Drizzle some maple syrup on top of the chaffles before serving.
Per serving: Calories: 350Kcal; Fat: 35g; Carbs: 6g; Protein: 25g

95. Maple Syrup and Vanilla Chaffles

Preparation time: 10 minutes
Cooking time: 12 minutes
Servings: 2
Ingredients:
- 1 egg, beaten
- ¼ cup mozzarella cheese, shredded
- 1 oz. cream cheese
- 1 tsp. vanilla
- 1 tbsp. keto maple syrup
- 1 tsp. sweetener
- 1 tsp. baking powder
- 4 tbsp. almond flour

Directions:
Preheat your waffle maker.
Add all the ingredients to a bowl.
Mix well.
Drop half of the mixture into the waffle maker, close the lid and cook for 4 minutes.
Transfer the chaffle to a plate and let it cool for 2 minutes.
Then, using the remaining mixture, repeat the operation.
Per serving: Calories: 515Kcal; Fat: 34g; Carbs: 3g; Protein: 23g

96. Easy Celery and Cottage Cheese Chaffles

Preparation time: 10 minutes
Cooking time: 15 minutes
Servings: 4
Ingredients:

- 4 eggs
- 2 cup grated cheddar cheese
- 1 cup fresh celery, chopped
- salt and pepper to taste
- ¼ cup cottage cheese for serving

Directions:
Preheat the waffle maker.
Add the eggs, grated mozzarella cheese, chopped celery, salt and pepper, chopped almonds, and baking powder to a bowl and mix them
Pour a few tbsp. of the batter into the maker.
Cook for about 4-5 minutes.
Serve each chaffle with cottage cheese on top.
Per serving: Calories: 392Kcal; Fat: 32g; Carbs: 3g; Protein: 26g

97. Mushroom and Almond Chaffles

Preparation time: 10 minutes
Cooking time: 15 minutes
Servings: 4
Ingredients:

- 4 eggs
- 2 cup grated mozzarella cheese
- 3 tbsp. chopped almonds
- 2 tsp. baking powder
- salt and pepper to taste
- 1 tsp. dried basil
- 1 tsp. chili flakes
- 2 tbsp. cooking spray to brush the waffle maker
- mushrooms

Directions:
Preheat the waffle maker.
Add the eggs, grated mozzarella, mushrooms, almonds, baking powder, salt and pepper, dried basil, and chili flakes to a bowl.
Mix with a fork.
Brush the heated waffle maker with cooking spray and add a few tbsp. of the batter.
Close the lid and cook for about 7 minutes, depending on your waffle maker.
Serve them and enjoy.
Per serving: Calories: 254Kcal; Fat: 33g; Carbs: 3g; Protein: 22g

98. Spinach and Artichoke Chaffles

Preparation time: 10 minutes
Cooking time: 15 minutes
Servings: 4
Ingredients:

- 4 eggs
- 2 cup grated provolone cheese
- 1 cup cooked and diced spinach
- ½ cup diced artichoke hearts
- salt and pepper to taste
- 2 tbsp. coconut flour
- 2 tsp. baking powder
- 2 tbsp. cooking spray to brush the waffle maker
- ¼ cup of cream cheese for serving

Directions:
Preheat the waffle maker.
Add the eggs, grated provolone cheese, diced spinach, artichoke hearts, salt and pepper, baking powder, and coconut flour into a bowl and mix well.
Spray the heated waffle maker with cooking spray and add a few tbsp. of the batter.
Close the lid and cook for about 7 minutes, depending on your waffle maker.
Serve each chaffle with cream cheese.
Per serving: Calories: 344Kcal; Fat: 35g; Carbs: 5g; Protein: 25g

99. Avocado Croque Madam Chaffle

Preparation time: 10 minutes
Cooking time: 15 minutes
Servings: 4
Ingredients:

- 4 eggs
- 1 avocado, mashed
- 1 avocado, mashed
- 2 cup grated mozzarella cheese
- 6 tbsp. almond flour
- 2 tsp. baking powder
- 1 tsp. dried dill
- 2 tbsp. cooking spray to brush the waffle maker

Toppings:

- 4 fried eggs
- 2 tbsp. chopped basil (fresh)
- salt and pepper to taste

Directions:
Plug in the waffle maker.
In a large bowl, mix well all the ingredients, except those for the topping.
Spray the heated waffle maker with cooking spray and add a few tbsp. of the batter.
Cook for about 5-6 minutes, depending on your waffle maker.
On top of each chaffle, place a fried egg and fresh basil. Serve and enjoy.
Per serving: Calories: 334Kcal; Fat: 33g; Carbs: 7g; Protein: 24g

100. Fruity Vegan Chaffles

Preparation time: 10 minutes
Cooking time: 5 minutes
Servings: 2
Ingredients:

- 1 tbsp. chia seeds
- 2 tbsp. warm water
- ¼ cup low carb vegan cheese
- 2 tbsp. strawberry puree
- 2 tbsp. Greek yogurt
- a pinch of salt

Directions:
Preheat the waffle maker to medium-high heat.
In a small bowl, mix together chia seeds and water and let it stand for a few minutes to be thickened.
Mix the rest of the ingredients in the chia seed and egg and mix well.
Spray the waffle machine with cooking spray.
Pour the vegan waffle batter into the center of the waffle iron.
Close the waffle maker and cook the chaffles for about 3-5 minutes.
Once cooked, remove from the maker and serve with berries on top.
Per serving: Calories: 335Kcal; Fat: 29g; Carbs: 4g; Protein: 24g

101. Almonds and Flaxseeds Chaffles

Preparation time: 10 minutes
Cooking time: 5 minutes
Servings: 2
Ingredients:

- ¼ cup coconut flour
- 1 tsp. stevia
- 1 tbsp. ground flaxseed
- ¼ tsp. baking powder
- ½ cup almond milk
- ¼ tsp. vanilla extract
- ½ cup low carb vegan cheese

Directions:
Mix together flaxseed in warm water and set it aside.
Add in the remaining ingredients.
Switch on the waffle iron and grease with cooking spray.
Drop half the mixture into the waffle maker and spread evenly.
Cook the chaffles for about 3-4 minutes.
Once cooked, remove it from the waffle machine.
Serve with berries and enjoy!
Per serving: Calories: 371Kcal; Fat: 28g; Carbs: 3g; Protein: 23g

102. Vegan Choco Chaffles

Preparation time: 10 minutes
Cooking time: 5 minutes
Servings: 2
Ingredients:

- ½ cup coconut flour
- 3 tbsp. cocoa powder
- 2 tbsp. whole psyllium husk
- ½ tsp. baking powder
- a pinch of salt
- ½ cup vegan cheese, softened
- ¼ cup coconut milk

Directions:
Preheat your waffle iron according to the manufacturer's directions.
Mix together the coconut flour, cocoa powder, baking powder, salt, and husk in a bowl and set aside.
Add melted cheese and milk and mix well. Let it stand for a few minutes before cooking.
Pour the batter into the waffle maker and cook for about 3-minutes.
Once the chaffles are cooked, carefully remove them from the waffle machine.
Serve with vegan ice cream and enjoy!
Per serving: Calories: 398Kcal; Fat: 34g; Carbs: 4g; Protein: 38g

103. Vegan Chaffles with Flaxseed

Preparation time: 10 minutes
Cooking time: 5 minutes
Servings: 2
Ingredients:

- 1 tbsp. flaxseed meal
- 2 tbsp. warm water
- ¼ cup low carb vegan cheese
- ¼ cup chopped minutest
- a pinch of salt
- 2 oz. blueberries chunks

Directions:
Warm up your waffle maker and then grease it with cooking spray.
Mix together the flaxseed meal and warm water and set it aside to be thickened.
After 5 minutes, mix together all the ingredients in flax-egg.
Pour the vegan waffle batter into the center of the waffle maker.
Close the lid and let it cook for 3-minutes

Once cooked, remove the vegan chaffle from the waffle maker and serve.
Per serving: Calories: 295Kcal; Fat: 27g; Carbs: 3g; Protein: 23g

104. Asparagus Chaffles

Preparation time: 10 minutes
Cooking time: 15 minutes
Servings: 4
Ingredients:

- 4 eggs
- 1½ cup mozzarella cheese, grated
- ½ cup parmesan cheese, grated
- 1 cup boiled asparagus, chopped
- salt and pepper to taste
- ¼ cup almond flour
- 2 tsp. baking powder
- 2 tbsp. cooking spray to brush the waffle maker
- ¼ cup Greek yogurt for serving
- ¼ cup chopped almonds for serving

Directions:
Preheat the waffle maker.
Add the eggs, grated mozzarella, grated parmesan, asparagus, salt and pepper, almond flour, and baking powder to a bowl.
Mix with a fork.
Grease your maker using a non-stick cooking spray and add a few tbsp. of the batter.
Cook for about 7 minutes or until golden brown.
Serve each chaffle with Greek yogurt and chopped almonds.
Per serving: Calories: 320Kcal; Fat: 35g; Carbs: 5g; Protein: 24g

105. Black Olives and Cheddar Chaffles

Preparation time: 10 minutes
Cooking time: 10 minutes
Servings: 1
Ingredients:

- 1 organic egg, beaten
- ½ cup sharp cheddar cheese, shredded
- 6/7 black olives, chopped

Directions:
Preheat your mini waffle iron and then grease it.
In a small bowl, place the egg and cheese and stir to combine.
Add olives into the batter
Spoon half of the prepared batter into the preheated waffle iron and cook for about 5 minutes or until golden brown.
Repeat with the remaining mixture.
Serve them warm.
Per serving: Calories: 300Kcal; Fat: 25g; Carbs: 1g; Protein: 20g

106. Egg-Free Almond Flour Chaffles

Preparation time: 10 minutes
Cooking time: 10 minutes
Servings: 2
Ingredients:

- 2 tbsp. cream cheese, softened
- 1 cup mozzarella cheese, shredded
- 2 tbsp. almond flour
- 1 tsp. organic baking powder

Directions:
Preheat the mini waffle iron and then grease it.
Place all the ingredients in a medium-sized bowl. Mix until smooth.
Place half of the mixture into the waffle iron and let it cook until golden brown (4-5 minutes)
Repeat with the remaining mixture.
Per serving: Calories: 345Kcal; Fat: 37g; Carbs: 1g; Protein: 20g

107. Mozzarella and Psyllium Husk Chaffles

Preparation time: 10 minutes
Cooking time: 8 minutes
Servings: 1
Ingredients:

- ½ cup mozzarella cheese, shredded
- 1 large organic egg, beaten
- 2 tbsp. blanched almond flour
- ½ tsp. psyllium husk powder
- ¼ tsp. organic baking powder

Directions:
Preheat the mini waffle iron and then grease it.
In a small-sized bowl, place all the ingredients and beat them until well combined.
Fill the waffle maker with half of the batter and close the lid. Cook for about 4 minutes or until golden brown.
Repeat with the remaining mixture.
Per serving: Calories: 314Kcal; Fat: 28g; Carbs: 2g; Protein: 25g

108. Pumpkin-Cinnamon Churro Sticks

Preparation time: 10 minutes
Cooking time: 14 minutes
Servings: 2
Ingredients:

- 3 tbsp. coconut flour
- ¼ cup pumpkin puree
- 1 egg, beaten
- ½ cup finely grated mozzarella cheese
- 2 tbsp. sugar-free maple syrup + more for serving
- 1 tsp. baking powder
- 1 tsp. vanilla extract
- ½ tsp. pumpkin spice seasoning
- ⅛ tsp. salt
- 1 tbsp. cinnamon powder

Directions:
Preheat the waffle iron.
Mix all the ingredients in a medium bowl until well combined.
Open the iron and add half of the mixture, and cook for about 7 minutes or until golden brown and crispy.
Remove the chaffle onto a plate and make one more with the remaining batter.
Cut each chaffle into sticks, drizzle the top with more maple syrup and serve after.
Per serving: Calories: 353Kcal; Fat: 26g; Carbs: 3g; Protein: 22g

109. Chicken Parmesan and Jalapeño Chaffles

Preparation time: 10 minutes
Cooking time: 14 minutes
Servings: 2
Ingredients:

- ⅛ cup finely grated parmesan cheese
- ¼ cup finely grated cheddar cheese
- 1 egg, beaten
- ½ cup cooked chicken breasts, diced
- 1 small jalapeño pepper, deseeded and minced
- ⅛ tsp. garlic powder
- ⅛ tsp. onion powder
- 1 tsp. cream cheese, softened

Directions:
Preheat the waffle iron.
In a medium bowl, mix all the ingredients until adequately combined.
Open the iron and add half of the mixture. Close and cook until crispy, 7 minutes.

Transfer the chaffle to a plate and make a second chaffle in the same manner.
Allow to cool and serve afterward.
Per serving: Calories: 450Kcal; Fat: 28g; Carbs: 4g; Protein: 25g

110. Chocolate and Almond Chaffles

Preparation time: 6 minutes
Cooking time: 12 minutes
Servings: 2
Ingredients:

- 1 egg
- ¼ cup mozzarella cheese, shredded
- 1 oz. cream cheese
- 2 tsp. sweetener
- 1 tsp. vanilla
- 2 tbsp. cocoa powder
- 1 tsp. baking powder
- 2 tbsp. almonds, chopped
- 4 tbsp. almond flour

Directions:
Blend all the ingredients in a bowl while the waffle maker is preheating.
Pour some of the mixture into the waffle maker.
Close and cook for 4 minutes.
Transfer the chaffle to a plate. Let cool for 2 minutes.
Repeat the steps using the remaining mixture.
Per serving: Calories: 428Kcal; Fat: 36g; Carbs: 2g; Protein: 23g

111. Chocolate Fudge Chaffles

Preparation time: 10 minutes
Cooking time: 14 minutes
Servings: 2
Ingredients:

- 1 egg, beaten
- ¼ cup finely grated gruyere cheese
- 2 tbsp. unsweetened cocoa powder
- ¼ tsp. baking powder
- ¼ tsp. vanilla extract
- 2 tbsp. erythritol
- 1 tsp. almond flour
- 1 tsp. Heavy whipping cream
- a pinch of salt

Directions:
Preheat the waffle iron.
Add all the ingredients to a medium bowl and mix well.
Open the iron and add half of the mixture. Let it cook until golden brown and crispy (about 6-7 minutes)
Remove the chaffle onto a plate and make another with the remaining batter.
Cut each chaffle into wedges and serve after.
Per serving: Calories: 329Kcal; Fat: 36g; Carbs: 3g; Protein: 25g

112. Brownie Sundae Chaffle

Preparation time: 9 minutes
Cooking time: 30 minutes
Servings: 2
Ingredients:
Chaffles:

- 2 eggs, beaten
- 1 tbsp. unsweetened cocoa powder
- 1 tbsp. erythritol
- 1 cup finely grated mozzarella cheese

Toppings:

- 3 tbsp. unsweetened chocolate, chopped
- 3 tbsp. unsalted butter

- ½ cup Swerve sugar
- low-carb ice cream
- 1 cup whipped cream
- 3 tbsp. sugar-free caramel sauce

Directions:
Preheat the waffle iron.
Meanwhile, in a medium bowl, mix all the ingredients for the chaffles.
Open the iron, pour in a quarter of the mixture, cover and cook until crispy, 7 minutes.
Remove the chaffle onto a plate and make 3 more with the remaining batter.
Plate and set them aside.
Meanwhile, melt the chocolate and butter in a medium saucepan with occasional stirring, 2 minutes.
Divide the chaffles into wedges and top with the ice cream, whipped cream, and swirl the chocolate sauce and caramel sauce on top.
Serve immediately.
Per serving: Calories: 548Kcal; Fat: 42g; Carbs: 6g; Protein: 20g

113. Cream Cheese Chaffles

Preparation time: 10 minutes
Cooking time: 8 minutes
Servings: 1
Ingredients:
- 1 egg, beaten
- 1 oz. cream cheese
- 4 tsp. sweetener
- ¼ tsp. baking powder
- cream cheese

Directions:
Preheat your waffle maker.
Add all the ingredients into a small-sized bowl and mix well.
Place half of the batter into the waffle maker.
Seal the device.
Cook for 4 minutes.
Remove the chaffle from the waffle maker.
Make the second one using the same steps.
Spread the remaining cream cheese on top before serving.
Per serving: Calories: 370Kcal; Fat: 28g; Carbs: 3g; Protein: 24g

114. Garlic Chaffles

Preparation time: 10 minutes
Cooking time: 5 minutes
Servings: 2
Ingredients:
- ½ cup mozzarella cheese, shredded
- 1/3 cup cheddar cheese
- 1 large egg
- ½ tbsp. garlic powder
- ½ tsp. Italian seasoning
- ¼ tsp. baking powder

Directions:
Switch on your waffle maker and lightly grease your waffle maker with a brush.
Beat the egg with garlic powder, Italian seasoning, and baking powder in a small mixing bowl.
Add mozzarella cheese and cheddar cheese to the egg mixture and mix well.
Pour half of the chaffles batter into the middle of your waffle iron and close the lid.
Cook the chaffles for about 2-3 minutes until crispy.
Once cooked, remove the chaffles from the maker.
Sprinkle garlic powder on top and enjoy!
Per serving: Calories: 342Kcal; Fat: 29g; Carbs: 7g; Protein: 23g

115. Cinnamon Powder Chaffles

Preparation time: 10 minutes
Cooking time: 5 minutes
Servings: 2
Ingredients:
- 1 large egg
- ¾ cup cheddar cheese, shredded
- 2 tbsp. coconut flour
- ½ tbsp. coconut oil melted
- 1 tsp. stevia
- ½ tsp. cinnamon powder
- ½ tsp. vanilla extract
- ½ tsp. psyllium husk powder
- ¼ tsp. baking powder

Directions:
Switch on your waffle iron.
With a cooking spray, grease your waffle maker
In a mixing bowl, beat the egg with coconut flour, oil, stevia, cinnamon powder, vanilla, husk powder, and baking powder.
Once the egg is beaten well, add in the cheese and mix again.
Pour half of the batter into the middle of your waffle iron and close the lid.
Cook the chaffles for about 2-3 minutes until crispy.
Once chaffles are cooked, carefully remove them from the maker.
Serve them with keto hot chocolate, and enjoy!
Per serving: Calories: 433Kcal; Fat: 28g; Carbs: 3g; Protein: 24g

116. Raspberry Syrup Chaffles

Preparation time: 9 minutes
Cooking time: 38 minutes
Servings: 2
Ingredients:
Chaffles:
- 1 egg, beaten
- ½ cup finely shredded cheddar cheese
- 1 tsp. almond flour
- 1 tsp. sour cream

Raspberry Syrup:
- 1 cup fresh raspberries
- ¼ cup Swerve sugar
- ¼ cup water
- 1 tsp. vanilla extract

Directions:
Chaffles:
Preheat the waffle iron.
Meanwhile, in a medium bowl, mix the egg, cheddar cheese, almond flour, and sour cream.
Open the iron, pour in half of the mixture, cover and cook until crispy, 7 minutes.
Remove the chaffle onto a plate and make another with the remaining batter.
Raspberry Syrup:
Meanwhile, add the raspberries, Swerve sugar, water, and vanilla extract to a medium pot. Set it over low heat and cook until the raspberries soften and sugar becomes syrupy.
Occasionally, stir while mashing the raspberries as you go. Turn the heat off when your desired consistency is achieved and set aside to cool.
Drizzle some syrup on the chaffles and enjoy when ready.
Per serving: Calories: 437Kcal; Fat: 41g; Carbs: 5g; Protein: 28g

117. Egg-Free Coconut Flour Chaffles

Preparation time: 10 minutes
Cooking time: 10 minutes
Servings: 2
Ingredients:

- 1 tbsp. flaxseed meal
- 2½ tbsp. water
- ¼ cup mozzarella cheese, shredded
- 1 tbsp. cream cheese, softened
- 2 tbsp. coconut flour

Directions:
Preheat the waffle iron and then grease it.
In a bowl, place the flaxseed meal and water and mix well.
Set aside for about 5 minutes or until thickened.
In the bowl of flaxseed mixture, add the remaining ingredients and mix them until well combined.
Use half of the mixture to create your first chaffles. Cook them for about 3 minutes or until golden brown.
Repeat with the remaining mixture.
Serve them warm.
Per serving: Calories: 224Kcal; Fat: 29g; Carbs: 1g; Protein: 15g

118. Cheeseburger Chaffle

Preparation time: 10 minutes
Cooking time: 15 minutes
Servings: 1
Ingredients:

- 1 lb. ground beef
- 1 onion, minced
- 1 tsp. parsley, chopped
- 1 egg, beaten
- 1 tbsp. olive oil
- 4 basic chaffles
- 2 lettuce leaves
- 2 cheese slices
- 1 tbsp. dill pickles
- ketchup
- mayonnaise
- salt and pepper to taste

Directions:
Use a large-sized bowl to combine the ground beef, onion, parsley, egg, onion, salt, and pepper. Mix well.
Form 2 thick patties.
Add olive oil to the pan.
Place the pan over medium heat.
Cook the patty for 3 to 5 minutes per side or until fully cooked.
Place the patty on top of each chaffle.
Top with lettuce, cheese, and pickles.
Squirt ketchup and mayo over the patty and veggies.
Top with another chaffle.
Per serving: Calories: 435Kcal; Fat: 32g; Carbs: 3g; Protein: 23g

119. Buffalo Hummus Chaffles

Preparation time: 9 minutes
Cooking time: 32 minutes
Servings: 2
Ingredients:

- 2 eggs
- 1 cup + ¼ cup finely grated cheddar cheese, divided
- 2 chopped fresh scallions
- salt and freshly ground black pepper to taste
- 2 chicken breasts, cooked and diced
- ¼ cup buffalo sauce
- 3 tbsp. low-carb hummus
- 2 celery stalks, chopped
- ¼ cup crumbled blue cheese for topping

Directions:
Preheat the waffle iron.
In a medium bowl, mix the eggs, 1 cup of cheddar cheese, scallions, salt, and black pepper.
Open the iron and add a quarter of the mixture. Close and cook until crispy, 7 minutes.
Transfer the chaffle to a plate and make 3 more chaffles in the same manner.
Preheat the oven to 400°F and line a baking sheet with parchment paper. Set aside.
Cut the chaffles into quarters and arrange them on the baking sheet.
In a medium bowl, mix the chicken with the buffalo sauce, hummus, and celery.
Spoon the chicken mixture onto each quarter of chaffles and top with the remaining cheddar cheese.
Place the baking sheet in the oven and bake them for about 4 minutes until the cheese melts.
Remove from the oven and top with the blue cheese.
Serve them afterward.
Per serving: Calories: 315Kcal; Fat: 31g; Carbs: 2g; Protein: 23g

120. Brie and Blackberry Chaffles

Preparation time: 9 minutes
Cooking time: 36 minutes
Servings: 2
Ingredients:
Chaffles:

- 2 eggs, beaten
- 1 cup finely grated mozzarella cheese

Toppings:

- 1½ cup blackberries
- 1 lemon, 1 tsp. zest and 2 tbsp. juice
- 1 tbsp. erythritol
- 4 slices Brie cheese

Directions:
Chaffles:
Preheat the waffle iron.
Meanwhile, in a medium bowl, mix the eggs and mozzarella cheese.
Open the iron, pour in a quarter of the mixture, cover and cook until crispy, 7 minutes.
Remove the chaffle onto a plate and make 3 more with the remaining batter.
Plate and set them aside.
Topping:
In a medium pot, add the blackberries, lemon zest, lemon juice, and erythritol. Cook until the blackberries break and the sauce thickens, 5 minutes. Turn the heat off.
Arrange the chaffles on the baking sheet and place two Brie cheese slices on each. Top with blackberry mixture and transfer the baking sheet to the oven.
Bake for about 2 to 3 minutes until the cheese melts.
Remove from the oven, allow cooling, and serve afterward.
Per serving: Calories: 468Kcal; Fat: 37g; Carbs: 4g; Protein: 22g

121. Turkey Burger Chaffle

Preparation time: 10 minutes
Cooking time: 10 minutes
Servings: 2
Ingredients:

- 2 cup ground turkey
- salt and pepper to taste
- 1 tbsp. olive oil
- 4 garlic chaffles

- 1 cup Romaine lettuce, chopped
- 1 tomato, sliced
- mayonnaise
- ketchup

Directions:

Combine ground turkey, salt, and pepper.

Form thick burger patties.

Add the olive oil to a pan over medium heat.

Cook the turkey burger until fully cooked on both sides.

Spread mayo on the chaffle.

Top with the turkey burger, lettuce, and tomato.

Squirt ketchup on top before topping with another chaffle.

Per serving: Calories: 404Kcal; Fat: 29g; Carbs: 1g; Protein: 22g

122. Double Choco Chaffle

Preparation time: 10 minutes
Cooking time: 10 minutes
Servings: 2
Ingredients:

- 1 egg
- 1 tsp. coconut flour
- 2 tbsp. sweetener
- 1 tbsp. cocoa powder
- ¼ tsp. baking powder
- 1 oz. cream cheese
- ½ tsp. vanilla
- 1 tbsp. sugar-free chocolate chips

Directions:

Place all the ingredients in a large-sized bowl.

Mix well, and then spoon half of the mixture into the waffle maker.

Seal the device.

Cook for 4 minutes.

Uncover and transfer to a plate to cool.

Repeat the procedure to make the second chaffle.

Per serving: Calories: 428Kcal; Fat: 32g; Carbs: 3g; Protein: 23g

123. Guacamole Chaffle Bites

Preparation time: 10 minutes
Cooking time: 14 minutes
Servings: 1
Ingredients:

- 1 large turnip, cooked and mashed
- 2 bacon slices, cooked and finely chopped
- ½ cup finely grated Monterey Jack cheese
- 1 egg, beaten
- 1 cup guacamole for topping

Directions:

Preheat the waffle iron.

Except for the guacamole, combine all of the ingredients in a medium bowl.

Open the iron and add half of the mixture. Close and cook for 4 minutes. Open the lid, flip the chaffle and cook further until golden brown and crispy, minutes.

Remove the chaffle onto a plate and make another in the same manner. Cut each chaffle into wedges, top with the guacamole and serve afterward.

Per serving: Calories: 346Kcal; Fat: 26g; Carbs: 2g; Protein: 24g

124. Mayonnaise and Cream Cheese Chaffles

Preparation time: 9 minutes
Cooking time: 20 minutes
Servings: 2

Ingredients:

- 4 organic eggs large
- 4 tbsp. mayonnaise
- 1 tbsp. almond flour
- 2 tbsp. cream cheese

Directions:

Preheat your waffle iron and then grease it.

In a bowl, place the eggs, mayonnaise, and almond flour, and with a hand mixer, mix until smooth.

Place about ¼ of the mixture into the preheated waffle iron.

Place about ¼ of the cream cheese cubes on top of the mixture evenly and cook for about 5 minutes or until golden brown.

Repeat with the remaining mixture and cream cheese cubes.

Per serving: Calories: 452Kcal; Fat: 34g; Carbs: 2g; Protein: 25g

125. Blue Cheese Chaffle Bites

Preparation time: 10 minutes
Cooking time: 14 minutes
Servings: 1
Ingredients:

- 1 egg, beaten
- ½ cup finely grated parmesan cheese
- ¼ cup crumbled blue cheese
- 1 tsp. erythritol

Directions:

Preheat the waffle iron.

Mix all the ingredients in a bowl.

Open the iron and add half of the mixture. Close and cook until crispy, 7 minutes.

Remove the chaffle onto a plate and make another with the remaining mixture.

Cut each chaffle into wedges and serve afterward.

Per serving: Calories: 364Kcal; Fat: 32g; Carbs: 2g; Protein: 26g

126. Raspberries Mozzarella Chaffles

Preparation time: 10 minutes
Cooking time: 5 minutes
Servings: 1
Ingredients:

- 1 egg
- ½ cup mozzarella cheese, shredded
- 1 tbsp. almond flour
- ¼ cup raspberry puree
- 1 tbsp. coconut flour for topping

Directions:

Preheat your waffle maker in line with the manufacturer's instructions.

Grease your waffle maker with cooking spray.

Mix together egg, almond flour, and raspberry purée.

Add cheese and mix until well combined.

Pour the batter into the waffle maker.

Close the lid.

Cook for about 3-4 minutes or until the waffles are cooked and not soggy.

Once cooked, remove it from the maker.

Sprinkle coconut flour on top and enjoy!

Per serving: Calories: 414Kcal; Fat: 30g; Carbs: 2g; Protein: 22g

127. Toast Chaffle

Preparation time: 10 minutes
Cooking time: 5 minutes
Servings: 1
Ingredients:

- 1 large egg
- ½ cup shredded cheddar cheese

Toppings:
- 1 egg
- 3-4 spinach leaves
- ¼ cup boil and shredded chicken

Directions:
Preheat your square waffle maker on medium-high heat.
Mix together the egg and cheese in a bowl and make two chaffles in a chaffle maker
Once the chaffles are cooked, carefully remove them from the maker.
Serve with spinach, boiled chicken, and fried egg.
Per serving: Calories: 354Kcal; Fat: 27g; Carbs: 4g; Protein: 26g

128. Beef Chaffle

Preparation time: 10 minutes
Cooking time: 15 minutes
Servings: 2
Ingredients:
- 1 tsp. olive oil
- 2 cup ground beef
- garlic salt to taste
- 1 red bell pepper, sliced into strips
- 1 green bell pepper, sliced into strips
- 1 onion, minced
- 1 bay leaf
- 2 garlic chaffles
- butter

Directions:
Put your pan over medium heat.
Add the olive oil and cook the ground beef until brown.
Season with garlic salt and add bay leaf.
Drain the fat, transfer to a plate and set it aside.
Discard the bay leaf.
In the same pan, cook the onion and bell peppers for 2 minutes.
Put the beef back in the pan.
Heat for 1 minute.
Spread the butter on top of the chaffle.
Add the ground beef and veggies.
Roll or fold the chaffle.
Per serving: Calories: 585Kcal; Fat: 34g; Carbs: 2g; Protein: 28g

129. Almond Flour Chaffles

Preparation time: 10 minutes
Cooking time: 5 minutes
Servings: 2
Ingredients:
- 2 large eggs
- ¼ cup almond flour
- ¾ tsp. baking powder
- 1 cup cheddar cheese, shredded
- cooking spray

Directions:
Switch on your waffle maker and grease with cooking spray.
Beat the eggs with almond flour and baking powder in a mixing bowl.
Once the eggs and flour are mixed together, add in cheese and mix again.
Pour ¼ cup of the batter in the dash mini waffle maker and close the lid.
Cook the chaffles for about 2-3 minutes until crispy and cooked.
Repeat with the remaining batter.
Carefully transfer the chaffles to the plate.
Serve with almonds and enjoy!
Per serving: Calories: 320Kcal; Fat: 27g; Carbs: 2g; Protein: 22g

130. Nutter Butter Chaffles

Preparation time: 10 minutes
Cooking time: 14 minutes
Servings: 2
Ingredients:
Chaffles:
- 2 tbsp. sugar-free peanut butter powder
- 2 tbsp. maple (sugar-free) syrup
- 1 egg, beaten
- ¼ cup finely grated mozzarella cheese
- ¼ tsp. baking powder
- ¼ tsp. almond butter
- ¼ tsp. peanut butter extract
- 1 tbsp. softened cream cheese

Frosting:
- ½ cup almond flour
- 1 cup peanut butter
- 3 tbsp. almond milk
- ½ tsp. vanilla extract
- ½ cup maple (sugar-free) syrup

Directions:
Preheat the waffle iron.
In a medium-sized bowl, mix all the ingredients until smooth.
Open the iron and pour in half of the mixture.
Close the iron and cook until crispy, 6 to 7 minutes.
Remove the chaffle onto a plate and set it aside.
Make a second chaffle with the remaining batter.
While the chaffles cool, make the frosting.
Pour the almond flour in a medium saucepan and stir-fry over medium heat until golden.
Transfer the almond flour to a blender and top with the remaining frosting ingredients. Process until smooth.
Spread the frosting on the chaffles and serve afterward.
Per serving: Calories: 283Kcal; Fat: 3g; Carbs: 8g; Protein: 14g

131. Reuben Chaffles

Preparation time: 9 minutes
Cooking time: 28 minutes
Servings: 2
Ingredients:
Chaffles:
- 2 eggs, beaten
- 1 cup finely grated Swiss cheese
- 2 tsp. caraway seeds
- ⅛ tsp. salt
- ½ tsp. baking powder

Sauce:
- 2 tbsp. sugar-free ketchup
- 3 tbsp. mayonnaise
- 1 tbsp. dill relish
- 1 tsp. hot sauce

Filling:
- 6 oz. pastrami
- 2 Swiss cheese slices
- ¼ cup pickled radishes

Directions:
Chaffles:
Preheat the waffle iron.
In a medium bowl, mix the eggs, Swiss cheese, caraway seeds, salt, and baking powder.
Open the iron and add a quarter of the mixture. Close and cook until crispy, 7 minutes.
Transfer the chaffle to a plate and make 3 more chaffles in the same manner.

Sauce:

In another bowl, mix the ketchup, mayonnaise, dill relish, and hot sauce.

To Assemble:

Divide into two chaffles; the sauce, the pastrami, Swiss cheese slices, and pickled radishes.

Cover with the other chaffles, divide the sandwich into halves, and serve.

Per serving: Calories: 426Kcal; Fat: 30g; Carbs: 3g; Protein: 27g

132. Easy Carrot Cake Chaffle

Preparation time: 10 minutes
Cooking time: 24 minutes
Servings: 2
Ingredients:

- 1 egg, beaten
- 2 tbsp. melted butter
- ½ cup carrot, shredded
- ¾ cup almond flour
- 1 tsp. baking powder
- 2 tbsp. heavy whipping cream
- 2 tbsp. sweetener
- 1 tbsp. walnuts, chopped
- 1 tsp. pumpkin spice
- 2 tsp. cinnamon

Directions:

Preheat your waffle maker.

Mix all the ingredients in a large-sized bowl.

Pour some of the mixture into the waffle maker.

Close and cook for 4 minutes.

Repeat the steps until all the remaining batter has been used.

Per serving: Calories: 381Kcal; Fat: 30g; Carbs: 3g; Protein: 27g

133. Monterrey Jack Chaffle

Preparation time: 8 minutes
Cooking time: 6 minutes
Servings: 1
Ingredients:

- 2 oz. Monterrey Jack cheese, cut into thin slices
- 1 large organic egg, beaten

Directions:

Preheat the waffle iron and then grease it.

Place one layer of cheese slices in the bottom of the preheated waffle iron.

Place the beaten egg on top of the cheese.

Now, place another layer of the cheese on top to cover evenly.

Cook until golden brown, about 6 minutes.

Per serving: Calories: 278Kcal; Fat: 25g; Carbs: 1g; Protein: 21g

134. Egg and Chives Sandwich Chaffle

Preparation time: 10 minutes
Cooking time: 0 minute
Servings: 1
Ingredients:

- 2 tbsp. mayonnaise
- 1 hard-boiled egg, chopped
- 1 tbsp. chives, chopped
- 2 basic chaffles

Directions:

In a bowl, mix the mayo, egg, and chives.

Spread the mixture on top of the chaffles.

Roll the chaffle.

Per serving: Calories: 360Kcal; Fat: 27g; Carbs: 2g; Protein: 22g

135. Mozzarella Sandwich Chaffle

Preparation time: 10 minutes
Cooking time: 5 minutes
Servings: 1
Ingredients:

- ½ cup mozzarella cheese, shredded
- 1 large egg
- 2 tbsp. almond flour
- ½ tsp. psyllium husk powder
- ¼ tsp. baking powder

Directions:

Grease your waffle maker with cooking spray.

Beat the egg with a fork; once the egg is beaten, add almond flour, husk powder, and baking powder.

Add cheese to the egg mixture and mix until combined.

Spoon the batter into the center of the waffle maker and close the lid.

Cook the chaffles for about 2-3 minutes until well cooked.

Carefully transfer the chaffles to the plate.

The chaffles are perfect for a sandwich base.

Per serving: Calories: 398Kcal; Fat: 33g; Carbs: 2g; Protein: 22g

136. Cereal Cake Chaffle

Preparation time: 10 minutes
Cooking time: 8 minutes
Servings: 2
Ingredients:

- 1 egg
- 2 tbsp. almond flour
- ½ tsp. coconut flour
- 1 tbsp. melted butter
- 1 tbsp. cream cheese
- 1 tbsp. plain cereal, crushed
- ¼ tsp. vanilla extract
- ¼ tsp. baking powder
- 1 tbsp. sweetener
- ⅛ tsp. xanthan gum

Directions:

Plug in your waffle maker to preheat.

Mix all the ingredients to a large-sized bowl until well combined.

Let the batter rest for 2 minutes before cooking.

Cook for about 4 minutes, half of the mixture into the waffle maker.

Make the next chaffle using the same steps.

Per serving: Calories: 463Kcal; Fat: 30g; Carbs: 3g; Protein: 25g

137. Okonomiyaki Chaffles with Sauces

Preparation time: 9 minutes
Cooking time: 28 minutes
Servings: 2
Ingredients:

Chaffles:

- 2 eggs, beaten
- 1 cup finely grated mozzarella cheese
- ½ tsp. baking powder
- ¼ cup shredded radishes

Sauce:

- 2 tsp. coconut aminos
- 2 tbsp. sugar-free ketchup
- 1 tbsp. sugar-free maple syrup
- 2 tsp. Worcestershire sauce

Toppings:

- 1 tbsp. mayonnaise
- 2 tbsp. chopped fresh scallions
- 2 tbsp. bonito flakes

- 1 tsp. dried seaweed powder
- 1 tbsp. pickled ginger

Directions:

Chaffles:

Preheat the waffle iron.

In a medium bowl, mix the eggs, mozzarella cheese, baking powder, and radishes.

Open the iron and add a quarter of the mixture. Close and cook until crispy, 7 minutes.

Transfer the chaffle to a plate and make 3 more chaffles in the same manner.

Sauce:

Combine the coconut aminos, ketchup, maple syrup, and Worcestershire sauce in a medium bowl and mix well.

Topping:

In another mixing bowl, mix the mayonnaise, scallions, bonito flakes, seaweed powder, and ginger.

Per serving: Calories: 371Kcal; Fat: 32g; Carbs: 4g; Protein: 21g

138. Bacon and Chicken Ranch Chaffles

Preparation time: 10 minutes
Cooking time: 8 minutes
Servings: 1
Ingredients:

- 1 egg
- ¼ cup chicken cubes, cooked
- 1 slice bacon, cooked and chopped
- ¼ cup cheddar cheese, shredded
- 1 tsp. ranch dressing powder

Directions:

Preheat your waffle maker.

In a bowl, mix all the ingredients.

Spoon half of the mixture into your waffle maker.

Cover and cook for 2 minutes.

Make the second chaffle using the same steps.

Per serving: Calories: 410Kcal; Fat: 38g; Carbs: 16g; Protein: 25g

139. Keto Cocoa Chaffles

Preparation time: 10 minutes
Cooking time: 5 minutes
Servings: 1
Ingredients:

- 1 large egg
- ½ cup shredded cheddar cheese
- 1 tbsp. cocoa powder
- 2 tbsp. almond flour
- vanilla

Directions:

Preheat your round waffle maker on medium-high heat.

Mix together the egg, cheese, almond flour, cocoa powder, and vanilla in a small mixing bowl.

Pour the chaffles mixture into the waffle iron.

Cook for 3-5 minutes or until the waffle is golden brown and set.

Carefully remove the chaffles from the waffle maker.

Per serving: Calories: 339Kcal; Fat: 24g; Carbs: 3g; Protein: 23g

140. Barbecue Chaffle

Preparation time: 10 minutes
Cooking time: 8 minutes
Servings: 1
Ingredients:

- 1 egg, beaten
- ½ cup cheddar cheese, shredded
- ½ tsp. barbecue sauce
- ¼ tsp. baking powder

Directions:

Plug in your waffle maker to preheat.

Mix all the ingredients in a bowl.

Spoon half of the mixture into the waffle maker, and cook for 4 minutes.

Repeat the same steps for the next barbecue chaffle.

Per serving: Calories: 345Kcal; Fat: 35g; Carbs: 2g; Protein: 22g

141. Chicken and Nachos Chaffle

Preparation time: 20 minutes
Cooking time: 33 minutes
Servings: 2
Ingredients:

Chaffles:

- 2 eggs, beaten
- 1 cup finely grated Mexican cheese blend

Toppings:

- 2 tbsp. butter
- 1 tbsp. almond flour
- ¼ cup unsweetened almond milk
- 1 cup finely grated cheddar cheese + more to garnish
- 3 bacon slices, cooked and chopped
- 2 cup cooked and diced chicken breasts
- 2 tbsp. hot sauce
- 2 tbsp. chopped fresh scallions

Directions:

Chaffles:

Preheat the waffle iron.

In a medium bowl, mix the eggs and Mexican cheese blend.

Open the iron and add a quarter of the mixture. Close and cook until crispy, 7 minutes.

Transfer the chaffle to a plate and make 3 more chaffles in the same manner.

Place the chaffles on serving plates and set them aside for serving.

Topping:

Melt the butter in a large skillet and mix in the almond flour until brown, 1 minute.

Pour the almond milk and whisk until well combined. Simmer until thickened, 2 minutes.

Stir in the cheese to melt, 2 minutes, and then mix in the bacon, chicken, and hot sauce.

Spoon the mixture onto the chaffles and top with some more cheddar cheese.

Garnish with the scallions and serve immediately.

Per serving: Calories: 492Kcal; Fat: 35g; Carbs: 3g; Protein: 33g

142. Ham, Cheese and Tomato Sandwich Chaffle

Preparation time: 10 minutes
Cooking time: 10 minutes
Servings: 2
Ingredients:

- 1 tsp. olive oil
- 2 slices ham
- 4 basic chaffles
- 1 tbsp. mayonnaise
- 2 slices provolone cheese
- 1 tomato, sliced

Directions:

Heat the olive oil in a saucepan over medium heat.

Cook the ham for 1 minute per side.

Spread the chaffles with mayonnaise.

Top with ham, cheese, and tomatoes.

Top with another chaffle to make a sandwich.

Per serving: Calories: 394Kcal; Fat: 36g; Carbs: 3g; Protein: 24g

143. Cereal and Butter Chaffles

Preparation time: 6 minutes
Cooking time: 6 minutes
Servings: 2
Ingredients:
- 1 ml cereal flavoring
- ¼ tsp. baking powder
- 1 tsp. sweetener
- 1 tbsp. butter (melted)
- ½ tsp. coconut flour
- 1 tbsp. cream cheese
- 2 tbsp. almond flour
- 1 large egg (beaten)
- ¼ tsp. cinnamon

Directions:
Preheat the mini waffle iron and then grease it.
In a mixing bowl, whisk the egg, and add cereal flavoring, cream cheese, and butter. Mix well.
In another mixing bowl, combine the coconut flour, almond flour, cinnamon, sweetener, and baking powder.
Pour the first mixture into the flour mixture and mix until you form a smooth batter.
Pour in an appropriate amount of batter into the waffle maker and spread out the batter to the edges to cover all the holes on the waffle maker.
Cook for about 4 minutes
Use a plastic or silicone utensil to remove the chaffle from the waffle maker.
Repeat steps 4 to 7 until you have cooked all the batter into chaffles.
Per serving: Calories: 369Kcal; Fat: 29g; Carbs: 3g; Protein: 28g

144. Cornbread Chaffles

Preparation time: 6 minutes
Cooking time: 12 minutes
Servings: 2
Ingredients:
- 1½ tbsp. melted butter
- 3 tbsp. almond flour
- 1 ml cornbread flavoring
- 2 tbsp. Mexican blend cheese
- 2 tbsp. shredded parmesan cheese
- 1 small jalapeño (seeded and sliced)
- 2 tsp. Swerve sweetener
- 1 large egg (beaten)
- ½ tsp. allspice
- baking powder

Directions:
Plug the waffle maker to preheat it and spray it with a non-stick cooking spray.
Combine the almond flour, jalapeño, allspice, baking powder, and Swerve into a mixing bowl.
In another medium-sized bowl, whisk the egg, and add the cornbread flavoring and the butter. Mix well
Pour the first mixture into the flour mixture and mix until you form a smooth batter. Stir in the cheese.
Sprinkle some parmesan cheese over the waffle maker. Pour some batter into the waffle maker.
Sprinkle some parmesan over the batter.
Cook for about 5 minutes or according to your waffle maker's settings.
After the baking cycle, remove the chaffle from the waffle maker with a plastic or silicone utensil.
Repeat until you have created all chaffles with the batter.
Serve warm with your desired topping and enjoy.
Per serving: Calories: 433Kcal; Fat: 29g; Carbs: 3g; Protein: 22g

145. Midday Chaffle Snack

Preparation time: 6 minutes
Cooking time: 5 minutes
Servings: 1
Ingredients:
- 2 oz. coconut flakes
- 2 oz. kiwi slice
- 2 oz. raspberry
- 2 oz. almonds chopped

Chaffles:
- 1 egg
- ½ cup mozzarella cheese
- 1 tsp. stevia
- 1 tsp. vanilla
- 2 tbsp. almond flour

Directions:
Make 4 chaffles with the chaffle ingredients.
Arrange the coconut flakes, kiwi, almonds, and raspberries on each chaffle.
Serve and enjoy the keto snacks.
Per serving: Calories: 434Kcal; Fat: 32g; Carbs: 3g; Protein: 24g

146. Spinach Chaffles

Preparation time: 6 minutes
Cooking time: 10 minutes
Servings: 1
Ingredients:
- 1 egg (beaten)
- ¼ tsp. pepper or to taste
- ½ tsp. Italian seasoning
- ⅛ tsp. thyme
- ½ cup finely chopped spinach
- ½ cup shredded cheddar cheese
- ¼ cup parmesan cheese for sprinkling

Directions:
Plug the waffle maker to preheat it and spray it with a non-stick cooking spray.
In a mixing bowl, combine the cheddar, spinach, Italian seasoning, thyme, and pepper. Add the egg and mix until the ingredients are well combined.
Sprinkle some parmesan cheese over the waffle maker and spoon ½ of the batter into the waffle maker, and spread out the batter to cover all the holes on the waffle maker. Sprinkle some more cheese over the batter.
Cook for about 5 minutes or according to your waffle maker's settings.
After the cooking cycle, use a silicone or plastic utensil to remove the chaffle from the waffle maker. Repeat to make the second chaffle.
Serve the chaffles and top with sour cream, or use the chaffles for the sandwich.
Per serving: Calories: 216Kcal; Fat: 34g; Carbs: 3g; Protein: 25g

147. Shirataki Rice Chaffle

Preparation time: 6 minutes
Cooking time: 20 minutes
Servings: 2
Ingredients:
- 2 tbsp. almond flour
- ½ tsp. oregano
- 1 bag shirataki rice
- 1 tsp. baking powder
- 1 cup shredded cheddar cheese
- 2 eggs (beaten)

Directions:

Rinse the shirataki rice with warm water for about 30 seconds and rinse it.

Plug the waffle maker to preheat it and spray it with a non-stick cooking spray.

In a mixing bowl, combine the rinsed rice, almond flour, baking powder, oregano, and shredded cheese. Add the eggs and mix until the ingredients are well combined.

Fill the waffle maker with an appropriate amount of batter and spread out the batter to the edges to cover all the holes on the waffle maker.

Cook for about 5 minutes or according to your waffle maker's settings.

After the cooking cycle, use a silicone or plastic utensil to remove the chaffles from the waffle maker.

Repeat steps 4 to 6 until you have cooked all the batter into chaffles.

Per serving: Calories: 468Kcal; Fat: 31g; Carbs: 3g; Protein: 22g

148. Basic Ham Chaffles

Preparation time: 6 minutes
Cooking time: 5 minutes
Servings: 1
Ingredients:
- 1 large egg
- 4 tbsp. chopped ham steak
- 1 scallion (chopped)
- ½ cup shredded mozzarella cheese ¼ tsp. garlic salt
- ⅛ tsp. Italian seasoning
- ½ jalapeño pepper (chopped)

Directions:

Plug the waffle maker to preheat it and spray it with a non-stick spray.

In a mixing bowl, combine the cheese, Italian seasoning, jalapeño, scallion, ham, and garlic salt. Add the egg and mix until the ingredients are well combined.

Fill the waffle maker with an appropriate amount of batter. Spread the batter to the edges of the waffle maker to cover all the holes on it.

Cook for about 5 minutes or according to the waffle maker's settings.

After the cooking cycle, remove the chaffle from the waffle maker with plastic or silicone utensil.

Per serving: Calories: 373Kcal; Fat: 3g; Carbs: 2g; Protein: 23g

149. Zucchini and Bacon Chaffles

Preparation time: 6 minutes
Cooking time: 12 minutes
Servings: 2
Ingredients:
- 1 cup grated zucchini
- 1 tbsp. bacon bits (finely chopped)
- ¼ cup shredded mozzarella cheese
- ½ cup shredded parmesan
- ½ tsp. salt or to taste
- ½ tsp. ground black pepper or to taste ½ tsp. onion powder
- ¼ tsp. nutmeg
- 2 eggs

Directions:

Add ¼ tsp. of salt to the grated zucchini and let it sit for about 5 minutes.

Squeeze off any extra water from the shredded zucchini using a clean cloth.

Plug the waffle maker and preheat it. Spray it with non-stick spray.

Whisk the eggs into a mixing bowl.

Add the grated zucchini, bacon bit, nutmeg, onion powder, pepper, salt, and mozzarella.

Add ¾ of the parmesan cheese. You have to set aside some parmesan cheese.

Mix until the ingredients are well combined.

Fill the preheated waffle maker with the batter and spread out the batter to the edge to cover all the holes on the waffle maker.

Close the waffle maker lid and cook until the chaffle is golden brown and crispy. The zucchini chaffle may take longer than other chaffles to get crispy.

After the baking cycle, use a plastic or silicone utensil to remove the chaffle from the waffle maker.

Repeat steps until you have cooked all the batter into chaffles.

Per serving: Calories: 435Kcal; Fat: 33g; Carbs: 3g; Protein: 23g

150. Spinach-Artichoke Chaffles with Bacon

Preparation time: 6 minutes
Cooking time: 8 minutes
Servings: 1
Ingredients:
- 4 slices of bacon
- ½ cup chopped spinach
- 1/3 cup marinated artichoke (chopped)
- 1 egg
- ¼ tsp. garlic powder
- ¼ tsp. smoked paprika
- 2 tbsp. cream cheese (softened)
- 1/3 cup shredded mozzarella

Directions:

Heat up a frying pan and add the bacon slices. Sear until both sides of the bacon slices are browned. Use a slotted spoon to transfer the bacon to a paper towel-lined plate to drain.

Once the bacon slices are cool, chop them into bits and set them aside.

Plug the waffle maker to preheat it and spray it with a non-stick cooking spray.

In a mixing bowl, combine mozzarella, garlic, paprika, cream cheese, and egg. Mix until the ingredients are well combined.

Add the spinach, artichoke, and bacon bit. Mix until they are well incorporated.

Pour some batter into the waffle maker and spread the batter to the edges to cover all the holes on the waffle maker.

Close the waffle maker and cook for 4 minutes or more, according to your waffle maker's settings.

After the cooking cycle, use a silicone or plastic utensil to remove the chaffle from the waffle maker.

Repeat steps 6 to 8 until you have cooked all the batter into chaffles.

Serve and top with sour cream as desired.

Per serving: Calories: 430Kcal; Fat: 36g; Carbs: 2g; Protein: 22g

151. Chocolate Cannoli Chaffle

Preparation time: 6 minutes
Cooking time: 10 minutes
Servings: 2
Ingredients:
Chaffles:
- 3 tbsp. almond flour
- 1 tbsp. Swerve
- 1 egg
- ⅛ tsp. baking powder
- ¾ tbsp. butter (melted)
- ½ tsp. nutmeg
- 1 tbsp. sugar-free chocolate chips
- ⅛ tsp. vanilla extract

Toppings:
- 2 tbsp. granulated Swerve
- 4 tbsp. cream cheese
- ¼ tsp. vanilla extract
- ¼ tsp. cinnamon

- 6 tbsp. Ricotta cheese
- 1 tsp. lemon juice

Directions:

Plug the waffle maker to preheat it and spray it with a non-stick spray. Whisk the egg in a medium-sized bowl, and add the butter and vanilla extract.

In another mixing bowl, combine the almond flour, baking powder, nutmeg, chocolate chips, and Swerve.

Pour the egg batter into the flour mixture and mix until the ingredients are well combined and you have formed a smooth batter.

Fill your waffle maker with an appropriate amount of batter and spread out the batter to the edges to cover all the holes on the waffle maker.

Cook for about 4 minutes or according to the waffle maker's settings.

After the baking cycle, remove the chaffle from the waffle maker with a plastic or silicone utensil.

Repeat until you have cooked all the batter into waffles.

For the topping, pour the cream cheese into a blender and add the ricotta, lemon juice, cinnamon, vanilla, and Swerve sweetener. Blend until smooth and fluffy.

Spread the cream over the chaffles and enjoy.

Per serving: Calories: 502Kcal; Fat: 38g; Carbs: 4g; Protein: 23g

152. Broccoli, Garlic and Onion Chaffles

Preparation time: 5 minutes
Cooking time: 15 minutes
Servings: 1
Ingredients:

- 1/3 cup broccoli (finely chopped)
- ½ tsp. oregano
- ⅛ tsp. salt or to taste
- ⅛ tsp. ground black pepper or to taste
- ½ tsp. garlic powder
- ½ tsp. onion powder
- 1 egg (beaten)
- 4 tbsp. shredded cheddar cheese

Directions:

Plug the waffle maker to preheat it and spray it with a non-stick cooking spray.

In a mixing bowl, combine the cheese, oregano, pepper, garlic, salt, onion, and egg. Mix until the ingredients are well combined.

Fold in the chopped broccoli.

Pour some batter into your waffle maker and spread out the batter to the edges to cover all the holes on the waffle maker.

Cook for about 6-8 minutes until the chaffle is browned. Cooking time may vary in some waffle makers.

After the cooking cycle, use a silicone or plastic utensil to remove the chaffle from the waffle maker.

Repeat the process until you have created all the chaffles.

Serve and top with sour cream as desired.

Per serving: Calories: 331Kcal; Fat: 26g; Carbs: 1g; Protein: 19g

153. Eggnog Chaffles

Preparation time: 5 minutes
Cooking time: 5 minutes
Servings: 1
Ingredients:

- 2 tbsp. coconut flour
- ½ tsp. baking powder
- 1 tsp. cinnamon
- 2 tbsp. cream cheese
- 2 tsp. Swerve
- ⅛ tsp. salt
- ⅛ tsp. nutmeg
- 1 egg (beaten)
- 4 tbsp. keto eggnog

Eggnog Filling:

- 4 tbsp. keto eggnog
- ¼ tsp. vanilla extract
- ¼ cup heavy cream
- 2 tsp. granulated Swerve
- ⅛ tsp. nutmeg

Directions:

Plug the waffle maker to preheat it and spray it with a non-stick cooking spray.

Combine the coconut flour, baking powder, Swerve, salt, cinnamon, and nutmeg in a mixing bowl.

In another mixing bowl, whisk together the eggnog, cream cheese, and egg.

Pour in the egg mixture into the flour mixture and mix until the ingredients are well combined.

Fill the waffle maker with an appropriate amount of batter. Spread out the batter to cover all the holes on the waffle maker.

Cook for about 5 minutes or according to your waffle maker's settings.

After the baking cycle, remove the chaffle from the waffle maker with a plastic or silicone utensil.

Repeat the process until you have cooked all the batter into chaffles.

For the eggnog cream, whisk together the cream cheese, heavy cream, vanilla, and eggnog. Add the Swerve and nutmeg; mix until the ingredients are well combined.

Top the chaffles with the eggnog cream and enjoy.

Per serving: Calories: 385Kcal; Fat: 36g; Carbs: 2g; Protein: 26g

154. Double Cheese Chaffles Plus Mayonnaise Dip

Preparation time: 5 minutes
Cooking time: 8 minutes
Servings: 1
Ingredients:

Chaffles:

- ½ cup mozzarella cheese, shredded
- 1 tbsp. parmesan cheese, shredded
- 1 organic egg
- ¾ tsp. coconut flour
- ¼ tsp. organic baking powder
- ⅛ tsp. Italian seasoning
- a pinch of salt

Sauce:

- ¼ cup mayonnaise
- a pinch of garlic powder
- a pinch of ground black pepper

Directions:

Preheat the mini waffle iron and then grease it.

For chaffles: In a medium bowl, put all the ingredients and, with a fork, mix until well combined.

Drop half of the mixture into the waffle iron and cook for about 3-4 minutes.

Repeat with the remaining mixture.

Meanwhile, for the dip: in a bowl, mix together the cream and stevia.

Serve them warm chaffles alongside the dip.

Per serving: Calories: 408Kcal; Fat: 38g; Carbs: 3g; Protein: 23g

155. Yellow Sweet Cake Chaffle

Preparation time: 5 minutes
Cooking time: 18 minutes
Servings: 1
Ingredients:

- 1 tbsp. toasted pecans (chopped)
- 2 tbsp. granulated Swerve
- 1 tsp. pumpkin spice

- ½ shredded carrots
- 2 tbsp. butter (melted)
- 1 tsp. cinnamon
- 1 tsp. vanilla extract (optional)
- 2 tbsp. heavy whipping cream ¾ cup almond flour
- 1 egg (beaten)

Buttercream Cheese Frosting:
- ½ cup cream cheese (softened)
- ¼ cup butter (softened)
- ½ tsp. vanilla extract
- ¼ cup granulated Swerve

Directions:

Plug the chaffle maker to preheat it and spray it with a non-stick cooking spray.

In a medium-sized bowl, combine the carrot, almond flour, cinnamon, Swerve, and pumpkin spice.

In another mixing bowl, whisk together the eggs, butter, heavy whipping cream, and vanilla extract.

Combine the flour and the egg compounds and mix them until you form a smooth batter.

Fold in the chopped pecans.

Pour in an appropriate amount of batter into your waffle maker and spread it out to the edges to cover all the holes on the waffle maker.

Cook for about 3 minutes or according to your waffle maker's settings.

After the cooking cycle, use a plastic or silicone utensil to remove the chaffle from the waffle maker.

Repeat the process until you have cooked all the batter into chaffles.

For the frosting, combine the cream cheese and butter in a mixer and mix until well combined.

Add the Swerve and vanilla extract slowly until the sweetener is well incorporated. Mix on high until the frosting is fluffy.

Place one chaffle on a flat surface and spread some cream frosting over it. Layer another chaffle over the first one a spread some cream over it, too.

Repeat step 12 until you have assembled all the chaffles into a cake. Cut and serve them.

Per serving: Calories: 575Kcal; Fat: 35g; Carbs: 4g; Protein: 23g

156. Chocolate Balls with Chaffles

Preparation time: 5 minutes
Cooking time: 5 minutes
Servings: 1
Ingredients:
- ¼ cup heavy cream
- ½ cup unsweetened cocoa powder
- ¼ cup coconut meat

Chaffles:
- 1 egg
- ½ cup mozzarella cheese

Directions:

Make 2 chaffles with the chaffle ingredients.

Meanwhile, blend all the ingredients in a mixing bowl.

Make two balls from the mixture and freeze them in the freezer for about 2 hours until set.

Per serving: Calories: 470Kcal; Fat: 34g; Carbs: 1g; Protein: 22g

157. Bacon Jalapeño Popper Chaffle

Preparation time: 5 minutes
Cooking time: 10 minutes
Servings: 3
Ingredients:
- 4 slices bacon (diced)
- 3 eggs
- 3 tbsp. coconut flour
- 1 tsp. baking powder

- ¼ tsp. salt
- ½ tsp. oregano
- a pinch of onion powder
- a pinch of garlic powder
- ½ cup cream cheese
- 1 cup shredded cheddar cheese
- 2 jalapeño peppers (deseeded and chopped)
- ½ cup sour cream

Directions:

Plug the waffle maker to preheat it and spray it with a non-stick cooking spray.

Heat up a frying pan over medium to high heat. Add the bacon and sauté until the bacon is brown and crispy.

Use a slotted spoon to transfer the bacon to a paper towel-lined plate to drain.

In a mixing bowl, combine the coconut flour, baking powder, salt, oregano, onion, and garlic.

In another medium-sized bowl, whisk together the egg and cream cheese until well combined.

Add the cheddar cheese and mix. Pour in the flour mixture and mix until you form a smooth batter.

Spoon some batter into the waffle maker and spread the batter to the edges to cover all the holes on the waffle maker.

Cook for about 5 minutes or according to the waffle maker's settings.

After the cooking cycle, use a plastic or silicone utensil to remove the chaffle from the waffle maker.

Repeat the process until you have transformed all the batter into the chaffles.

Serve them warm and top with sour cream, crispy bacon, and jalapeño slices.

Per serving: Calories: 451Kcal; Fat: 37g; Carbs: 3g; Protein: 27g

158. Apple Pie Chaffle

Preparation time: 5 minutes
Cooking time: 6 minutes
Servings: 1
Ingredients:
- 1 egg (beaten)
- 1 tbsp. almond flour
- 1 big apple (finely chopped)
- 1 tbsp. heavy whipping cream
- 1 tsp. cinnamon
- 1 tbsp. Swerve granular
- ½ tsp. vanilla extract
- 1/3 cup mozzarella cheese

Toppings:
- ¼ tbsp. sugar-free maple syrup

Directions:

Plug the waffle maker and preheat it. Spray it with non-stick spray.

In a large mixing bowl, combine the Swerve, almond flour, mozzarella, cinnamon, and chopped apple.

Add the egg, vanilla extract, and heavy whipping cream. Mix until all the ingredients are well combined.

Pour some batter into the waffle maker, and spread out the batter to the edges of the waffle maker to all the holes on it.

Cook for about 4 minutes or according to the waffle maker's settings.

After the cooking cycle, remove the chaffle from the waffle maker with a plastic or silicone utensil.

Repeat the process until you have cooked all the batter into chaffles.

Serve and top with maple syrup.

Per serving: Calories: 347Kcal; Fat: 34g; Carbs: 3g; Protein: 25g

159. French Toast Chaffle Sticks

Preparation time: 5 minutes
Cooking time: 40 minutes
Servings: 4
Ingredients:

- 6 organic eggs
- 2 cup mozzarella cheese, shredded
- ¼ cup coconut flour
- 2 tbsp. powdered erythritol
- 1 tsp. ground cinnamon
- 1 tbsp. butter, melted

Directions:

Preheat your oven to 350°F and line a large baking sheet with a greased piece of foil.

Preheat the waffle iron and then grease it.

In a bowl, add 4 eggs and beat well.

Add the cheese, coconut flour, erythritol, and ½ tsp. of cinnamon and mix until well combined.

Place ¼ of the mixture into the preheated waffle iron and cook for about 6-8 minutes.

Repeat with the remaining mixture.

Set the chaffles aside to cool.

Cut each chaffle into 4 strips.

In a large bowl, add the remaining eggs and cinnamon and beat until well combined.

Dip the chaffle sticks in the egg mixture evenly.

Arrange the chaffle sticks onto the prepared baking sheet in a single layer.

Bake for about 10 minutes.

Remove the baking sheet from the oven and brush the top of each stick with the melted butter.

Flip the stick and bake for about 6-8 minutes.

Serve them immediately.

Per serving: Calories: 396Kcal; Fat: 35g; Carbs: 7g; Protein: 22g

160. Ginger Brownie Chaffles

Preparation time: 5 minutes
Cooking time: 14 minutes
Servings: 2
Ingredients:

- 1 large egg
- ¼ tsp. baking powder
- ½ tsp. vanilla extract
- ½ tsp. ginger
- 2 tbsp. cream cheese (melted)
- 1½ tsp. cocoa powder
- 1 tbsp. Swerve

Toppings:

- ½ tsp. vanilla extract.
- ½ tsp. cinnamon
- ¼ tsp. liquid stevia
- 2 tbsp. heavy cream
- 6 tbsp. cream cheese (melted)

Directions:

Plug the waffle maker to preheat it and spray it with a non-stick cooking spray.

In a mixing bowl, combine the Swerve, cocoa powder, ginger, and baking powder.

In another mixing bowl, whisk together the cream cheese, egg, and vanilla.

Pour the cocoa powder mixture into the egg mixture and mix until the ingredients are well combined.

Fill the waffle maker with an appropriate amount of batter and spread it to the edges to cover all the holes on the waffle maker.

Cook for about 7 minutes or according to your waffle maker's settings.

After the cooking cycle, use a silicone or plastic utensil to remove the chaffle from the waffle maker. Set aside to cool completely.

Repeat the process with the remaining batter to create more chaffles.

For the filling, combine the vanilla, cream cheese, stevia, cinnamon, and heavy cream in a mixing bowl. Mix until well combined.

Spread the cream frosting over the surface of one chaffle and cover with another chaffle.

Place the filled chaffles in a refrigerator and chill for about 15 minutes.

Per serving: Calories: 365Kcal; Fat: 23g; Carbs: 3g; Protein: 23g

161. Savory Chaffle Stick

Preparation time: 5 minutes
Cooking time: 25 minutes
Servings: 4
Ingredients:

- 6 eggs
- 2 cup mozzarella cheese, shredded
- ½ tsp. ground black pepper or to taste ½ tsp. baking powder
- 4 tbsp. coconut flour
- 1 tsp. onion powder
- 1 tsp. garlic powder
- 1 tsp. oregano
- ¼ tsp. Italian seasoning
- 1 tbsp. olive oil
- 1 tbsp. melted butter
- a pinch of salt

Directions:

Plug the waffle maker to preheat it and spray it with a non-stick cooking spray.

Break 4 of the eggs into a mixing bowl and beat. Add the coconut flour, baking powder, salt, cheese, and Italian seasoning. Combine until the ingredients are well combined. Add more flour if the mixture is too thick.

Pour some batter into the waffle maker and spread out the batter to cover all the holes on the waffle maker.

Cover the waffle maker and cook for about 7 minutes or according to your waffle maker's settings. Make sure the chaffle is browned.

After the cooking cycle, use a plastic or silicone utensil to remove the chaffle from the waffle maker.

Repeat steps 3 to 5 until you have cooked all the batter into chaffles.

Cut the chaffles into sticks. Each mini chaffle should make about 4 sticks.

Preheat the oven to 350°F. Line a baking sheet with parchment paper and grease it with melted butter.

Break the remaining two eggs into another mixing bowl and beat.

In another mixing bowl, combine the oregano, pepper, garlic, and onion.

Dip one chaffle stick into the egg. Bring it out and hold it for a few seconds to allow excess liquid to drip off.

Dip the wet chaffle stick into the seasoning mixture and make sure it is coated with seasoning. Drop it on the baking sheet.

Repeat the process until all the chaffle sticks are coated.

Arrange the chaffle sticks into the baking sheet in a single layer.

Place the baking sheet in the oven and bake for 10 minutes.

Remove the baking sheet from the oven, brush the oil over the sticks and flip them.

Return it to the oven and bake for an additional 6 minutes or until the stick are golden brown.

After removing the sticks from the oven, let them cool for a few minutes.

Per serving: Calories: 406 Kcal; Fat: 14g; Carbs: 8g; Protein: 25g

162. Grain-Free Chaffles

Preparation time: 5 minutes
Cooking time: 15 minutes
Servings: 2
Ingredients:
- 1 tsp. almond flour
- 1 shake cinnamon
- 1 tsp. baking powder
- 1 egg
- 1 cup mozzarella cheese
- 1 tsp. vanilla

Directions:
In a bowl, combine the egg and vanilla concentrate.

Blend in the baking powder, almond flour and cinnamon.

Finally, include the mozzarella cheddar and coat it equitably with the blend.

Shower your Chaffle maker with oil and let it heat up to its most noteworthy setting.

Cook the Chaffle, minding it at regular intervals until it gets crunchy and brilliant.

Making it a muddled procedure. I recommend putting down a spat tangle for simple cleanup.

Take it out cautiously, and top it with spread and your preferred low-carb syrup.

Per serving: Calories: 421Kcal; Fat: 27g; Carbs: 3g; Protein: 22g

CHAPTER 2:

Breakfast and Brunch

163. Cinnamon Garlic Chaffles

Preparation time: 5 minutes
Cooking time: 10 minutes
Servings: 1
Ingredients:

- 1 egg
- ½ cup mozzarella cheese, shredded
- ½ tbsp. ground garlic
- ½ tsp. ground cinnamon
- 1 tsp. powdered erythritol
- ¼ tsp. ground nutmeg
- 2 tbsp. almond flour
- ½ tsp. baking powder

Directions:
Mix all the ingredients well together.
Pour a layer on a preheated waffle iron.
Cook the chaffle for around 5 minutes.
Make as many chaffles as your mixture allow.
Serve with your favorite topping.
Per serving: Calories: 370Kcal; Fat: 28g; Carbs: 3g; Protein: 23g

164. Creamy Cinnamon Chaffles

Preparation time: 5 minutes
Cooking time: 10 minutes
Servings: 2
Ingredients:

- 2 eggs
- 1 cup shredded mozzarella
- 2 tbsp. cream cheese
- 1 tbsp. cinnamon powder
- 2 tbsp. almond flour
- ¾ tbsp. baking powder
- 2 tbsp. water (optional)

Directions:
Preheat your mini waffle iron if needed.
Mix all the ingredients in a medium-sized bowl.
Grease your waffle iron lightly.
Cook your mixture in the mini waffle iron for at least 4 minutes or till the desired crisp is achieved and serve hot.
Make as many chaffles as your mixture allow.
Per serving: Calories: 423Kcal; Fat: 28g; Carbs: 3g; Protein: 23g

165. Crispy Chaffles with Egg and Asparagus

Preparation time: 5 minutes
Cooking time: 10 minutes
Servings: 1
Ingredients:

- 1 egg
- ¼ cup cheddar cheese
- 2 tbsp. almond flour
- ½ tsp. baking powder

Toppings:

- 1 egg
- 4-5 stalks of asparagus
- 1 tsp. avocado oil

Directions:
Preheat the waffle maker to medium-high heat.
Whisk together the egg, mozzarella cheese, almond flour, and baking powder.
Spoon the chaffles mixture into the waffle iron. Close the lid and let cook for 5 minutes or until the waffle is golden brown and set.
Remove the chaffles from the waffle maker and serve them.
While you're cooking your chaffles, heat the oil in a non-stick pan.
Once the pan is hot, fry asparagus for about 4-5 minutes until golden brown.
Poach the egg in boiling water for about 2-3 minutes.
Once the chaffles are cooked, remove them from the maker.
Serve the chaffles with the poached egg and asparagus.
Per serving: Calories: 347Kcal; Fat: 32g; Carbs: 3g; Protein: 26g

166. Gingerbread Chaffle

Preparation time: 5 minutes
Cooking time: 10 minutes
Servings: 1
Ingredients:

- 1 egg
- ½ cup mozzarella cheese (shredded)
- ½ tsp. ground ginger
- 1 tsp. powdered erythritol
- ½ tsp. ground cinnamon
- ¼ tsp. ground nutmeg
- ⅛ tsp. ground cloves
- 2 tbsp. almond flour
- ½ tsp. baking powder

Directions:
Mix all the ingredients well together.
Pour a layer on a preheated waffle iron.
Cook the chaffle for around 5 minutes.
Make as many chaffles as your mixture allow.
Serve with your favorite topping.
Per serving: Calories: 523Kcal; Fat: 28g; Carbs: 3g; Protein: 23g

167. Hot Ham Chaffles

Preparation time: 5 minutes
Cooking time: 10 minutes
Servings: 1
Ingredients:

- 1 egg
- 1 cup shredded Swiss cheese
- ¼ cup chopped deli ham
- 1 tbsp. mayonnaise
- 2 tsp. Dijon mustard
- 1 tsp. garlic salt

Directions:
Preheat your mini waffle iron and grease it.
Add the egg, cheese, garlic salt, and ham to a bowl and whisk.
Cook your mixture in the mini waffle iron for at least 4 minutes.
Make as many chaffles as your mixture allow.
Combine together the Dijon mustard and mayonnaise and serve with the dip.
Per serving: Calories: 423Kcal; Fat: 31g; Carbs: 4g; Protein: 23g

168. Jalapeño Grilled Cheese Bacon Chaffle

Preparation time: 15 minutes
Cooking time: 20 minutes
Servings: 2
Ingredients:
- 2 eggs
- 1 cup mozzarella cheese (shredded)
- 2 sliced jalapeños with seeds removed along with the skin
- ½ cup cream cheese
- 2 slices Monterey Jack
- 2 slices cheddar cheese
- 4 slices cooked bacon

Directions:
Add over two tbsp. of cream cheese to the half-cut jalapeños.
Bake them for around 10 minutes and set them aside.
Preheat the waffle maker and grease it.
In a mixing bowl, beat the eggs and add mozzarella cheese to them and mix well.
Pour the mixture into the lower plate of the waffle maker and spread it evenly to cover the plate properly.
Cook for about 4 minutes until crunchy.
After cooking, keep the chaffle aside for around one minute.
Make as many chaffles as your mixture allow.
Make a sandwich by placing a slice of Monterey Jack, a cheese slice, 2 bacon slices in between two chaffles, and enjoy!
Per serving: Calories: 423Kcal; Fat: 38g; Carbs: 2g; Protein: 23g

169. Japanese Styled Breakfast Chaffles

Preparation time: 5 minutes
Cooking time: 10 minutes
Servings: 1
Ingredients:
- 1 egg
- ½ cup mozzarella cheese (shredded)
- 1 slice bacon
- 2 tbsp. Kewpie mayo
- 1 stalk green onion

Directions:
Preheat the waffle maker if needed and grease it.
In a mixing bowl, beat an egg and put 1 tbsp. of Kewpie Mayo.
Chop the green onion and put half of it in the mixing bowl and half aside.
Cut the bacon into pieces of ¼ inches and add in the mixing bowl and mix well.
Sprinkle around ⅛ cup of shredded mozzarella cheese to the lower plate of the waffle maker and pour the mixture over it.
Again, sprinkle ⅛ cup of shredded mozzarella cheese to the top of the mixture.
Cook for at least 4 minutes to get the desired crunch.
Remove the chaffle from the heat and drizzle Kewpie mayo.
Serve by sprinkling the remaining green onions.
Make as many chaffles as your mixture allow.
Per serving: Calories: 423Kcal; Fat: 28g; Carbs: 1g; Protein: 23g

170. Lemon Almonds Chaffles

Preparation time: 15 minutes
Cooking time: 20 minutes
Servings: 1
Ingredients:
- 1/3 cup cheddar cheese
- 1 egg
- 2 tbsp. lemon juice
- 2 tbsp. almond flour
- ¼ tsp. baking powder
- 1/3 cup mozzarella cheese

Directions:
Mix the cheddar cheese, egg, lemon juice, almond flour, almond ground, and baking powder together in a bowl.
Preheat your mini waffle maker and grease it.
In your mini waffle iron, shred some of the mozzarella cheese.
Add half of the mixture to your mini waffle iron.
Shred some mozzarella cheese again on the mixture.
Cook till the desired crisp is achieved.
Repeat the process to create the next chaffle
Per serving: Calories: 423Kcal; Fat: 28g; Carbs: 2g; Protein: 24g

171. Mini Breakfast Chaffles

Preparation time: 5 minutes
Cooking time: 15 minutes
Servings: 2
Ingredients:
- 6 tsp. coconut flour
- 1 tsp. stevia
- ¼ tsp. baking powder
- 2 eggs
- 3 oz. cream cheese
- ½. tsp. vanilla extract

Toppings:
- 1 egg
- 6 slice bacon
- 2 oz. raspberries
- 2 oz. blueberries
- 2 oz. strawberries

Directions:
Heat up your square waffle maker and grease with cooking spray.
Mix together coconut flour, stevia, egg, baking powder, cheese, and vanilla in a mixing bowl.
Pour ½ of the chaffles mixture in a waffle maker.
Close the lid and cook the chaffles for about 3-5 minutes.
Meanwhile, fry the bacon slices in a pan at medium heat for about 2-3 minutes until cooked and transfer them to the plate.
In the same pan, fry the eggs one by one in the leftover grease of bacon.
Once the chaffles are cooked, carefully transfer them to the plate.
Serve with fried eggs and bacon slice and berries on top.
Per serving: Calories: 372Kcal; Fat: 38g; Carbs: 2g; Protein: 27g

172. Minty Mini Chaffles

Preparation time: 5 minutes
Cooking time: 10 minutes
Servings: 2
Ingredients:
- 2 eggs
- 1 cup shredded mozzarella
- 2 tbsp. cream cheese
- ¼ cup chopped mint
- 2 tbsp. almond flour

- ¾ tbsp. baking powder
- 2 tbsp. water (optional)

Directions:
Preheat your mini waffle iron if needed.
Mix all the ingredients in a medium-sized bowl.
Grease your waffle iron lightly.
Cook your mixture in the mini waffle iron for at least 4 minutes or till the desired crisp is achieved and serve hot.
Create as many chaffles as your mixture allow.
Per serving: Calories: 353Kcal; Fat: 28g; Carbs: 3g; Protein: 23g

173. Monte Cristo Chaffle

Preparation time: 5 minutes
Cooking time: 10 minutes
Servings: 2
Ingredients:
Chaffles:
- 2 eggs
- 2 tbsp. cream cheese
- 1 tbsp. vanilla extract
- 2 tbsp. almond flour
- 1 tsp. heavy cream
- 1 tsp. cinnamon powder
- 1 tbsp. Swerve sweetener

Assembling:
- 2 slices cheese
- 2 slices ham
- 2 slices turkey

Directions:
Preheat your waffle maker and grease it.
In a mixing bowl, add all the ingredients for the chaffles and mix them well.
Pour the mixture into the lower plate of the waffle maker and spread it evenly to cover the plate properly.
Cook for about 4 minutes to get the desired crunch.
Once the chaffle is done, keep it aside for around one minute.
Repeat the process to create the rest of the chaffles.
Serve with a cheese slice, a turkey, and a ham.
You can also serve with any of your favorite low-carb raspberry jam on top.
Per serving: Calories: 423Kcal; Fat: 28g; Carbs: 2g; Protein: 23g

174. Mushroom Stuffed Chaffles

Preparation time: 15 minutes
Cooking time: 40 minutes
Servings: 2
Ingredients:
Chaffles:
- 2 eggs
- ½ cup mozzarella cheese (shredded)
- ½ tsp. onion powder
- ¼ tsp. garlic powder
- ¼ tsp. salt or as per your taste
- ¼ tsp. black pepper or as per your taste
- ½ tsp. dried poultry seasoning

Stuffing:
- 1 small diced onion
- 4 oz. mushrooms
- 3 celery stalks
- 4 tbsp. butter
- 3 eggs

Directions:
Preheat your waffle maker and grease it.
Combine all the chaffle ingredients in a mixing bowl. Mix well.
Drop the mixture into the waffle maker and spread it evenly to cover the plate properly, and close the lid.
Cook the batter for about 4 minutes or until the chaffle becomes crunchy.
Once the chaffle is cooked, keep it aside.
Repeat the process to create more chaffles.
Into a frying pan, melt the butter (medium-low heat).
Sauté celery, onion, and mushrooms to make them soft.
Take another bowl and tear the chaffles down into minute pieces.
Add the eggs and the veggies to it.
Take a casserole dish, and add this new stuffing mixture to it.
Bake it at 350°F for around 30 minutes and serve hot.
Per serving: Calories: 423Kcal; Fat: 38g; Carbs: 1g; Protein: 26g

175. Zucchini Nut Bread Chaffle

Preparation time: 5 minutes
Cooking time: 10 minutes
Servings: 2
Ingredients:
Chaffles:
- 1 egg
- 1 cup zucchini (shredded)
- 2 tbsp. softened cream cheese
- ½ tsp. cinnamon
- 1 tsp. erythritol blend
- 1 tbsp. nutmeg (grounded)
- 2 tsp. butter
- ½ tsp. baking powder
- 3 tbsp. walnuts
- 2 tsp. coconut flour

Frosting:
- 4 tbsp. cream cheese
- ¼ tsp. cinnamon
- 2 tbsp. butter
- 2 tbsp. caramel (sugar-free)
- 1 tbsp. walnuts (chopped)

Directions:
Grate the zucchini and leave it in a colander for 10 minutes.
Squeeze with your hands as well to drain excess water.
Plug in your waffle maker and grease it.
In a mixing bowl, beat an egg, zucchini, and other chaffle ingredients.
Pour the mixture into the lower plate of the waffle maker and spread it evenly to cover the plate properly, and close the lid.
Cook for at least 4 minutes to get the desired crunch.
Repeat the process to create the rest of the chaffles.
Whisk all the frosting ingredients together except for walnuts and give a uniform consistency.
Serve the chaffles with frosting on top and chopped nuts.
Per serving: Calories: 523Kcal; Fat: 41g; Carbs: 8g; Protein: 26g

176. Coconut Chaffles

Preparation time: 5 minutes
Cooking time: 5 minutes
Servings: 2
Ingredients:
- 2 eggs
- 1 oz. cream cheese
- 1 oz. cheddar cheese
- 2 tbsp. coconut flour
- 1 tsp. stevia

- 1 tbsp. coconut oil, melted
- ½ tsp. coconut extract
- 2 eggs, soft boil for serving

Directions:
Heat your Mini Dash waffle maker and grease with cooking spray.
Mix together all the chaffles ingredients in a bowl.
Pour the chaffle batter into a preheated waffle maker.
Close the lid.
Cook the chaffles for about 2-3 minutes until golden brown.
Serve them with boiled egg and enjoy!
Per serving: Calories: 342Kcal; Fat: 28g; Carbs: 7g; Protein: 21g

177. Avocado Toast Chaffle

Preparation time: 5 minutes
Cooking time: 7 minutes
Servings: 2
Ingredients:
- 4 tbsp. avocado mash
- ½ tsp. lemon juice
- ⅛ tsp. salt
- ⅛ tsp. black pepper
- 2 eggs
- ½ cup shredded cheese

For Serving:
- 2 eggs
- ½ avocado thinly sliced
- 1 tomato, sliced

Directions:
Mash the avocado mash with lemon juice, salt, and black pepper in a mixing bowl, until well combined.
Beat the eggs in a small bowl, and pour them in the avocado mixture, and mix well.
Switch on the waffle maker to Preheat.
Pour ⅛ of shredded cheese in a waffle maker and then pour ½ of the egg and avocado mixture, and then ⅛ of the shredded cheese.
Close the lid and cook the chaffles for about 3-4 minutes.
Repeat with the remaining mixture.
Meanwhile, fry the eggs in a pan for about 1-2 minutes.
For serving, arrange the fried egg on the chaffle toast with the avocado slice and tomatoes.
Sprinkle salt and pepper on top for your taste, and enjoy!
Per serving: Calories: 358Kcal; Fat: 30g; Carbs: 2g; Protein: 26g

178. Crispy Chaffles with Pork Sausage

Preparation time: 5 minutes
Cooking time: 10 minutes
Servings: 1
Ingredients:
Chaffles:
- ½ cup cheddar cheese
- ½ tsp. baking powder
- 1 egg
- 2 tsp. pumpkin spice

Others:
- 1 egg, whole
- 2 pork sausages
- 2 slices of bacon
- avocado oil
- salt and pepper to taste

Directions:
Mix together all the ingredients in a bowl.
Allow the batter to sit while the waffle iron warms.
Spray the waffle iron with non-stick spray.
Cook for around 4 minutes half of the mixture on the mini waffle iron.

Repeat to cook the second chaffle.
Meanwhile, in a pan, heat the oil and cook the egg according to your choice and transfer it to a plate.
In the same pan, fry the bacon slices and sausage on medium heat for about 2-3 minutes until cooked.
Once the chaffles are cooked thoroughly, remove them from the maker.
Serve with the fried egg, bacon slice, sausages, and enjoy!
Per serving: Calories: 510Kcal; Fat: 43g; Carbs: 1g; Protein: 22g

179. Chili Chaffles

Preparation time: 5 minutes
Cooking time: 10 minutes
Servings: 4
Ingredients:
- 4 eggs
- ½ cup grated parmesan cheese
- 1½ cup grated yellow cheddar cheese
- 1 hot red chili pepper
- salt and pepper to taste
- ½ tsp. dried garlic powder
- 1 tsp. dried basil
- 2 tbsp. almond flour
- 2 tbsp. olive oil for brushing the waffle maker

Directions:
Preheat the waffle maker.
Beat the eggs into a medium-sized bowl, and add the grated parmesan and cheddar cheese.
Mix until just combined and add the chopped chili pepper. Season with salt and pepper, dried garlic powder, and dried basil. Stir in the almond flour.
Mix until everything is combined.
Brush the heated waffle maker with olive oil and add a few tbsp. of the batter.
Cook for about 6-7 minutes depending on your waffle maker.
Per serving: Calories: 336Kcal; Fat: 30g; Carbs: 2g; Protein: 22g

180. Sugar-Free Marshmallow Chaffles

Preparation time: 30 minutes
Cooking time: 20 minutes
Servings: 1
Ingredients:
Chaffles:
- 1 egg
- ½ tsp. vanilla extract
- ¼ cup cream cheese
- 2 tbsp. almond flour
- 1 tbsp. sweetener of choice
- 1 tbsp. protein powder, unflavored
- ½ tsp. baking powder
- 1 tsp. ground cinnamon

Sugar-Free Marshmallow:
- 100g (3.5 oz.) xylitol, or other baking friendly sweetener
- 3 tbsp. water
- 4 gelatin sheets, or 7g gelatin powder

Chocolate Dip:
- 10g cacao butter
- 80g sugar-free chocolate

Directions:
If you do not have sugar-free marshmallow fluff, then it is suggested that you make this up to eight hours or even the day before making the chaffle.
Choose a container to set the marshmallow in later. This container needs to be lined with cling film.

Gelatin sheets need to be placed in water for a few minutes before use.

Melt the sugar in a cooking pot and allow it to boil for up to 3 minutes before adding the gelatin sheets or powder.

Dissolve the gelatin fully.

Now that the liquid is ready pour it into an electric mixer.

Mix the mixture until the liquid bulks up and starts to form a white marshmallow-like fluff.

Pour the marshmallow fluff into the previously prepared container and smooth the surface.

Allow the mixture to sit on a kitchen surface for no less than eight hours. For the best possible setting, let the fluff rest overnight so that it sets into the marshmallow form. Cover with cling film once cool to prevent insects from getting into the mixture.

Once fully set, the marshmallow can be cut into the desired shape.

Dust the marshmallow pieces with powdered sweetener if you want to keep it softer for longer.

Chaffles:

Preheat the waffle iron.

Beat the egg, and add the cinnamon and the remaining chaffle ingredients. At the end add a few drops of vanilla.

Divide the batter in half and cook each portion for 3 minutes.

Set the chaffles aside to cool.

If you want to prepare the s'mores at home, take the marshmallow fluff and spread it to the thickness of choice on one chaffle before adding the second chaffle on top.

Set aside the chaffles to prepare the chocolate dip.

Chocolate Dip:

Make use of a double boiler or instant pot to melt the cocoa butter and sugar-free chocolate together.

Make sure the mixture is completely smooth before dipping the chaffles edges in it. Coat all the marshmallow fluff.

Put aside and allow the chocolate to harden.

Whether you are making this as a snack at home or you take the individual parts with you to go camping, this chaffle is something that is a must in your collection.

Per serving: Calories: 368Kcal; Fat: 23g; Carbs: 3g; Protein: 21g

181. Thin Mint Cookie Chaffles

Preparation time: 20 minutes
Cooking time: 16 minutes
Servings: 2
Ingredients:

- 1 cup grated mozzarella cheese
- 2 tbsp. unsweetened cocoa powder
- 2 large eggs
- 3 tbsp. Swerve confectioners' sugar

Filling:

- 6 oz. cream cheese, softened
- 2 tbsp. unsweetened cocoa powder
- ½ cup almond flour
- ¼ cup Swerve confectioners' sugar or sweeteners of choice
- 1 tsp. peppermint extract
- ½ tsp. vanilla extract

Toppings:

- 3 tbsp. sugar-free chocolate chips
- 1 tbsp. coconut oil

Directions:

Preheat the waffle iron.

Mix all the chaffle ingredients in a bowl and make sure everything is mixed well.

Cook ¼ of the batter in the waffle iron for two to four minutes. The longer it is cooked, the crispier it becomes.

Continue to make chaffles until the batter is finished.

Filling and Topping:

Combine all the filler ingredients and beat with a hand mixer.

Apply the filling to the three cooled chaffles, stack, and set aside.

Heat the coconut oil and chocolate chips at 30-second intervals in a microwave until melted together.

Drizzle this over the stacked chaffles and serve.

Anyone who is a fan of chocolate will be delighted by this delicacy!

Per serving: Calories: 431Kcal; Fat: 38g; Carbs: 2g; Protein: 23g

182. Chocolate Cake Chaffle

Preparation time: 2 minutes
Cooking time: 8 minutes
Servings: 1
Ingredients:

- 2 tbsp. cocoa powder, keto-friendly
- 1 tbsp. heavy whipping cream
- 2 tbsp. granulated Swerve, or sweetener of choice
- 1 egg
- ¼ tsp. baking powder
- ½ tsp. vanilla extract
- 1 tbsp. almond flour

Cream Cheese Frosting:

- 1 tsp. heavy cream
- 2 tbsp. cream cheese
- ⅛ tsp. vanilla extract
- 2 tsp. Swerve confectioners' sugar

Directions:

Preheat the waffle iron.

Whisk the baking powder, almond flour, cocoa powder, and sweetener together.

Then, add the heaving whipping cream and vanilla extract.

Add the egg and mix very well, scraping the sides to get all the ingredients.

Allow the mixture to sit for about 3 minutes before cooking.

Pour the mixture into the waffle iron and cook it for about 4 minutes.

Repeat the process with the other half of the batter.

Start on the frosting while the second chaffle is cooking.

Cream Cheese Frosting:

In a bowl that is microwave-safe, put 2 tbsp of cream cheese.

Microwave for about eight seconds to soften.

Using a hand mixer, combine the heavy cream, vanilla extract, and softened cream cheese.

Add confectioners' sugar with a hand mixer to make the frosting fluffy.

Building the Cake:

Apply the frosting to one chaffle with a knife or piping bag.

Place the second chaffle on top of the first and finish adding the remaining frosting.

Don't feel that you need to build the chaffle cake if you only want one chaffle. You can just as easily add the frosting.

Per serving: Calories: 451Kcal; Fat: 38g; Carbs: 3g; Protein: 26g

183. Chocolate Ice Cream Sundae Chaffle

Preparation time: 5 minutes
Cooking time: 20 minutes
Servings: 3 mini chaffles
Ingredients:

- 1 egg
- ½ tsp. baking powder
- 1 tsp. vanilla extract
- ½ cup grated mozzarella cheese
- 2 tbsp. unsweetened cocoa powder
- 3 tbsp. Swerve sweetener, or sweetener of choice

Toppings:

- 2 cup keto-friendly vanilla ice cream
- pecans
- keto-friendly chocolate sauce

Directions:
Preheat the waffle iron.
Mix all the ingredients well.
Use ⅓ of the batter to make a mini chaffle and cook for between five to seven minutes. Allow each cooked chaffle to cool completely. Depending on your taste, add the ice cream, pecans and drizzle some chocolate sauce over the top.
Per serving: Calories: 390Kcal; Fat: 28g; Carbs: 1g; Protein: 22g

184. Fudgy Dark Chocolate Dessert Chaffle
Preparation time: 5 minutes
Cooking time: 20 minutes
Servings: 2
Ingredients:

- 2 large eggs
- 2 tsp. coconut flour
- 4 tbsp. grated mozzarella cheese
- 2 tbsp. heavy whipping cream
- ½ tsp. baking powder
- ½ tsp. vanilla extract
- 1 tbsp. dark cacao (70% cocoa or higher)
- a pinch of salt
- ¼ tsp. Stevia powder, or powdered sweetener of choice

Directions:
Preheat the waffle iron.
Beat the eggs and cream together before adding the other ingredients to the mixture.
Divide the batter into four parts and add to the waffle iron.
Cook the chaffles for about three to five minutes, then remove them from the waffle iron.
Continue until all the batter is gone.
This chaffle has a wide range of toppings that can accompany it. Try some berries with whipped cream and a dash of powdered sweetener.
Per serving: Calories: 383Kcal; Fat: 26g; Carbs: 3g; Protein: 22g

185. Birthday Cake Chaffle
Preparation time: 3 minutes
Cooking time: 12 minutes
Servings: 2
Ingredients:

- 2 eggs
- 2 tbsp. cream cheese room temp
- 2 tbsp. melted butter
- ¼ cup almond flour
- 1 tsp. coconut flour
- ½ tsp. baking powder
- 2 tbsp. Swerve confectioners' sugar, or sweetener of choice
- ¼ tsp. xanthan powder
- 1 tsp. cake batter extract
- ½ tsp. vanilla extract

Whipped Cream Frosting:

- ½ cup heavy whipping cream
- ½ tsp. vanilla extract
- 2 tbsp. Swerve confectioners' sugar or any sweetener of choice

Directions:
Preheat the waffle iron.
Use a blender to mix all the chaffle ingredients. The batter may look a little watery so let it rest for a minute before use.
Add about 3 tbsp of the batter to the waffle maker.
Cook until golden brown or about three minutes.
Remove the cooked chaffle and repeat until the batter is finished.
While the fourth chaffle is cooking, start on the frosting.

Frosting:
In a clean bowl, add all the frosting ingredients with a hand mixer.
The whipped cream is perfect when peaks are formed.
Once the chaffles are cool, add the frosting.
The chaffles must be cool, or the frosting will melt.
Per serving: Calories: 344Kcal; Fat: 33g; Carbs: 3g; Protein: 25g

186. Chicken Cauli Chaffles
Preparation time: 27 minutes
Cooking time: 25 minutes
Servings: 2
Ingredients:

- 3-4 pieces chicken, or ½ cup when done
- 2 cloves garlic (finely grated)
- 2 eggs
- salt as per your taste
- 1 stalk green onion
- 1 tbsp. soy sauce
- 1 cup cauliflower rice
- 1 cup mozzarella cheese
- ¼ tsp. black pepper, or as per your taste
- ¼ tsp. white pepper, or as per your taste

Directions:
Melt some butter in an oven and set aside, then cook the chicken in a skillet using salt and a cup of water to boil.
With the lid closed, cook for 18 minutes.
Once done, put off the heat and shred the chicken into pieces, then discard all the bones.
Using another mixing bowl, prepare a mix containing peppers (white and black), soy sauce, cauliflower rice, grated garlic, beaten egg with the shredded chicken pieces. Mix evenly.
Preheat and grease the waffle maker. Pour ⅛ cup of mozzarella into the waffle maker with the mixture on the cheese, add another cup (⅛) of mozzarella to the chaffle.
With a closed lid, heat the waffle for 5 minutes to a crunch, and then remove the chaffle.
Repeat for the remaining chaffles mixture to make more batter.
Serve by garnishing the chaffle with chopped green onions and enjoy.
Per serving: Calories: 344Kcal; Fat: 28g; Carbs: 2g; Protein: 25g

187. Garlic Chicken Chaffles
Preparation time: 27 minutes
Cooking time: 25 minutes
Servings: 1
Ingredients:

- 3-4 pieces chicken
- 1 garlic clove
- 1 egg
- salt
- ½ tbsp. lemon juice
- 2 tbsp. Kewpie mayo
- ½ cup mozzarella cheese

Directions:
Cook the chicken in a skillet using salt and a cup of water to boil.
With the lid closed, cook for 18 minutes. Once done, put off the heat and shred the chicken into pieces, then discard all the bones.
Using another mixing bowl, prepare a mix containing ⅛ cup of cheese, Kewpie mayo, lemon juice, and grated garlic. Mix evenly.
Preheat and grease the waffle maker. Arrange the chaffles on a baking tray with the chicken, then sprinkle cheese on the chaffles. With a closed lid, heat the waffle for 5 minutes until cheese melts, and then remove the chaffle.

Repeat for the remaining chaffles mixture to make more batter. Serve and warm.

Per serving: Calories: 344Kcal; Fat: 30g; Carbs: 2g; Protein: 25g

188. Chicken Mozzarella Chaffles

Preparation time: 12 minutes
Cooking time: 6 minutes
Servings: 2
Ingredients:

- 1 cup chicken
- 1 cup and 4 tbsp. mozzarella cheese
- ½ tsp. basil
- 1 tsp. butter
- 2 eggs
- 6 tbsp. tomato sauce
- ½ tbsp. garlic

Directions:

Melt some butter in a pan with shredded chicken added into it and stir for a few minutes. Add basil with garlic and set aside.

Using a mixing bowl, prepare a mixture containing the eggs with cooked chicken and mozzarella cheese, then mix evenly.

Preheat and grease a waffle maker. Spread the mixture on the base of the mini-waffle maker evenly, then heat for 5 minutes to a crispy form. Repeat the process for the remaining batter.

On a baking tray, arrange the chaffles with tomato sauce and grated cheese to garnish the top. Heat the oven at 399°F to melt the cheese. Then, serve hot.

Per serving: Calories: 340Kcal; Fat: 30g; Carbs: 2g; Protein: 26g

189. Chicken BBQ Chaffles

Preparation time: 32 minutes
Cooking time: 30 minutes
Servings: 1
Ingredients:

- ½ cup chicken
- 1 tbsp. BBQ sauce (sugar-free)
- 1 egg
- 2 tbsp. almond flour
- ½ cup cheddar cheese
- 1 tbsp. butter

Directions:

Melt some butter in a pan with shredded chicken added into it and stir for 11 minutes.

Using a mixing bowl, prepare a mixture containing all the ingredients with the cooked chicken, then mix evenly.

Preheat and grease a waffle maker.

Fill the waffle maker with half of the batter and close the lid. Cook for 5-6 minutes to a crispy form.

Repeat the process for the remaining batter.

Per serving: Calories: 350Kcal; Fat: 75g; Carbs: 1g; Protein: 20g

190. Chicken Spinach Chaffles

Preparation time: 41 minutes
Cooking time: 20 minutes
Servings: 1
Ingredients:

- ½ cup spinach
- pepper, as per your taste
- 1 tsp. basil
- ½ cup boneless chicken
- ½ cup shredded mozzarella
- 1 tbsp. garlic powder
- salt, as per your taste

- 1 egg
- 1 tbsp. onion powder

Directions:

Heat the chicken in water to boil, then shred it into pieces and keep aside. Heat the spinach for 9 minutes to strain.

Using a mixing bowl, prepare a mixture containing all the ingredients with the cooked chicken, then mix evenly.

Preheat and grease a waffle maker. Spread the mixture on the waffle maker evenly and then heat for 7 minutes to a crispy form.

Repeat the process for the remaining batter. Serve the best crispy with your desired keto sauce.

Per serving: Calories: 3200Kcal; Fat: 25g; Carbs: 1g; Protein: 24g

191. Chicken and Provolone Chaffles

Preparation time: 30 minutes
Cooking time: 5 minutes
Servings: 1
Ingredients:

- ½ cup canned chicken breast
- ¼ cup cheddar cheese
- ⅛ cup parmesan cheese
- 1 egg
- 1 tsp. Italian seasoning
- ⅛ tsp. garlic powder
- 1 tsp. cream cheese, room temperature

Toppings:

- 2 slices provolone cheese
- 1 tbsp. sugar-free pizza sauce

Directions:

Warm up the waffle maker.

Heat 1 tsp. of shredded cheese for 30 seconds before adding the ingredients.

Mix all the ingredients in a medium-sized mixing basin and stir until well combined.

This will provide the greatest crust and make it simpler to remove the chaffle when it's cooked.

Spoon half of the batter into the waffle maker and cook for about 4-5 minutes.

Repeat the process to cook the second chaffle in the same way.

Top the chaffles with a slice of provolone cheese and a sugar-free pizza sauce. I love to top it with even more Italian seasoning!

Per serving: Calories: 440Kcal; Fat: 33g; Carbs: 2g; Protein: 28g

192. Mexican Cheese Flavor Corndog Chaffles

Preparation time: 45 minutes
Cooking time: 5 minutes
Servings: 2
Ingredients:

- 2 eggs
- 1 cup Mexican cheese blend
- 1 tbsp. almond flour
- ½ tsp. cornbread extract
- ¼ tsp. salt
- hotdogs with hot dog sticks

Directions:

Plug in the corndog waffle maker.

In a small-sized bowl, whip the eggs and add the remaining ingredients, mixing well, except for the hotdogs.

Use a non-stick cooking spray to grease the corndog waffle maker.

Pour the batter into the corndog waffle maker (halfway filled). Adding a small amount of cheese 30 seconds before cooking the batter will make your corndog crispy,

Insert a stick into the hotdog.

Place the hot dog in the batter and push down gently.

Spread a layer of batter on top of the hot dog, just enough to cover it. Cook for about 4-5 minutes, or until golden brown.

When done, use a pair of tongs to take them from the corndog waffle maker.

Top with mustard, mayonnaise, or sugar-free ketchup!

Optional: for extra added spice, I love to add diced jalapeños to this recipe!

Per serving: Calories: 234Kcal; Fat: 60g; Carbs: 2g; Protein: 25g

193. Burger Bun Chaffle

Preparation time: 3 minutes
Cooking time: 5 minutes
Servings: 1
Ingredients:

- 1 large egg, beaten
- ½ cup shredded mozzarella
- 1 tbsp. almond flour
- ¼ tsp. baking powder
- 1 tsp. sesame seeds
- 1 a pinch of onion powder

Directions:
Plug in the mini waffle maker.
Combine all the ingredients to form the batter.
Spoon half of the batter into the mini waffle maker.
Cook for about 5 minutes or until you no longer see steam coming from the waffle maker.
Remove to a wire rack and allow to cool.
Per serving: Calories: 330Kcal; Fat: 30g; Carbs: 2g; Protein: 24g

194. Halloumi Cheese Chaffle

Preparation time: 5 minutes
Cooking time: 5 minutes
Servings: 1
Ingredients:

- 3 oz. halloumi cheese
- 2 tbsp. pasta sauce optional
- 2 classic chaffles

Directions:
Cut Halloumi cheese into ½ inch thick slices.
Place cheese in the unheated waffle maker.
Place the chaffle on top of the halloumi
Turn the waffle maker on.
Let it cook for about 3-6 minutes or until golden brown and to your liking.
Let it cool for some time on a rack.
Add low-carb marinara or pasta sauce.
Per serving: Calories: 330g; Fat: 27g; Carbs: 1g; Protein: 22g

195. Sausage Balls with Chaffle

Preparation time: 10 minutes
Cooking time: 5 minutes
Servings: 1
Ingredients:

- 1 lb. Italian sausage balls
- salt and pepper
- 6 tbsp. pasta sauce
- 1 cup sharp cheddar
- 1 cup almond flour
- ¼ cup parmesan
- 2 tsp. baking powder
- 1 egg

Directions:
Preheat the mini chaffle maker.
Mix all the ingredients in a large mixing bowl and blend well using your hands.
Scoop 3 tbsp of the blend onto the warmed chaffle maker.
Cook for at least 3 minutes. Flip over and cook for 2 additional minutes for even firmness.
Repeat to make all the rest of the chaffles
Add salt and pepper to the sausage and create meatballs of about 1 inch.
Heat a bit of oil in a frying pan and cook the meatballs until golden brown.
Add pasta sauce to the meatballs and cook for about other 2 minutes
Serve chaffles with the meatballs
Per serving: Calories: 530Kcal; Fat: 45g; Carbs: 2g; Protein: 23g

196. Pumpkin Cake Chaffle

Preparation time: 10 minutes
Cooking time: 10 minutes
Servings: 1
Ingredients:

- 1 egg
- ½ cup mozzarella cheese

Frosting:

- 2 tbsp. cream cheese
- ½ tsp. pumpkin pie
- 2 tbsp. monk fruit spice
- stevia sweetener
- 1 tbsp. pumpkin
- ½ tsp. clear vanilla extract

Directions:
Preheat the mini chaffle maker. In a small bowl, whip the egg.
Include the cheddar, pumpkin pie flavor, and the pumpkin.
Include ½ of the blend to the mini chaffle maker and cook it for about 3 to 4 minutes until it's golden brown.
While the chaffle is cooking, include the entirety of the cream cheddar icing ingredients in a bowl and blend it until it's smooth and rich.
On the off chance that you need a rich taste of this icing, you can likewise include one tbsp. of genuine margarine that has been cooled down to room temperature.
Add the cream cheddar icing to the hot chaffle and serve it right away.
Per serving: Calories: 395Kcal; Fat: 30g; Carbs: 1g; Protein: 20g

197. Breakfast Sandwich Chaffle

Preparation time: 10 minutes
Cooking time: 6 minutes
Servings: 1
Ingredients:

- 1 egg
- ½ cup Monterey Jack cheese
- 1 tbsp. almond flour
- 2 tbsp. butter

Directions:
Preheat your mini waffle maker
In a small-sized bowl, beat the egg, and add the almond flour and Monterey Jack cheese.
Spoon half of the batter into your waffle maker. Cook it for 3-4 minutes. Repeat for the second chaffle.
In a small pan, melt 2 tbsp. of butter, and then add the chaffles.
Cook them on each side for 2 minutes pressing down lightly on the top of them, so they crisp up better.
Let them sit for 2 minutes before serving.
Per serving: Calories: 340Kcal; Fat: 33g; Carbs: 1g; Protein: 21g

198. Super Easy Cream Cheese Cinnamon Roll Chaffles

Preparation time: 10 minutes
Cooking time: 10 minutes
Servings: 1
Ingredients:

Roll Chaffles:
- ½ cup mozzarella cheese
- 1 tbsp. coconut flour
- ¼ tsp. baking powder
- 1 egg
- 1 tsp. cinnamon
- 1 tsp. sweetener

Roll Swirl:
- 1 tbsp. butter
- 1 tsp. cinnamon
- 2 tsp. sweetener

Directions:
Preheat the waffle iron.
In a small bowl, mix all the roll chaffles ingredients and set aside.
In another small bowl, add a tbsp. of butter, 1 tsp. of cinnamon and 2 tsp of sweetener.
Microwave for 15 seconds and mix well.
Grease the waffle maker using a non-stick spray.
Pour ½ of the batter to your waffle maker and swirl in ½ of the cinnamon, Swerve, and butter mixture.
Let it cook for 3-4 minutes.
Once the first cinnamon roll chaffle is cooked, proceed with the second one.
Per serving: Calories: 420Kcal; Fat: 36g; Carbs: 3g; Protein: 77g

199. Lily's Chocolate Chip Chaffle

Preparation time: 10 minutes
Cooking time: 8 minutes
Servings: 1
Ingredients:
- 1 egg
- 1 tbsp. heavy whipping cream
- ½ tsp. coconut flour
- 1¾ tsp. Lakanto monk fruit golden to adjust sweetness
- ¼ tsp. baking powder
- a pinch of salt
- 1 tbsp. Lily's chocolate chips

Directions:
Preheat the waffle maker.
In a small bowl, mix all the ingredients except the chocolate chips, and stir well until combined.
Grease the waffle maker using a non-stick spray. Drop into the maker half of the batter and sprinkle a few chocolate chips on top of it.
Cook for 3 minutes or until the chocolate chip chaffle dessert is golden brown, then remove from the waffle maker with a fork, being careful not to burn your fingers.
Repeat with the rest of the batter.
Let the chaffle sit for a couple of minutes so that it begins to crisp.
I love to serve them with sugar-free whipped topping.
Per serving: Calories: 396Kcal; Fat: 30g; Carbs: 3g; Protein: 12g

200. Cheesy Garlic Bread Chaffle

Preparation time: 10 minutes
Cooking time: 14 minutes
Servings: 1
Ingredients:
- 1 egg
- ½ cup mozzarella cheese, shredded
- 1 tbsp. parmesan cheese
- ¾ tsp. coconut flour
- ¼ tsp. baking powder
- ⅛ tsp. Italian seasoning
- a pinch of salt

Filling and Seasoning:
- 1 tbsp. butter, melted
- ¼ tsp. garlic powder
- ½ cup mozzarella cheese, shredded
- ¼ tsp. basil seasoning

Directions:
Preheat the oven to 400°F and preheat the Dash Mini Waffle Maker.
Lightly grease waffle maker with a non-stick spray.
Mix the first 7 ingredients in a small-sized bowl and mix well to obtain a homogeneous mixture.
Cook half of the batter into the waffle maker for about 4 minutes or until golden brown.
Carefully remove the chaffle bread from the waffle maker.
Repeat the process with the remaining batter to create more chaffles.
Melt the butter in a bowl. Add garlic powder and mix well.
Cut each chaffle in half and place them on a baking tray, then brush the tops with the garlic butter mixture.
Top with the mozzarella cheese and pop in the oven for 4-5 minutes.
Preheat the oven to broil and place the baking pan on the top rack for 1-2 minutes, or until the cheese bubbles and becomes golden brown.
Keep a close eye on it since broiling might cause it to burn rapidly. (check every 30 seconds).
Remove from the oven and sprinkle basil seasoning on top. Enjoy!
Per serving: Calories: 370Kcal; Fat: 21g; Carbs: 3g; Protein: 16g

201. Pizza Chaffle

Preparation time: 10 minutes
Cooking time: 15 minutes
Servings: 2
Ingredients:
- 1 tsp. coconut flour
- 1 egg white
- ½ cup mozzarella cheese, shredded
- 1 tsp. cream cheese, softened
- ¼ tsp. baking powder
- ⅛ tsp. Italian seasoning
- ⅛ tsp. garlic powder
- a pinch of salt
- 3 tsp. low carb marinara sauce
- ½ cup mozzarella cheese
- 6 pepperonis cut in half
- 1 tbsp. parmesan cheese, shredded
- ¼ tsp. basil seasoning

Directions:
Preheat the oven to 400°F. and plug in the waffle maker so that it gets hot.
In a small-sized bowl, add the coconut flour, baking powder, garlic powder, mozzarella cheese, egg white, softened cream cheese, Italian seasonings, and a pinch of salt. Mix well.
Spoon ½ of the batter into the waffle maker, close the lid, and cook for 4 minutes or until the chaffle reaches the desired doneness.
Repeat the process to make the second chaffle.
Top each chaffle with marinara sauce (I used 1½ tsp. per), pepperoni, mozzarella cheese, and parmesan cheese.
Bake the chaffles in the oven, on the top baking rack, for 5 minutes.
Then, turn the oven to broil so that the cheese begins to bubble and

brown. Keep a close eye as it can burn quickly. I broiled my pizza chaffle for approx. 1 minute and 30 seconds.

Remove it from the oven and sprinkle basil on top.

Per serving: Calories: 480Kcal; Fat: 28g; Carbs: 4g; Protein: 17g

202. Sausage Gravy and Chaffles

Preparation time: 10 minutes
Cooking time: 10 minutes
Servings: 2
Ingredients:

For the Chaffles:

- 1 egg
- ½ cup mozzarella cheese, grated
- 1 tsp. coconut flour
- 1 tsp. water
- ¼ tsp. baking powder
- a pinch of salt

For the Keto Sausage Gravy:

- ¼ cup breakfast sausage, browned
- 1½ tsp. cream cheese, softened
- 1½ tbsp. heavy whipping cream
- 4 tbsp. chicken broth
- pepper to taste
- dash of onion powder (optional)
- dash garlic powder

Directions:

Preheat your Dash Mini Waffle Maker or any other waffle maker you got.

Grease it using a cooking spray.

Into a medium-sized bowl, mix all the ingredients for the chaffle and stir to combine well.

Put half of the chaffle batter onto the waffle maker, close the lid and cook for about 4 minutes.

Repeat the process to cook the second chaffle. Set them aside for about 2-3 minutes before serving to crisp.

For the Keto Sausage Gravy:

Cook ¼ cup of breakfast sausage in a skillet.

If you've never cooked the breakfast sausage, note that it is crumbled like ground beef.

Remove the excess of the grease from the skillet, add the rest of the ingredients, and bring to a boil stirring continuously.

Reduce the heat to medium and continue to simmer with the lid off for about 5-7 minutes, or until the sauce thickens.

Add some salt and pepper to taste and spoon some keto sausage gravy over chaffles.

Per serving: Calories: 426Kcal; Fat: 37g; Carbs: 5g; Protein: 21g

203. Sausage Biscuits and Gravy Breakfast Chaffle

Preparation time: 10 minutes
Cooking time: 20 minutes
Servings: 2
Ingredients:

- 2 eggs
- 1 cup mozzarella cheese
- ¼ tbsp. onion (granulated)
- ¼ tbsp. garlic (granulated)
- 2 tbsp. butter
- 1 tbsp. garlic (finely minced)
- 1 tbsp. almond flour
- 10 drops cornbread starch

- 1 tsp. baking powder
- 1 tsp. dried parsley
- 1 batch keto sausage biscuit and gravy

Directions:

Preheat your waffle maker if needed and grease it.

Beat the eggs in a medium-sized bowl and add all the chaffle ingredients, except the last one, and mix well.

Pour the mixture into the lower plate of the waffle maker and spread it evenly to cover the plate properly.

Cooking for about 4 minutes or until to get the desired crunch.

When the chaffle is done, remove it from the waffle maker and keep it aside.

Repeat the process to create as many chaffles as the mixture allow Sausage Gravy recipe and serve with yummy chaffles.

Per serving: Calories: 443Kcal; Fat: 24g; Carbs: 3g; Protein: 23g

204. Bagel Chaffle with Peanut Butter

Preparation time: 5 minutes
Cooking time: 10 minutes
Servings: 1
Ingredients:

Chaffles:

- 1 egg
- ½ cup shredded mozzarella cheese
- 1 tsp. coconut flour
- 1 tsp. everything bagel seasoning

For the Filling:

- 3 tbsp. peanut butter
- 1 tbsp. butter
- 2 tbsp. powdered sweetener

Directions:

Preheat your mini waffle iron and grease it.

Add all the Chaffles ingredients into a bowl and whisk well.

Cook your mixture in the waffle iron for about 4 minutes.

Make as many chaffles as your batter allow.

Mix the filling ingredients until a creamy mixture is obtained.

When the chaffles cool down, spread peanut butter.

Per serving: Calories: 450Kcal; Fat: 37; Carbs: 17g; Protein: 26g

205. Ground Cinnamon Bread Chaffle

Preparation time: 5 minutes
Cooking time: 10 minutes
Servings: 1
Ingredients:

- 1 egg
- ½ cup mozzarella cheese (shredded)
- ½ tsp. ground ginger
- 1 tsp. powdered erythritol
- ½ tsp. ground cinnamon
- ¼ tsp. ground nutmeg
- ⅛ tsp. ground cloves
- 2 tbsp. almond flour
- ½ tsp. baking powder

Directions:

Mix all the ingredients well together.

Pour a layer on a preheated waffle iron.

Cook the chaffle for around 5 minutes.

Repeat the process for the rest of the chaffles.

Serve with your favorite topping.

Per serving: Calories: 332Kcal; Fat: 23g; Carbs: 2g; Protein: 21g

206. Italian Bread Chaffle

Preparation time: 15 minutes
Cooking time: 20 minutes
Servings: 2
Ingredients:

For the Chaffles:
- 2 eggs
- 1 cup mozzarella cheese (shredded)
- ½ tsp. garlic powder
- 1 tsp. Italian seasoning
- 1 tsp. cream cheese

For the Garlic Butter Topping:
- ½ tsp. garlic powder
- ½ tsp. Italian seasoning
- 1 tbsp. butter

For the Cheesy Bread:
- 2 tbsp. mozzarella cheese (shredded)
- 1 tbsp. parsley

Directions:

Preheat your mini waffle maker and grease it.
In a mixing bowl, add all the ingredients of the chaffle and mix well.
Pour the mixture into the lower plate of the waffle maker and spread it evenly to cover the plate properly, and close the lid.
Cook for at least 4 minutes to get the desired crunch.
In the meanwhile, melt the butter and add the garlic butter ingredients.
Remove the chaffle from the heat and apply the garlic butter immediately.
Make as many chaffles as your batter allow.
Put the chaffles on the baking tray and sprinkle the mozzarella cheese on the chaffles.
Bake for 5 minutes in an oven at 350°F to melt the cheese.
Per serving: Calories: 481Kcal; Fat: 39g; Carbs: 2g; Protein: 25g

207. Blueberries Compote and Mozzarella Chaffle

Preparation time: 20 minutes
Cooking time: 30 minutes
Servings: 2
Ingredients:

Chaffles:
- 2 eggs
- ¼ cup mozzarella
- 1 tbsp. vanilla extract
- 2 tbsp. coconut flour
- ¼ tsp. baking powder
- 1 tsp. cinnamon powder
- 1 tbsp. Swerve sweetener

Blueberry Compote:
- 1 cup blueberries
- ½ tsp. lemon zest
- 1 tsp. lemon juice
- ⅛ tsp. xanthan gum
- 2 tbsp. water
- 1 tbsp. Swerve sweetener

Directions:

Blueberry compote:
Combine all of the ingredients, except the xanthan gum, in a small-sized saucepan and bring to a boil.
Reduce the heat to low and continue to cook for 8-10 minutes; the sauce will start to thicken.
Add the xanthan gum now and stir.
Remove the pan from the heat, let the compote cool, and after 6-7 minutes, put it in the refrigerator.

Preheat a mini waffle maker and grease it with a non-stick cooking spray.
In a medium-sized bowl, add all the chaffle ingredients and mix well.
Pour the mixture into the lower plate of the waffle maker and spread it evenly to cover the plate properly.
Close the lid and cook for about 4 minutes or until the desired crunch.
Take the chaffle off the heat and set it aside.
Repeat with the remaining batter.
Serve it with the blueberry compote and enjoy!
Per serving: Calories: 375Kcal; Fat: 25g; Carbs: 5g; Protein: 22g

208. Peanut Buttercup Chaffles

Preparation time: 5 minutes
Cooking time: 15 minutes
Servings: 1
Ingredients:

For the Chaffles:
- 1 egg
- ½ cup shredded mozzarella cheese
- 2 tbsp. cocoa powder
- ¼ tsp. espresso powder
- 1 tbsp. sugar-free chocolate chips

For the Filling:
- 3 tbsp. peanut butter
- 1 tbsp. butter
- 2 tbsp. powdered sweetener

Directions:

Preheat your waffle iron and grease it.
Put all the chaffles ingredients into a bowl and mix well.
Cook your mixture in the mini waffle iron for at least 4 minutes.
Make two chaffles.
Mix the filling ingredients together.
When the chaffles cool down, spread peanut butter on them to make a sandwich.
Per serving: Calories: 448Kcal; Fat: 34g; Carbs: 3g; Protein: 24g

209. Chocolaty Chaffles

Preparation time: 5 minutes
Cooking time: 15 minutes
Servings: 1
Ingredients:
- 1 egg
- ½ cup shredded mozzarella cheese
- 2 tbsp. cocoa powder
- ¼ tsp. espresso powder
- 1 tbsp. sugar-free chocolate chips

Directions:

Preheat your waffle iron and grease it.
Put all the chaffles ingredients into a bowl and mix well.
Cook your mixture in the mini waffle iron for at least 4 minutes.
Make as many chaffles as you can.
Per serving: Calories: 350Kcal; Fat: 23g; Carbs: 1g; Protein: 22g

210. McGriddles Chaffle

Preparation time: 5 minutes
Cooking time: 10 minutes
Servings: 1
Ingredients:
- 1 egg
- 1½ cup mozzarella cheese (shredded)
- 2 tbsp. maple syrup (sugar-free)
- 2 sausages

- 2 slices American cheese
- 2 tbsp. Swerve sweetener

Directions:
Plug in your mini waffle maker to preheat it. Grease it if needed
In a mixing bowl, beat the eggs and add shredded mozzarella cheese, Swerve/monk fruit, and maple syrup.
Mix them all well and pour the mixture into the lower plate of the waffle maker.
Close the lid.
Cook for at least 4 minutes to get the desired crunch.
Remove the chaffle from the heat.
Make the sausage patty by following the instruction given on the packaging.
Place a cheese slice on the patty immediately when removing it from the heat.
Take two chaffles and put the sausage patty and cheese in between.
Repeat the process to create all the McGriddles chaffles.
Per serving: Calories: 431Kcal; Fat: 20g; Carbs: 2g; Protein: 22g

211. Super Easy Cinnamon Swirl Chaffles

Preparation time: 5 minutes
Cooking time: 10 minutes
Servings: 2
Ingredients:
Chaffles:
- 2 eggs
- 2 oz. softened cream cheese
- 2 tbsp. almond flour
- 2 tsp. vanilla extract
- 2 tsp. cinnamon
- 2 tsp. vanilla extract
- 2 tbsp. Splenda sweetener

Cinnamon Drizzle:
- 2 tbsp. Splenda
- 1 tbsp. butter
- 2 tsp. cinnamon

Directions:
Preheat the waffle maker.
Grease it lightly.
Mix all the chaffle ingredients together.
Pour the mixture into the waffle maker.
Cook for around 4 minutes or till the chaffles become crispy.
In a small-sized bowl, mix the ingredients of cinnamon drizzle.
Spread the drizzle on cooled chaffles and enjoy!
Per serving: Calories: 423Kcal; Fat: 38g; Carbs: 3g; Protein: 25g

212. Raspberries Jack and Chaddar Cheese Chaffle

Preparation time: 15 minutes
Cooking time: 15 minutes
Servings: 1
Ingredients:
- 1 egg white
- ¼ cup Jack cheese, shredded
- ¼ cup cheddar cheese, shredded
- 1 tsp. coconut flour
- ¼ tsp. baking powder
- ½ tsp. stevia

Toppings:
- 4 oz. raspberries
- 2 tbsp. coconut flour
- 2 oz. unsweetened raspberry sauce

Directions:
Switch on your round waffle maker and grease it with cooking spray once it is hot.
Mix together all the chaffle ingredients in a bowl and combine with a fork.
Pour the chaffle batter into a preheated maker and close the lid.
Once the chaffle is done, remove it from the maker.
Dip the raspberries in the sauce and arrange them on the chaffle.
Drizzle coconut flour on top.
Repeat for the rest of the batter.
Enjoy your chaffles.
Per serving: Calories: 386Kcal; Fat: 37g; Carbs: 4g; Protein: 25g

213. Scrambled Eggs and Spring Onions Chaffle

Preparation time: 10 minutes
Cooking time: 7-9 minutes
Servings: 4
Ingredients:
Batter:
- 4 eggs
- 2 cup grated mozzarella cheese
- ½ tsp. dried garlic powder
- 2 spring onions, finely chopped
- 2 tbsp. almond flour
- 2 tbsp. coconut flour
- salt and pepper to taste

Other:
- 2 tbsp. butter for brushing the waffle maker
- 6-8 eggs
- salt and pepper
- 1 tsp. Italian spice mix
- 1 tbsp. olive oil
- 1 tbsp. freshly chopped parsley

Directions:
Preheat the waffle maker.
Beat the eggs into a bowl and add the grated cheese.
Mix until just combined, then add the chopped spring onions and season with salt and pepper and dried garlic powder.
Stir in the almond flour and mix until everything is combined.
Brush the waffle maker (at this point, it should be warm) with butter and add some batter.
Close the lid and cook for about 7-8 minutes, depending on your waffle maker.
While the chaffles are cooking, scramble the eggs by whisking the eggs in a bowl until frothy, about 2 minutes. Season with salt and black pepper to taste and add the Italian spice mix. Whisk to blend in the spices.
Warm the oil in a non-stick pan over medium heat.
Pour the eggs in the pan and cook until the eggs are set to your liking.
Serve each chaffle and top with some scrambled eggs. Top with freshly chopped parsley.
Per serving: Calories: 365Kcal; Fat: 35g; Carbs: 5g; Protein: 26g

214. Egg and Cheddar Cheese Chaffle

Preparation time: 10 minutes
Cooking time: 7-9 minutes
Servings: 4
Ingredients:
Batter:
- 4 eggs
- 2 cup shredded white cheddar cheese
- a pinch salt and pepper

Other:
- 2 tbsp. butter for brushing the waffle maker
- 4 large eggs
- 2 tbsp. olive oil

Directions:

Preheat the waffle maker.

Beat the eggs into a medium-sized bowl and whisk them with a fork.

Stir in the grated cheddar cheese and season with salt and pepper.

Brush the heated waffle maker with butter and add a few tbsp. of the batter.

Close the lid and cook for about 7-8 minutes, depending on your waffle maker.

While chaffles are cooking, cook the eggs.

Warm the oil in a large non-stick pan that has a lid over medium-low heat for 2-3 minutes

Crack an egg in a small ramekin and gently add it to the pan. Repeat the same way for the other 3 eggs.

Cover and let cook for 2 to 2½ minutes for set eggs but with runny yolks.

Remove from the heat.

To serve, place a chaffle on each plate and top with an egg. Season with salt and black pepper to taste.

Per serving: Calories: 374Kcal; Fat: 37g; Carbs: 3g; Protein: 25g

215. Simple Savory Provolone Chaffle

Preparation time: 10 minutes
Cooking time: 7-9 minutes
Servings: 4
Ingredients:
Batter:
- 4 eggs
- 1 cup grated mozzarella cheese
- 1 cup grated provolone cheese
- ½ cup almond flour
- 2 tbsp. coconut flour
- 2½ tsp. baking powder
- salt and pepper to taste

Other:
- 2 tbsp. butter to brush the waffle maker

Directions:

Preheat the waffle maker.

Add the grated mozzarella and provolone cheese to a bowl and mix.

Add the almond and coconut flour and baking powder and season with salt and pepper.

Mix with a wire whisk and crack in the eggs.

Stir everything together until you have a creamy batter.

Brush the heated waffle maker with butter and add a few tbsp. of the batter.

Close the lid and cook for about 8 minutes, depending on your waffle maker.

Per serving: Calories: 348Kcal; Fat: 28g; Carbs: 3g; Protein: 21g

216. Pizza Chaffle with Almond Flour

Preparation time: 10 minutes
Cooking time: 7-9 minutes
Servings: 4
Ingredients:
Batter:
- 4 eggs
- 1½ cup mozzarella cheese, grated
- ½ cup parmesan cheese, grated
- 2 tbsp. tomato sauce
- ¼ cup almond flour
- 1½ tsp. baking powder

- salt and pepper to taste
- 1 tsp. dried oregano
- ¼ cup sliced salami

Other:
- 2 tbsp. olive oil for brushing the waffle maker
- ¼ cup tomato sauce for serving

Directions:

Preheat the waffle maker.

Add the grated mozzarella and grated parmesan to a bowl and mix.

Add the almond flour and baking powder. Season with salt and pepper and dried oregano.

Mix with a wooden spoon and crack in the eggs.

Stir everything together until you have a creamy batter.

Stir in the chopped salami.

Brush the heated waffle maker with olive oil and add a few tbsp. of the batter.

Close the lid and cook for about 7-minutes depending on your waffle maker.

Serve with extra tomato sauce on top and enjoy.

Per serving: Calories: 383Kcal; Fat: 34g; Carbs: 3g; Protein: 21g

217. Mozzarella Chaffle with Chopped Bacon

Preparation time: 10 minutes
Cooking time: 7-9 minutes
Servings: 4
Ingredients:
Batter:
- 4 eggs
- 2 cup shredded mozzarella
- 2 oz. finely chopped bacon
- salt and pepper to taste
- 1 tsp. dried oregano

Other:
- 2 tbsp. olive oil for brushing the waffle maker

Directions:

Preheat the waffle maker.

Crack the eggs into a bowl and add the grated mozzarella cheese.

Mix until just combined and stir in the chopped bacon.

Season with salt and pepper and dried oregano.

Brush the heated waffle maker with olive oil and add a few tbsp. of the batter.

Cook for about 7-8 minutes, depending on your waffle maker.

Per serving: Calories: 280Kcal; Fat: 20g; Carbs: 2g; Protein: 19g

218. Mouth-Watering Chaffle

Preparation time: 10 minutes
Cooking time: 5 minutes
Servings: 2
Ingredients:
- 1 cup egg whites
- 1 cup cheddar cheese, shredded
- ¼ cup almond flour
- ¼ cup heavy cream
- 4 oz. raspberries
- 4 oz. strawberries
- 1 oz. Keto chocolate flakes
- 1 oz. feta cheese

Directions:

Preheat your square waffle maker and grease with cooking spray.

Beat the egg white in a small bowl with flour.

Add shredded cheese to the egg whites and flour mixture and mix well.

Add cream and cheese to the egg mixture.

Pour the chaffles batter into a waffle maker and close the lid.

Cook the chaffles for about 4 minutes until crispy and brown.

Carefully remove the chaffles from the maker.

Serve with berries, cheese, and chocolate on top.

Per serving: Calories: 354Kcal; Fat: 29g; Carbs: 3g; Protein: 21g

219. Breakfast Bowl with Chaffles

Preparation time: 15 minutes
Cooking time: 5 minutes
Servings: 1
Ingredients:

- 1 egg
- ½ cup cheddar cheese shredded
- a pinch of Italian seasoning
- ½ avocado sliced
- 2 eggs boiled
- 1 tomato, halves

Directions:

Preheat your waffle maker and grease with cooking spray.

Crack an egg in a small bowl and beat it with Italian seasoning.

Add shredded cheese to the egg and spices mixture.

Pour 1 tbsp. of shredded cheese in a waffle maker and cook for 30 seconds.

Pour the chaffles batter into the waffle maker

Cook the chaffles for about 4 minutes until crispy and brown.

Carefully remove the chaffles from the maker.

Serve with boiled egg, avocado slice, and tomatoes.

Per serving: Calories: 349Kcal; Fat: 32g; Carbs: 2g; Protein: 25g

220. Cajun and Feta Chaffles

Preparation time: 30 minutes
Cooking time: 10 minutes
Servings: 1
Ingredients:

- 1 egg white
- ¼ cup shredded mozzarella cheese
- 2 tbsp. almond flour
- 1 tsp. Cajun Seasoning
  For Serving:
- 1 egg
- 4 oz. feta cheese
- 1 tomato, sliced

Directions:

Whisk together egg, cheese, and seasoning in a bowl.

Switch on and grease waffle maker with cooking spray.

Pour the batter into a preheated waffle maker.

Cook the chaffles for about 2-3 minutes until the chaffle is cooked through.

Meanwhile, fry the egg in a non-stick pan for about 1-2 minutes.

Set the fried egg on chaffles with feta cheese and tomato slices for serving.

Per serving: Calories: 303Kcal; Fat: 19g; Carbs: 2g; Protein: 17g

221. Hot Chocolate Breakfast Chaffle

Preparation time: 15 minutes
Cooking time: 14 minutes
Servings: 1

Ingredients:

- 1 egg, beaten
- 2 tbsp. almond flour
- 1 tbsp. unsweetened cocoa powder
- 2 tbsp. cream cheese, softened
- ¼ cup finely grated Monterey Jack cheese
- 2 tbsp. sugar-free maple syrup
- 1 tsp. vanilla extract

Directions:

Preheat the waffle iron.

In a medium bowl, mix all the ingredients.

Open the iron, lightly grease with cooking spray, and pour in half of the mixture.

Close the iron and cook until crispy, 7 minutes.

Remove the chaffle onto a plate and set it aside.

Pour the remaining batter into the iron and make the second chaffle.

Allow cooling and serve afterward.

Per serving: Calories: 403Kcal; Fat: 30g; Carbs: 2g; Protein: 18g

222. Garlic and Parsley Chaffles

Preparation time: 15 minutes
Cooking time: 5 minutes
Servings: 1
Ingredients:

- 1 large egg
- ¼ cup mozzarella cheese
- 1 tsp. coconut flour
- ¼ tsp. baking powder
- ½ tsp. garlic powder
- 1 tbsp. minced parsley
  For Serving:
- 1 poach egg
- 4 oz. Smoked salmon

Directions:

Switch on your Dash mini waffle maker and let it preheat.

Grease waffle maker with cooking spray.

Mix together the egg, mozzarella, coconut flour, baking powder, garlic powder, and parsley into a mixing bowl until combined well.

Pour the batter into a round chaffle maker.

Close the lid.

Cook for about 2-3 minutes or until the chaffles are cooked.

Serve with smoked salmon and poached egg.

Per serving: Calories: 287Kcal; Fat: 34g; Carbs: 4g; Protein: 15g

223. Blueberry Taco Chaffles

Preparation time: 20 minutes
Cooking time: 15 minutes
Servings: 1
Ingredients:

- 1 egg white
- ½ cup mozzarella cheese, shredded
- 1 tsp. almonds flour
- ¼ tsp. baking powder
- ½ tsp. stevia
  Toppings:
- 4 oz. blueberries
- 2 oz. unsweetened blueberry sauce

Directions:

Switch on your round waffle maker and grease it with cooking spray once it is hot.

Mix together all the chaffle ingredients in a bowl and combine with a fork.

Pour the chaffle batter into a preheated maker and close the lid.

Roll the taco chaffle around using a kitchen roller, set it aside, and let it stand for a few minutes.

Once the taco chaffle is set, remove it from the roller.

Dip the blueberries in the sauce and arrange them on a taco chaffle. Enjoy!

Per serving: Calories: 454Kcal; Fat: 34g; Carbs: 3g; Protein: 23g

224. Cinnamon Swirls Chaffles

Preparation time: 12 minutes
Cooking time: 6 minutes
Servings: 2
Ingredients:
Icing:
- 2 tbsp. unsalted butter
- 2 oz. softened cream cheese
- 1 tsp. vanilla
- 2 tbsp. Splenda

Chaffles:
- 2 eggs
- 2 tbsp. almond flour
- 2 tsp. cinnamon
- 2 tbsp. Splenda
- 2 oz. softened cream cheese
- 2 tsp. vanilla extract

Cinnamon Drizzle:
- 2 tbsp. Splenda
- 2 tsp. cinnamon
- 1 tbsp. butter

Directions:
Preheat and grease a waffle maker. Make a combined mixture of all ingredients, evenly mixed and pour into the waffle maker.

Cook for 4 minutes till the chaffles turn crispy, and then set aside. Using a mixing bowl, mix all the ingredients for icing and the cinnamon drizzle, then heat using a microwave for 12 seconds to soften.

Pour heated icing and cinnamon on the cool chaffles to enjoy.

Per serving: Calories: 494Kcal; Fat: 37g; Carbs: 5g; Protein: 29g

225. Japanese Styled Chaffles

Preparation time: 12 minutes
Cooking time: 6 minutes
Servings: 1
Ingredients:
- 1 egg
- 1 slice bacon
- 1 stalk green onion
- ½ cup mozzarella cheese (shredded)
- 2 tbsp. Kewpie mayo

Directions:
Preheat and grease the waffle maker. Using a mixing bowl, mix Kewpie mayo with the beaten egg, then add in ½ of chopped green onion with the other ½ kept aside and ¼ inches of cut bacon into the mixture.

Mix evenly. Sprinkle the base of the waffle maker with ⅛ cup of shredded mozzarella and pour in the mixture, then top with more shredded mozzarella. With a closed lid, heat the waffle for 5 minutes to a crunch and then remove the chaffle and allow cooking for a few minutes.

Repeat for the remaining chaffles mixture to make more batter. Serve by garnishing the chaffle with the leftover chopped green onions.

Per serving: Calories: 192Kcal; Fat: 7g; Carbs: 1g; Protein: 2g

226. Strawberry Chaffles

Preparation time: 10 minutes
Cooking time: 5 minutes
Servings: 1
Ingredients:
- 1 egg
- ¼ cup mozzarella cheese
- 1 tbsp. cream cheese
- ¼ tsp. baking powder
- 2 sliced strawberries
- 1 tsp. strawberry extract

Directions:
Preheat the waffle maker.

In a little bowl, beat the egg.

Add the rest of the ingredients.

The waffle maker is sprayed with non-stick cooking spray.

Divide the mix into two equal parts.

Cook a portion of the mix for around 4 minutes or until golden brown colored.

Per serving: Calories: 380Kcal; Fat: 25g; Carbs: 1g; Protein: 15g

227. Crunchy Chaffles

Preparation time: 15 minutes
Cooking time: 8 minutes
Servings: 2
Ingredients:
- 2 large eggs
- ½ cup shredded mozzarella cheese (pressed firmly)
- ½ tsp. baking powder
- 1 tbsp. erythritol (powder), or sweetener (however powder is better than sweetener)
- ½ tsp. vanilla extract

Directions:
Heat your waffle iron on the high heat setting. I used a 7-inch waffle iron, and this formula fits nicely for one huge waffle. If you have a smaller waffle maker, split the recipe into two waffles.

Put all the ingredients into a Blender and mix for 10 seconds.

Pour the mix into a very hot and dry waffle Iron. It will look thin once poured but have no fear; it significantly increases in size when cooking (and you'll need to keep an eye on it to avoid overflow when cooking)! Let the waffle cook for 3-4 minutes or much more! The waffle is done once the entire waffle is golden dark-colored, which takes longer than a normal waffle would.

Flip your waffle with a fork to ensure that each side has even colors if it doesn't look done after some time. Let the waffle cool for 3-4 minutes before eating since it may become brown on cooling.

Serve with gobs of grass-fed butter and sugar-free syrup or whatever topping you want.

Per serving: Calories: 285Kcal; Fat: 23g; Carbs: 2g; Protein: 18g

228. Silver Dollar Chaffles

Preparation time: 10 minutes
Cooking time: 5 minutes
Servings: 2
Ingredients:
- 3 eggs
- ½ cup Cottage cheese
- 1/3 cup almond Flour
- ¼ cup unsweetened almond milk
- 2 tbsp. sweetener
- vanilla extract
- 1 tsp. baking powder
- cooking oil spray

Directions:

Place the ingredients in a blender in the order listed above. Mix until you have a smooth, fluid batter.

Heat a non-stick pan at medium-high temperature. Spray with oil or margarine.

Place 2 tbsp. of batter at once to make little, dollar hotcakes. This is an extremely fluid, sensitive batter, so don't attempt to make big pancakes with this one as they won't flip over easily.

Cook every pancake until the top of the hotcake has made little air pockets, and the air pockets have vanished around 1-2 minutes.

Using a spatula, tenderly loosen the pancake and afterward flip over.

Make the remainder of the pancakes and serve hot.

Per serving: Calories: 310Kcal; Fat: 28g; Carbs: 2g; Protein: 22g

229. Chaffle Waffle

Preparation time: 10 minutes
Cooking time: 6 minutes
Servings: 1
Ingredients:

- 1 egg
- ½ cup shredded mozzarella cheese
- 1½ tbsp. almond flour
- a pinch of baking powder

Directions:

Turn your waffle maker on and preheat it.

Meanwhile, in a bowl, whisk the egg and shredded mozzarella cheese together. If you do not have shredded mozzarella cheese, you can use the shredder to shred your cheese, then add the almond powder and baking powder to the bowl and whisk them until the mixture is consistent.

Then, pour the mixture onto the waffle machine. Make sure you pour it to the center of the mixture will come out of the edges on closing the machine. Close the machine and let the waffles cook until golden brown. Then, you can serve your tasty chaffle waffles.

Per serving: Calories: 300Kcal; Fat: 25g; Carbs: 2g; Protein: 21g

230. Salted Caramel Syrup Chaffles

Preparation time: 15 minutes
Cooking time: 10 minutes
Servings: 2
Ingredients:

- 2 eggs
- ½ cup mozzarella cheese
- ¼ cup cream
- 2 tbsp. collagen powder
- 1½ tbsp. almond flour
- 1½ tbsp. unsalted butter
- a pinch of salt
- ¾ tbsp. powdered erythritol
- a pinch of baking powder

Directions:

Begin by preheating your waffle machine by switching it on and turning the heat to medium. Whisk together the chaffle ingredients that include the egg, mozzarella cheese, almond flour, and baking powder.

Pour the mixture on the waffle machine. Let it cook until golden brown. You can make up to two chaffles with this method.

To make the caramel syrup, you will need to turn on the flame under a pan to medium heat Melt the unsalted butter on the pan. Then, turn the heat low and add collagen powder and erythritol to the pan and whisk them.

Gradually add the cream and remove it from the heat. Then, add the salt and continue to whisk. Pour the syrup onto the chaffle, and here you go.

Per serving: Calories: 425Kcal; Fat: 37g; Carbs: 3g; Protein: 19g

231. Bacon Sandwich Chaffle

Preparation time: 15 minutes
Cooking time: 10 minutes
Servings: 1
Ingredients:

- 1 egg
- ½ cup shredded mozzarella cheese
- 2 tbsp. coconut flour
- 2 strips pork or beef bacon
- 1 slice of any type of Swiss cheese
- 2 tbsp. coconut oil

Directions:

To make the chaffle, you will be following the typical recipe for making a chaffle. Start by warming your waffle machine to medium heat.

In a bowl, beat 1 egg, ½ cup of mozzarella cheese, and almond flour. Pour the mixture on the waffle machine. Let it cook until it is golden brown. Then, remove it to a plate.

Warm the coconut oil in a pan over medium heat. Then, place the bacon strips in the pan. Cook until crispy over medium heat. Assemble the bacon and cheese on the chaffle.

Per serving: Calories: 325Kcal; Fat: 39g; Carbs: 6g; Protein: 18g

232. Crispy Zucchini and Onions Chaffles

Preparation time: 15 minutes
Cooking time: 5 minutes
Servings: 2
Ingredients:

- 2 eggs
- 1 fresh zucchini
- 1 cup shredded or grated cheddar cheese
- 2 pinches of salt
- 1 tbsp. onion (chopped)
- 1 garlic clove

Directions:

Preheat the waffle maker to medium heat.

Start by dicing the onions and mashing the garlic. Then, use the grater to grate the zucchini. Then, take a bowl and add 2 eggs and add the grated zucchini to the bowl.

Also, add the onions, salt, and garlic for extra flavor. You can also add other herbs to give your chaffle a crispier flavor. Then, sprinkle ½ cup of cheese on top of the waffle machine.

Transfer the mixture from the bowl to the waffle machine. Add the remaining cheese on top of the waffle machine and close it. Cook for about 3 to 5 minutes until it turns golden brown.

By the layering method, you will achieve the perfect crisp. Take out your zucchini chaffles and serve them hot and fresh.

Per serving: Calories: 330Kcal; Fat: 28g; Carbs: 2g; Protein: 23g

233. Peanut Butter Vanilla Chaffle

Preparation time: 15 minutes
Cooking time: 10 minutes
Servings: 1
Ingredients:

- 1 egg
- ½ cup cheddar cheese
- 2 tbsp. peanut butter
- few drops of vanilla extract

Directions:

Take a grater and grate some cheddar cheese. Add one egg, cheddar cheese, 2 tbsp of peanut butter, and a few drops of vanilla extract. Beat these ingredients together until the batter is consistent enough.

Then, sprinkle some shredded cheese as a base on the waffle maker. Pour the mixture on top of the waffle machine.

Sprinkle more cheese on top of the mixture and close the waffle machine. Ensure that the waffle is cooked thoroughly for a few minutes until they are golden brown. Then, remove it and enjoy your deliciously cooked chaffles.
Per serving: Calories: 465Kcal; Fat: 30g; Carbs: 5g; Protein: 26g

234. Feta Breakfast Chaffles
Preparation time: 5 minutes
Cooking time: 5 minutes
Servings: 2
Ingredients:
- 1 cup egg whites
- 1 cup cheddar cheese, shredded
- ¼ cup coconut flour
- ¼ cup heavy cream
- 1 oz. feta cheese

Directions:
Preheat your square waffle maker and grease with cooking spray.
Beat the egg white in a small-sized bowl and add the flour. Mix well.
Add shredded cheese to the egg whites and flour mixture and mix well.
Add the cream and cheese to the egg mixture.
Pour the chaffles batter into a waffle maker and close the lid.
Cook the chaffles for about 4 minutes until crispy and brown.
Carefully remove the chaffles from the maker.
Serve with feta cheese on top.
Per serving: Calories: 345Kcal; Fat: 32g; Carbs: 3g; Protein: 15g

235. Breakfast Bowl Pizza Chaffle
Preparation time: 10 minutes
Cooking time: 5 minutes
Servings: 1
Ingredients:
- 1 egg
- ½ cup cheddar cheese shredded
- a pinch of Italian seasoning
- 1 tbsp. pizza sauce

Toppings:
- 2 eggs boiled
- 4 oz. fresh spinach leaves

Directions:
Preheat your waffle maker and grease with cooking spray.
Crack an egg in a small bowl and beat with Italian seasoning and pizza sauce.
Add the shredded cheese to the egg and spices mixture.
Pour 1 tbsp. of shredded cheese in a waffle maker and cook for 30 seconds.
Pour the chaffles batter into the waffle maker and close the lid.
Cook the chaffles for about 4 minutes until crispy and brown.
Carefully remove the chaffles from the maker.
Serve on the bed of spinach with boiled egg and a few drops of pizza sauce.
Per serving: Calories: 375Kcal; Fat: 26g; Carbs: 2g; Protein: 22g

236. Sausage and Chaffle
Preparation time: 5 minutes
Cooking time: 10 minutes
Servings: 1
Ingredients:
- ½ cup cheddar cheese
- ½ tsp. baking powder
- ¼ cup egg whites
- 2 tsp. pumpkin spice
- 1 egg, whole

- 2 chicken sausages
- 2 slices bacon
- a pinch salt and pepper
- 1 tsp. avocado oil

Directions:
Mix together all the ingredients in a bowl.
Allow batter to sit while the waffle iron warms.
Spray the waffle iron with non-stick spray.
Cook the batter into the waffle maker for about 4-5 minutes.
Meanwhile, heat the oil in a pan and fry the egg according to your choice and transfer it to a plate.
In the same pan, fry the bacon slice and sausage on medium heat for about 2-3 minutes until cooked.
Once the chaffles are cooked thoroughly, remove them from the maker.
Serve them with fried egg, bacon slice, sausages, and enjoy!
Per serving: Calories: 419Kcal; Fat: 54g; Carbs: 2g; Protein: 25g

237. Raspberry-Yogurt Chaffle Bowl
Preparation time: 10 minutes
Cooking time: 14 minutes
Servings: 2
Ingredients:
- 1 egg, beaten
- 1 tbsp. almond flour
- ¼ cup finely grated mozzarella cheese
- ¼ tsp. baking powder
- 1 cup Greek yogurt
- 1 cup fresh raspberries
- 2 tbsp. almonds, chopped

Directions:
Preheat a waffle bowl maker and grease lightly with cooking spray.
Meanwhile, in a medium bowl, whisk all the ingredients, except the yogurt, raspberries until smooth batter forms.
Open the iron; pour in half of the mixture, cover, and cook until crispy, 6 to 7 minutes.
Remove the chaffle bowl onto a plate and set it aside.
Make the second chaffle bowl with the remaining batter.
To serve, divide the yogurt into the chaffle bowls and top with the raspberries and almonds.
Per serving: Calories: 320Kcal; Fat: 29g; Carbs: 2g; Protein: 23g

238. Egg and Asparagus Chaffles
Preparation time: 10 minutes

Cooking time: 10 minutes
Servings: 1
Ingredients:
- 1 egg
- ¼ cup mozzarella cheese
- 2 tbsp. almond flour
- ½ tsp. baking powder

Toppings:
- 1 egg
- 4-5 stalks of asparagus
- 2 tsp. avocado oil

Directions:
Preheat the waffle maker to medium-high heat.
Whisk together the egg, mozzarella cheese, almond flour, and baking powder
Pour the chaffles batter into the waffle iron.
Close the waffle maker and let cook for 5 minutes or until the waffle is golden brown and set.
Remove the chaffles from the waffle maker and serve them.

Meanwhile, heat the oil in a non-stick pan.
Once the pan is hot, fry the asparagus for about 4-5 minutes until golden brown.
Poach the egg in boiling water for about 2-3 minutes.
Once the chaffles are cooked, remove them from the maker.
Serve the chaffles with the poached egg and asparagus.
Per serving: Calories: 343Kcal; Fat: 25g; Carbs: 27g; Protein: 16g

239. Raspberries Taco Chaffle

Preparation time: 10 minutes
Cooking time: 15 minutes
Servings: 1
Ingredients:

- 1 egg white
- ½ cup Jack cheese, shredded
- 1 tsp. coconut flour
- ¼ tsp. baking powder
- ½ tsp. Swerve confectioners' sugar

Toppings:

- 4 oz. raspberries
- Swerve confectioners' sugar
- 2 oz. unsweetened raspberry sauce

Directions:
Switch on your round waffle maker and grease it with cooking spray once it is hot.
Mix together all the chaffle ingredients in a bowl and combine with a fork.
Pour the chaffle batter into a preheated maker and close the lid.
Roll the taco chaffle around using a kitchen roller, set it aside, and let it stand for a few minutes.
Once the taco chaffle is set, remove it from the roller.
Dip the raspberries in the sauce and arrange them on a taco chaffle.
Drizzle confectioners' sugar on top.
Enjoy the raspberries taco chaffle with keto coffee.
Per serving: Calories: 386Kcal; Fat: 25g; Carbs: 37g; Protein: 28g

240. Egg, Salmon and Cherry Tomatoes Chaffles

Preparation time: 10 minutes
Cooking time: 7-9 minutes
Servings: 4
Ingredients:
Batter:

- 4 eggs
- 2 cup shredded white cheddar cheese
- a pinch salt and pepper

Other:

- 2 tbsp. butter for brushing the waffle maker
- 4 large eggs
- 4 smoked salmon slices
- 4 oz cherry tomatoes
- 2 tbsp. olive oil

Directions:
Preheat the waffle maker.
Beat the eggs into a medium-sized bowl and whisk them with a fork.
Stir in the grated cheddar cheese and season with salt and pepper.
Grease the heated waffle maker with butter and add a few tbsp. of the batter.
Cook for about 7-8 minutes.
While chaffles are cooking, cook the eggs.
Heat the oil in a large non-stick pan that has a lid over medium-low heat for 2-3 minutes.

Beat an egg in a small ramekin and gently add it to the pan.
Repeat the same way for the other 3 eggs.
Cover and let cook for 2 to 2½ minutes for set eggs but with runny yolks.
Remove from the heat.
Cut cherry tomatoes
To serve, place a chaffle on each plate and top with an egg, a slice of salmon, and a few cherry tomatoes. Season with salt, black pepper, and a sprinkle of lemon to taste.
Per serving: Calories: 546Kcal; Fat: 54g; Carbs: 3g; Protein: 26g

241. Crispy Chaffle with Chicken Sausage

Preparation time: 10 minutes
Cooking time: 10 minutes
Servings: 2
Ingredients:

- ½ cup mozzarella cheese
- ½ tsp. baking powder
- ¼ cup egg whites
- 1 egg, whole
- 2 chicken sausages
- salt and pepper to taste
- 1 tsp. avocado oil

Directions:
Mix together all the ingredients in a bowl.
Allow the batter to sit while the waffle iron warms.
Spray waffle iron with non-stick spray.
Cook the batter into the waffle maker for about 5 minutes.
Meanwhile, heat the oil in a pan and fry the egg and the sausage on medium heat until cooked.
Once the chaffles are cooked thoroughly, remove them from the maker.
Serve Chaffles with fried egg and sausages
Per serving: Calories: 332Kcal; Fat: 23g; Carbs: 2g; Protein: 18g

242. Provolone and Mozzarella Chaffle

Preparation time: 10 minutes
Cooking time: 7-9 minutes
Servings: 4
Ingredients:
Batter:

- 4 eggs
- 1 cup grated mozzarella cheese
- 1 cup grated provolone cheese
- ½ cup almond flour
- 2 tbsp. coconut flour
- 2½ tsp. baking powder
- salt and pepper to taste

Other:

- 2 tbsp. butter to brush the waffle maker

Directions:
Preheat the waffle maker.
Add the grated mozzarella and provolone cheese to a bowl and mix.
Add the almond and coconut flour and baking powder and season with salt and pepper.
Mix with a wire whisk and crack in the eggs.
Stir everything together until a creamy batter.
Grease the heated waffle maker with butter and add a few tbsp. of the batter.
Cook for about 8 minutes, depending on your waffle maker.
Repeat the process to create more chaffles.
Per serving: Calories: 352Kcal; Fat: 30g; Carbs: 8g; Protein: 15g

243. Oregano and Mozzarella Chaffles

Preparation time: 10 minutes
Cooking time: 7-9 minutes
Servings: 4
Ingredients:
Batter:
- 4 eggs
- 2 cup shredded mozzarella
- 2 oz. finely chopped bacon
- salt and pepper to taste
- 1 tsp. dried oregano

Other:
- 2 tbsp. olive oil for brushing the waffle maker

Directions:
Preheat the waffle maker.
Crack the eggs into a bowl and add the grated mozzarella cheese.
Mix until just combined and stir in the chopped bacon.
Season with salt and pepper and dried oregano.
Brush the heated waffle maker with olive oil and add a few tbsp. of the batter.
Cook for about 7-8 minutes, depending on your waffle maker.
Repeat the process with the remaining batter.
Per serving: Calories: 380Kcal; Fat: 34g; Carbs: 2g; Protein: 24g

244. Avocado and Boiled Eggs Chaffles

Preparation time: 10 minutes
Cooking time: 5 minutes
Servings: 2
Ingredients:
- 2 eggs
- ½ cup cheddar cheese shredded
- a pinch of Italian seasoning
- 1 tbsp. pizza sauce

Toppings:
- ½ avocado sliced
- 2 eggs boiled
- 1 tomato, halves
- 4 oz. fresh spinach leaves

Directions:
Preheat your waffle maker and grease with cooking spray.
Crack an egg in a small bowl and beat with Italian seasoning and pizza sauce.
Add shredded cheese to the egg and spices mixture.
Pour 1 tbsp. of shredded cheese in a waffle maker and cook for 30 seconds.
Pour the chaffles batter into the waffle maker and close the lid.
Cook the chaffles for about 4 minutes until crispy and brown.
Carefully remove the chaffles from the maker.
Serve on the bed of spinach with the boiled egg, avocado slice, and tomatoes.
Per serving: Calories: 355Kcal; Fat: 26g; Carbs: 3g; Protein: 20g

245. Berries and Heavy Cream Chaffles

Preparation time: 10 minutes
Cooking time: 5 minutes
Servings: 2
Ingredients:
- 1 cup egg whites
- 1 cup cheddar cheese, shredded
- ¼ cup almond flour
- ¼ cup heavy cream

Toppings:
- 4 oz. raspberries
- 4 oz. strawberries
- 1 oz. keto chocolate flakes
- 1 oz. feta cheese

Directions:
Preheat your square waffle maker and grease with cooking spray.
Beat the egg white in a small bowl with flour.
Add shredded cheese to the egg whites and flour mixture and mix well.
Add the cream and cheese to the egg mixture.
Pour the chaffles batter into a waffle maker and close the lid.
Cook the chaffles for about 4 minutes until crispy and brown.
Carefully remove the chaffles from the maker.
Serve with berries, cheese, and chocolate on top.
Per serving: Calories: 380Kcal; Fat: 6g; Carbs: 2g; Protein: 20g

246. Berries and Vanilla Chaffles

Preparation time: 10 minutes
Cooking time: 28 minutes
Servings: 1
Ingredients:
- 1 egg, beaten
- ½ cup finely grated mozzarella cheese
- 1 tbsp. cream cheese, softened
- 1 tbsp. sugar-free maple syrup
- 2 strawberries, sliced
- 2 raspberries, slices
- ¼ tsp. blackberry extract
- ¼ tsp. vanilla extract
- ½ cup plain yogurt for serving

Directions:
Preheat the waffle iron.
In a medium bowl, mix all the ingredients except the yogurt.
Open the iron, lightly grease with cooking spray, and pour in a quarter of the mixture.
Close the iron and cook for 7 minutes.
Remove the chaffle onto a plate and set it aside.
Make three more chaffles with the remaining mixture.
To serve: top with the yogurt and enjoy.
Per serving: Calories: 385Kcal; Fat: 27g; Carbs: 1g; Protein: 16g

247. Ham and Spices Chaffles

Preparation time: 15 minutes
Cooking time: 28 minutes
Servings: 2
Ingredients:
- 1 cup finely shredded parsnips, steamed
- 8 oz. ham, diced
- 2 eggs, beaten
- 1½ cup finely grated cheddar cheese
- ½ tsp. garlic powder
- 2 tbsp. chopped fresh parsley leaves
- ¼ tsp. smoked paprika
- ½ tsp. dried thyme
- salt and freshly ground black pepper to taste

Directions:
Preheat the waffle iron.
In a medium bowl, mix all the ingredients.
Open the iron, lightly grease with cooking spray, and pour in a quarter of the mixture.
Close the iron and cook until crispy, 7 minutes.
Remove the chaffle onto a plate and set it aside.
Make three more chaffles using the remaining mixture.
Serve them afterward.
Per serving: Calories: 420Kcal; Fat: 28g; Carbs: 1g; Protein:14g

248. Gruyere and Chives Chaffles

Preparation time: 15 minutes
Cooking time: 14 minutes
Servings: 2
Ingredients:

- 2 eggs, beaten
- 1 cup finely grated gruyere cheese
- 2 tbsp. finely grated cheddar cheese
- ⅛ tsp. freshly ground black pepper
- 3 tbsp. minced fresh chives + more for garnishing
- 2 sunshine fried eggs for topping

Directions:
Preheat the waffle iron.
In a medium bowl, mix the eggs, cheeses, black pepper, and chives.
Open the iron and pour in half of the mixture.
Close the iron and cook until brown and crispy, 7 minutes.
Remove the chaffle onto a plate and set it aside.
Make another chaffle using the remaining mixture.
Top the chaffles with the fried egg, garnish with the chives, and serve.
Per serving: Calories: 355Kcal; Fat: 38g; Carbs: 2g; Protein: 15g

249. Chicken Quesadilla Chaffle

Preparation time: 10 minutes
Cooking time: 14 minutes
Servings: 1
Ingredients:

- 1 egg, beaten
- ¼ tsp. taco seasoning
- 1/3 cup finely grated cheddar cheese
- 1/3 cup cooked chopped chicken

Directions:
Preheat the waffle iron.
In a medium bowl, mix the eggs, taco seasoning, and cheddar cheese.
Add the chicken and combine well.
Grease the iron with cooking spray and pour in half of the mixture.
Close the iron and cook until brown and crispy, 7 minutes.
Remove the chaffle onto a plate and set it aside.
Make another chaffle using the remaining mixture.
Per serving: Calories: 310Kcal; Fat: 28g; Carbs: 1g; Protein: 24g

250. Bacon-Cheddar Biscuit Chaffle

Preparation time: 10 minutes
Cooking time: 28 minutes
Servings: 1
Ingredients:

- 1 egg, beaten
- 2 tbsp. almond flour
- 2 tbsp. ground flaxseed
- 3 bacon slices, cooked and chopped
- ¼ cup heavy cream
- 1½ tbsp. melted butter
- ½ cup finely grated gruyere cheese
- ½ cup finely grated cheddar cheese
- ¼ tsp. erythritol
- ½ tsp. onion powder
- ½ tsp. garlic salt
- ½ tbsp. dried parsley
- ½ tbsp. baking powder
- ¼ tsp. baking soda

Directions:
Preheat the waffle iron.
Meanwhile, in a medium bowl, whisk all the ingredients until the batter becomes smooth.

Open the iron, pour a quarter of the mixture into the iron, close and cook until crispy, 6 to 7 minutes.
Remove the chaffle onto a plate and set it aside.
Make three more Chaffles with the remaining batter.
Allow cooling and serve afterward.
Per serving: Calories: 407Kcal; Fat: 31g; Carbs: 2g; Protein: 22g

251. Turnip Hash Brown Chaffles

Preparation time: 10 minutes
Cooking time: 42 minutes
Servings: 2
Ingredients:

- 1 large turnip, peeled and shredded
- ½ medium white onion, minced
- 2 garlic cloves, pressed
- 1 cup finely grated gouda cheese
- 2 eggs, beaten
- salt and freshly ground black pepper to taste

Directions:
Pour the turnips in a medium microwave-safe bowl, sprinkle with 1 tbsp. of water, and steam in the microwave until softened, 1 to 2 minutes.
Remove the bowl and mix in the remaining ingredients, except for a quarter cup of the Gouda cheese.
Preheat the waffle iron.
Once heated, open and sprinkle some of the reserved cheese in the iron and top with 3 tbsp. of the mixture. Close the lid and cook for about 5 minutes or until crispy.
Open the lid, flip the chaffle and cook further for 2 more minutes.
Remove the chaffle onto a plate and set it aside.
Make five more chaffles with the remaining batter in the same proportion.
Allow cooling and serve afterward.
Per serving: Calories: 580Kcal; Fat: 50g; Carbs: 2g; Protein: 30g

252. Parmesan Bagel Chaffle

Preparation time: 10 minutes
Cooking time: 28 minutes
Servings: 1
Ingredients:

- 1 egg, beaten
- ½ cup finely grated parmesan cheese
- 1 tsp. everything bagel seasoning

Directions:
Preheat the waffle iron.
In a medium-sized bowl, mix all the ingredients.
Open the iron, pour in a quarter of the mixture, close, and cook until crispy, 6 to 7 minutes.
Remove the chaffle onto a plate and set it aside.
Make three more chaffles, allow cooling, and enjoy!.
Per serving: Calories: 310Kcal; Fat: 25g; Carbs: 1g; Protein: 20g

253. Blueberry Shortcake Chaffle

Preparation time: 10 minutes
Cooking time: 14 minutes
Servings: 1
Ingredients:

- 1 egg, beaten
- 1 tbsp. cream cheese, softened
- ¼ cup finely grated mozzarella cheese
- ¼ tsp. baking powder
- 4 fresh blueberries
- 1 tsp. blueberry extract

Directions:
Preheat the waffle iron.
In a medium-sized bowl, mix all the ingredients.
Open the iron, pour in half of the batter, close and cook until crispy, 6 to 7 minutes.
Remove the chaffle onto a plate and set it aside.
Make the other chaffle with the remaining batter.
Allow cooling and enjoy after.
Per serving: Calories: 368Kcal; Fat: 26g; Carbs: 1g; Protein: 22g

254. Raspberry-Pecan Chaffles

Preparation time: 10 minutes
Cooking time: 14 minutes
Servings: 1
Ingredients:

- 1 egg, beaten
- ½ cup finely grated mozzarella cheese
- 1 tbsp. cream cheese, softened
- 1 tbsp. sugar-free maple syrup
- ¼ tsp. raspberry extract
- ¼ tsp. vanilla extract
- 2 tbsp. sugar-free caramel sauce for topping
- 3 tbsp. chopped pecans for topping

Directions:
Preheat the waffle iron.
In a medium bowl, mix all the ingredients.
Open the iron, pour in half of the batter, close and cook until crispy, 6 to 7 minutes.
Remove the chaffle onto a plate and set it aside.
Make another chaffle with the remaining batter.
To serve: drizzle the caramel sauce on the chaffles and top with the pecans.
Per serving: Calories: 395Kcal; Fat: 30g; Carbs: 1g; Protein: 23g

255. Ricotta and Spinach Chaffles

Preparation time: 10 minutes
Cooking time: 28 minutes
Servings: 2
Ingredients:

- 4 oz. frozen spinach, thawed, squeezed dry
- 1 cup ricotta cheese
- 2 eggs, beaten
- ½ tsp. garlic powder
- ¼ cup finely grated pecorino Romano cheese
- ½ cup finely grated mozzarella cheese
- salt and freshly ground black pepper to taste

Directions:
Preheat the waffle iron.
In a medium-sized bowl, mix all the ingredients.
Open the iron, lightly grease with cooking spray, and spoon in a quarter of the mixture.
Close the iron and cook until brown and crispy, 7 minutes.
Remove the chaffle onto a plate and set it aside.
Make three more chaffles with the remaining mixture.
Allow cooling and serve afterward.
Per serving: Calories: 590Kcal; Fat: 35g; Carbs: 11g; Protein: 31g

256. Scrambled Egg Chaffles

Preparation time: 15 minutes
Cooking time: 28 minutes
Servings: 2
Ingredients:
   Chaffles:
- 1 cup finely grated cheddar cheese
- 2 eggs, beaten
   For the Egg Stuffing:
- 1 tbsp. olive oil
- 2 large eggs
- 1 small green bell pepper, deseeded and chopped
- 1 small red bell pepper, deseeded and chopped
- salt and freshly ground black pepper to taste
- 2 tbsp. grated parmesan cheese

Directions:
For the chaffles:
Preheat the waffle iron.
In a mixing bowl, mix the eggs and cheddar cheese.
Open the iron, pour in a quarter of the mixture, close, and cook until crispy, 6 to 7 minutes.
Plate and make three more chaffles using the remaining mixture.
For the egg stuffing:
Meanwhile, warm the olive oil in a medium skillet over medium heat on a stovetop.
In a medium bowl, beat the eggs with bell peppers, salt, black pepper, and parmesan cheese.
Pour the mixture into the skillet and scramble until set to your likeness, 2 minutes.
Between two chaffles, spoon half of the scrambled eggs and repeat with the second set of chaffles.
Per serving: Calories: 380Kcal; Fat: 32g; Carbs: 2g; Protein: 25g

257. Onions and Gruyere Chaffles

Preparation time: 15 minutes
Cooking time: 14 minutes
Servings: 2
Ingredients:

- 2 eggs, beaten
- 1 cup finely grated gruyere cheese
- 2 tbsp. finely grated cheddar cheese
- ⅛ tsp. freshly ground black pepper
- 3 tbsp. fresh onions thin chopped
   Toppings:
- 2 fried eggs
- ⅛ tsp. chives

Directions:
Preheat the waffle iron.
In a medium bowl, mix the eggs, cheeses, black pepper, and onions.
Pour half of the mixture into your waffle maker.
Cook until brown and crispy. It will take about 6 or 7 minutes.
Make another chaffle using the remaining mixture.
Top each chaffle with one fried egg each, garnish with the chives and serve.
Per serving: Calories: 750Kcal; Fat: 66g; Carbs: 2g; Protein: 58g

CHAPTER 3:

Lunch

258. Pumpkin Spice Chaffles
Preparation time: 30 minutes
Cooking time: 14 minutes
Servings: 1
Ingredients:
- 1 egg, beaten
- ½ tsp. pumpkin pie spice
- ½ cup finely grated mozzarella cheese
- 1 tbsp. sugar-free pumpkin puree

Directions:
Preheat the waffle iron.
In a small bowl, mix all the ingredients.
Open the iron, pour in half of the batter, close and cook until crispy, 6 to 7 minutes.
Remove the chaffle onto a plate and set it aside.
Make another chaffle with the remaining batter.
Allow cooling and serve afterward.
Per serving: Calories: 280Kcal; Fat: 23g; Carbs: 1g; Protein: 18g

259. Ham and Black Olives Sandwich Chaffle
Preparation time: 20 minutes
Cooking time: 10 minutes
Servings: 1
Ingredients:
- 2 slices ham
- cooking spray
- 1 green bell pepper, sliced into strips
- 2 slices cheddar cheese
- 1 tbsp. black olives, pitted and sliced
- 2 basic chaffles

Directions:
Cook the ham in a pan coated with oil over medium heat.
Next, cook the bell pepper.
Assemble the open-faced sandwich by topping each chaffle with ham and cheese, bell pepper, and olives.
Bake it in the oven until the cheese has melted a little.
Per serving: Calories: 486Kcal; Fat: 38g; Carbs: 3g; Protein: 22g

260. Lt. Sandwich Chaffle
Preparation time: 20 minutes
Cooking time: 15 minutes
Servings: 2
Ingredients:
- cooking spray
- 4 slices bacon
- 1 tbsp. mayonnaise
- 4 basic chaffles
- 2 lettuce leaves
- 2 tomato slices

Directions:
Coat your pan with foil and place it over medium heat.
Cook the bacon until golden and crispy.
Spread the mayo on top of the chaffle.
Top with lettuce, bacon, and tomato.
Top with another chaffle.
Per serving: Calories: 428Kcal; Fat: 32g; Carbs: 1g; Protein: 24g

261. Mozzarella Peanut Chaffle
Preparation time: 20 minutes
Cooking time: 15 minutes
Servings: 2
Ingredients:
- 1 egg, lightly beaten
- 2 tbsp. peanut butter
- 2 tbsp. Swerve
- ½ cup mozzarella cheese, shredded

Directions:
Preheat your waffle maker.
In a bowl, mix the egg, cheese, Swerve, and peanut butter until well combined.
Spray the waffle maker with cooking spray.
Pour half of the batter into the hot waffle maker and cook for 7-8 minutes or until golden brown. Repeat with the remaining batter.
Per serving: Calories: 415Kcal; Fat: 34g; Carbs: 4g; Protein: 20g

262. Cinnamon and Vanilla Chaffle
Preparation time: 10 minutes
Cooking time: 7-9 minutes
Servings: 4
Ingredients:
Batter:
- 4 eggs
- 4 oz. sour cream
- 1 tsp. vanilla extract
- 1 tsp. cinnamon
- ¼ cup stevia
- 5 tbsp. coconut flour

Other:
- 2 tbsp. coconut oil to brush the waffle maker
- ½ tsp. cinnamon for garnishing the chaffles

Directions:
Preheat the waffle maker.
Add the eggs and sour cream to a bowl and stir with a wire whisk until just combined.
Add the vanilla extract, cinnamon, and stevia and mix until combined.
Stir in the coconut flour and stir until combined.
Brush the heated waffle maker with coconut oil and add a few tbsp of the batter.
Close the lid and cook for about 7-8 minutes, depending on your waffle maker.
Repeat the process to cook more chaffles.
Per serving: Calories: 430Kcal; Fat: 15g; Carbs: 5g; Protein: 12g

263. New Year Chaffle with Coconut Cream

Preparation time: 7 minutes
Cooking time: 5 minutes
Servings: 2
Ingredients:
- 2 large eggs
- ⅛ cup almond flour
- 1 tsp. cinnamon powder
- 1 tsp. sea salt
- ½ tsp. baking soda
- 1 cup shredded mozzarella

Toppings:
- 2 tbsp. coconut cream
- 1 tbsp. unsweetened chocolate sauce

Directions:
Preheat the waffle maker.
Mix together the recipe ingredients in a mixing bowl.
Add cheese and mix well.
Pour about ½ cup of the mixture into the center of the waffle maker and cook for about 2-3 minutes until golden and crispy.
Repeat with the remaining batter.
For serving, coat coconut cream over the chaffles. Drizzle chocolate sauce over the chaffle.
Freeze the chaffle in the freezer for about 10 minutes
Serve on Christmas morning and enjoy!
Per serving: Calories: 325Kcal; Fat: 33g; Carbs: 2g; Protein: 17g

264. Choco Chips Pumpkin Chaffles

Preparation time: 20 minutes
Cooking time: 15 minutes
Servings: 1
Ingredients:
- 1 egg, lightly beaten
- 1 tbsp. almond flour
- 1 tbsp. unsweetened chocolate chips
- ¼ tsp. pumpkin pie spice
- 2 tbsp. Swerve
- 1 tbsp. pumpkin puree
- ½ cup mozzarella cheese, shredded

Directions:
Plug in your waffle maker to preheat it.
In a small bowl, mix the egg and pumpkin puree.
Add the pumpkin pie spice, Swerve, almond flour, and cheese and mix well.
Stir in chocolate chips.
Spray the waffle maker with cooking spray.
Cook half of the batter into the hot waffle maker for about 4 minutes.
Repeat with the remaining batter.
Per serving: Calories: 453Kcal; Fat: 31g; Carbs: 2g; Protein: 23g

265. Sausage and Pepperoni Sandwich Chaffle

Preparation time: 15 minutes
Cooking time: 10 minutes
Servings: 4
Ingredients:
- cooking spray
- 2 cervelat sausage, sliced into rounds
- 12 slices pepperoni
- 6 mushroom slices
- 4 tsp. mayonnaise
- 4 big white onion rings
- 4 basic chaffles

Directions:
Spray your skillet with oil.
Place it over medium heat.
Cook the sausage until brown on both sides.
Transfer to a plate.
Cook the pepperoni and mushrooms for 2 minutes.
Spread mayo on top of the chaffle.
Top with the sausage, pepperoni, mushrooms, and onion rings.
Top with another chaffle.
Per serving: Calories: 452Kcal; Fat: 36g; Carbs: 3g; Protein: 24g

266. Pizza Flavored Chaffle

Preparation time: 15 minutes
Cooking time: 12 minutes
Servings: 1
Ingredients:
- 1 egg, beaten
- ½ cup cheddar cheese, shredded
- 2 tbsp. pepperoni, chopped
- 1 tbsp. keto marinara sauce
- 4 tbsp. almond flour
- 1 tsp. baking powder
- ½ tsp. dried Italian seasoning
- parmesan cheese, grated

Directions:
Preheat your waffle maker.
In a bowl, mix the egg, cheddar cheese, pepperoni, marinara sauce, almond flour, baking powder, and Italian seasoning.
Add the mixture to the waffle maker.
Close the device and cook for 4 minutes.
Open it and transfer the chaffle to a plate.
Let it cool for 2 minutes.
Repeat the steps with the remaining batter.
Top with the grated parmesan and serve.
Per serving: Calories: 485Kcal; Fat: 35g; Carbs: 2g; Protein: 26g

267. Maple Chaffles

Preparation time: 20 minutes
Cooking time: 15 minutes
Servings: 2
Ingredients:
- 1 egg, lightly beaten
- 2 egg whites
- ½ tsp. maple extract
- 1 tsp. Swerve
- ½ tsp. baking powder, gluten-free
- 2 tbsp. almond milk
- 2 tbsp. coconut flour

Directions:
Preheat your waffle maker.
Into a bowl, using a whisk, beat the egg whites until stiff peaks form.
Stir in the maple extract, Swerve, baking powder, almond milk, coconut flour, and egg.
Spray the waffle maker with cooking spray.
Cook half of the batter into the hot waffle maker for 3 minutes or until golden brown. Repeat with the remaining batter.
Per serving: Calories: 390Kcal; Fat: 27g; Carbs: 5g; Protein: 22g

268. Pumpkin Chaffles with Choco Chips

Preparation time: 15 minutes
Cooking time: 12 minutes
Servings: 1

Ingredients:
- 1 egg
- ½ cup shredded mozzarella cheese
- 4 tsp. pureed pumpkin
- ¼ tsp. pumpkin pie spice
- 2 tbsp. sweetener
- 1 tbsp. almond flour
- 4 tsp. chocolate chips (sugar-free)

Directions:
Turn your waffle maker on.
In a medium-sized bowl, beat the egg and stir in the pureed pumpkin. Mix well.
Add the rest of the ingredients one by one.
Pour half of the mixture into your waffle maker.
Cook for 4 minutes.
Repeat the same steps with the remaining mixture.
Per serving: Calories: 343Kcal; Fat: 25g; Carbs: 4g; Protein: 18g

269. Walnuts Chaffles

Preparation time: 10 minutes
Cooking time: 5 minutes
Servings: 1
Ingredients:
- 2 tbsp. cream cheese
- ½ tsp. almonds flour
- ¼ tsp. baking powder
- 1 large egg
- ¼ cup chopped walnuts
- a pinch of stevia extract powder

Directions:
Preheat your waffle maker.
Spray the waffle maker with cooking spray.
In a bowl, add cream cheese, almond flour, baking powder, egg, walnuts, and stevia.
Mix all ingredients.
Spoon walnut batter in the waffle maker and cook for about 2-3 minutes.
Let chaffles cool at room temperature before serving.
Per serving: Calories: 202Kcal; Fat: 16g; Carbs: 1g; Protein: 12g

270. Holidays Chaffles

Preparation time: 10 minutes
Cooking time: 5 minutes
Servings: 4
Ingredients:
- 1 cup egg whites
- 2 tsp. coconut flour
- ½ tsp. vanilla
- 1 tsp. baking powder
- 1 tsp. baking soda
- ⅛ tsp. cinnamon powder
- 1 cup mozzarella cheese, grated

Toppings:
- cranberries
- keto Chocolate sauce

Directions:
Make 4 mini chaffles from the chaffle ingredients.
Top with chocolate sauce and cranberries.
Serve hot and enjoy!
Per serving: Calories: 421Kcal; Fat: 28g; Carbs: 3g; Protein: 15g

271. Cherry Chocolate Chaffles

Preparation time: 15 minutes
Cooking time: 10 minutes
Servings: 1
Ingredients:
- 1 egg, lightly beaten
- 1 tbsp. unsweetened chocolate chips
- 2 tbsp. sugar-free cherry pie filling
- 2 tbsp. heavy whipping cream
- ½ cup mozzarella cheese, shredded
- ½ tsp. baking powder, gluten-free
- 1 tbsp. Swerve
- 1 tbsp. unsweetened cocoa powder
- 1 tbsp. almond flour

Directions:
Preheat the waffle maker.
In a bowl, whisk together egg, cheese, baking powder, Swerve, cocoa powder, and almond flour.
Spray the waffle maker with cooking spray.
Cook the batter into the waffle maker until golden brown. It will take about 4-5 minutes.
Top with cherry pie filling, heavy whipping cream, and chocolate chips and serve.
Per serving: Calories: 468Kcal; Fat: 39g; Carbs: 2g; Protein: 21g

272. Bacon, Egg and Avocado Sandwich Chaffle

Preparation time: 15 minutes
Cooking time: 10 minutes
Servings: 2
Ingredients:
- cooking spray
- 4 slices bacon
- 2 eggs
- ½ avocado, mashed
- 4 basic chaffles
- 2 leaves lettuce

Directions:
Coat your skillet with cooking spray.
Cook the bacon until golden and crisp.
Transfer it into a paper towel-lined plate.
Crack the eggs into the same pan and cook until firm.
Flip and cook until the yolk is set.
Spread the avocado on the chaffle.
Top with lettuce, egg, and bacon.
Top with another chaffle.
Per serving: Calories: 350Kcal; Fat: 11g; Carbs: 2g; Protein: 34g

273. Sausage and Egg Sandwich Chaffle

Preparation time: 15 minutes
Cooking time: 10 minutes
Servings: 1
Ingredients:
- 2 basics cooked chaffles
- 1 tbsp. olive oil
- 1 sausage, sliced into rounds
- 1 egg

Directions:
Pour olive oil into your pan over medium heat.
Put it over medium heat.
Add the sausage and cook until brown on both sides.
Put the sausage rounds on top of one chaffle.
Cook the egg in the same pan without mixing.

Place on top of the sausage rounds.
Top with another chaffle.
Per serving: Calories: 365Kcal; Fat: 29g; Carbs: 3g; Protein: 26g

274. Choco Chips Chaffles

Preparation time: 20 minutes
Cooking time: 15 minutes
Servings: 2
Ingredients:

- 2 eggs, lightly beaten
- 1 tbsp. unsweetened chocolate chips
- 2 tsp. Swerve
- ½ tsp. vanilla
- ½ tsp. lemon extract
- ½ cup mozzarella cheese, shredded
- 2 tsp. almond flour

Directions:
Preheat your waffle maker.
In a bowl, whisk the eggs, Swerve, vanilla, lemon extract, cheese, and almond flour. Add chocolate chips and stir well.
Spray the waffle maker with cooking spray.
Pour ½ of the batter in the hot waffle maker and cook for 4 minutes or until golden brown. Repeat with the remaining batter.
Per serving: Calories: 311Kcal; Fat: 24g; Carbs: 2g; Protein: 18g

275. Coconut Cake Chaffle

Preparation time: 20 minutes
Cooking time: 15 minutes
Servings: 2
Ingredients:

- 2 large eggs
- 1 cup shredded cheese
- 2 tbsp. coconut cream
- 2 tbsp. coconut flour
- 1 tsp. stevia

Toppings:
- 1 cup heavy cream
- 8 oz. raspberries
- 4 oz. blueberries
- 2 oz. cherries

Directions:
Make 4 thin round chaffles with the chaffle ingredients.
Once the chaffles are cooked, set them in layers on a plate, and spread heavy cream in each layer.
Top with raspberries, then blueberries and cherries.
Per serving: Calories: 491Kcal; Fat: 36g; Carbs: 4g; Protein: 26g

276. Coffee Flavored Chaffles

Preparation time: 10 minutes
Cooking time: 7-9 minutes
Servings: 4
Ingredients:

Batter:
- 4 eggs
- 4 oz. cream cheese
- ½ tsp. vanilla extract
- 6 tbsp. strong boiled espresso
- ¼ cup stevia
- ½ cup almond flour
- 1 tsp. baking powder
- a pinch of salt

Other:
- 2 tbsp. butter to brush the waffle maker

Directions:
Preheat the waffle maker.
Add the eggs and cream cheese to a bowl and stir in the vanilla extract, espresso, stevia, almond flour, baking powder, and a pinch of salt.
Stir just until everything is combined and fully incorporated.
Grease the heated waffle maker with butter and add a few tbsp. of the batter.
Cook for about 7-8 minutes, depending on your waffle maker.
Per serving: Calories: 371Kcal; Fat: 45g; Carbs: 2g; Protein: 41g

277. Chicken Bites with Chaffles

Preparation time: 10 minutes
Cooking time: 10 minutes
Servings: 1
Ingredients:

- 1 chicken breast cut into 2x2 inch chunks
- 1 egg
- ¼ cup almond flour
- 2 tbsp. onion powder
- 2 tbsp. garlic powder
- 1 tsp. dried oregano
- 1 tsp. paprika powder
- 1 tsp. salt
- ½ tsp. black pepper
- 2 tbsp. avocado oil

Directions:
Combine all the dry ingredients into a bowl. Mix well.
Whisk the egg into a separate bowl.
Dip each chicken piece into the egg and then into the dry ingredients.
Heat the oil in the 10-inch skillet, add oil.
Once the avocado oil is hot, place the coated chicken nuggets onto a skillet and cook them for 6-8 minutes until cooked and golden brown.
Serve them with chaffles and raspberries.
Per serving: Calories: 401Kcal; Fat: 29g; Carbs: 2g; Protein: 26g

278. Fish and Chaffle

Preparation time: 10 minutes
Cooking time: 15 minutes
Servings: 2
Ingredients:

- 1 lb. cod fillets, sliced into 4 slices
- 1 tsp. sea salt
- 1 tsp. garlic powder
- 1 egg, whisked
- 1 cup almond flour
- 2 tbsp. avocado oil

Chaffles:
- 2 eggs
- ½ cup cheddar cheese
- 2 tbsp. almond flour
- ½ tsp. Italian seasoning

Directions:
Mix together the chaffle ingredients in a bowl and make 4 squares
Put the chaffles in a preheated chaffle maker.
Blend together the salt, pepper, and garlic powder in a mixing bowl.
Toss the cod cubes in this mixture and let sit for 10 minutes.
Then, dip each cod slice into the egg mixture and then into the almond flour.
Heat the oil in the skillet and fish cubes for about 2-3 minutes, until cooked and browned
Serve on the chaffles and enjoy!
Per serving: Calories: 340Kcal; Fat: 29g; Carbs: 3g; Protein: 16g

279. Grilled Pork Chaffle Sandwich

Preparation time: 10 minutes
Cooking time: 15 minutes
Servings: 1
Ingredients:

- ½ cup mozzarella, shredded
- 1 egg
- a pinch garlic powder
- **Pork Patty:**
- ½ cup pork, minutes
- 1 tbsp. green onion, diced
- ½ tsp. Italian seasoning
- lettuce leaves

Directions:
Preheat the square waffle maker and grease it.
Mix together the egg, cheese, and garlic powder in a small mixing bowl.
Pour the batter into a preheated waffle maker and close the lid.
Make 2 chaffles from this batter.
Cook the chaffles for about 2-3 minutes until cooked through.
Meanwhile, mix together the pork patty ingredients in a bowl and make 1 large patty.
Grill the pork patty in a preheated grill for about 3-4 minutes per side until cooked through.
Arrange the pork patty between two chaffles with lettuce leaves. Cut the sandwich to make a triangular sandwich.
Per serving: Calories: 396Kcal; Fat: 34g; Carbs: 1g; Protein: 18g

280. Chicken Lunch Plate with Chaffles

Preparation time: 10 minutes
Cooking time: 15 minutes
Servings: 1
Ingredients:

- 1 large egg
- ½ cup Jack cheese, shredded
- a pinch of salt
- 1 chicken leg
- salt
- pepper
- 1 tsp. garlic, minutes
- 1 egg
- 1 tsp. avocado oil

Directions:
Heat your square waffle maker and grease with cooking spray.
Pour the chaffle batter into the skillet and cook for about 3 minutes.
Meanwhile, heat the oil in a pan over medium heat.
Once the oil is hot, add chicken thigh and garlic then, cook for about 5 minutes. Flip and cook for another 3-4 minutes.
Season with salt and pepper and give them a good mix.
Transfer the cooked thigh to a plate.
Fry the egg in the same pan for about 1-2 minutes according to your choice.
Once the chaffles are cooked, serve with the fried egg and chicken thigh.
Per serving: Calories: 375Kcal; Fat: 36g; Carbs: 1g; Protein: 23g

281. Omelet Sandwich Chaffle

Preparation time: 10 minutes
Cooking time: 10 minutes
Servings: 1

Ingredients:

- 2 classic chaffles
- 2 slice cheddar cheese
- 1 simple egg omelet

Directions:
Prepare your oven on 400°F.
Arrange the egg omelet and cheese slice between chaffles.
Bake the sandwich in the preheated oven for about 4-5 minutes until the cheese is melted.
Once the cheese is melted, remove it from the oven.
Per serving: Calories: 350Kcal; Fat: 27g; Carbs: 2g; Protein: 25g

282. Minutes Sandwich Chaffle

Preparation time: 10 minutes
Cooking time: 10 minutes
Servings: 1
Ingredients:

- 1 large egg
- ⅛ cup almond flour
- ½ tsp. garlic powder
- ¾ tsp. baking powder
- ½ cup shredded cheese
- **Sandwich Filling:**
- 2 slices deli ham
- 2 slices tomatoes
- 1 slice cheddar cheese

Directions:
Grease your square waffle maker and preheat it on medium heat.
Mix together the chaffle ingredients in a mixing bowl until well combined.
Pour the batter into a square waffle and make two chaffles.
Once the chaffles are cooked, remove them from the maker.
For a sandwich, arrange deli ham, tomato slice, and cheddar cheese between two chaffles.
Cut the sandwich from the center.
Per serving: Calories: 337Kcal; Fat: 29g; Carbs: 2g; Protein: 23g

283. Cheese Sandwich Chaffle

Preparation time: 10 minutes
Cooking time: 10 minutes
Servings: 1
Ingredients:

- 2 classic chaffles
- 2 slice cheddar cheese
- 2 lettuce leaves

Directions:
Prepare your oven on 400°F.
Arrange the lettuce leaves and cheese slices between chaffles.
Bake in the preheated oven for about 4-5 minutes until the cheese is melted.
Once the cheese is melted, remove it from the oven.
Per serving: Calories: 346Kcal; Fat: 28g; Carbs: 1g; Protein: 23g

284. Chicken Zinger Chaffle

Preparation time: 10 minutes
Cooking time: 15 minutes
Servings: 2
Ingredients:

- 1 chicken breast, cut into 2 pieces
- ½ cup coconut flour
- ¼ cup finely grated parmesan
- 1 tsp. paprika
- ½ tsp. garlic powder

- ½ tsp. onion powder
- 1 tsp. salt and pepper
- 1 egg beaten
- avocado oil for frying
- lettuce leaves
- BBQ sauce

Chaffles:
- 4 oz. cheese
- 2 whole eggs
- 2 oz. almond flour
- ¼ cup almond flour
- 1 tsp. baking powder

Directions:
Mix together the chaffle ingredients in a bowl.
Pour the chaffle batter into the preheated, greased square chaffle maker.
Cook the chaffles for about 2 minutes until cooked through.
Make square chaffles from this batter.
Meanwhile, mix together the coconut flour, parmesan, paprika, garlic powder, onion powder, salt, and pepper in a bowl.
Dip the chicken first in the coconut flour mixture, then in the beaten egg.
Heat the avocado oil in a skillet and cook the chicken from both sides until lightly brown and cooked.
Set the chicken zinger between two chaffles with lettuce and BBQ sauce.
Per serving: Calories: 574Kcal; Fat: 5g; Carbs: 10g; Protein: 31g

285. Double Chicken Chaffle

Preparation time: 10 minutes
Cooking time: 5 minutes
Servings: 1
Ingredients:
- ½ cup boil shredded chicken
- ¼ cup cheddar cheese
- ⅛ cup parmesan cheese
- 1 egg
- 1 tsp. Italian seasoning
- ⅛ tsp. garlic powder
- 1 tsp. cream cheese

Directions:
Preheat the Belgian waffle maker.
Mix together the chaffle ingredients in a bowl and mix together.
Sprinkle 1 tbsp. of cheese in a waffle maker and pour in the chaffle batter.
Pour 1 tbsp. of cheese over the batter and close the lid.
Cook the chaffles for about 4 to minutes.
Serve with a chicken zinger and enjoy the double chicken flavor.
Per serving: Calories: 228Kcal; Fat: 6g; Carbs: 3g; Protein: 7g

286. Swiss Cheese and Vegetables Chaffles

Preparation time: 10 minutes
Cooking time: 10 minutes
Servings: 1
Ingredients:
- 1 large egg
- 1 tbsp. almond flour
- 1 tbsp. full-fat Greek yogurt
- ⅛ tsp. baking powder
- ¼ cup shredded Swiss cheese

Toppings:
- 4 oz. grill prawns
- 4 oz. steamed cauliflower mash

- ½ zucchini sliced
- 3 lettuce leaves
- 1 tomato, sliced
- 1 tbsp. flax seeds

Directions:
Make 3 chaffles with the given chaffles ingredients.
For serving, arrange lettuce leaves on each chaffle.
Top with the zucchini slice, grill prawns, cauliflower mash, and a tomato slice.
Drizzle flax seeds on top.
Per serving: Calories: 395Kcal; Fat: 27g; Carbs: 2g; Protein: 22g

287. Parmesan and Bacon Chaffles

Preparation time: 10 minutes
Cooking time: 15 minutes
Servings: 1
Ingredients:
- 1 egg
- ½ cup cheddar cheese, shredded
- 1 tbsp. parmesan cheese
- ¾ tsp. coconut flour
- ¼ tsp. baking powder
- ⅛ tsp. Italian seasoning
- a pinch of salt
- ¼ tsp. garlic powder

Toppings:
- 1 bacon sliced, cooked, and chopped
- ½ cup mozzarella cheese, shredded
- ¼ tsp. parsley, chopped

Directions:
Preheat the oven to 400°F.
Switch on your mini waffle maker and grease with cooking spray.
Mix together the chaffle ingredients in a mixing bowl until combined.
Spoon half of the batter in the center of the waffle maker and close the lid. Cook the chaffles for about 3 minutes until cooked.
Carefully remove the chaffles from the maker.
Arrange chaffles in a greased baking tray.
Top with mozzarella cheese, chopped bacon, and parsley and bake in the oven for 4-5 minutes.
Once the cheese is melted, remove it from the oven.
Per serving: Calories: 358Kcal; Fat: 32g; Carbs: 2g; Protein: 22g

288. Grill Beefsteak Chaffle

Preparation time: 10 minutes
Cooking time: 10 minutes
Servings: 1
Ingredients:
- 1 beefsteak rib eye
- 1 tsp. salt
- 1 tsp. pepper
- 1 tbsp. lime juice
- 1 tsp. garlic
- 1 classic chaffle

Directions:
Prepare your grill for direct heat.
Mix together allspice and rub over beefsteak evenly.
Place the beef on the grill rack over medium heat.
Cover and cook the steak for about 6 to 8 minutes.
Flip and cook for another 5 minutes until cooked through.
Serve with the simple keto chaffle and enjoy!
Per serving: Calories: 450Kcal; Fat: 34g; Carbs: 1g; Protein: 24g

289. Cauliflower and Tomatoes Chaffles

Preparation time: 10 minutes
Cooking time: 15 minutes
Servings: 1
Ingredients:

- ½ cup cauliflower
- ¼ tsp. garlic powder
- ¼ tsp. black pepper
- ¼ tsp. salt
- ½ cup shredded cheddar cheese
- 1 egg

Toppings:

- 1 lettuce leave
- 1 tomato sliced
- 4 oz. cauliflower steamed, mashed
- 1 tsp. sesame seeds

Directions:
Add all the chaffle ingredients into a blender and mix well.
Sprinkle ⅛ of shredded cheese on the waffle maker and pour the cauliflower mixture in a preheated waffle maker and sprinkle the rest of the cheese over it.
Cook the chaffles for about 4-5 minutes until cooked.
For serving, lay lettuce leaves over the chaffle top with steamed cauliflower and tomato.
Drizzle sesame seeds on top.
Per serving: Calories: 335Kcal; Fat: 26g; Carbs: 1g; Protein: 22g

290. Rosemary Pork Chops Chaffles

Preparation time: 10 minutes
Cooking time: 15 minutes
Servings: 4
Ingredients:

- 4 eggs
- 2 cup mozzarella cheese, grated
- a pinch of nutmeg
- 2 tbsp. sour cream
- 6 tbsp. almond flour
- 2 tsp. baking powder
- salt and pepper to taste

Pork Chops:

- 2 tbsp. olive oil
- 1 lb. pork chops
- salt and pepper to taste
- 1 tsp. freshly chopped rosemary

Other:

- 2 tbsp. cooking spray to brush the waffle maker
- 2 tbsp. freshly chopped basil for decoration

Directions:
Preheat the waffle maker.
Add the eggs, mozzarella cheese, salt and pepper, nutmeg, sour cream, almond flour, and baking powder to a bowl.
Mix until combined.
Add some of the batter into the waffle maker after greasing it with a non-stick cooking spray.
Cook for about 7 minutes or until golden brown.
Meanwhile, heat the butter in a non-stick grill pan and season the pork chops with salt and pepper and freshly chopped rosemary.
Cook the pork chops for about 4-5 minutes on each side.
Serve each chaffle with a pork chop and sprinkle some freshly chopped basil on top.
Per serving: Calories: 466Kcal; Fat: 35g; Carbs: 3g; Protein: 22g

291. Beef and Cream Cheese Classic Chaffle

Preparation time: 10 minutes
Cooking time: 10 minutes
Servings: 2
Ingredients:
Batter:

- ½ lb. ground beef
- 2 eggs
- 4 oz. cream cheese
- 1 cup mozzarella cheese, grated
- garlic clove, minced
- ½ tsp. Freshly chopped rosemary
- salt and pepper to taste

Other:

- 2 tbsp. butter to brush the waffle maker
- ¼ cup sour cream
- 2 tbsp. freshly chopped parsley for garnish

Directions:
Preheat the waffle maker.
Add the ground beef, eggs, cream cheese, grated mozzarella cheese, salt and pepper, minced garlic, and freshly chopped rosemary to a bowl.
Grease the waffle maker with butter and add a few tbsp. of the batter.
Cook for about 8-10 minutes, depending on your waffle maker.
Serve each chaffle with a tbsp. of sour cream and freshly chopped parsley on top.
Per serving: Calories: 368Kcal; Fat: 24g; Carbs: 3g; Protein: 22g

292. Beef and Tomato Chaffle

Preparation time: 10 minutes
Cooking time: 15 minutes
Servings: 2
Ingredients:
Batter:

- 2 eggs
- ¼ cup cream cheese
- 1 cup mozzarella cheese, grated
- salt and pepper to taste
- ¼ cup almond flour
- 1 tsp. freshly chopped dill

Beef:

- 1 lb. beef loin
- salt and pepper to taste
- 1 tbsp. balsamic vinegar
- 2 tbsp. olive oil
- 1 tsp. freshly chopped rosemary

Other:

- 2 tbsp. cooking spray to brush the waffle maker
- 4 tomato slices for serving

Directions:
Preheat the waffle maker.
Add the eggs, cream cheese, grated mozzarella cheese, salt and pepper, almond flour, and freshly chopped dill to a bowl.
Mix until combined and a creamy batter.
Grease your waffle maker and add a few tbsp. of the batter.
Cook for about 8-10 minutes, depending on your waffle maker.
Meanwhile, heat the olive oil in a non-stick frying pan and season the beef loin with salt and pepper and freshly chopped rosemary.
Cook the beef on each side for about 5 minutes and drizzle with some balsamic vinegar.
Serve each chaffle with a slice of tomato and cooked beef loin slices.
Per serving: Calories: 496Kcal; Fat: 33g; Carbs: 2g; Protein: 28g

293. Ground Pork Chaffles

Preparation time: 10 minutes
Cooking time: 15 minutes
Servings: 2
Ingredients:

- ½ lb. ground pork
- 2 eggs
- ½ cup grated mozzarella cheese
- salt and pepper to taste
- 1 garlic clove, minced
- 1 tsp. dried oregano

Other:

- 2 tbsp. butter to brush the waffle maker
- 2 tbsp. freshly chopped parsley for garnish

Directions:
Preheat the waffle maker.
Add the ground pork, eggs, mozzarella cheese, salt and pepper, minced garlic, and dried oregano to a bowl and mix until combined.
Grease the waffle maker with butter and add some batter.
Cook for about 7-8 minutes, depending on your waffle maker.
Cook more chaffles with the same process and serve them with freshly chopped parsley.
Per serving: Calories: 330Kcal; Fat: 11g; Carbs: 1g; Protein: 20g

294. Spicy Jalapeño Popper Chaffles

Preparation time: 10 minutes
Cooking time: 10 minutes
Servings: 1
Ingredients:

For the Chaffles:

- 1 egg
- 1 oz. cream cheese, softened
- 1 cup cheddar cheese, shredded

Toppings:

- 2 tbsp. bacon bits
- ½ tbsp. jalapeños

Directions:
Turn on the waffle maker and preheat it.
Mix the chaffle ingredients.
Pour the batter onto the waffle maker.
Cook the batter for 3-4 minutes until it's brown and crispy.
Remove the chaffle and repeat the steps until all the remaining batter have been used up.
Sprinkle bacon bits and a few jalapeño slices as toppings.
Per serving: Calories: 2331Kcal; Fat: 31g; Carbs: 1g; Protein: 23g

295. Eggnog Cinnamon Chaffles

Preparation time: 15 minutes
Cooking time: 10 minutes
Servings: 1
Ingredients:

- 1 egg, separated
- 1 egg yolk
- ½ cup mozzarella cheese shredded
- ½ tsp. spiced rum
- 1 tsp. vanilla extract
- ¼ tsp. nutmeg, dried
- a dash of cinnamon
- 1 tsp. coconut flour

For the Icing:

- 2 tbsp. cream cheese
- 1 tbsp. powdered sweetener
- 2 tsp. rum or rum extract

Directions:
Preheat the mini waffle maker.
Mix the egg yolk in a small bowl until smooth.
Add in the sweetener and mix until the powder is completely dissolved.
Add the coconut flour, cinnamon, and nutmeg. Mix well.
In another bowl, mix the rum, egg white, and vanilla. Whisk until well combined.
Throw in the yolk mixture with the egg white mixture. You should be able to form a thin batter.
Add the mozzarella cheese and combine it with the mixture.
Separate the batter into two batches. Put ½ of the batter into the waffle maker and let it cook for 6 minutes until it's solid.
Repeat until you've used up the remaining batter.
In a separate bowl, mix all the icing ingredients.
Top the cooked chaffles with the icing, or you can use this as a dip.
Per serving: Calories: 266Kcal; Fat: 23g; Carbs: 2g; Protein: 21g

296. Cheddar Jalapeño Chaffles

Preparation time: 15 minutes
Cooking time: 10 minutes
Servings: 1
Ingredients:

- 1 egg
- ½ cup cheddar cheese shredded
- 1 tbsp. almond flour
- 1 tbsp. jalapeños
- 1 tbsp. olive oil

Directions:
Preheat the waffle maker.
While waiting for the waffle maker to heat up, mix the jalapeño, egg, cheese, and almond flour in a small mixing bowl.
Lightly grease the waffle maker with olive oil.
In the center of the waffle maker, carefully pour the chaffle batter. Spread the mixture evenly toward the edges.
Close the waffle maker lid and wait for 3-4 minutes for the mixture to cook. For an even crispier texture, wait for another 1-2 minutes.
Remove the chaffle. Let it cool before serving.
Per serving: Calories: 345Kcal; Fat: 28g; Carbs: 2g; Protein: 21g

CHAPTER 4:

Dinner

297. Chicken Green Butter Chaffle

Preparation time: 10 minutes
Cooking time: 25 minutes
Servings: 2
Ingredients:

- 1/3 cup chicken, boiled and shredded
- 1/3 cup cabbage
- 1/3 cup broccoli
- 1/3 cup zucchini
- 2 eggs
- 1 cup mozzarella cheese (shredded)
- 1 tbsp. butter
- 2 tbsp. almond flour
- ¼ tsp. baking powder
- a pinch onion powder
- a pinch garlic powder
- a pinch salt

Directions:
In a deep saucepan, boil cabbage, broccoli, and zucchini for five minutes or till they tender, then strain and blend.
Mix all the remaining ingredients well together.
Pour a thin layer of the mixture on a preheated waffle iron.
Add a layer of the blended vegetables to the mixture.
Again, add more mixture over the top.
Cook the chaffle for around 5 minutes.
Serve them with your favorite sauce.
Per serving: Calories: 319Kcal; Fat: 24g; Carbs: 2g; Protein: 25g

298. Artichoke and Spinach Chicken Chaffle

Preparation time: 10 minutes
Cooking time: 25 minutes
Servings: 1
Ingredients:

- 1/3 cup chicken, cooked and diced
- ½ cup spinach, cooked and chopped
- 1/3 cup chopped artichokes
- 1 egg
- 1/3 cup mozzarella cheese (shredded)
- 1 oz. cream cheese
- ¼ tsp. garlic powder

Directions:
Preheat your waffle maker and grease it.
In a mixing bowl, add all the ingredients.
Mix them all well.
Pour the mixture into the waffle maker and spread it evenly to cover the plate properly.
Cook for about 4 minutes or until the required crunch is obtained.

Remove the chaffle from the heat and set it aside for one minute.
Repeat the process with the rest of the batter
Per serving: Calories: 320Kcal; Fat: 24g; Carbs: 2g; Protein: 22g

299. Halloumi and Boiled Chicken Chaffle

Preparation time: 15 minutes
Cooking time: 20 minutes
Servings: 1
Ingredients:

- 1 cup shredded boiled chicken
- ½ tsp. pepper
- a pinch of salt
- 3 oz. halloumi cheese
- 1 tbsp. oregano

Directions:
Take a bowl and add the chicken, pepper, and salt.
Make ½-inch thick slices of Halloumi cheese and divide each further into two.
Put one slice of cheese in the unheated waffle maker and spread the chicken on it.
Top with another cheese slice and sprinkle oregano.
Cook the cheese for over 4-6 minutes till it turns golden brown.
Remove from the heat when a bit cool, and serve it with your favorite sauce.
Per serving: Calories: 333Kcal; Fat: 16g; Carbs: 1g; Protein: 19g

300. Mozzarella Chicken Chaffle

Preparation time: 15 minutes
Cooking time: 20 minutes
Servings: 1
Ingredients:

- 1/3 cup cheddar cheese
- 1 egg
- 2 small pieces chicken, sautéed in butter
- ¼ tsp. baking powder
- ¼ tsp. salt
- 2 tbsp. yogurt
- 1/3 cup mozzarella cheese

Directions:
Mix the cheddar cheese, egg, yogurt, chicken, baking powder, and salt together.
Preheat your waffle iron and grease it.
In your mini waffle iron, shred a quarter of the mozzarella cheese.
Add the mixture to your mini waffle iron.
Again, shred another quarter of mozzarella cheese on the mixture.
Cook till the desired crisp is achieved.
Repeat the process to create the last chaffle.
Per serving: Calories: 310Kcal; Fat: 22g; Carbs: 1g; Protein: 21g

301. Sautéed Chicken Chaffles

Preparation time: 10 minutes
Cooking time: 25 minutes
Servings: 1
Ingredients:

- 1 cup chicken boneless, sautéed in butter
- 1 egg
- 2 cup mozzarella cheese (shredded)
- 1 tbsp. butter
- ¼ tsp. turmeric
- ¼ tsp. baking powder
- a pinch onion powder
- a pinch garlic powder
- salt: a pinch

Directions:
Mix all the remaining ingredients well together, except the mince.
Pour a thin layer on a preheated waffle iron.
Add a layer of chicken mince to the mixture.
Again, add more mixture over the top.
Cook the chaffle for around 5 minutes.
Serve them hot with your favorite keto sauce.
Per serving: Calories: 407Kcal; Fat: 32g; Carbs: 2g; Protein: 29g

302. Aromatic Chicken Chaffles

Preparation time: 10 minutes
Cooking time: 40 minutes
Servings: 2
Ingredients:

- 2 leg pieces of chicken
- 1 dried bay leaves
- 1 cardamom
- 4 whole black peppers
- 4 cloves
- 2 cup water
- 2 eggs
- ¼ tsp. salt
- 1 cup shredded mozzarella
- ¾ tbsp. baking powder

Directions:
Boil water in a large pan.
Add in the chicken, bay leaves, black pepper, cloves, and cardamom, and cover and boil for 20 minutes at least.
Remove the chicken and shred it finely and discard the bones.
Preheat your mini waffle iron if needed.
Mix all the above-mentioned remaining ingredients in a bowl and add in the chicken.
Grease your waffle iron lightly.
Cook your mixture in the mini waffle iron for at least 4 minutes or till the desired crisp is achieved and serve hot.
Repeat the process to create the remaining chaffles.
Per serving: Calories: 410Kcal; Fat: 25g; Carbs: 1g; Protein: 25g

303. Pumpkin Chicken Chaffles

Preparation time: 10 minutes
Cooking time: 20 minutes
Servings: 1
Ingredients:

- ½ cup boiled chicken
- ½ cup pumpkin puree
- ¼ tsp. pepper
- 1 egg
- ½ cup mozzarella cheese (shredded)
- 2 tbsp. almond flour
- a pinch onion powder
- a pinch garlic powder
- salt: as per your taste

Directions:
Mix all the ingredients well together in a bowl.
Pour a layer of the mixture on a preheated waffle iron.
Cook for 5 minutes.
Serve with your favorite sauce.
Per serving: Calories: 435Kcal; Fat: 32g; Carbs: 1g; Protein: 30g

304. Garlicky Chicken Pepper Chaffles

Preparation time: 5 minutes
Cooking time: 10 minutes
Servings: 1
Ingredients:

- 1 egg
- ½ cup mozzarella cheese (shredded)
- 2 chopped garlic cloves
- ½ cup finely chopped pepper
- ½ cup chicken, boiled and shredded
- 1 tsp. onion powder
- salt and pepper: as per your taste

Directions:
Mix all the ingredients well together.
Pour a layer on a preheated waffle iron.
Cook the chaffle for around 5 minutes.
Create as many chaffles as your batter will allow.
Per serving: Calories: 390Kcal; Fat: 29g; Carbs: 1g; Protein: 22g

305. Sliced Chicken and Chaffles

Preparation time: 15 minutes
Cooking time: 25 minutes
Servings: 2
Ingredients:

- 2 eggs
- 1½ cup mozzarella cheese (shredded)
- 2 slices American cheese
- 2 boneless sliced chicken breast
- ¼ tsp. salt
- ¼ tsp. black pepper
- 2 tbsp. butter

Directions:
Plug in your mini waffle maker to preheat it and then grease it.
In a mixing bowl, beat the eggs and add the shredded mozzarella cheese and mix.
Pour the mixture into the plate of the waffle maker.
Cook for at least 4 minutes to get the desired crunch.
Remove the chaffle from the heat.
Add the chicken, salt, and pepper together and mix.
Fry the chicken in the butter from both sides till they turn golden.
Place a cheese slice on the chicken immediately when removing it from the heat.
Take two chaffles and put chicken and cheese in between.
Repeat the process with the remaining ingredients.
Per serving: Calories: 468Kcal; Fat: 30g; Carbs: 1g; Protein: 18g

306. Garlic Chicken Cucumber Roll Chaffle

Preparation time: 20 minutes
Cooking time: 30 minutes
Servings: 2

Ingredients:

Garlic Chicken:
- 1 cup chicken mince
- ¼ tsp. salt, or as per your taste
- ¼ tsp. black pepper, or as per your taste
- 1 tbsp. lemon juice
- 2 tbsp. butter
- 2 tbsp. fresh garlic
- 1 tsp. garlic powder
- 1 tbsp. soy sauce

Chaffle:
- 2 eggs
- 1 cup mozzarella cheese (shredded)
- 1 tsp. garlic powder

To Serve:
- ½ cup cucumber (diced)
- 1 tbsp. parsley

Directions:

In a frying pan, melt the butter and add fresh garlic and sauté for 1 minute.

Now, add chicken mince and cook until they are tender.

When done, add the rest of the ingredients and set them aside.

In a medium-sized bowl, beat the eggs and add mozzarella cheese to them with garlic powder.

Mix them all well and pour them into the greasy mini waffle maker.

Cook for at least 4 minutes to get the desired crunch.

Remove the chaffle from the heat, add the chicken mixture in between with cucumber, and fold.

Make as many chaffles as your mixture allow.

Serve hot and top with parsley.

Per serving: Calories: 356Kcal; Fat: 6g; Carbs: 1g; Protein: 38g

307. Spiced Chicken Chaffles with Special Sauce

Preparation time: 5 minutes
Cooking time: 15 minutes
Servings: 1
Ingredients:

- 1 egg
- ½ cup shredded mozzarella cheese
- ½ tsp. dried basil
- ½ tsp. smoked paprika
- 1 cup chicken, boiled and shredded
- ½ tsp. salt

Sauce:
- ¼ cup mayonnaise
- 1 tsp. vinegar
- 3 tbsp. sweet chili sauce
- 1 tbsp. hot sauce

Directions:

Plug in your mini waffle iron and grease it.

Add the egg, dried basil, smoked paprika, chicken, salt, and cheese in a medium-sized bowl and whisk well.

Cook your mixture in the mini waffle iron for at least 4 minutes.

Make as many chaffles as you can.

Combine the sauce ingredients well together.

Serve spicy chaffles with the sauce.

Per serving: Calories: 360Kcal; Fat: 35g; Carbs: 1g; Protein: 37g

308. Strawberry Frosty Chaffles

Preparation time: 10 minutes
Cooking time: 5 minutes
Servings: 1

Ingredients:
- 1 cup frozen strawberries
- ½ cup heavy cream
- 1 tsp. stevia
- 1 scoop protein powder
- 2 basic chaffles

Directions:

Mix together all the ingredients in a mixing bowl.

Pour the mixture into silicone molds and freeze in a freezer for about 4 hours to set.

Once the frosty is set, top on chaffles and enjoy!

Per serving: Calories: 325Kcal; Fat: 27g; Carbs: 1g; Protein: 2g

309. Pecan Pumpkin Chaffles

Preparation time: 20 minutes
Cooking time: 15 minutes
Servings: 1
Ingredients:

- 1 egg
- 2 tbsp. pecans, toasted and chopped
- 2 tbsp. almond flour
- 1 tsp. erythritol
- ¼ tsp. pumpkin pie spice
- 1 tbsp. pumpkin puree
- ½ cup mozzarella cheese, grated

Directions:

Preheat your waffle maker.

Beat the egg in a small bowl.

Add the remaining ingredients and mix well.

Spray the waffle maker with cooking spray.

Pour half of the batter into the hot waffle maker and cook for 7-8 minutes or until golden brown. Repeat with the remaining batter.

Per serving: Calories: 290Kcal; Fat: 23g; Carbs: 2g; Protein: 21g

310. Swiss Bacon Chaffle

Preparation time: 10 minutes
Cooking time: 8 minutes
Servings: 1
Ingredients:

- 1 egg
- ½ cup Swiss cheese
- 2 tbsp. cooked crumbled bacon

Directions:

Preheat your waffle maker.

Beat the egg in a bowl.

Stir in the cheese and bacon.

Pour half of the mixture into the device.

Close and cook for 4 minutes.

Cook the second chaffle using the same steps.

Per serving: Calories: 1250Kcal; Fat: 21g; Carbs: 2g; Protein: 17g

311. Bacon, Olives and Cheddar Chaffle

Preparation time: 10 minutes
Cooking time: 8 minutes
Servings: 1
Ingredients:

- 1 egg
- ½ cup cheddar cheese, shredded
- 1 tbsp. black olives, chopped
- 1 tbsp. bacon bits

Directions:

Plug in your waffle maker.

In a bowl, beat the egg and stir in the cheese.

Add the black olives and bacon bits.
Mix well.
Add half of the mixture into the waffle maker.
Cover and cook for 4 minutes.
Open and transfer it to a plate.
Let it cool for 2 minutes.
Cook the other chaffle using the remaining batter.
Per serving: Calories: 433Kcal; Fat: 35g; Carbs: 1g; Protein: 21g

312. Garlic and Coconut Flour Chaffle

Preparation time: 10 minutes
Servings: 1
Cooking time: 8 minutes
Ingredients:

- 1 egg
- ½ cup cheddar cheese, beaten
- 1 tsp. coconut flour
- a pinch garlic powder

Directions:
Plug in your waffle maker.
Beat the egg in a bowl.
Stir in the rest of the ingredients.
Cook for about 4 minutes half of the batter into the waffle maker.
Remove the waffle and let it sit for 2 minutes.
Do the same steps with the remaining batter.
Per serving: Calories: 318Kcal; Fat: 26g; Carbs: 3g; Protein: 21g

313. Herby Chaffle Snacks

Preparation time: 30 minutes
Cooking time: 28 minutes
Servings: 1
Ingredients:

- 1 egg, beaten
- ½ cup finely grated Monterey Jack cheese
- ¼ cup finely grated parmesan cheese
- ½ tsp. dried mixed herbs

Directions:
Preheat the waffle iron.
Mix all the ingredients in a medium bowl.
Open the iron and pour in a quarter of the mixture. Close and cook until crispy, 7 minutes.
Remove the chaffle onto a plate and make 3 more with the rest of the ingredients.
Cut each chaffle into wedges.
Allow cooling and serve.
Per serving: Calories: 295Kcal; Fat: 20g; Carbs: 2g; Protein: 13g

314. Frosting Pumpkin Chaffles

Preparation time: 20 minutes
Cooking time: 15 minutes
Servings: 1
Ingredients:

- 1 egg, lightly beaten
- 1 tbsp. sugar-free pumpkin puree
- ¼ tsp. pumpkin pie spice
- ½ cup mozzarella cheese, shredded
For Frosting:
- ½ tsp. vanilla
- 2 tbsp. Swerve
- 2 tbsp. cream cheese, softened

Directions:
Preheat your waffle maker.
Add the egg to a bowl and whisk well.

Add the pumpkin puree, pumpkin pie spice, and cheese, and stir well.
Spray the waffle maker with cooking spray.
Pour ½ of the batter in the hot waffle maker and cook for 3-4 minutes or until golden brown. Repeat with the remaining batter.
In a small-sized bowl, combine all the frosting ingredients until smooth.
Add frosting on top of hot chaffles and serve.
Per serving: Calories: 296Kcal; Fat: 20g; Carbs: 1g; Protein: 16g

315. Strawberry Sandwich Chaffle

Preparation time: 10 minutes
Cooking time: 5 minutes
Servings: 1
Ingredients:

- ¼ cup heavy cream
- 4 oz. strawberry slice
Chaffles:
- 1 egg
- ½ cup mozzarella cheese

Directions:
Make 2 chaffles with the chaffle ingredients.
Meanwhile, mix together the cream and strawberries.
Spread this mixture over the chaffle slice.
Drizzle chocolate sauce over a sandwich.
Per serving: Calories: 310Kcal; Fat: 20g; Carbs: 1g; Protein: 14g

316. Cranberries Cake Chaffle

Preparation time: 20 minutes
Cooking time: 15minutes
Servings: 5
Ingredients:

- 4 oz. almond flour
- 2 cup cheddar cheese
- 5 eggs
- 1 tsp. stevia
- 2 tsp. baking powder
- 2 tsp. vanilla extract
- ¼ cup almond butter, melted
- 3 tbsp. almond milk
- 1 cup cranberries
- 1 cup coconut cream

Directions:
Beat the eggs in a small-sized bowl, and combine them with stevia, almond flour, and baking powder.
While you are mixing the flour mixture, add little by little the melted butter. Mix well to ensure a smooth consistency.
Add the cheese, almond milk, cranberries, and vanilla to the flour and butter mixture and make sure to mix well.
Preheat the waffles maker according to the manufacturer's instructions and grease it with avocado oil.
Cook the mixture into the waffle maker for about 4-5 minutes or until golden brown.
Create all the chaffles that your batter allows.
Place chaffles on a plate. Spread the cream all around. Cut in slices and serve.
Per serving: Calories: 357Kcal; Fat: 30g; Carbs: 3g; Protein: 19g

317. Thanksgiving Pumpkin Latte with Chaffles

Preparation time: 10 minutes
Cooking time: 5minutes
Servings: 1

Ingredients:

- ¾ cup unsweetened coconut milk
- 2 tbsp. heavy cream
- 2 tbsp. pumpkin puree
- 1 tsp. stevia
- ¼ tsp. pumpkin spice
- ¼ tsp. vanilla extract
- ¼ cup espresso
- 1 classic chaffle

Toppings:

- 2 scoop whipped cream
- pumpkin spice
- 2 heart shape chaffles

Directions:

Mix together all the recipe ingredients in a mug and microwave for 5 minutes.

Pour the latte into a serving glass.

Top with a heavy cream scoop, pumpkin spice, and chaffle.

Per serving: Calories: 398Kcal; Fat: 25g; Carbs: 2g; Protein: 20g

318. Choco and Strawberries Chaffles

Preparation time: 10 minutes
Cooking time: 5 minutes
Servings: 1
Ingredients:

- 1 tbsp. almond flour
- ½ cup strawberry puree
- ½ cup cheddar cheese
- ½ tsp. baking powder
- 1 large egg
- 1 tbsp. chocolate
- 2 tbsp. coconut oil. melted
- ½ tsp. vanilla extract optional

Directions:

Preheat your waffle maker while you are mixing all the ingredients.

Melt coconut oil in a microwave.

In a medium-sized bowl, mix together the flour, baking powder, and vanilla until well combined.

Add the egg, melted oil, ½ cup of cheese, chocolate, and strawberry puree to the flour mixture.

Pour ⅛ cup cheese in a waffle maker and then pour the mixture in the center of the greased waffle.

Again, sprinkle cheese on the batter.

Close the waffle maker.

Cook chaffles for about 4-5 minutes until crispy.

Once chaffles are cooked, remove and enjoy them!

Per serving: Calories: 420Kcal; Fat: 34g; Carbs: 2g; Protein: 22g

319. Lemon and Paprika Chaffles

Preparation time: 30 minutes
Cooking time: 28 minutes
Servings: 1
Ingredients:

- 1 egg, beaten
- 1 oz. cream cheese, softened
- 1/3 cup finely grated mozzarella cheese
- 1 tbsp. almond flour
- 1 tsp. butter, melted
- 1 tsp. maple (sugar-free) syrup
- ½ tsp. sweet paprika
- ½ tsp. lemon extract

Directions:

Preheat the waffle iron.

Mix all the ingredients in a medium bowl.

Open the iron and pour in a quarter of the mixture. Close and cook until crispy, 7 minutes.

Remove the chaffle onto a plate and make 3 more with the remaining mixture.

Cut each chaffle into wedges, plate, allow cooling, and serve.

Per serving: Calories: 342Kcal; Fat: 24g; Carbs: 2g; Protein: 18g

320. Triple Chocolate Chaffle

Preparation time: 10 minutes
Cooking time: 7-9 minutes
Servings: 4
Ingredients:

- 4 eggs
- 4 oz. cream cheese, softened
- 1 oz. dark unsweetened chocolate, melted
- 1 tsp. vanilla extract
- 5 tbsp. almond flour
- 3 tbsp. cocoa powder
- 1½ tsp. baking powder
- ¼ cup dark unsweetened chocolate chips
- 2 tbsp. butter to brush the waffle maker

Directions:

Preheat the waffle maker.

Add the eggs and cream cheese to a bowl and stir with a wire whisk until just combined.

Add the vanilla extract and mix well until combined.

Stir in the almond flour, cocoa powder, and baking powder and mix until combined.

Add the chocolate chips and stir.

Grease the heated waffle maker with butter and add a few tbsp. of the batter.

Cook for about 8 minutes or until golden brown.

Per serving: Calories: 463Kcal; Fat: 26g; Carbs: 2g; Protein: 16g

321. 'Nduja Pesto Chaffles

Preparation time: 5 minutes
Cooking time: 8 minutes
Servings: 1
Ingredients:

- cooking spray
- 1 egg
- ½ cup cheddar cheese, shredded
- ½ tsp. 'nduja pesto

Directions:

Turn your mini waffle maker on and grease both sides with cooking spray.

Beat the egg in a bowl.

Stir in the cheddar cheese and add 'nduja pesto.

Spoon half of the batter into the waffle maker.

Seal and cook for 4 minutes.

Remove the chaffle slowly from the waffle maker.

Let it sit for 3 minutes.

Repeat the steps to create another chaffle

Per serving: Calories: 343Kcal; Fat: 26g; Carbs: 1g; Protein: 20g

322. Nut Butter Chaffles

Preparation time: 10 minutes
Cooking time: 8 minutes
Servings: 1

Ingredients:

- 1 egg
- ½ cup mozzarella cheese, shredded
- 2 tbsp. almond flour
- ½ tsp. baking powder
- 1 tbsp. sweetener
- 1 tsp. vanilla
- 2 tbsp. nut butter

Directions:

Turn on the waffle maker.

Beat the egg in a bowl and combine with the cheese.

In another bowl, mix the almond flour, baking powder, and sweetener.

In the third bowl, blend the vanilla extract and nut butter.

Gradually, add the almond flour mixture into the egg mixture.

Then, stir in the vanilla extract.

Pour the batter into the waffle maker and cook for about 4 minutes.

Transfer to a plate and let it cool for 2 minutes.

Repeat the steps with the remaining batter.

Per serving: Calories: 420Kcal; Fat: 31g; Carbs: 2g; Protein: 26g

323. Beef Taco Chaffle

Preparation time: 10 minutes
Cooking time: 158 minutes
Servings: 2
Ingredients:

Batter:

- 4 eggs
- 2 cup grated cheddar cheese
- ¼ cup heavy cream
- salt and pepper to taste
- ¼ cup almond flour
- 2 tsp. baking powder

Beef:

- 2 tbsp. butter
- ½ onion, diced
- 1 lb. ground beef
- 1 tsp. dried oregano
- 1 tbsp. sugar-free ketchup
- salt and pepper to taste

Other:

- 2 tbsp. cooking spray to brush the waffle maker
- 2 tbsp. freshly chopped parsley

Directions:

Preheat the waffle maker.

Add the eggs, grated cheddar cheese, heavy cream, salt and pepper, almond flour, and baking powder to a bowl.

Grease your waffle maker using a non-stick cooking spray and add a few tbsp. of the batter.

Cook for about 5-7 minutes, depending on your waffle maker.

Once the chaffle is ready, place it in a napkin holder to harden into the shape of a taco as it cools.

Meanwhile, melt and heat the butter in a non-stick frying pan and start cooking the diced onion.

Once the onion is tender, add the ground beef. Season with salt and pepper and dried oregano and stir in the sugar-free ketchup.

Cook for about 7 minutes.

Serve the cooked ground meat in each taco chaffle sprinkled with some freshly chopped parsley.

Per serving: Calories: 520Kcal; Fat: 40g; Carbs: 3g; Protein: 26g

324. Ground Chicken Chaffles

Preparation time: 10 minutes
Cooking time: 8-10 minutes
Servings: 2

Ingredients:

Batter

- ½ lb. ground chicken
- 4 eggs
- 3 tbsp. tomato sauce
- salt and pepper to taste
- 1 cup grated mozzarella cheese
- 1 tsp. dried oregano

Other:

- 2 tbsp. butter to brush the waffle maker

Directions:

Preheat the waffle maker.

Add the ground chicken, eggs, and tomato sauce to a bowl and season with salt and pepper.

Combine everything with a fork and stir in the mozzarella cheese and dried oregano.

Blend again until fully combined.

Brush the heated waffle maker with butter and add a few tbsp. of the batter.

Cook for about 8-10 minutes, depending on your waffle maker.

Per serving: Calories: 352Kcal; Fat: 26g; Carbs: 2g; Protein: 21g

325. Turkey Sandwich Chaffle

Preparation time: 10 minutes
Cooking time: 15 minutes
Servings: 2
Ingredients:

Batter:

- 4 eggs
- 1 lb., turkey
- ¼ cup cream cheese
- 1 cup grated mozzarella cheese
- 1 tsp. dried dill
- ½ tsp. onion powder
- ½ tsp. garlic powder
- juicy chicken
- 2 tbsp. butter
- 1 lb. chicken breast
- 1 tsp. dried dill
- 2 tbsp. heavy cream
- salt and pepper to taste

Other:

- 2 tbsp. butter to brush the waffle maker
- 4 lettuce leaves to garnish the sandwich
- 4 tomato slices to garnish the sandwich

Directions:

Preheat the waffle maker.

Add the eggs, cream cheese, mozzarella cheese, turkey, salt and pepper, dried dill, onion powder, and garlic powder to a bowl.

Mix everything with a fork just until a creamy batter.

Brush the heated waffle maker with butter and add a few tbsp. of the batter.

Cook for 5-6 minutes, or until golden and crunchy.

Meanwhile, heat some butter in a non-stick pan.

Season the chicken with salt and pepper and sprinkle with dried dill.

Pour the heavy cream on top.

Cook the chicken slices for about 10 minutes or until golden.

Cut each chaffle in half.

On one half, add a lettuce leaf, tomato slice, and chicken slice. Cover with the other chaffle half to make a sandwich.

Per serving: Calories: 510Kcal; Fat: 33g; Carbs: 4g; Protein: 31g

326. BBQ Sauce Pork Chaffle

Preparation time: 10 minutes
Cooking time: 15 minutes
Servings: 2
Ingredients:

- ½ lb. ground pork
- 3 eggs
- 1 cup grated mozzarella cheese
- 1 clove garlic, minced
- 1 tsp. dried rosemary
- 3 tbsp. sugar-free BBQ sauce
- pinch salt and pepper

Other:

- 2 tbsp. butter to brush the waffle maker
- ½ lb. pork rinds for serving
- ¼ cup sugar-free BBQ sauce for serving

Directions:

Preheat the waffle maker.

Add the ground pork, eggs, mozzarella, salt and pepper, minced garlic, dried rosemary, and BBQ sauce to a bowl.

Mix until combined.

Brush the heated waffle maker with butter and add a few tbsp. of the batter.

Cook for about 7-8 minutes, depending on your waffle maker.

Serve each chaffle with some pork rinds and a tbsp. of BBQ sauce.

Per serving: Calories: 270Kcal; Fat: 28g; Carbs: 1g; Protein: 20g

327. Chicken Taco Chaffle

Preparation time: 10 minutes
Cooking time: 20 minutes
Servings: 4
Ingredients:

Chaffles:

- 4 eggs
- 2 cup grated provolone cheese
- 6 tbsp. almond flour
- 2½ tsp. baking powder
- a pinch salt and pepper

Toppings:

- 2 tbsp. olive oil
- ½ lb. ground chicken
- salt and pepper to taste
- 1 garlic clove, minced
- 2 tsp. dried oregano

Other:

- 2 tbsp. butter to brush the waffle maker
- 2 tbsp. freshly chopped spring onion for garnishing

Directions:

Preheat the waffle maker.

Add the eggs, grated provolone cheese, almond flour, baking powder, and salt and pepper to a bowl.

Mix until just combined.

Grease your waffle maker using a non-stick cooking spray and add a few tbsp. of the batter.

Close the lid and cook for about 7-9 minutes, depending on your waffle maker.

Meanwhile, heat the olive oil in a non-stick pan over medium heat and start cooking the ground chicken.

Add a pinch of salt and pepper and stir in the minced garlic and dried oregano. Cook for 10 minutes.

Add some of the cooked ground chicken to each chaffle and serve with freshly chopped spring onion.

Per serving: Calories: 450Kcal; Fat: 30g; Carbs: 2g; Protein: 31g

328. Italian Chicken and Basil Chaffle

Preparation time: 10 minutes
Cooking time: 7-9 minutes
Servings: 2
Ingredients:

Batter:

- ½ lb. ground chicken
- 4 eggs
- 3 tbsp. tomato sauce
- salt and pepper to taste
- 1 cup grated mozzarella cheese
- 1 tsp. dried oregano
- 3 tbsp. freshly chopped basil leaves
- ½ tsp. dried garlic

Other:

- 2 tbsp. butter to brush the waffle maker
- ¼ cup tomato sauce for serving
- 1 tbsp. freshly chopped basil for serving

Directions:

Preheat the waffle maker.

Add the ground chicken, eggs, and tomato sauce to a bowl and season with salt and pepper.

Add the mozzarella cheese and season with dried oregano, freshly chopped basil, and dried garlic.

Mix until fully combined and creamy batter.

Brush the heated waffle maker with butter and add a few tbsp. of the chaffle batter.

Close the lid and cook for about 7-9 minutes, depending on your waffle maker.

Repeat with the rest of the batter.

Serve with tomato sauce and freshly-chopped basil on top.

Per serving: Calories: 450Kcal; Fat: 30g; Carbs: 1g; Protein: 31g

329. Beef Meatballs on Chaffle

Preparation time: 10 minutes
Cooking time: 20 minutes
Servings: 2
Ingredients:

Batter:

- 4 eggs
- 2½ cup grated gouda cheese
- ¼ cup heavy cream
- 1 spring onion, finely chopped
- a pinch salt and pepper

Beef Meatballs:

- 1 lb. ground beef
- Pinch salt and pepper
- 2 tsp. Dijon mustard
- 1 spring onion, finely chopped
- 5 tbsp. almond flour
- 2 tbsp. butter

Other:

- 2 tbsp. cooking spray to brush the waffle maker
- 2 tbsp. freshly chopped parsley

Directions:

Preheat the waffle maker.

Add the eggs, grated gouda cheese, heavy cream, salt and pepper, and finely chopped spring onion to a bowl.

Mix until combined and a batter form.

Use a cooking spray to grease the heated waffle maker and add a few tbsp. of the batter.

Cook for about 7 minutes or until golden.

Meanwhile, mix the ground beef meat, salt and pepper, Dijon mustard, chopped spring onion, and almond flour in a large bowl.

Form small meatballs with your hands.

Warm the butter in a non-stick frying pan and cook the beef meatballs for about 3-4 minutes on each side.

Serve each chaffle with a couple of meatballs and some freshly chopped parsley on top.

Per serving: Calories: 478Kcal; Fat: 35g; Carbs: 2g; Protein: 18g

330. Leftover Turkey Chaffle

Preparation time: 10 minutes
Cooking time: 7-9 minutes
Servings: 2
Ingredients:
   Batter:
   - ½ lb. shredded leftover turkey meat
   - 4 eggs
   - 1 cup grated provolone cheese
   - salt and pepper to taste
   - 1 tsp. dried basil
   - ½ tsp. dried garlic
   - 3 tbsp. sour cream
   - 2 tbsp. coconut flour
   Other:
   - 2 tbsp. cooking spray for greasing the chaffle maker
   - ¼ cup cream cheese for serving the chaffles

Directions:
Preheat the waffle maker.

Add the leftover turkey, eggs, and provolone cheese to a bowl and season with salt and pepper, dried basil, and dried garlic.

Add the sour cream and coconut flour and mix until a batter form.

Grease your waffle maker with cooking spray and add a few tbsp. of the chaffle batter.

Close the lid and cook for about 7-9 minutes, depending on your waffle maker.

Repeat with the rest of the batter.

Serve with cream cheese on top of each chaffle.

Per serving: Calories: 370Kcal; Fat: 36g; Carbs: 6g; Protein: 26g

331. Beef Meatza Chaffle

Preparation time: 10 minutes
Cooking time: 15 minutes
Servings: 2
Ingredients:
   Meatza Chaffle Batter:
   - ½ lb. ground beef
   - 4 eggs
   - 2 cup cheddar cheese, grated
   - 1 tsp. Italian seasoning
   - 2 tbsp. tomato sauce
   - salt and pepper to taste
   Other:
   - 2 tbsp. cooking spray to brush the waffle maker
   - ¼ cup tomato sauce for serving
   - 2 tbsp. freshly chopped basil for serving

Directions:
Preheat the waffle maker.

Add the ground beef, eggs, grated cheddar cheese, salt and pepper, Italian seasoning, and tomato sauce to a bowl.

Mix until everything is fully combined.

With cooking spray, grease your waffle maker and add a few tbsp. of the batter.

Cook for about 7-10 minutes, depending on your waffle maker.

Serve with tomato sauce and freshly-chopped basil on top.

Per serving: Calories: 384Kcal; Fat: 28g; Carbs: 2g; Protein: 22g

332. Chicken Jalapeño Chaffles

Preparation time: 10 minutes
Cooking time: 8-10 minutes
Servings: 2
Ingredients:
   Batter:
   - ½ lb. ground chicken
   - 4 eggs
   - 1 cup grated mozzarella cheese
   - 2 tbsp. sour cream
   - 1 green jalapeño, chopped
   - salt and pepper to taste
   - 1 tsp. dried oregano
   - ½ tsp. dried garlic
   Other:
   - 2 tbsp. butter to brush the waffle maker
   - ¼ cup sour cream to garnish
   - 1 green jalapeño, diced, to garnish

Directions:
Preheat the waffle maker.

Add the ground chicken, eggs, mozzarella cheese, sour cream, chopped jalapeño, salt and pepper, dried oregano, and dried garlic to a bowl.

Mix everything until you have a creamy batter.

Brush the heated waffle maker with butter and add a few tbsp. of the batter.

Close the lid and cook for about 8-10 minutes, depending on your waffle maker.

Serve with a tbsp. of sour cream and sliced jalapeño on top.

Per serving: Calories: 502Kcal; Fat: 34g; Carbs: 2g; Protein: 18g

333. Lamb Chops on Chaffle

Preparation time: 10 minutes
Cooking time: 15 minutes
Servings: 2
Ingredients:
   - 4 eggs
   - 2 cup mozzarella cheese, grated
   - 1 tsp. garlic powder
   - ¼ cup heavy cream
   - 6 tbsp. almond flour
   - 2 tsp. baking powder
   - a pinch salt and pepper
   Lamb Chops:
   - 2 tbsp. herbed butter
   - 1 lb. lamb chops
   - salt and pepper to taste
   - 1 tsp. freshly chopped rosemary
   Other:
   - 2 tbsp. butter to brush the waffle maker
   - 2 tbsp. freshly chopped parsley for garnish

Directions:
Preheat the waffle maker.

Add the eggs, mozzarella cheese, salt and pepper, garlic powder, heavy cream, almond flour, and baking powder to a bowl and mix until combined.

Brush the heated waffle maker with butter and add a few tbsp. of the batter.

Close the lid and cook for about 7 minutes, depending on your waffle maker.

Meanwhile, heat a non-stick frying pan and rub the lamb chops with herbed butter, salt and pepper, and freshly chopped rosemary.

Cook the lamb chops for about 3-4 minutes on each side.

Serve each chaffle with a few lamb chops and sprinkle on some freshly chopped parsley for a nice presentation.

Per serving: Calories: 466Kcal; Fat: 39g; Carbs: 2g; Protein: 26g

334. Chicken Parmesan Chaffles

Preparation time: 10 minutes
Cooking time: 8 minutes
Servings: 1
Ingredients:

- 1/3 cup chicken
- 1 egg
- 1/3 cup parmesan
- ¼ tsp. basil
- ¼ garlic
- 2 tbsp. tomato sauce
- 2 tbsp. mozzarella cheese

Directions:

Heat up your Mini Dash waffle maker.

In a small-sized bowl, mix the egg, cooked chicken, basil, garlic, parmesan, and mozzarella cheese.

Add ½ of the batter into your mini waffle maker and cook for 4 minutes. If it is still not cooked properly, let it cook for another 2 minutes.

Use the rest of the batter to make a second chaffle.

Remove from the pan after cooking and set aside for 2 minutes.

Top with 1-2 tbsp. of sauce on each chicken parmesan chaffle. Then sprinkle 1-2 tbsp. mozzarella cheese.

Put the chaffles in the oven or a toaster oven at 400°F and cook until the cheese is melted.

Per serving: Calories: 352Kcal; Fat: 33g; Carbs: 1g; Protein: 25g

335. Pork Tzatziki Chaffle

Preparation time: 10 minutes
Cooking time: 25 minutes
Servings: 4
Ingredients:

- 4 eggs
- 2 cup grated provolone cheese
- salt and pepper to taste
- 1 tsp. dried rosemary
- 1 tsp. dried oregano

Pork Loin:

- 2 tbsp. olive oil
- 1 lb. pork tenderloin
- salt and pepper to taste

Tzatziki Sauce:

- 1 cup sour cream
- salt and pepper to taste
- 1 cucumber, peeled and diced
- 1 tsp. garlic powder
- 1 tsp. dried dill

Other:

- 2 tbsp. butter to brush the waffle maker

Directions:

Preheat the waffle maker.

Add the eggs, grated provolone cheese, dried rosemary, and dried oregano to a bowl; season with salt and pepper to taste.

Mix until combined.

Brush the heated waffle maker with butter and add a few tbsp. of the batter.

Cook for about 7 minutes or until golden.

Meanwhile, warm the olive oil in a non-stick frying pan.

Season the pork tenderloin generously with salt and pepper and cook for 7 minutes on each side. Mix the sour cream, salt and pepper, diced cucumber, garlic powder, and dried dill in a bowl.

Serve each chaffle with a few tbsp. of tzatziki sauce and slices of pork tenderloin.

Per serving: Calories: 513Kcal; Fat: 35g; Carbs: 2g; Protein: 21g

336. Lamb Kebabs on Chaffles

Preparation time: 10 minutes
Cooking time: 15 minutes
Servings: 4
Ingredients:

- 4 eggs
- 2 cup grated mozzarella cheese
- 1 tsp. garlic powder
- ¼ cup Greek yogurt
- ½ cup coconut flour
- 2 tsp. baking powder
- a pinch salt and pepper

Lamb Kebabs:

- 1 lb. ground lamb meat
- salt and pepper to taste
- 1 egg
- 2 tbsp. almond flour
- 1 spring onion, finely chopped
- ½ tsp. dried garlic
- 2 tbsp. olive oil

Other:

- 2 tbsp. butter to brush the waffle maker
- ¼ cup sour cream for serving
- 4 sprigs of fresh dill for garnish

Directions:

Preheat the waffle maker.

Add the eggs, mozzarella cheese, salt and pepper, garlic powder, Greek yogurt, coconut flour, and baking powder to a bowl.

Mix until combined.

Brush the heated waffle maker with butter and add a few tbsp. of the batter.

Close the lid and cook for about 7 minutes, depending on your waffle maker.

Meanwhile, add the ground lamb, salt and pepper, egg, almond flour, chopped spring onion, and dried garlic to a bowl. Mix and form medium-sized kebabs.

Impale each kebab on a skewer. Heat the olive oil in a frying pan.

Cook the lamb kebabs for about 3 minutes on each side.

Serve each chaffle with a tbsp. of sour cream and one or two lamb kebabs. Decorate with fresh dill.

Per serving: Calories: 486Kcal; Fat: 36g; Carbs: 2g; Protein: 18g

337. Creamy Bacon Salad on a Chaffle

Preparation time: 10 minutes
Cooking time: 15 minutes
Servings: 4
Ingredients:

- 4 eggs
- 1½ cup mozzarella cheese, grated
- ½ cup parmesan cheese
- salt and pepper to taste
- 1 tsp. dried oregano
- ¼ cup almond flour
- 2 tsp. baking powder

Bacon Salad:

- ½ lb. cooked bacon
- 1 cup cream cheese
- 1 tsp. dried oregano
- 1 tsp. dried basil
- 1 tsp. dried rosemary
- 2 tbsp. lemon juice

Other:

- 2 tbsp. butter to brush the waffle maker
- 2 spring onions, finely chopped, for serving

Directions:

Preheat the waffle maker.

Add the eggs, mozzarella cheese, parmesan cheese, salt and pepper, dried oregano, almond flour, and baking powder to a bowl.

Mix until combined.

Brush the heated waffle maker with butter and add a few tbsp of the batter.

Close the lid and cook for about 7 minutes, depending on your waffle maker.

Meanwhile, chop the cooked bacon into smaller pieces and place them in a bowl with the cream cheese. Season with dried oregano, dried basil, dried rosemary, and lemon juice.

Mix until combined and spread each chaffle with the creamy bacon salad.

To serve, sprinkle some freshly chopped spring onion on top.

Per serving: Calories: 366Kcal; Fat: 23g; Carbs: 2g; Protein: 18g

338. Beef and Sour Cream Chaffles

Preparation time: 10 minutes
Cooking time: 15 minutes
Servings: 4
Ingredients:
  Batter:

- 4 eggs
- 2 cup grated mozzarella cheese
- 3 tbsp. coconut flour
- 3 tbsp. almond flour
- 2 tsp. baking powder
- salt and pepper to taste
- 1 tbsp. freshly chopped parsley

  Seasoned Beef:

- 1 lb. beef tenderloin
- salt and pepper to taste
- 2 tbsp. olive oil
- 1 tbsp. Dijon mustard

  Other:

- 2 tbsp. olive oil to brush the waffle maker
- ¼ cup sour cream for garnish
- 2 tbsp. freshly chopped spring onion for garnish

Directions:

Preheat the waffle maker.

Add the eggs, grated mozzarella cheese, coconut flour, almond flour, baking powder, salt and pepper, and freshly chopped parsley to a bowl.

Mix until just combined, and you have a creamy batter.

Brush the heated waffle maker with olive oil and add a few tbsp of the batter.

Close the lid and cook for about 7 minutes, depending on your waffle maker.

Meanwhile, warm the olive oil in a non-stick pan over medium heat.

Use salt and pepper to season the beef tenderloin and spread the whole piece of beef tenderloin with Dijon mustard.

Cook on each side for about 4-5 minutes.

Serve each chaffle with sour cream and slices of the cooked beef tenderloin.

Garnish with freshly chopped spring onion.

Per serving: Calories: 255Kcal; Fat: 10g; Carbs: 6g; Protein: 34g

339. Pork Loin Sandwich Chaffle

Preparation time: 10 minutes
Cooking time: 15 minutes
Servings: 4
Ingredients:

- 4 eggs
- 1 cup mozzarella cheese, grated
- 1 cup parmesan cheese, grated
- salt and pepper to taste
- 2 tbsp. cream cheese
- 6 tbsp. coconut flour
- 2 tsp. baking powder

Pork Loin:

- 2 tbsp. olive oil
- 1 lb. pork loin
- salt and pepper to taste
- 2 garlic cloves, minced
- 1 tbsp. freshly chopped thyme

Other:

- 2 tbsp. cooking spray to brush the waffle maker
- 4 lettuce leaves for serving
- 4 slices of tomato for serving
- ¼ cup sugar-free mayonnaise for serving

Directions:

Preheat the waffle maker.

Add the eggs, mozzarella cheese, parmesan cheese, salt and pepper, cream cheese, coconut flour, and baking powder to a bowl.

Mix until combined.

With cooking spray, grease your waffle maker and add a few tbsp. of the batter.

Close the lid and cook for about 7 minutes, depending on your waffle maker.

Meanwhile, heat the olive oil in a non-stick frying pan and season the pork loin with salt and pepper, minced garlic, and freshly chopped thyme.

Cook the pork loin for about 5 minutes on each side.

Cut each chaffle in half and add some mayonnaise, lettuce leaf, tomato slice, and sliced pork loin on one half.

Cover the sandwich with the other chaffle half and serve.

Per serving: Calories: 486Kcal; Fat: 34g; Carbs: 8g; Protein: 22g

340. Beef Chaffles Tower

Preparation time: 10 minutes
Cooking time: 15 minutes
Servings: 4
Ingredients:
  Batter:

- 4 eggs
- 2 cup mozzarella cheese, grated
- salt and pepper to taste
- 2 tbsp. almond flour
- 1 tsp. Italian seasoning

  Beef:

- 2 tbsp. butter
- 1 lb. beef tenderloin

- salt and pepper to taste
- 1 tsp. chili flakes

Other:
- 2 tbsp. cooking spray to brush the waffle maker

Directions:
Preheat the waffle maker.

Add the eggs, grated mozzarella cheese, salt and pepper, almond flour, and Italian seasoning to a bowl.

Mix until everything is fully combined.

Grease your waffle maker using a non-stick cooking spray and add a few tbsp. of the batter.

Cook for about 7 minutes or until golden.

Meanwhile, heat the butter in a non-stick frying pan and season the beef tenderloin with salt and pepper and chili flakes.

Cook the beef tenderloin for about 5 minutes on each side.

When serving, assemble the chaffle tower by placing one chaffle on a plate, a layer of diced beef tenderloin, another chaffle, another layer of beef, and so on until you finish with the chaffles and beef.

Per serving: Calories: 442Kcal; Fat: 34g; Carbs: 2g; Protein: 23g

341. Red Peppers BBQ Sauce Chaffles

Preparation time: 10 minutes
Cooking time: 8-10 minutes
Servings: 2

Ingredients:
Batter:
- 4 red peppers
- 2 eggs
- 1 cup grated cheddar cheese
- ¼ cup cream cheese
- ¼ cup BBQ sauce
- salt and pepper to taste
- 2 cloves garlic, minced

Other:
- 2 tbsp. butter to brush the waffle maker
- ¼ cup BBQ sauce for serving
- 2 tbsp. freshly chopped parsley for garnish

Directions:
Preheat your oven to 220 degrees C (430 F)

Slice the peppers into thin strips

Roast the peppers strips in the oven for about 20 minutes

Preheat the waffle maker.

Add the eggs, cheddar cheese, cream cheese, BBQ sauce, salt and pepper, and minced garlic to a bowl.

Mix everything to have your batter.

Brush the heated waffle maker with butter and add a few tbsp of the batter.

Close the lid and cook for about 8-10 minutes, depending on your waffle maker.

Serve each chaffle with a tbsp. of BBQ sauce and red peppers strips with a sprinkle of freshly chopped parsley.

Per serving: Calories: 370Kcal; Fat: 28g; Carbs: 1g; Protein: 21g

CHAPTER 5:

Dessert and Cake Chaffles

342. Butter and Cream Cheese Chaffles

Preparation time: 10 minutes
Cooking time: 16 minutes
Servings: 2
Ingredients:

- 2 tbsp. butter, melted and cooled
- 2 large organic eggs
- 2 oz. cream cheese, softened
- ¼ cup powdered erythritol
- 1½ tsp. organic vanilla extract
- a pinch of salt
- ¼ cup almond flour
- 2 tbsp. coconut flour
- 1 tsp. organic baking powder

Directions:
Preheat a mini waffle iron and then grease it.
In a bowl, add the butter and eggs and beat until creamy.
Add the cream cheese, erythritol, vanilla extract, and salt, and beat until well combined.
Add the flours and baking powder and beat until well combined.
Place ¼ of the mixture into the preheated waffle iron and cook for about 4 minutes.
Repeat with the remaining mixture.
Serve warm.
Per serving: Calories: 287Kcal; Fat: 22g; Carbs: 3g; Protein: 15g

343. Peanut Butter Chaffles

Preparation time: 5 minutes
Cooking time: 8 minutes
Servings: 2
Ingredients:

- 1 organic egg, beaten
- ½ cup mozzarella cheese, shredded
- 3 tbsp. granulated erythritol
- 2 tbsp. peanut butter

Directions:
Preheat the mini waffle iron and then grease it.
In a medium-sized bowl, put all the ingredients, and with a fork, mix until a homogeneous mixture is formed.
Spoon half of the batter into the preheated waffle iron and cook for about 4 minutes.
Repeat with the remaining mixture.
Serve warm.
Per serving: Calories: 245Kcal; Fat: 20g; Carbs: 4g; Protein: 18g

344. Almond Butter Chaffles

Preparation time: 5 minutes
Cooking time: 10 minutes
Servings: 2
Ingredients:

- 1 large organic egg, beaten
- 1/3 cup mozzarella cheese, shredded
- 1 tbsp. erythritol
- 2 tbsp. almond butter
- 1 tsp. organic vanilla extract

Directions:
Preheat a mini waffle iron and then grease it.
Combine all the ingredients in a medium-sized bowl. Mix until thoroughly blended.
Spoon half of the batter into your waffle iron and cook for about 3-5 minutes.
Repeat with the remaining mixture.
Per serving: Calories: 270Kcal; Fat: 21g; Carbs: 1g; Protein: 18g

345. Cinnamon Chaffles

Preparation time: 10 minutes
Cooking time: 8 minutes
Servings: 2
Ingredients:
Chaffles:

- 1 large organic egg, beaten
- ¾ cup mozzarella cheese, shredded
- ½ tbsp. unsalted butter, melted
- 2 tbsp. blanched almond flour
- 2 tbsp. erythritol
- ½ tsp. ground cinnamon
- ½ tsp. Psyllium husk powder
- ¼ tsp. organic baking powder
- ½ tsp. organic vanilla extract

Toppings:

- 1 tsp. powdered erythritol
- ¾ tsp. ground cinnamon

Directions:
Preheat the waffle iron and then grease it.
For chaffles: In a medium bowl, put all the ingredients and, with a fork, mix until thoroughly blended.
Cook half of the mixture into the preheated waffle iron for about 3-5 minutes.
Repeat with the remaining mixture.
Meanwhile, for topping: In a small bowl, mix together the erythritol and cinnamon.
Place the chaffles onto serving plates and set them aside to cool slightly.
Sprinkle with the cinnamon mixture and serve immediately.
Per serving: Calories: 342Kcal; Fat: 10g; Carbs: 2g; Protein: 18g

346. Layered Chaffles

Preparation time: 5 minutes
Cooking time: 10 minutes
Servings: 1
Ingredients:

- 1 organic egg, beaten and divided
- ½ cup cheddar cheese, shredded and divided
- ½ tsp. capers, chopped

Directions:
Preheat the mini waffle iron and then grease it.
Mix the egg and capers.
Place about ⅛ cup of cheese in the bottom of the waffle iron and top with half of the beaten egg and capers.
Now, place ⅛ cup of cheese on top and cook for about 4-5 minutes.
Repeat with the remaining cheese and egg.
Per serving: Calories: 300Kcal; Fat: 25g; Carbs: 1g; Protein: 20g

347. Blueberry Cream Cheese Chaffles

Preparation time: 10 minutes
Cooking time: 8 minutes
Servings: 1
Ingredients:
- 1 organic egg, beaten
- 1/3 cup mozzarella cheese, shredded
- 1 tsp. cream cheese, softened
- 1 tsp. coconut flour
- ¼ tsp. organic baking powder
- ¾ tsp. powdered erythritol
- ¼ tsp. ground cinnamon
- ¼ tsp. organic vanilla extract
- a pinch of salt
- 1 tbsp. fresh blueberries

Directions:
Preheat the mini waffle iron and then grease it.
In a mixing bowl, combine all the ingredients except for blueberries, and stir until well combined.
Fold in the blueberries.
Cook half of the mixture into the preheated waffle iron for about 4 minutes.
Repeat with the remaining mixture.
Serve them warm.
Per serving: Calories: 280Kcal; Fat: 19g; Carbs: 3g; Protein: 15g

348. Raspberry and Cream Cheese Chaffles

Preparation time: 10 minutes
Cooking time: 8 minutes
Servings: 1
Ingredients:
- 1 organic egg, beaten
- 1 tbsp. cream cheese, softened
- ½ cup mozzarella cheese, shredded
- 1 tbsp. powdered erythritol
- ¼ tsp. organic raspberry extract
- ¼ tsp. organic vanilla extract

Directions:
Preheat your mini waffle iron and then grease it.
In a medium-sized bowl, put all the ingredients, and with a fork, mix until fully blended.
Spoon half of the mixture into your waffle iron and cook for about 4 minutes.
Repeat with the remaining mixture.
Serve them warm.
Per serving: Calories: 260Kcal; Fat: 19g; Carbs: 1g; Protein: 15g

349. Easy Red Velvet Chaffles

Preparation time: 10 minutes
Cooking time: 8 minutes
Servings: 1
Ingredients:
- 2 tbsp. cacao powder
- 2 tbsp. erythritol
- 1 organic egg, beaten
- 2 drops super red food coloring
- ¼ tsp. organic baking powder
- 1 tbsp. heavy whipping cream

Directions:
Preheat your mini waffle iron and then grease it.
In a medium-sized bowl, put all the ingredients, and with a fork, mix until thoroughly blended.
Pour half of the mixture into the preheated waffle iron and cook for about 4 minutes.
Repeat with the remaining mixture.
Serve them warm.
Per serving: Calories: 170Kcal; Fat: 16g; Carbs: 1g; Protein: 8g

350. Walnut Pumpkin Chaffles

Preparation time: 10 minutes
Cooking time: 10 minutes
Servings: 1
Ingredients:
- 1 organic egg, beaten
- ½ cup mozzarella cheese, shredded
- 2 tbsp. almond flour
- 1 tbsp. sugar-free pumpkin puree
- 1 tsp. erythritol
- ¼ tsp. ground cinnamon
- 2 tbsp. walnuts, toasted and chopped

Directions:
Preheat your mini waffle iron and then grease it.
Add all the ingredients in a medium-sized bowl, except pecans, and mix until fully blended.
Fold in the walnuts.
Fill the waffle maker with half of the batter and close the lid. Cook for about 5 minutes.
Repeat with the remaining mixture.
Serve them warm.
Per serving: Calories: 254Kcal; Fat: 22g; Carbs: 2g; Protein: 20g

351. Nutmeg Cream Cheese Chaffles

Preparation time: 10 minutes
Cooking time: 10 minutes
Servings: 1
Ingredients:
- 1 organic egg, beaten
- ½ cup mozzarella cheese, shredded
- 2 tsp. heavy cream
- 1 tsp. cream cheese, softened
- 1 tbsp. almond flour
- 1 tbsp. erythritol
- ½ tsp. ground nutmeg
- ½ tsp. organic baking powder
- 1 tsp. organic vanilla extract

Directions:
Preheat the mini waffle iron and then grease it.
In a medium bowl, put all the ingredients, and with a fork, mix until fully blended.
Pour half of the mixture into the preheated waffle iron and cook for about 3-5 minutes.
Repeat with the remaining mixture.
Serve them warm.
Per serving: Calories: 270Kcal; Fat: 23g; Carbs: 3g; Protein: 21g

352. Mozzarella Basic Chaffles

Preparation time: 1 Minute
Cooking time: 6 minutes
Servings: 1
Ingredients:
- 1 large egg
- ½ cup mozzarella cheese finely chopped

Directions:
Connect a waffle maker and heat.
Break the eggs into small bowls and beat with a fork. Add mozzarella cheese and mix.
Spray the non-stick spray on the waffle iron.
Pour half of the egg mixture into your heated waffle iron and cook for 2-3 minutes.
Carefully remove the waffle and cook the remaining dough.
Serve them warm with butter and sugar-free syrup.
Note: Try adding a little vanilla or cinnamon for the next level of breakfast chaffle!
Per serving: Calories: 220Kcal; Fat: 16g; Carbs: 3g; Protein: 20g

353. Pumpkin Chaffle

Preparation time: 5 minutes
Cooking time: 5 minutes
Servings: 1
Ingredients:
- ½ oz. cream cheese
- 1 large egg
- ½ cup mozzarella cheese (shredded)
- 2 tbsp. pumpkin puree
- 2½ tbsp. erythritol
- 3 tsp. coconut flour
- ½ tbsp. pumpkin pie spice
- ½ tsp. of vanilla essence (optional)
- ¼ tsp. baking powder (optional)

Directions:
Preheat the waffle iron for about 5 minutes until hot.
If your recipe includes cream cheese, put it in a bowl first. Gently heat in a microwave (15-30 seconds) or double boiler until soft and stir.
Stir all the remaining ingredients (except toppings, if any).
Pour a sufficient amount of chaffle dough into the waffle maker and cover the surface firmly (For a normal waffle maker, about ½ cup, for a mini waffle maker, about ¼ cup).
Cook for about 3-4 minutes until brown and crisp.
Remove the chaffle from the waffle maker with care and leave it aside for a crisp noise (cooling is important for the texture!) If there is any dough, repeat with the remaining dough.
Per serving: Calories: 308Kcal; Fat: 19g; Carbs: 5g; Protein: 23g

354. Pecan Pie Cake Chaffle

Preparation time: 15 minutes
Cooking time: 25 minutes
Servings: 1
Ingredients:
Pecan Pie Chaffle:
- 1 egg
- 2 tbsp. cream cheese
- ½ tbsp. maple extract
- 4 tbsp. almond flour
- 1 tbsp. Sukrin Gold
- ½ tbsp. baking powder
- 2 tbsp. chopped pecan
- 1 tbsp. heavy whipping cream

Pecan Pie Filling:
- 2 tbsp. butter
- 1 tbsp. Sukrin Gold
- 2 tbsp. chopped pecan
- 2 tbsp. heavy whipping cream
- 2 tbsp. maple syrup
- 2 large egg yolks
- a pinch of salt

Directions:
In a small saucepan, add sweetener, butter, syrups, and heavy whipping cream and use a low flame to heat.
Mix all the ingredients well together.
Remove from the heat and add egg yolks and mix.
Now, put it on the heat again and stir.
Add pecan and salt to the mixture and let it simmer.
It will thicken, then remove from the heat and let it rest.
For the chaffles, add all the ingredients, except pecans, and blend.
Now, add pecan with a spoon.
Preheat your waffle maker and grease it.
Pour the mixture into the lower plate of the waffle maker and spread it evenly to cover the plate properly, and close the lid.
Cook for about 4 minutes to achieve the desired crunch.
Take the chaffle off the heat and set it aside for around one minute.
Use the remaining ingredients to create as many chaffle as you can.
Add 1/3 of the previously-prepared pecan pie filling to the chaffle and arrange it like a cake.
Per serving: Calories: 405Kcal; Fat: 32g; Carbs: 2g; Protein: 23g

355. German Chocolate Chaffle Cake

Preparation time: 5 minutes
Cooking time: 10 minutes
Servings: 1
Ingredients:
Chocolate Chaffles:
- 1 egg
- 2 tbsp. cream cheese
- 1 tbsp. powdered sweetener
- ½ tbsp. vanilla extract
- ¼ tsp. instant coffee powder
- 1 tbsp. almond flour
- 1 tbsp. cocoa powder (unsweetened)

Filling:
- 1 egg yolk
- ¼ cup heavy cream
- 1 tbsp. butter
- 2 tbsp. powdered sweetener
- ½ tsp. caramel
- ¼ cup coconut flakes
- 1 tsp. coconut flour
- ¼ cup chopped pecans

Directions:
Preheat your waffle maker and grease it.
In a mixing bowl, beat the eggs and add the remaining chaffle ingredients.
Mix them all well.
Pour the mixture into the lower plate of the waffle maker and spread it evenly to cover the plate properly, and close the lid.
Cook for at least 4 minutes to get the desired crunch.
Remove the chaffle from the heat and let them cool completely.
Repeat the process to create more chaffles.
In a small pan, mix the heavy cream, egg yolk, sweetener, and butter at low heat for around 5 minutes.
Remove from the heat and add the remaining ingredients to make the filling.

Stack chaffles on one another and add filling in between to enjoy the cake.

Per serving: Calories: 460Kcal; Fat: 39g; Carbs: 3g; Protein: 19g

356. Chocolate Cake Almond Chaffle

Preparation time: 5 minutes
Cooking time: 10 minutes
Servings: 1
Ingredients:

Chocolate Chaffles:
- 1 egg
- 2 tbsp. cream cheese
- 1 tbsp. powdered sweetener
- ½ tbsp. vanilla extract
- ¼ tsp. instant coffee powder
- 1 tbsp. almond flour
- 1 tbsp. cocoa powder (unsweetened)

Coconut Filling:
- 1½ tbsp. melted coconut oil
- 1 tbsp. heavy cream
- 4 tbsp. cream cheese
- 1 tbsp. powdered sweetener
- ½ tbsp. vanilla extract
- ¼ cup finely shredded coconut
- 14 whole almonds

Directions:
Plug in your waffle maker to preheat it and grease it.
Add all the chaffle ingredients n a medium-sized bowl and mix them well.
Pour the mixture into the lower plate of the waffle maker and spread it evenly to cover the plate properly.
Close the lid.
Cook for about 4 minutes to achieve the desired crunch.
Take the chaffle off the heat and set it aside for around one minute.
Repeat the steps to create as many chaffle as the batter allow.
Except for almonds, add all the filling ingredients in a bowl and mix well.
Spread the filling on the chaffle and spread almonds on top with another chaffle at almonds—stack the chaffles and fillings like a cake and enjoy.

Per serving: Calories: 385Kcal; Fat: 25g; Carbs: 1g; Protein: 14g

357. Easy Peanut Butter Cake Chaffle

Preparation time: 5 minutes
Cooking time: 10 minutes
Servings: 2
Ingredients:

Chaffles:
- 1 egg
- 2 tbsp. peanut butter (sugar-free)
- 2 tbsp. monk fruit
- ¼ tsp. baking powder
- ¼ tsp. peanut butter extract
- 1 tsp. heavy whipping cream
- 4 tbsp. peanut butter for the assembling (sugar-free)

Directions:
Grease your waffle maker and preheat it.
In a mixing bowl, beat eggs and add all the chaffle ingredients.
Mix them all well and pour the mixture into the lower plate of the waffle maker.
Close the lid and cook for about 4 minutes or until golden and crispy.
Remove the chaffle from the heat and keep it aside for around a few minutes.
Repeat the process to create more chaffles.

Assemble the chaffles in a way that in between two chaffles, you put the peanut butter and make the cake.

Per serving: Calories: 264Kcal; Fat: 23g; Carbs: 4g; Protein: 14g

358. Nuts and Cream Cake Chaffle

Preparation time: 8 minutes
Cooking time: 12 minutes
Servings: 2
Ingredients:

Chaffles:
- 4 eggs
- 5 tbsp. almond flour
- 1 tbsp. sweetener
- 1½ tsp. baking powder
- 1 tbsp. butter (melted)
- 1 tsp. almond (chopped)
- 1 tsp. walnuts (chopped)
- 1 tsp. pecans (chopped)

Cream Frosting:
- 4 tbsp. cream cheese
- 2 tbsp. butter
- 2 tbsp. sweetener

Directions:
Blend the eggs, cream cheese, sweetener, almond flour, melted butter, and baking powder.
Make the mixture creamy.
Plug in your waffle maker to preheat it and grease it.
Pour the mixture into the lower plate of the waffle maker.
Close the lid.
Cook for about 4 minutes to get the desired crunch.
Once the chaffle is done, keep it aside to cool it.
Repeat the steps to create as many chaffle as the batter allow.
Garnish with chopped almonds, walnuts, and pecans.

Per serving: Calories: 230Kcal; Fat: 24g; Carbs: 2g; Protein: 12g

359. Banana Cake Pudding Chaffle

Preparation time: 1 hour
Cooking time: 10 minutes
Servings: 2
Ingredients:

Banana Chaffles:
- 2 tbsp. cream cheese
- 1 tsp. banana extract
- ¼ cup mozzarella cheese
- 1 egg
- 2 tbsp. sweetener
- 4 tbsp. almond flour
- 1 tsp. baking powder

Banana Pudding:
- 1 large egg yolk
- 3 tbsp. powdered sweetener
- ½ tsp. xanthan gum
- ½ cup heavy whipping cream
- ½ tsp. banana extract
- a pinch salt

Directions:
In a pan, add the powdered sweetener, heavy cream, and egg yolk and whisk continuously, so the mixture thickens.
Simmer for a minute only.
Add xanthan gum to the mixture and whisk again.
Remove the pan from the heat and add banana extract and salt and mix them all well.
Shift the mixture to a glass dish and refrigerate the pudding.

Grease your waffle maker and preheat it.

In a medium-sized bowl, add all the chaffle ingredients, and stir them well.

Pour the mixture into the lower plate of the waffle maker.

Cook for at least 5 minutes to achieve the required crunch.

Take the chaffle off the maker and keep it aside to cool it down.

Stack the chaffles and pudding one by one to form a cake.

Per serving: Calories: 287Kcal; Fat: 23; Carbs: 2g; Protein: 14g

360. Cream Coconut Cake Chaffle

Preparation time: 20 minutes
Cooking time: 4 minutes (+1 hour in refrigerator)
Servings: 2
Ingredients:

Chaffles:

- 2 eggs
- 2 tbsp. powdered sweetener
- 2 tbsp. cream cheese
- ½ tsp. vanilla extract
- 1 tbsp. butter (melted)
- 2 tbsp. coconut (shredded)
- ½ tsp. coconut extract

Filling:

- ¼ cup coconut (shredded)
- 2 tsp. butter
- 2 tbsp. monk fruit sweetener
- ¼ tsp. xanthan gum
- a pinch of salt
- 2 egg yolks
- 1/3 cup unsweetened almond
- 1/3 cup coconut milk

Garnishing:

- Whipped cream as per your taste
- 1 tbsp. Coconut (shredded)

Directions:
Plug in your waffle maker to preheat it and grease it.

In a medium-sized bowl, add all the chaffle ingredients, and stir them well.

Pour the mixture into the lower plate of the waffle maker. Close the lid.

Cook for about 4 minutes to get the desired crunch.

Take the chaffle off the heat and set it aside for around a few minutes.

Repeat the process to create as many chaffle as the mixture allow.

For the filling, in a small pan, cook almond milk and coconut together on medium heat in such a way that it only steams but doesn't boil.

In another bowl, lightly whisk the egg yolks and add milk to it continuously.

Heat the mixture, so it thickens; again, it must not boil.

Add the sweetener and whisk while adding the xanthan gum bit by bit.

Remove from the heat and mix all the other ingredients.

Mix well and refrigerate; the mixture will further thicken when cool.

Assemble the prepared chaffles and cream on top of one another to make the cake-like shape.

Garnish with coconuts and whipped cream at the end.

Per serving: Calories: 368Kcal; Fat: 24g; Carbs: 3g; Protein: 17g

361. Fluffy Mozzarella Chaffles

Preparation time: 10 minutes
Cooking time: 5 minutes
Servings: 2
Ingredients:

- 1 large egg
- 1 large egg white
- 2 tbsp. cream cheese

- ½ cup grated mozzarella cheese
- 2 tbsp. coconut flour
- ¼ cup almond flour
- ¼ tsp. vanilla extract
- ½ tsp. baking powder
- ¼ cup Swerve

Directions:
Preheat the mini waffle maker.

Place the egg, egg white, cream cheese, and mozzarella into a blender. Process until smooth. Add the remaining ingredients and process again.

Spoon one-quarter of the batter into the waffle maker. Cook for 2 to 4 minutes or until golden brown. Transfer the chaffle onto a cooling rack to cool. Repeat with the remaining batter.

Serve immediately.

Per serving: Calories: 325Kcal; Fat: 21g; Carbs: 3g; Protein: 14g

362. Blueberry Keto Chaffles

Preparation time: 3 minutes
Cooking time: 15 minutes
Servings: 2
Ingredients:

- 2 eggs
- 1 cup mozzarella cheese
- 2 tbsp. almond flour
- 2 tsp. Swerve, plus additional for serving
- 1 tsp. baking powder
- 1 tsp. cinnamon
- 3 tbsp. blueberries
- Non-stick cooking spray

Directions:
Preheat the mini waffle maker and grease it.

Stir together the eggs, mozzarella cheese, almond flour, Swerve, baking powder, cinnamon, and blueberries in a mixing bowl.

Pour in a little bit less than ¼ cup of blueberry waffle batter at a time. Cook the chaffle for 3 to 5 minutes.

Check it at the 3-minute mark to see if it is crispy and brown.

If it is not well cooked, let it cook for another 2 minutes.

Serve sprinkled with additional Swerve.

Per serving: Calories: 370Kcal; Fat: 22g; Carbs: 2g; Protein: 15g

363. Sprinkles Birthday Cake Chaffle

Preparation time: 10 minutes
Cooking time: 7 minutes
Servings: 2
Ingredients:

Cake Chaffle:

- 2 eggs
- ¼ almond flour
- 1 cup coconut powder
- 1 cup melted butter
- 2 tbsp. cream cheese
- 1 tsp. cake butter extract
- 1 tsp. vanilla extract
- 2 tsp. baking powder
- 2 tsp. confectionery sweetener or monk fruit
- ¼ tsp. xanthan powder whipped cream

Vanilla Frosting

- ½ cup heavy whipped cream
- 2 tbsp. sweetener or monk fruit
- ½ tsp. vanilla extract

Directions:

The mini waffle maker is preheated.

Add all the ingredients of the chaffle cake to a medium-sized blender and blend it to the top until it is smooth and creamy. Allow only a minute to sit with the batter. It may seem a little watery, but it's going to work well.

Cook 2 to 3 tbsp. of the batter into your waffle maker, and cook for about 2 to 3 minutes or until golden brown

Start to frost the whipped vanilla cream in a separate bowl.

Add all the ingredients and mix with a hand mixer until thick and soft peaks are formed by the whipping cream.

Until frosting your cake, allow the cake to cool completely. If you frost it too soon, the frosting will be melted.

Per serving: Calories: 238Kcal; Fat: 32g; Carbs: 2g; Protein: 16g

364. Chocolate Waffle Cake

Preparation time: 5 minutes
Cooking time: 5 minutes
Servings: 1
Ingredients:

- 2 tbsp. cocoa
- 2 tbsp. sweetener
- 1 egg
- ¼ tsp. baking powder
- 1 tbsp. heavy whipped cream

Frosted:

- 2 tbsp. monk fruit sweetener
- 2 tbsp. cream cheese softens, room temperature
- ¼ tsp. transparent vanilla

Directions:

Whip the egg in a small bowl.

Add the rest of the ingredients and mix well until smooth and creamy. Pour half of the batter into a mini waffle maker and cook until fully cooked for 2½ to 3 minutes.

Add the sweetener, cream cheese, and vanilla in a separate small bowl. Mix the frosting until all is well embedded.

Spread the frosting on the cake after it has cooled down to room temperature.

Per serving: Calories: 232Kcal; Fat: 15g; Carbs: 1g; Protein: 12g

365. Vanilla Twinkie Chaffle

Preparation time: 5 minutes
Cooking time: 4 minutes
Servings: 2
Ingredients:

- 2 tbsp. butter (cooled)
- 2 oz. cream cheese softened
- 2 large egg room temperature
- 1 tsp. vanilla essence
- optional ½ tsp. vanilla cupcake extract
- ¼ cup Lakanto monk fruit sweetener
- a pinch of salt
- ¼ cup almond flour
- 2 tbsp. coconut powder
- 1 tsp. baking powder

Directions:

Preheat the corndog maker.

Melt the butter and let it cool for 1 minute.

Whisk the butter until the eggs are creamy.

Add vanilla, extract, sweetener and salt and mix well.

Add almond flour, coconut flour, baking powder.

Mix until well incorporated.

Add ~2 tbsp of batter to each well and spread evenly.

Close and lock the lid and cook for 4 minutes.

Per serving: Calories: 210Kcal; Fat: 18g; Carbs: 1g; Protein: 11g

366. Apple Cake Chaffle

Preparation time: 5 minutes
Cooking time: 5 minutes
Servings: 1
Ingredients:

- ½ cup shredded apple
- 1 egg
- 2 tsp. butter melted
- 2 tsp. heavy whipped cream
- ¾ cup almond flour
- 1 walnut chopped
- 2 tsp. powder sweetener
- 2 tsp. cinnamon
- 1 tsp. pumpkin spice
- 1 tsp. baking powder

Cream Cheese Frosting:

- 4 oz. cream cheese softened
- ¼ cup powdered sweetener
- 1 tsp. of vanilla essence
- 1-2 tsp. heavy whipped cream according to your preferred consistency

Directions:

Mix the dry ingredients such as almond flour, cinnamon, pumpkin spices, baking powder, powdered sweeteners, and walnut pieces.

Add the grated carrots, eggs, melted butter, and cream.

Add 3 tsp. of batter to a preheated mini waffle maker. Cook for 2 ½-3 minutes.

Mix the frosted ingredients with a hand mixer.

Stack waffles and add a frost between each layer.

Per serving: Calories: 180Kcal; Fat: 8g; Carbs: 1g; Protein: 5g

367. Cinnamon Rolls Chaffle Cake

Preparation time: 5 minutes
Cooking time: 12 minutes
Servings: 1
Ingredients:

- 1 egg
- ½ cup mozzarella cheese
- ½ tsp. vanilla
- ½ tsp. cinnamon
- 1 tbsp. sweetener

Directions:

Crack the egg into a small bowl and beat it while preheating your waffle maker.

Add the remaining ingredients and stir well.

Grease the waffle maker with a non-stick cooking spray.

Cook half of the mixture for about 4 minutes or until golden.

Additional glaze: 1 tbsp. of cream cheese melted in a microwave for 15 seconds and 1 tbsp. of sweetener. Mix it and spread it over the oiled maker.

Additional frosting: 1 tbsp. of cream cheese (high temp), 1 tbsp. of room temp butter (low temp) and 1 tbsp. of sweetener. Mix all the ingredients together and spread to the top of the maker.

Top with optional frosting, glaze, nuts, sugar-free syrup, whipped cream, or simply dust with monk fruit sweets.

Per serving: Calories: 220Kcal; Fat: 16g; Carbs: 3g; Protein: 20g

368. Banana Pudding Chaffle Cake

Preparation time: 5 minutes
Cooking time: 5 minutes
Servings: 2
Ingredients:
- 1 large egg yolk
- ½ cup fresh cream
- 3 tsp. powder sweetener
- ¼-½ tsp. xanthan gum
- ½ tsp. banana extract

Banana Chaffles:
- 1 oz. softened cream cheese
- ¼ cup mozzarella cheese shredded
- 1 egg
- 1 tsp. banana extract
- 2 tsp. sweetener
- 1 tsp. baking powder
- 4 tsp. almond flour

Directions:
Mix the heavy cream, powdered sweetener, and egg yolk in a small pot.
Constantly whisk until the sweetener has dissolved and the mixture is thick.
Cooking for 1 minute. Add the xanthan gum and whisk.
Remove from the heat, add a pinch of salt and banana extract and stir well.
Transfer to a glass dish and cover the pudding with plastic wrap. Refrigerate.
Mix all the ingredients together. Cook in a preheated mini waffle maker.
Per serving: Calories: 188Kcal; Fat: 19g; Carbs: 1g; Protein: 12g

369. Peanut Butter Cake

Preparation time: 5 minutes
Cooking time: 5 minutes
Servings: 2
Ingredients:
- 2 tbsp. sugar-free peanut butter powder
- 2 tbsp. monk fruit confectioners' sugar
- 1 egg
- ¼ tsp. baking powder
- 1 tbsp. heavy whipped cream
- ¼ tsp. peanut butter extract

Peanut Butter Frosting:
- 2 tbsp. monk fruit confectioners' sugar
- 1 tbsp. butter softens, room temperature
- 1 tbsp. unsweetened natural peanut butter or peanut butter powder
- 2 tbsp. cream cheese softens, room temperature
- ¼ tsp. vanilla

Directions:
Serve the eggs in a small bowl.
Add the remaining ingredients and mix well until the dough is smooth and creamy.
If you don't have peanut butter extract, you can skip it. It adds absolutely wonderful, more powerful peanut butter flavor and is worth investing in this extract.
Pour half of the butter into a mini waffle maker and cook for 2-3 minutes until it is completely cooked.
In another small bowl, add vanilla, sweetener, cream cheese, and sugar-free natural peanut butter. Stir the frosting until everything is well incorporated.
When the waffle cake has completely cooled to room temperature, spread the frosting.
Per serving: Calories: 287Kcal; Fat: 17g; Carbs: 1g; Protein: 15g

370. Coconut Cream Cake Chaffle

Preparation time: 5 minutes
Cooking time: 3 minutes
Servings: 2
Ingredients:
Chaffles:
- 4 oz. cream cheese softens, room temperature
- 2 eggs
- 1 tbsp. butter
- 1½ tsp. vanilla essence
- 1 tbsp. favorite keto-approved sweetener
- 5 tbsp. coconut flour
- 1½ cup baking powder
- 1 tbsp. coconut

Cream Frosting:
- 2 oz. cream cheese softens, room temperature
- 2 cup butter room temp

Directions:
In a medium blender, add the cream cheese, eggs, melted butter, vanilla, sweetener, coconut flour, and baking powder.
Optional: add shredded coconut to the mixture or save them for topping. Both methods are great!
Mix the ingredients high until smooth and creamy.
Preheat the mini waffle maker.
Add the ingredients to the preheated waffle maker.
Cook for about 2-3 minutes until the waffle is complete.
Remove the chaffle and let cool.
In a separate bowl, add all the frosting ingredients together and start frosting. Stir until smooth and creamy.
When the chaffle has cooled completely, frost the cake.
Per serving: Calories: 398Kcal; Fat: 15g; Carbs: 5g; Protein: 8g

371. Boston Cream Pie Chaffle Cake

Preparation time: 10 minutes
Cooking time: 5 minutes
Servings: 2
Ingredients:
Cake Chaffle:
- 2 eggs
- ¼ cup almond flour
- 1 tsp. coconut flour
- 2 tbsp. melted butter
- 2 tbsp. cream cheese
- 20 drops Boston cream extract
- ½ tsp. vanilla essence
- ½ tsp. baking powder
- 2 tbsp. sweetener or monk fruit
- ¼ tsp. xanthan powder

Custard:
- ½ cup fresh cream
- ½ tsp. of vanilla essence
- ½ tbsp. Swerve confectioners' sugar
- 2 yolks
- ⅛ tsp. xanthan gum

For Ganache:
- 2 tbsp. Heavy Whipped cream
- 2 tbsp. unsweetened baking chocolate bar chopped
- 1 tbsp. Swerve confectioners' sugar

Directions:
Preheat the mini waffle iron to render the cake chops first.
Mix all the ingredients of the cake in a blender until smooth and fluffy. It's only supposed to take a few minutes.

Warm the heavy whipping cream to a boil on the stovetop. While it's dry, whisk the egg yolks together in a small separate dish.

Once the cream is boiling, add half of it to the egg yolks. Make sure you're whisking it together while you're slowly pouring it into the mixture.

Add the milk and egg mixture to the rest of the cream in the stovetop pan and stir vigorously for 2-3 minutes more.

Take the custard off the heat and whisk in your vanilla and xanthan gum. Then, set aside to cool and thicken.

Place the ganache ingredients in a small bowl. Microwave for about 20 seconds, stir. Repeat, if necessary. Careful not to overheat and roast the ganache. Just do it 20 seconds at a time until it's completely melted.

Assemble and enjoy your Boston cream pie chaffle cake!

Per serving: Calories: 4; Fat: 25g; Carbs: 2g; Protein: 7g

372. Easy Cake Chaffle with Fruits

Preparation time: 10 minutes
Cooking time: 5 minutes
Servings: 2
Ingredients:

Cake Chaffle:
- 2 eggs
- ¼ cup almond flour
- 1 tsp. coconut flour
- 2 tbsp. melted butter
- 2 tbsp. cream cheese
- 1 tsp. cake batter extract
- ½ tsp. vanilla essence
- ½ tsp. baking powder
- 2 tbsp. sweetener or monk fruit
- ¼ tsp. xanthan powder
- your favorite fruits, chopped

Directions:
Preheat the mini waffle maker.

In a medium-sized blender, add all the ingredients of the chaffle cake and blend high until smooth and creamy. Let the dough sit for only one minute. It may look a bit watery, but it works.

Add 2-3 tbsp of the dough to the waffle maker and cook for about 2-3 minutes until golden.

Add all the ingredients and mix with a hand mixer until whipped cream thickens and soft peaks form.

Let the cake chaffle cool completely and serve with the fruits beside.

Per serving: Calories: 245Kcal; Fat: 16g; Carbs: 2g; Protein: 7g

373. Shortcake Chaffles

Preparation time: 2 minutes
Cooking time: 4 minutes
Servings: 1
Ingredients:

- 1 egg
- 1 tbsp. heavy whipped cream
- 1 tsp. coconut flour
- 2 tbsp. Lakanto golden sweetener (use off wine)
- ½ tsp. cake batter extract
- ¼ tsp. baking powder

Directions:
Preheat the mini waffle maker.

Combine all the ingredients of the chaffle in a small bowl.

Pour half of the mixture of the chaffle into the waffle iron center. Allow 3-5 minutes of cooking. If the chaffle rises, lift the lid slightly for a couple of seconds until it begins to go back down and restore the lid as it finishes.

Carefully remove the second chaffle and repeat it. Let the chaffles sit for a couple of minutes to crisp up.

Add your desired amount of whipped cream and strawberries!
Note: The recipe is perfect in a standard waffle maker for either two mini chaffles or one chaffle.

Per serving: Calories: 176Kcal; Fat: 12g; Carbs: 2g; Protein: 6g

374. Pumpkin Cake Chaffle with Cream Cheese Frosting

Preparation time: 15 minutes
Cooking time: 28 minutes
Servings: 2
Ingredients:

Pumpkin chaffles:
- 2 eggs, beaten
- ½ tsp. pumpkin pie spice
- 1 cup finely grated mozzarella cheese
- 1 tbsp. pumpkin puree

Cream Cheese Frosting:
- 2 tbsp. cream cheese, softened
- 2 tbsp. Swerve confectioners' sugar
- ½ tsp. vanilla extract

Directions:
Chaffles:
Preheat the waffle iron.

In a medium bowl, mix the eggs, pumpkin pie spice, mozzarella cheese, and pumpkin puree.

Open the iron and add a quarter of the mixture. Close and cook until crispy, 7 minutes.

Transfer the chaffle to a plate and make 3 more chaffles with the remaining batter.

Cream Cheese Frosting:
Add the cream cheese, Swerve sugar and vanilla to a medium bowl, and whisk using an electric mixer until smooth and fluffy.

Layer the chaffles one on another, but with some frosting spread between the layers. Top with a bit of frosting.

Slice and serve them.

Per serving: Calories: 340Kcal; Fat: 17g; Carbs: 1g; Protein: 5g

375. S'mores Chaffles

Preparation time: 15 minutes
Cooking time: 28 minutes
Servings: 2
Ingredients:

- 2 eggs, beaten
- 1 cup finely grated gruyere cheese
- ½ tsp. vanilla extract
- 2 tbsp. Swerve brown sugar
- a pinch of salt
- ¼ cup unsweetened chocolate chips, melted
- 2 tbsp. low carb marshmallow fluff

Directions:
Preheat the waffle iron.

In a medium bowl, mix the eggs, gruyere cheese, vanilla, Swerve sugar, and salt.

Open the iron and add a quarter of the mixture. Close and cook until crispy, 7 minutes.

Transfer the chaffle to a plate and make 3 more chaffles with the remaining batter.

Spread half of the chocolate on two chaffles, add the marshmallow fluff, and cover with the other chaffles.

Swirl the remaining chocolate, slice in half, and serve them.

Per serving: Calories: 303Kcal; Fat: 14g; Carbs: 1g; Protein: 7g

376. Chocolate Cake Chaffles with Cream Cheese Frosting

Preparation time: 10 minutes
Cooking time: 28 minutes
Servings: 2
Ingredients:
    Chaffles:
- 2 eggs, beaten
- 1 cup finely grated gouda cheese
- 2 tsp. unsweetened cocoa powder
- ¼ tsp. sugar-free maple syrup
- 1 tbsp. cream cheese, softened

    Frosting:
- 3 tbsp. cream cheese, softened
- ¼ tsp. vanilla extract
- 2 tbsp. sugar-free maple syrup

Directions:
Chaffles:
Preheat the waffle iron.
In a medium bowl, mix all the ingredients for the chaffles.
Open the iron and add a quarter of the mixture. Close and cook until crispy, 7 minutes.
Transfer the chaffle to a plate and make 3 more chaffles with the remaining batter.
Frosting:
In a medium bowl, beat the cream cheese, vanilla extract, and maple syrup with a hand mixer until smooth.
Assemble the chaffles with the frosting to make the cake making sure to top the last layer with some frosting.
Slice and serve them.
Per serving: Calories: 350Kcal; Fat: 12g; Carbs: 1g; Protein: 5g

377. Lemon Cake Chaffle with Frosting

Preparation time: 10 minutes
Cooking time: 28 minutes
Servings: 22
Ingredients:
    Chaffles:
- 2 eggs, beaten
- ½ cup finely grated Swiss cheese
- 2 oz. cream cheese, softened
- ½ tsp. lemon extract
- 20 drops cake batter extract

    Frosting:
- ½ cup heavy cream
- 1 tbsp. sugar-free maple syrup
- ¼ tsp. lemon extract

Directions:
Chaffles:
Preheat the waffle iron.
In a medium bowl, mix all the ingredients for the chaffles.
Open the iron and add a quarter of the mixture. Close and cook until crispy, 7 minutes.
Transfer the chaffle to a plate and make 3 more chaffles with the remaining batter.
Frosting:
In a medium-sized bowl, using a hand mixer, beat the heavy cream, maple syrup, and lemon extract until fluffy.
Assemble the chaffles with the frosting to make the cake.
Slice and serve them.
Per serving: Calories: 210Kcal; Fat: 16g; Carbs: 2g; Protein: 12g

378. Butter Cake Almond Chaffle with Chocolate Butter Frosting

Preparation time: 20 minutes
Cooking time: 28 minutes
Servings: 1
Ingredients:
    Chaffles:
- 1 egg, beaten
- ⅓ cup finely grated mozzarella cheese
- 1 tbsp. almond flour
- 2 tbsp. almond butter
- 1 tbsp. Swerve confectioners' sugar
- ½ tsp. vanilla extract

    Chocolate Butter Frosting:
- 1½ cup butter, room temperature
- 1 cup unsweetened cocoa powder
- ½ cup almond milk
- 5 cup Swerve confectioners' sugar
- 2 tsp. vanilla extract

Directions:
Chaffles:
Preheat the waffle iron.
In a medium bowl, mix the egg, mozzarella cheese, almond flour, almond butter, Swerve confectioners' sugar, and vanilla extract.
Open the iron and add a quarter of the mixture. Close and cook until crispy, 7 minutes.
Transfer the chaffle to a plate and make 3 more chaffles with the remaining batter.
Frosting:
In a medium-sized bowl, stir the butter and cocoa powder until smooth.
Gradually, whisk in the almond milk and Swerve confectioners' sugar until smooth.
Add the vanilla extract and mix well.
Assemble the chaffles with the frosting to make the cake.
Slice and serve them.
Per serving: Calories: 280Kcal; Fat: 21g; Carbs: 1g; Protein: 20g

379. Tiramisu Chaffle

Preparation time: 20 minutes
Cooking time: 28 minutes
Servings: 2
Ingredients:
    Chaffles:
- 2 eggs, beaten
- 3 tbsp. cream cheese, softened
- ½ cup finely grated gouda cheese
- 1 tsp. vanilla extract
- ¼ tsp. erythritol

    Coffee Syrup:
- 2 tbsp. strong coffee, room temperature
- 3 tbsp. sugar-free maple syrup

    Filling:
- ¼ cup heavy cream
- 2 tsp. vanilla extract
- ¼ tsp. erythritol
- 4 tbsp. mascarpone cheese, room temperature
- 1 tbsp. cream cheese, softened

    Dusting:
- ½ tsp. unsweetened cocoa powder

Directions:

Chaffles:

Preheat the waffle iron.

In a medium bowl, mix all the ingredients for the chaffles.

Open the iron and add a quarter of the mixture. Close and cook until crispy, 7 minutes.

Transfer the chaffle to a plate and make 3 more with the remaining batter.

Coffee Syrup:

In a small bowl, mix the coffee and maple syrup. Set it aside.

Filling:

Beat the heavy cream, vanilla, and erythritol in a medium bowl using an electric hand mixer until stiff peaks form.

In another bowl, beat the mascarpone cheese and cream cheese until well combined. Add the heavy cream mixture and fold in. Spoon the mixture into a piping bag.

To Assemble:

Spoon 1 tbsp. of the coffee syrup on one chaffle and pipe some of the cream cheese mixture on top. Cover with another chaffle and continue the assembling process.

Generously dust with cocoa powder and refrigerate overnight.

When ready to enjoy, slice and serve them.

Per serving: Calories: 279Kcal; Fat: 22g; Carbs: 1g; Protein: 7g

380. Coconut Chaffles with Frosting

Preparation time: 15 minutes
Cooking time: 28 minutes
Servings: 2
Ingredients:

Chaffles:
- 2 eggs, beaten
- 2 tbsp. cream cheese, softened
- 1 cup finely grated Monterey Jack cheese
- 2 tbsp. coconut flour
- ¼ tsp. baking powder
- 1 tbsp. unsweetened shredded coconut
- 1 tbsp. walnuts, chopped

Frosting:
- ¼ cup unsalted butter, room temperature
- 3 tbsp. almond milk
- 2 tsp. mint extract
- 1 drops green food coloring
- 3 cup Swerve confectioners' sugar

Directions:

Chaffles:

Preheat the waffle iron.

In a medium bowl, mix all the ingredients for the chaffles.

Open the iron and add a quarter of the mixture. Close and cook until crispy, 7 minutes.

Transfer the chaffle to a plate and make 3 more with the remaining batter.

For the Frosting:

In a medium bowl, cream the butter using an electric hand mixer until smooth.

Gradually mix in the almond milk until smooth.

Add the mint extract and green food coloring; whisk until well combined.

Finally, mix in the Swerve confectioners' sugar a cup at a time until smooth.

Layer the chaffles with the frosting.

Slice and serve afterward.

Per serving: Calories: 352Kcal; Fat: 12g; Carbs: 3g; Protein: 8g

381. Ice Cream and Chaffles

Preparation time: 10 minutes
Cooking time: 14 minutes
Servings: 1
Ingredients:

- 1 egg, beaten
- ½ cup finely grated mozzarella cheese
- ¼ cup almond flour
- 2 tbsp. keto-approved sweetener
- ⅛ tsp. xanthan gum
- low-carb ice cream (flavor of your choice) for serving

Directions:

Preheat the waffle iron.

In a medium bowl, mix all the ingredients, except the ice cream.

Open the iron and add half of the mixture. Close and cook until crispy, 7 minutes.

Transfer the chaffle to a plate and make a second one with the remaining batter.

On each chaffle, add a scoop of low-carb ice cream, fold into half-moons and enjoy.

Per serving: Calories: 286Kcal; Fat: 18g; Carbs: 1g; Protein: 15g

CHAPTER 6:

Sandwich Chaffles

382. Strawberry Cream Sandwich Chaffle

Preparation time: 6 minutes
Cooking time: 6 minutes
Servings: 1
Ingredients:
Chaffles:
- 1 large organic egg, beaten
- ½ cup mozzarella cheese, shredded finely

Filling:
- 4 tsp. heavy cream
- 2 tbsp. powdered erythritol
- 1 tsp. fresh lemon juice
- a pinch of fresh lemon zest, grated
- 2 fresh strawberries, hulled and sliced

Directions:
Preheat your mini waffle iron and then grease it.
For chaffles: In a small bowl, add the egg and mozzarella cheese and stir to combine.
Cook for about 2 minutes half of the mixture into the preheated waffle iron.
Repeat with the remaining mixture to create the second chaffle.
Meanwhile, for the filling: in a bowl, place all the ingredients, except the strawberry, slices and with a hand mixer, beat until well combined.
Serve each chaffle with cream mixture and strawberry slices.
Per serving: Calories: 260Kcal; Fat: 18g; Carbs: 1g; Protein: 22g

383. Ham and Tomatoes Sandwich Chaffle

Preparation time: 6 minutes
Cooking time: 8 minutes
Servings: 1
Ingredients:
- 1 organic egg, beaten
- ½ cup Monterrey Jack cheese, shredded
- 1 tsp. coconut flour
- a pinch of garlic powder

Filling:
- 2 sugar-free ham slices
- 1 small tomato, sliced
- 2 lettuce leaves

Directions:
Preheat the mini waffle iron and then grease it.
In a medium bowl, put all the ingredients, and with a fork, mix until well combined.
Cook half of the mixture into the waffle iron for about 3-4 minutes.
Repeat with the remaining mixture.
Serve each chaffle with the filling ingredients.
Per serving: Calories: 275Kcal; Fat: 18g; Carbs: 3g; Protein: 12g

384. Salmon and Cheese Sandwich Chaffle

Preparation time: 6 minutes
Cooking time: 24 minutes
Servings: 2

Ingredients:
Chaffles:
- 2 organic eggs
- ½ oz. butter, melted
- 1 cup mozzarella cheese, shredded
- 2 tbsp. almond flour
- a pinch of salt

Filling:
- ½ cup smoked salmon
- 1/3 cup avocado, peeled, pitted, and sliced
- 2 tbsp. feta cheese, crumbled

Directions:
Preheat your mini waffle iron and then grease it.
For chaffles: In a medium bowl, put all the ingredients and, with a fork, mix until well combined. Place ¼ of the mixture into the preheated waffle iron and cook for about 5-6 minutes.
Repeat with the remaining mixture.
Serve each chaffle with the filling ingredients.
Per serving: Calories: 252Kcal; Fat: 16g; Carbs: 2g; Protein: 14g

385. Strawberry Cream Cheese Sandwich Chaffle

Preparation time: 6 minutes
Cooking time: 10 minutes
Servings: 2
Ingredients:
Chaffles:
- 2 organic eggs, beaten
- 1 tsp. organic vanilla extract
- 1 tbsp. almond flour
- 1 tsp. organic baking powder
- a pinch of ground cinnamon
- 1 cup mozzarella cheese, shredded

Filling:
- 2 tbsp. cream cheese, softened
- 2 tbsp. erythritol
- ¼ tsp. organic vanilla extract
- 2 fresh strawberries, hulled and chopped

Directions:
Preheat the mini waffle iron and then grease it.
For chaffles: in a bowl, add the egg and vanilla extract and mix well.
Add the flour, baking powder, and cinnamon, then mix until well combined.
Add the mozzarella cheese and stir well to combine.
Cook for around 4 minutes a quarter of the mixture on the mini waffle iron.
Repeat with the remaining mixture.
Meanwhile, for the filling: in a bowl, place all the ingredients, except the strawberry, pieces and with a hand mixer, beat until well combined.
Serve each chaffle with the cream cheese mixture and strawberry pieces.
Per serving: Calories: 282Kcal; Fat: 18g; Carbs: 2g; Protein: 21g

386. Egg and Bacon Sandwich Chaffle

Preparation time: 6 minutes
Cooking time: 20 minutes
Servings: 2
Ingredients:
Chaffles:
- 2 large organic eggs, beaten
- 4 tbsp. almond flour
- 1 tsp. organic baking powder
- 1 cup mozzarella cheese, shredded

Filling:
- 4 organic fried eggs
- 4 cooked bacon slices

Directions:
Preheat the mini waffle iron and then grease it.
In a medium-sized bowl, put all the ingredients, and with a fork, stir them until properly combined.
Cook for around 4 minutes a quarter of the mixture on the mini waffle iron.
Repeat with the remaining mixture.
Serve each chaffle with the filling ingredients.
Per serving: Calories: 340Kcal; Fat: 26g; Carbs: 2g; Protein: 24g

387. Blueberry Peanut Butter Sandwich Chaffle

Preparation time: 6 minutes
Cooking time: 10 minutes
Servings: 1
Ingredients:
- 1 organic egg, beaten
- ½ cup cheddar cheese, shredded

Filling
- 2 tbsp. erythritol
- ½ tbsp. butter, softened
- 1 tbsp. natural peanut butter
- 2 tbsp. cream cheese, softened
- ¼ tsp. organic vanilla extract
- 2 tsp. fresh blueberries

Directions:
Preheat the mini waffle iron and then grease it.
For chaffles: In a small bowl, add the egg and cheddar cheese and stir to combine.
Drop half of the mixture into the waffle maker and cook for about 5 minutes.
Repeat with the remaining mixture.
Meanwhile, for the filling: In a medium bowl, put all the ingredients and mix until well combined.
Serve each chaffle with the peanut butter mixture.
Per serving: Calories: 420Kcal; Fat: 26g; Carbs: 2g; Protein: 16g

388. Chocolate and Vanilla Sandwich

Preparation time: 6 minutes
Cooking time: 10 minutes
Servings: 2
Ingredients:
Chaffles:
- 1 organic egg, beaten
- 1 oz. cream cheese, softened
- 2 tbsp. almond flour
- 1 tbsp. cacao powder
- 2 tsp. erythritol
- 1 tsp. organic vanilla extract

Filling:
- 2 tbsp. cream cheese, softened
- 2 tbsp. erythritol
- ½ tbsp. cacao powder
- ¼ tsp. organic vanilla extract

Directions:
Preheat your mini waffle iron and then grease it.
For the chaffles: In a medium bowl, put all the ingredients and, with a fork, mix until well combined. Drop half of the mixture into the waffle maker and cook for about 3-5 minutes.
Repeat with the remaining mixture.
Meanwhile, for the filling: In a medium bowl, put all the ingredients, and with a hand mixer, beat until well combined.
Serve each chaffle with the chocolate mixture.
Per serving: Calories: 302Kcal; Fat: 22g; Carbs: 2g; Protein: 12g

389. Berry Sauce Sandwich Chaffle

Preparation time: 6 minutes
Cooking time: 12 minutes
Servings: 2
Ingredients:
Filling:
- 3 oz. frozen mixed berries, thawed with the juice
- 1 tbsp. erythritol
- 1 tbsp. water
- ¼ tbsp. fresh lemon juice
- 2 tsp. cream

Chaffles:
- 1 large organic egg, beaten
- ½ cup cheddar cheese, shredded
- 2 tbsp. almond flour

Directions:
For the berry sauce: in a pan, add the berries, erythritol, water, and lemon juice over medium heat and cook for about 8- minutes, pressing with the spoon occasionally.
Remove the pan of the sauce from the heat and set it aside to cool before serving.
Preheat a mini waffle iron and then grease it.
In a bowl, add the egg, cheddar cheese, and almond flour and beat until properly blended. Drop half of the mixture into the preheated waffle iron and cook for about 3-5 minutes.
Repeat with the remaining mixture.
Serve each chaffle with cream and berry sauce.
Per serving: Calories: 348Kcal; Fat: 26g; Carbs: 1g; Protein: 20g

390. Pork and Tomato Sandwich

Preparation time: 6 minutes
Cooking time: 16 minutes
Servings: 2
Ingredients:
Chaffles:
- 2 large organic eggs
- ¼ cup superfine blanched almond flour
- ¾ tsp. organic baking powder
- ½ tsp. garlic powder
- 1 cup cheddar cheese, shredded

Filling:
- 12 oz. cooked pork, cut into slices
- 1 tomato, sliced
- 4 lettuce leaves

Directions:
Preheat a mini waffle iron and then grease it.
For chaffles: in a bowl, add the eggs, almond flour, baking powder, and garlic powder, and beat until well combined.

Add the cheese and stir to combine.
Place ¼ of the mixture into the preheated waffle iron and cook for about 3 minutes.
Repeat with the remaining mixture.
Serve each chaffle with the filling ingredients.
Per serving: Calories: 367Kcal; Fat: 28g; Carbs: 1g; Protein: 20g

391. Tomato Sandwich Chaffle

Preparation time: 6 minutes
Cooking time: 6 minutes
Servings: 2
Ingredients:
   Chaffles:
   - 1 large organic egg, beaten
   - ½ cup Jack cheese, shredded finely
   - ⅛ tsp. organic vanilla extract
   Filling:
   - 1 small tomato, sliced
   - 2 tsp. fresh basil leaves

Directions:
Preheat a mini waffle iron and then grease it.
For the chaffles: In a small bowl, place all the ingredients and stir to combine.
Drop half of the mixture into the preheated waffle iron and cook for about 3 minutes.
Repeat with the remaining mixture.
Serve each chaffle with tomato slices and basil leaves.
Per serving: Calories: 315Kcal; Fat: 25g; Carbs: 1g; Protein: 15g

392. Salmon and Cream Sandwich Chaffle

Preparation time: 6 minutes
Cooking time: 8 minutes
Servings: 1
Ingredients:
   Chaffles:
   - 1 organic egg, beaten
   - ½ cup cheddar cheese, shredded
   - 1 tbsp. almond flour
   - 1 tbsp. fresh rosemary, chopped
   Filling:
   - ¼ cup smoked salmon
   - 1 tsp. fresh dill, chopped
   - 2 tbsp. cream

Directions:
Preheat a mini waffle iron and then grease it.
For chaffles: In a medium bowl, put all the ingredients and, with a fork, mix until well combined. Pour half of the mixture into the preheated waffle iron and cook for about 3-4 minutes.
Repeat with the remaining mixture.
Serve each chaffle with the filling ingredients.
Per serving: Calories: 209Kcal; Fat: 25g; Carbs: 1g; Protein: 21g

393. Tuna Sandwich Chaffle

Preparation time: 6 minutes
Cooking time: 8 minutes
Servings: 1
Ingredients:
   Chaffles:
   - 1 organic egg, beaten
   - ½ cup cheddar cheese, shredded
   - 1 tbsp. almond flour
   - a pinch of salt

Filling
   - ¼ cup water-packed tuna, flaked
   - 2 lettuce leaves

Directions:
Preheat a mini waffle iron and then grease it.
For chaffles: In a medium bowl, put all the ingredients and, with a fork, mix until well combined. Drop half of the mixture into the waffle iron and cook for about 3-4 minutes.
Repeat with the remaining mixture.
Serve each chaffle with the filling ingredients.
Per serving: Calories: 311Kcal; Fat: 26g; Carbs: 1g; Protein: 21g

394. Beef Sandwich Chaffle

Preparation time: 10 minutes
Cooking time: 15 minutes
Servings: 2
Ingredients:
   Batter:
   - 2 eggs
   - 2 cup mozzarella cheese, grated
   - 1 tsp. Italian seasoning
   - salt and pepper to taste
   Beef:
   - 2 tbsp. butter
   - 1 lb. beef tenderloin
   - salt and pepper to taste
   - 2 tsp. Dijon mustard
   - 1 tsp. dried paprika
   Other:
   - 2 tbsp. cooking spray to brush the waffle maker
   - 4 lettuce leaves for serving
   - 4 tomato slices for serving
   - 4 leaves fresh basil

Directions:
Preheat the waffle maker.
Add the eggs, grated mozzarella cheese, salt and pepper, and Italian seasoning to a bowl.
Mix until you have a creamy batter.
Grease your waffle maker using a non-stick cooking spray and add a few tbsp. of the batter.
Let it cook for about 7 minutes.
Meanwhile, melt and heat the butter in a non-stick frying pan.
Season the beef loin with salt and pepper, brush it with Dijon mustard, and sprinkle some dried paprika on top.
Cook the beef on each side for about 5 minutes.
Thinly slice the beef and assemble the chaffle sandwiches.
Cut each chaffle in half. On one half, place a lettuce leaf, tomato slice, basil leaf, and some sliced beef.
Cover with the other chaffle half and serve.
Per serving: Calories: 296Kcal; Fat: 26g; Carbs: 2g; Protein: 14g

395. Sloppy Joe Chaffles

Preparation time: 10 minutes
Cooking time: 5 minutes
Servings: 4
Ingredients:
   Sloppy Jaw:
   - 1 lb. ground beef
   - 1 tsp. onion powder
   - 1 tsp. garlic
   - 3 tbsp. tomato paste
   - ½ tsp.

- ¼ tsp. pepper
- 1 tbsp. chili powder
- 1 tsp. cocoa powder
- ½ cup bone soup beef flavor
- 1 tsp. coconut amino or soy sauce as you like
- 1 tsp. mustard powder
- 1 tsp. brown or screen golden
- ½ tsp. paprika

Corn Bread Chaffle:

- 1 egg
- ½ cup cheddar cheese
- 5 slice jalapeño, very small diced (pickled or fresh)
- 1 tsp. Frank's red-hot sauce
- ¼ tsp. corn extract is optional but tastes like real cornbread!
- a pinch salt

Directions:

First, cook the minced meat with salt and pepper.

Add all the remaining ingredients.

Cook the mixture while making the chaffle.

Preheat the waffle maker.

Put the eggs in a small bowl and add the remaining ingredients.

Spray to the waffle maker with a non-stick cooking spray.

Divide the mixture in half.

Simmer half of the mixture for about 4 minutes or until golden.

For a chaffle crispy rind, add 1 tsp. of cheese to the waffle maker for 30 seconds before adding the mixture.

Pour the warm stubby Joe mix into the hot chaffle and finish! Dinner is ready!

Note: You can also add diced jalapeños (fresh or pickled) to this basic chaffle recipe to make a jalapeño cornbread chaffle recipe!

Per serving: Calories: 396Kcal; Fat: 33g; Carbs: 2g; Protein: 17g

396. Broccoli and Cheese Sandwich Chaffle

Preparation time: 2 minutes
Cooking time: 8 minutes
Servings: 1
Ingredients:

- ½ cup cheddar cheese
- ¼ cup fresh chopped broccoli
- 1 egg
- ¼ tsp. garlic powder
- 1 tbsp. almond flour

Directions:

Preheat your waffle maker.

Beat the egg in a mixing bowl, and add the almond flour, cheddar cheese, and garlic powder. I find it easier to mix everything using a fork.

Add half of the broccoli and cheese batter to the waffle maker at a time.

Cook the batter for about 4 minutes or until

Allow each chaffle to firm up for 1-2 minutes on a plate. Enjoy alone or dipping in sour cream or ranch dressing.

Per serving: Calories: 220Kcal; Fat: 22g; Carbs: 1g; Protein: 18g

397. Dip Keto Chaffle Sandwich

Preparation time: 5 minutes
Cooking time: 12 minutes
Servings: 1
Ingredients:

- 1 egg white
- ¼ cup mozzarella cheese, shredded (packed)
- ¼ cup sharp cheddar cheese, shredded (packed)
- ¾ tsp. water

- 1 tsp. coconut flour
- ¼ tsp. baking powder
- a pinch of salt

Directions:

Preheat the oven to 425°F.

Plug in your waffle maker to preheat it and grease lightly once it is hot.

Blend all the ingredients in a medium-sized bowl until properly mixed.

Spoon out ½ of the batter on the waffle maker and close the lid.

Let it cook for about 4 minutes, and do not lift the lid until the cooking time is complete. Lifting the lid ahead of time can cause the batter to stick to the pan and ruin the recipe.

Set the chaffle aside after removing it from the waffle iron. Repeat the procedures with the remaining chaffle batter.

Add your favorite keto-friendly filling between two chaffles, and your sandwich is ready.

Tip: Before filling, add a slice of deli cheese or shredded cheese on top of the chaffles. Swiss and provolone are both great options.

Place the chaffles on the top rack of the oven for 5 minutes so that the cheese can melt.

Per serving: Calories: 240Kcal; Fat: 20g; Carbs: 3g; Protein: 20g

398. Blackberry Almond Chaffles

Preparation time: 5 minutes
Cooking time: 8 minutes
Servings: 1
Ingredients:

- ¼ cup cream cheese, soft
- ¼ cup blackberries
- 2 tbsp. almond flour
- 1 egg, whisked
- 1 tbsp. stevia
- ½ tsp. baking soda

Directions:

In a medium-sized bowl, mix the cream cheese with the berries and the other ingredients and whisk well.

Heat up the waffle iron over high heat, pour ¼ of the batter, close the waffle maker, cook for 8 minutes and transfer to a plate.

Repeat the process to create more chaffles and serve the chaffles warm.

Per serving: Calories: 229Kcal; Fat: 23g; Carbs: 1g; Protein: 15g

399. Coconut Sandwich Chaffle

Preparation time: 5 minutes
Cooking time: 10 minutes
Servings: 2
Ingredients:

- ½ cup cream cheese, soft
- 1 tbsp. coconut flesh, unsweetened and shredded
- 2 tsp. coconut oil, melted
- 1 tbsp. coconut flour
- 2 eggs, whisked
- 1 tbsp. erythritol
- 1 tsp. vanilla extract
- ½ tsp. almond extract

Directions:

In a bowl, combine the cream cheese with the melted coconut oil and the other ingredients and whisk well.

Heat up the waffle iron over high heat, pour ¼ of the batter, close the waffle maker, cook for 10 minutes and transfer it to a plate.

Repeat with the rest of the batter and serve the chaffles warm.

Per serving: Calories: 259Kcal; Fat: 25; Carbs: 2g; Protein: 15g

400. Nuts Chaffle

Preparation time: 5 minutes
Cooking time: 8 minutes
Servings: 2
Ingredients:

- 2 tbsp. almonds, chopped
- 2 tbsp. walnuts, chopped
- 1 tbsp. stevia
- ½ cup cream cheese, soft
- 2 eggs, whisked
- 1 tbsp. almond flour
- 1 tbsp. coconut flour
- ½ tsp. almond extract

Directions:
In a blender, mix the almonds with the walnuts, cream cheese, and the other ingredients and pulse well.
Heat up the waffle iron over high heat, pour ¼ of the batter, close the waffle maker, cook for 5 minutes and transfer it to a plate.
Repeat with the other part of the batter and serve them.
Per serving: Calories: 151Kcal; Fat: 5g; Carbs: 8g; Protein: 26g

401. Rhubarb Vanilla and Nutmeg Chaffles

Preparation time: 5 minutes
Cooking time: 6 minutes
Servings: 2
Ingredients:

- ½ cup rhubarb, chopped
- ¼ cup heavy cream
- 3 tbsp. cream cheese, soft
- 2 tbsp. almond flour
- 2 eggs, whisked
- 2 tbsp. Swerve
- ½ tsp. vanilla extract
- ½ tsp. nutmeg, ground

Directions:
In a bowl, mix the rhubarb with the cream, cream cheese, and the other ingredients and whisk well.
Heat up the waffle iron over high heat, pour 1/3 of the batter, close the waffle maker, cook for 5 minutes and transfer it to a plate.
Repeat the process with the remaining batter and serve them.
Per serving: Calories: 180Kcal; Fat: 14g; Carbs: 1g; Protein: 8g

402. Rosemary Cherry Tomatoes Chaffles

Preparation time: 5 minutes
Cooking time: 6 minutes
Servings: 1
Ingredients:

- 1 egg, whisked
- ½ cup mozzarella, shredded
- 1 cup cherry tomatoes, cubed
- 2 tbsp. cream cheese, soft
- 1 tsp. coriander, ground
- ½ tsp. rosemary, dried
- 3 tbsp. tomato pasta sauce

Directions:
In a bowl, mix the egg with the cheese, cream cheese, coriander, and rosemary and stir well. Preheat the waffle iron over high heat, pour half of the chaffle mix, cook for 6 minutes and transfer it to a plate.
Repeat with the rest of the batter, divide the tomatoes, tomato pasta sauce, and rosemary over the chaffles, and serve.
Per serving: Calories: 220Kcal; Fat: 20g; Carbs: 1g; Protein: 20g

403. Jalapeño and Garlic Chaffles

Preparation time: 5 minutes
Cooking time: 10 minutes
Servings: 2
Ingredients:

- 2 eggs, whisked
- 2 cup almond milk
- 2 tbsp. avocado oil
- ½ cup cheddar, shredded
- 1 cup almond flour
- 1 tbsp. baking powder
- a pinch of salt and black pepper
- ½ tsp. garlic powder
- 1 jalapeño, minced

Directions:
In a medium-sized bowl, whisk the eggs and combine with the milk, oil, and the other ingredients and whisk well.
Preheat the waffle iron, pour 1/6 of the batter, cook for 8 minutes and transfer it to a plate.
Repeat with the rest of the batter and serve them.
Per serving: Calories: 368Kcal; Fat: 28g; Carbs: 1g; Protein: 22g

404. Green Chili Chaffle

Preparation time: 10 minutes
Cooking time: 10 minutes
Servings: 2
Ingredients:

- 2 eggs, whisked
- 1½ cup almond flour
- ½ cup cream cheese, soft
- ½ cup almond milk
- 1 tsp. baking soda
- a pinch of salt and black k pepper
- ½ cup green chilies, minced
- 1 tbsp. chives, chopped

Directions:
Whisk the eggs in a mixing bowl and combine with the flour, cream cheese, and the other ingredients. Mix well
Preheat the waffle iron, pour a quarter of the batter, close the lid and cook for 8 minutes. After cooking, transfer the chaffle to a plate.
Repeat the process with the remaining batter to create more chaffles.
Per serving: Calories: 220Kcal; Fat: 16g; Carbs: 1g; Protein: 12g

405. Okonomiyaki Style Chaffle

Preparation time: 5 minutes
Cooking time: 8 minutes
Servings: 2
Ingredients:

- 4 tbsp. finely shredded cabbage
- 2 eggs (beaten)
- 1/3 cup shredded mozzarella cheese
- 1 slice bacon (finely chopped)
- a pinch of salt
- 1 tsp. tamari sauce
- 1 tbsp. chopped green onion
- ⅛ tsp. ground black pepper or to taste

Toppings:

- 1 tbsp. kewpie mayonnaise or American mayonnaise
- 2 tbsp. bonito flakes
- 2 tsp. Worcestershire sauce

Directions:

Heat up a frying pan over medium to high heat and add the chopped bacon.

Sear until the bacon is brown and crispy. Use a slotted spoon to transfer the bacon to a paper towel-lined plate to drain.

Plug the waffle maker to preheat it and spray it with a non-stick spray. In a mixing bowl, combine the crispy bacon, cabbage, cheese, onion, pepper, and salt. Add the egg and tamari. Mix until the ingredients are well combined.

Spon some of the batter into the waffle maker and spread out it to cover all the holes on the waffle maker.

Cook for about 4 minutes or according to your waffle maker's settings. After the cooking cycle, use a silicone or plastic utensil to remove the chaffle from the waffle maker.

Repeat the process until you have cooked all the batter into chaffles.

Top the chaffles with sauce, mayonnaise, and bonito flakes.

Per serving: Calories: 167Kcal; Fat: 18g; Carbs: 1g; Protein: 20g

406. BLT Sandwich Chaffle

Preparation time: 5 minutes
Cooking time: 10 minutes
Servings: 1
Ingredients:
  Sandwich Filling:
  - 2 strips bacon
  - a pinch of salt
  - 2 slices tomato
  - 1 tbsp. mayonnaise
  - 3 pieces lettuce
  Chaffles:
  - 1 egg (beaten)
  - ½ cup shredded mozzarella cheese
  - ¼ tsp. onion powder
  - ¼ tsp. garlic powder
  - ½ tsp. curry powder

Directions:

Plug the waffle maker and preheat it and spray it with a non-stick spray.

In a medium-sized bowl, combine the cheese, onion powder, garlic, and curry powder.

Add the egg and stir until the ingredients are properly mixed.

Drop some of the mixture into the waffle maker and spread the batter to the edges of the waffle maker.

Cook for about 5 minutes or according to the waffle maker's settings. After the cooking cycle, remove the chaffle from the waffle maker using a silicone or plastic utensil.

Repeat the process until you have transformed all the batter into chaffles. Set the chaffles aside to cool.

Heat up a skillet over medium heat. Add the bacon strips and sear until all the sides of the bacon have browned, turning and pressing the bacon while searing.

Use a slotted spoon to transfer the bacon to a paper towel-lined plate to drain.

Place the chaffles on a flat surface and spread mayonnaise over the face of the chaffles.

Divide the lettuce into two and layer it on one portion on both chaffles.

Layer the tomatoes on one of the chaffles and sprinkle with salt.

Layer the bacon over the tomatoes and place the other chaffle over the one containing the bacon.

Press and serve immediately. Enjoy!

Per serving: Calories: 220Kcal; Fat: 18g; Carbs: 1g; Protein: 16g

407. Cinnamon Rolls Chaffles

Preparation time: 10 minutes
Cooking time: 10 minutes
Servings: 1
Ingredients:
  Cinnamon Roll Chaffle:
  - ½ cup mozzarella cheese
  - 1 tbsp. almond flour
  - ¼ tsp. baking powder
  - 1 egg
  - 1 tsp. cinnamon
  - 1 tsp. granulated Swerve
  Cinnamon Roll Swirl:
  - 1 tbsp. butter
  - 1 tsp. cinnamon
  - 2 tsp. Swerve confectioners' sugar
  Keto Cinnamon Roll Glaze:
  - 1 tbsp. butter
  - 1 tbsp. cream cheese
  - ¼ tsp. vanilla extract
  - 2 tsp. Swerve confectioners' sugar

Directions:

Plug in your Dash Mini Waffle Maker and let it heat up.

Mix the egg, almond flour, mozzarella cheese, baking powder, 1 tsp. of cinnamon, and 1 tsp. of Swerve granulated into a medium-sized bowl. Mix until well combined, and set it aside.

In another small bowl, add a tbsp. of butter, 1 tsp. of cinnamon, and 2 tsp. of Swerve confectioners' sugar.

Microwave for about 15 seconds and mix well.

Spray the waffle maker with non-stick spray.

Pour half of the batter into your waffle maker. Swirl in half of the cinnamon, Swerve, and butter mixture on top. Allow the waffle machine to cook for 3-4 minutes.

Repeat the process to make the second one.

While the last chaffle is cooking, place 1 tbsp. of butter and 1 tbsp. of cream cheese in a small-sized bowl. Heat in the microwave for 10-20 seconds until it's all melted.

Add the Swerve confectioners' sugar and vanilla extract to the butter and cream cheese mixture. Mix well.

Use the keto cream cheese glaze to garnish the chaffles.

Per serving: Calories: 482Kcal; Fat: 28g; Carbs: 2g; Protein: 18g

408. Coconut Flour Garlic Bread Chaffles

Preparation time: 10 minutes
Cooking time: 14 minutes
Servings: 1
Ingredients:
  Chaffles:
  - 1 egg
  - ½ cup mozzarella cheese, shredded
  - 1 tbsp. parmesan cheese
  - ¾ tsp. coconut flour
  - ¼ tsp. baking powder
  - ⅛ tsp. Italian Seasoning
  - a pinch of salt
  Filling:
  - 1 tbsp. butter, melted
  - ¼ tsp. garlic powder
  - ½ cup mozzarella cheese, shredded
  - ¼ tsp. basil seasoning

Directions:

Preheat the oven to 400°F.

Plug in your waffle maker to preheat it and grease it.

In a small-sized bowl, combine the chaffles ingredients and stir well to combine.

Drop half of the mixture into the waffle maker and cook for about 4 minutes or until golden brown.

Repeat the process to create a second chaffles.

In a small-sized bowl, melt the butter and add garlic powder.

Place each chaffle on a baking sheet after cutting them in half, then sprinkle the surface with the garlic butter mixture.

Top the chaffles with some mozzarella cheese and pop in the oven for 5-6 minutes.

Turn the oven to broil and move the baking pan to the top shelf for 1-2 minutes. You will see then the cheese begins to bubble and turns golden brown. Check it often, as it can burn quickly on broil (check every 30 seconds).

Remove from the oven and sprinkle basil seasoning on top.

Per serving: Calories: 285Kcal; Fat: 24g; Carbs: 2g; Protein: 13g

409. Easy Keto Chaffle Sausage Gravy

Preparation time: 10 minutes
Cooking time: 10 minutes
Servings: 1
Ingredients:
Chaffle:

- 1 egg
- ½ cup mozzarella cheese, grated
- 1 tsp. coconut flour
- 1 tsp. water
- ¼ tsp. baking powder
- a pinch of salt

Keto Sausage Gravy:

- ¼ cup breakfast sausage, browned
- 3 tbsp. chicken broth
- 2 tbsp. heavy whipping cream
- 2 tsp. cream cheese, softened
- Dash garlic powder
- Pepper to taste
- Dash of onion powder (optional)

Directions:
Plug in your waffle maker to preheat it and grease it.

In a medium-sized bowl, add all the chaffle ingredients, and stir them well.

Spoon half of the chaffle batter onto the waffle maker, then shut the lid and cook for approximately 4 minutes.

Repeat the same process to make another chaffle. Set aside to crisp.

Keto Sausage Gravy:
Cook 1 pound of breakfast sausage and drain. Reserve ¼ cup for this recipe.

Tip: Make sausage patties with the remaining sausage, reserving 14 cups to brown for this dish. If you're not experienced with breakfast sausage, it's crushed like ground beef.

Wipe the excess grease from the skillet and add ¼ cup of browned breakfast sausage and the rest of the ingredients listed.

Bring to a boil.

Reduce the heat to medium and continue to simmer with the lid off for about 5-7 minutes, or until it starts to thicken.

Tip: If you want it particularly thick, add a touch of xanthan gum, but if you wait long enough, the keto sausage gravy will thicken anyway.

Season with salt and pepper to taste, then ladle the keto sausage gravy over the chaffles.

Per serving: Calories: 477Kcal; Fat: 31g; Carbs: 2g; Protein: 21g

410. Fudgy Chocolate Chaffles

Preparation time: 10 minutes
Cooking time: 8 minutes
Servings: 1

Ingredients:

- 1 egg
- 2 tbsp. mozzarella cheese, shredded
- 2 tbsp. cocoa
- 2 tbsp. Lakanto monk fruit powdered
- 1 tsp. coconut flour
- 1 tsp. heavy whipping cream
- ¼ tsp. baking powder
- ¼ tsp. vanilla extract
- a pinch of salt

Directions:
Turn on the waffle or chaffle maker. I use the Dash Mini Waffle Maker. Grease lightly or use a cooking spray.

In a small-sized bowl, combine all the ingredients.

Cover the dash mini waffle maker with ½ of the batter and cook for about 4 minutes. Remove the chaffle carefully from the maker as it's very hot.

Repeat the process to create more chaffles.

Serve with keto ice cream or sugar-free whipped topping.

Per serving: Calories: 365Kcal; Fat: 22g; Carbs: 2g; Protein: 20g

411. Raspberries and Cream Cheese Chaffles

Preparation time: 10 minutes
Cooking time: 8 minutes
Servings: 1
Ingredients:

- 1 egg
- 1/3 cup mozzarella cheese, shredded
- 1 tbsp. raspberries
- 1 tsp. cream cheese
- 1 tsp. coconut flour
- ¼ tsp. baking powder
- ¼ tsp. vanilla extract
- ¾ tsp. sweetener
- ¼ tsp. cinnamon
- a pinch of salt

Directions:
Turn on the waffle or chaffle maker. Grease lightly or use a cooking spray.

In a small bowl, combine all the ingredients except the raspberries.

Cover the dash mini waffle maker with ½ of the batter, then sprinkle a couple of raspberries on top.

Cook for 4 minutes and then remove the chaffle from the waffle maker carefully.

Repeat the steps above to create the next chaffle.

Serve with sugar-free maple syrup, whipped cream, or keto ice cream.

Per serving: Calories: 366Kcal; Fat: 13g; Carbs: 1g; Protein: 12g

412. Jack Cheese and Bacon Sandwich Chaffle

Preparation time: 10 minutes
Cooking time: 12 minutes
Servings: 1
Ingredients:

- 1 egg white
- ½ cup Monterey Jack cheese, shredded
- ¾ tsp. water
- 1 tsp. almond flour
- ¼ tsp. baking powder
- a pinch of salt
- 2 slices bacon
- ¼ cup provolone cheese

Directions:
Preheat the oven to 425°F.

Warm your waffle maker and grease it if needed.

In a medium-sized mixing bowl, combine all the chaffles ingredients. Stir until homogeneous.

Spoon out ½ of the batter on the waffle maker and close the lid.

Let it cook for about 4 minutes. Do not remove the cover before. Lifting the Chaffle keto sandwich recipe beforehand may cause it to split and adhere to the waffle iron. Allow it to cook for the full 4 minutes before removing the cover.

Set the chaffle aside after removing it from the waffle iron. Repeat the previous procedures with the remaining chaffle batter.

Meanwhile, cook the bacon in a pan until it is golden and crunchy

Place the chaffles a few inches apart on a cookie sheet lined with parchment paper.

Put the bacon and the provolone cheese on top of the chaffles.

Place the pan on the top shelf of the oven for 5 minutes to allow the cheese to melt.

Turn the oven to broil for 1 minute if you want the cheese to bubble and golden.

Enjoy with some of the beef broth for dipping.

Per serving: Calories: 256Kcal; Fat: 17g; Carbs: 3g; Protein: 20g

413. Taco Chaffle Shells

Preparation time: 10 minutes
Cooking time: 20 minutes
Servings: 2
Ingredients:
- 1 tbsp. almond flour
- 1 cup taco blend cheese
- 2 eggs
- ¼ tsp. taco seasoning

Directions:
Preheat your waffle maker.

In a bowl, mix the almond flour, taco blend cheese, eggs, and taco seasoning. I find it easier to mix everything using a fork.

Add a quarter of the batter to the waffle maker at a time.

Cook for about 4 minutes.

Remove the taco chaffle shell from the maker and drape it over a bowl's edge.

I used a pie plate since that's what I had on hand, but any bowl would do.

Continue forming the chaffle taco shells until the batter runs out.

Fill your taco shells with taco meat and your chosen toppings, and serve.

Per serving: Calories: 240Kcal; Fat: 3g; Carbs: 1g; Protein: 22g

414. Peanut Butter and Chocolate Chips Chaffles

Preparation time: 10 minutes
Cooking time: 8 minutes
Servings: 1
Ingredients:
- 1 egg
- ¼ cup shredded mozzarella cheese
- 2 tbsp. creamy peanut butter
- 1 tbsp. almond flour
- 1 tbsp. granulated Swerve
- 1 tsp. vanilla extract
- 1 tbsp. low carb chocolate chips

Directions:
Plug in your waffle maker.

Add the peanut butter and egg into a mixing bowl, and stir them well. Make sure the peanut butter is well blended with the egg.

Add in the previous mixture the almond flour, mozzarella cheese, Swerve, and chocolate chips. Mix until the ingredients are well combined

Add half of the keto peanut butter chocolate chip chaffle mix to the waffle maker at a time. Cook the chaffle batter in the waffle maker for 4 minutes.

When the first one is completely done cooking, cook the second one. Enjoy with some Swerve confectioners' sugar or whipped cream on top.

Per serving: Calories: 273Kcal; Fat: 10g; Carbs: 2g; Protein: 22g

415. Mini Pizza Chaffle

Preparation time: 10 minutes
Cooking time: 10 minutes
Servings: 1
Ingredients:
- ½ cup shredded mozzarella cheese
- 1 tbsp. almond flour
- ½ tsp. baking powder
- 1 egg
- ¼ tsp. garlic powder
- ¼ tsp. basil
- 2 tbsp. low-carb pasta sauce
- 2 tbsp. mozzarella cheese

Directions:
Heat up your waffle maker

In a mixing bowl, add garlic, basil, egg, mozzarella cheese, almond flour, and baking powder.

Pour half of the mixture into your waffle maker.

Cook for about 5 minutes.

Allow it to cook for another minute or two if the waffle sticks to the waffle machine.

Then, pour the remaining batter into the waffle maker and cook it.

Place both pizza crusts on the baking sheet of your toaster oven once they're done.

Put 1 tbsp. of low-carb pasta sauce on top of each pizza crust.

Sprinkle 1 tbsp. of mozzarella cheese on top of each chaffle.

Bake at 350°F in the toaster oven for about 5 minutes, just until the cheese is melted.

Per serving: Calories: 240Kcal; Fat: 18g; Carbs: 2g; Protein: 22g

416. Maple Pumpkin Chaffle

Preparation time: 10 minutes
Cooking time: 16 minutes
Servings: 2
Ingredients:
- 2 eggs
- ¾ tsp. baking powder
- 2 tsp. pumpkin puree (100% pumpkin)
- ¾ tsp. pumpkin pie spice
- 4 tsp. heavy whipping cream
- 2 tsp. Lakanto Sugar-Free Maple Syrup
- 1 tsp. coconut flour
- ½ cup mozzarella cheese, shredded
- ½ tsp. vanilla
- a pinch of salt
- maple syrup

Directions:
Turn on the chaffle maker.

In a small bowl, combine all ingredients.

Cover the waffle maker with ¼ of the batter and cook for 4 minutes.

Repeat the process to create the rest of the chaffles.

Serve with sugar-free maple syrup or keto ice cream.

Per serving: Calories: 244Kcal; Fat: 19g; Carbs: 1g; Protein: 22g

417. Shrimp and Avocado Sandwich Chaffle

Preparation time: 8 minutes
Cooking time: 32 Minutes
Servings: 4
Ingredients:

- 2 cups shredded mozzarella cheese
- 4 large eggs
- ½ tsp. curry powder
- ½ tsp. oregano

Shrimp Sandwich Filling:

- 1-pound raw shrimp (peeled and deveined)
- 1 large avocado (diced)
- 4 slices cooked bacon
- 2 tbsp. sour cream
- ½ tsp. paprika
- 1 tsp. Cajun seasoning
- 1 tbsp. olive oil
- ¼ cup onion (finely chopped)
- 1 red bell pepper (diced)

Directions:

Plug the waffle maker to preheat it and spray it with a non-stick cooking spray.

Break the eggs into a mixing bowl and beat. Add the cheese, oregano and curry. Mix until the ingredients are well combined.

Pour an appropriate amount of the batter into the waffle maker and spread out the batter to the edges to cover all the holes on the waffle maker. This should make 8 mini waffles. 4. Close the waffle maker and cook for about minutes or according to your waffle maker's settings.

After the cooking cycle, use a silicone or plastic utensil to remove the chaffle from the waffle maker.

Repeat step 3 to 5 until you have cooked all the batter into chaffles.

Heat up the olive oil in a large skillet over medium to high heat.

Add the shrimp and cook until the shrimp is pink and tender.

Remove the skillet from heat and use a slotted spoon to transfer the shrimp to a paper towel lined plate to drain for a few minutes.

Put the shrimp in a mixing bowl. Add paprika and Cajun seasoning. Toss until the shrimps are all coated with seasoning.

To assemble the sandwich, place one chaffle on a flat surface and spread some sour cream over it. Layer some shrimp, onion, avocado, diced pepper and one slice of bacon over it. Cover with another chaffle.

Repeat step 10 until you have assembled all the ingredients into sandwiches.

Per serving: Calories: 294Kcal; Fat: 18g; Carbs: 3g; Protein: 22g

CHAPTER 7:

Sweet Chaffles

418. Chocolate Sauce Chaffles

Preparation time: 7 minutes
Cooking time: 5 minutes
Servings: 1
Ingredients:
- 2 classic chaffles
- 2 scoop vanilla keto ice cream
- 8 oz. strawberries, sliced
- keto chocolate sauce

Directions:
Arrange the chaffles, ice cream, strawberries slice in a serving plate.
Drizzle the chocolate sauce on top.
Per serving: Calories: 333Kcal; Fat: 32g; Carbs: 1g; Protein: 20g

419. Mango Chaffles

Preparation time: 5 minutes
Cooking time: 6 minutes
Servings: 2
Ingredients:
- 1 cup grated cheddar cheese
- 2 eggs
- ½ mango, chopped

Directions:
Preheat the waffle iron.
Beat the eggs, then add the grated cheddar cheese and mango.
Make sure that the mixture is well combined.
Cook the mixture for about six minutes.
Per serving: Calories: 340Kcal; Fat: 26g; Carbs: 1g; Protein: 22g

420. French Toast Chaffle

Preparation time: 5 minutes
Cooking time: 10 minutes
Servings: 1
Ingredients:
- 1 egg
- ½ cup grated mozzarella cheese
- 2 tbsp. almond flour
- 1 tsp. vanilla extract
- 1 tsp. cinnamon
- 1 tsp. granulated sweetener of choice

Directions:
Preheat your waffle iron.
Mix all the chaffle ingredients well.
Use half of the mixture and cook the chaffle for about five minutes.
Add an extra minute to the cooking if you want a crispier chaffle.
Repeat until all the batter is used.
Add some sugar-free cinnamon syrup and enjoy these chaffles still warm.
Per serving: Calories: 280Kcal; Fat: 12g; Carbs: 2g; Protein: 11g

421. Banana Nut Chaffle

Preparation time: 3 minutes
Cooking time: 8 minutes
Servings: 1
Ingredients:
- 1 egg
- ¼ tsp. vanilla extract
- ¼ tsp. banana extract
- 1 tbsp. cream cheese, room temperature, and softened
- ½ cup grated mozzarella cheese
- 1 tbsp. monk fruit confectioners' sugar, or confectioners' sweetener of choice
- 1 tbsp. sugar-free cheesecake pudding, optional

Toppings:
- Pecans
- Sugar-free caramel sauce. or keto-safe sauce of preference

Directions:
Preheat the waffle iron.
Beat the egg in a medium-sized mixing bowl and add the other ingredients. Mix well, making sure that everything is coated in the egg mixture.
Use half of the batter and cook for about four minutes.
Remove the chaffle to rest while cooking the second mini chaffle.
Top the chaffle with pecans and caramel sauce.
Per serving: Calories: 240Kcal; Fat: 20g; Carbs: 1g; Protein: 20g

422. Banana Foster Pancakes Chaffle

Preparation time: 5 minutes
Cooking time: 20 minutes
Servings: 2
Ingredients:
- 2 large eggs
- 1 cup almond flour
- ⅓ cup flaxseed meal
- 1 tsp. vanilla extract
- ½ medium banana, slightly overripe
- 4 oz. cream cheese
- 2 tsp. baking powder
- ½ tsp. banana extract, optional
- liquid stevia or sweetener of choice, optional

Toppings:
- 8 tbsp. salted butter
- ½ tsp. cinnamon
- ½ tsp. vanilla extract
- ½ tsp. banana extract
- ¼ cup sugar-free maple syrup
- ½ cup brown sugar substitute or granulated sweetener with maple extract
- ½ medium banana, sliced into discs
- ⅛-¼ tsp. xanthan gum, optional

- 2 tbsp. dark rum or bourbon, optional
- ¼ cup pecans chopped, optional

Directions:
Preheat the waffle iron or skillet.
Add all the chaffle ingredients to a blender and blend until smooth.
Add ¼ of the batter to the waffle iron and cook for about 2-3 minutes; add an extra minute to cooking if the chaffle isn't set.
Repeat until all the batter is used.

Topping:
At a medium temperature, combine the banana extract, rum or bourbon, butter, and vanilla in a skillet.
As the mixture starts to bubble, add the sliced bananas in a single layer and allow them to cook for between two to three minutes. Do not stir.
After the time has passed, add the cinnamon, brown sugar substitute, and sugar-free maple syrup.
Stir and let the mixture simmer until all the brown sugar substitute has become melted and incorporated into the butter.
If the brown sugar substitute isn't blending with the butter, then add the xanthan gum to the simmering mixture. This will also help to thicken up the sauce.
Depending on your preference, you can either add the pecans to the simmering sauce or add them after pouring the source on the chaffles.
Add the warm sauce to the cooled chaffles.
Add a scoop or two of keto-friendly ice cream to make a unique taste experience. Or simply enjoy the chaffle with no sauce.
Per serving: Calories: 380Kcal; Fat: 26g; Carbs: 3g; Protein: 20g

423. Chocolate Chips Cinnamon Chaffles

Preparation time: 3 minutes
Cooking time: 8 minutes
Servings: 1
Ingredients:
- ½ cup grated mozzarella cheese
- ½ tbsp. granulated Swerve, or sweetener of choice
- 1 tbsp. almond flour
- 2 tbsp. low-carb, sugar-free chocolate chips
- 1 egg
- ¼ tsp. cinnamon

Directions:
Preheat your waffle iron.
In a bowl, mix the almond flour, egg, cinnamon, mozzarella cheese, Swerve, chocolate chips.
Drop half of the mixture into the waffle maker and cook for 4 minutes.
Remove the chaffle and cook the remaining batter.
Let the chaffles cool before serving.
Enjoy these chaffles with some keto-safe chocolate sauce and some whipped cream.
Per serving: Calories: 246Kcal; Fat: 10g; Carbs: 1g; Protein: 20g

424. Chocolate Chaffles

Preparation time: 3 minutes
Cooking time: 5 minutes
Servings: 1
Ingredients:
- 1 tsp. vanilla extract
- 1 tbsp. cocoa powder, unsweetened
- 1 egg
- 2 tbsp. almond flour
- 2 tsp. monk fruit
- 1 oz. cream cheese

Directions:
Preheat the waffle iron.
Soften the cream cheese, then whisk together the other ingredients well.

Pour the batter into the center of the waffle iron and spread out.
Cook the batter for between three and five minutes.
Remove the chaffle once set and serve.
Consider making your own keto-friendly ice cream to go with the chaffles; the combination will be delicious.
Per serving: Calories: 242Kcal; Fat: 18g; Carbs: 1g; Protein: 20g

425. Basic Chaffles with Papaya

Preparation time: 5 minutes
Cooking time: 5 minutes
Servings: 1
Ingredients:
- 1 egg
- ½ cup shredded cheddar cheese
- 2 tsp papaya, chopped

Directions:
Turn on the waffle maker to heat and oil it with cooking spray.
Whisk the egg in a bowl until well beaten.
Add the cheese to the egg and stir well to combine. Add the chopped papaya too
Pour ½ of batter into the waffle maker and close the top. Cook for 3-5 minutes.
Transfer the chaffle to a plate and set aside for 2-3 minutes to crisp up.
Repeat for the remaining batter.
Per serving: Calories: 280Kcal; Fat: 22g; Carbs: 1g; Protein: 18g

426. Chocolate and Peanut Butter Chaffles

Preparation time: 5 minutes
Cooking time: 10 minutes
Servings: 1
Ingredients:
- ½ cup shredded mozzarella cheese
- 1 tbsp. cocoa powder
- 2 tbsp. powdered sweetener
- 2 tbsp. peanut butter
- ½ tsp. vanilla
- 1 egg
- 2 tbsp. crushed peanuts
- 2 tbsp. whipped cream
- ¼ cup sugar-free chocolate syrup

Directions:
Combine the mozzarella, egg, vanilla, peanut butter, cocoa powder, and sweetener in a bowl.
Add in the peanuts and mix well.
Turn on the waffle maker and oil it with cooking spray.
Pour one-half of the batter into the waffle maker and cook for 5 minutes, then transfer it to a plate.
Top with whipped cream, peanuts, and sugar-free chocolate syrup.
Per serving: Calories: 245Kcal; Fat: 19g; Carbs: 1g; Protein: 22g

427. Lemon Curd Chaffles

Preparation time: 5 minutes
Cooking time: 5 minutes
Servings: 2
Ingredients:
- 2 large eggs
- 4 oz. cream cheese, softened
- 1 tbsp. low carb sweetener
- 1 tsp. vanilla extract
- ¾ cup mozzarella cheese, shredded
- 3 tbsp. coconut flour
- 1 tsp. baking powder
- ⅓ tsp. salt

Lemon Curd:
- ½-1 cup water
- 5 egg yolks
- ½ cup lemon juice
- ½ cup powdered sweetener
- 2 tbsp. fresh lemon zest
- 1 tsp. vanilla extract
- a pinch of salt
- 8 tbsp. cold butter, cubed

Directions:
Pour water into a saucepan and heat at medium until it reaches a soft boil. Start with ½ cup and add more if needed.
Whisk the yolks, lemon juice, lemon zest, powdered sweetener, vanilla, and salt in a medium heat-proof bowl. Leave to sit for 5-6 minutes.
Place the bowl onto the saucepan and heat. The bowl shouldn't be touching the water.
Whisk the mixture for 8-10 minutes or until it begins to thicken.
Add the butter cubes and whisk for 7 minutes until it thickens.
When it lightly coats the back of a spoon, remove it from the heat.
Refrigerate until cool, allowing it to continue thickening.
Turn on the waffle maker to heat and oil it with cooking spray.
Add the baking powder, coconut flour, and salt to a small bowl. Mix well and set it aside.
Add the eggs, cream cheese, sweetener, and vanilla in a separate bowl. Using a hand beater, beat until frothy.
Add mozzarella to the egg mixture and beat again.
Add the dry ingredients and mix until well-combined.
Drop the batter into the waffle maker. Cook for about 3-4 minutes.
Transfer it to a plate and top with lemon curd before serving.
Per serving: Calories: 305Kcal; Fat: 19g; Carbs: 3g; Protein: 11g

428. Rich Mozzarella Chaffles

Preparation time: 8 minutes
Cooking time: 20 minutes
Servings: 2
Ingredients:
- ½ scoop unsweetened protein powder
- 2 large organic eggs
- ½ cup mozzarella cheese, shredded
- 1 tbsp. erythritol
- ¼ tsp. organic vanilla extract

Directions:
Preheat the mini waffle iron and then grease it.
In a medium bowl, place all the ingredients, and with a fork, mix until well combined.
Place ¼ of the mixture into the preheated waffle iron and cook for about 4-5 minutes or until golden brown.
Repeat with the remaining mixture.
Serve them warm.
Per serving: Calories: 2616Kcal; Fat: 18g; Carbs: 1g; Protein: 20g

429. Dark Chocolate Chips Chaffles

Preparation time: 5 minutes
Cooking time: 8 minutes
Servings: 1
Ingredients:
- 1 organic egg, beaten
- ¼ cup mozzarella cheese, shredded
- 2 tbsp. creamy peanut butter
- 1 tbsp. almond flour
- 1 tbsp. granulated erythritol
- 1 tsp. organic vanilla extract
- 1 tbsp. 70% dark chocolate chips

Directions:
Preheat the mini waffle iron and then grease it.
In a bowl, place all the ingredients except chocolate chips, and beat until well combined.
Gently, fold in the chocolate chips.
Drop half of the mixture into the preheated waffle iron and cook for about 2 minutes or until golden brown.
Repeat with the remaining mixture.
Per serving: Calories: 386Kcal; Fat: 22g; Carbs: 2g; Protein: 18g

430. Pumpkin Chaffles

Preparation time: 5 minutes
Cooking time: 12 minutes
Servings: 1
Ingredients:
- 1 organic egg, beaten
- ½ cup mozzarella cheese, shredded
- 1½ tbsp. homemade pumpkin puree
- ½ tsp. erythritol
- ½ tsp. organic vanilla extract
- ¼ tsp. pumpkin pie spice

Directions:
Preheat a mini waffle iron and then grease it.
In a bowl, place all the ingredients and beat until well combined.
Place ¼ of the mixture into the preheated waffle iron and cook for about 4-6 minutes or until golden brown.
Repeat with the remaining mixture.
Serve them warm.
Per serving: Calories: 246Kcal; Fat: 14g; Carbs: 1g; Protein: 22g

431. Shredded Mozzarella Chaffles

Preparation time: 5 minutes
Cooking time: 8 minutes
Servings: 1
Ingredients:
- 1 large organic egg
- 1 tsp. coconut flour
- 1 tsp. erythritol
- ½ tsp. organic vanilla extract
- ½ cup mozzarella cheese, shredded finely
- 1 tbsp. dried basil

Directions:
Preheat your mini waffle iron and then grease it.
In a bowl, place the egg, coconut flour, sweetener, and vanilla extract and beat until well combined.
Add the cheese and stir to combine.
Spoon half of the batter into the preheated waffle iron and top with dried basil.
Cook for about 3-4 minutes or until golden brown.
Repeat the process with the remaining mixture and chocolate chips.
Serve them warm.
Per serving: Calories: 230Kcal; Fat: 16g; Carbs: 2g; Protein: 21g

432. Cream Cake Chaffle

Preparation time: 8 minutes
Cooking time: 12 minutes
Servings: 2
Ingredients:
Chaffles:
- 4 oz. cream cheese, softened
- 4 eggs
- 4 tbsp. coconut flour
- 1 tbsp. almond flour

- 1½ tsp. baking powder
- 1 tbsp. butter, softened
- 1 tsp. vanilla extract
- ½ tsp. cinnamon
- 1 tbsp. sweetener
- 1 tbsp. shredded coconut, colored and unsweetened
- 1 tbsp. walnuts, chopped
- **Italian Cream Frosting:**
- 2 oz. cream cheese, softened
- 2 tbsp. butter, room temperature
- 2 tbsp. sweetener
- ½ tsp. vanilla

Directions:
Preheat your waffle maker and add ¼ of the batter.
Cook for 3 minutes and repeat the process until you have 4 chaffles. Remove and set them aside.
In the meantime, mix all the frosting ingredients, and stir until you have a smooth and creamy mixture.
Cool, frost the cake, and enjoy.
Per serving: Calories: 431Kcal; Fat: 36g; Carbs: 10g; Protein: 24g

433. Protein Nuts Chaffles

Preparation time: 10 minutes
Cooking time: 48 minutes
Servings: 2
Ingredients:
- ½ cup golden flax seeds meal
- ½ cup almond flour
- 2 tbsp. unflavored whey protein powder
- 1 tsp. organic baking powder
- ¾ cup mozzarella cheese, shredded
- 1/3 cup unsweetened almond milk
- 2 tbsp. unsalted butter, melted
- 2 large organic eggs, beaten
- 2 tbsp. walnuts, chopped
- 2 tbsp. almonds, chopped
- 2 tbsp. pecans, chopped
- sugar-free maple syrup

Directions:
Preheat the mini waffle iron and then grease it.
In a bowl, mix the flax seeds meal, flour, protein powder, and baking powder.
Stir in the cheddar cheese.
In another bowl, add the remaining ingredients and beat until well combined. Use only half of the chopped nuts for the batter
Add the egg mixture into the bowl with the flax seeds meal mixture and mix until well combined.
Place the desired amount of the mixture into the preheated waffle iron. Cook for 5 minutes.
Repeat with the remaining mixture.
Serve them warm with the remaining chopped nuts and maple syrup on top
Per serving: Calories: 248Kcal; Fat: 26g; Carbs: 2g; Protein: 18

434. Simple Sweet Mozzarella Chaffle

Preparation time: 5 minutes
Cooking time: 8 minutes
Servings: 1
Ingredients:
- ½ cup mozzarella cheese, shredded
- 1 large organic egg
- 2 tbsp. blanched almond flour
- ¼ tsp. organic baking powder

- 2-3 drops liquid stevia

Directions:
Preheat a mini waffle iron and then grease it.
Put all the ingredients in a medium-sized mixing bowl, and mix until well combined.
Pour half of the mixture into the preheated waffle iron and cook for about 3-4 minutes.
Repeat the process with the remaining mixture, and serve the chaffles warm. Enjoy
Per serving: Calories: 222Kcal; Fat: 16g; Carbs: 3g; Protein: 20g

435. Cream Mini-Chaffle

Preparation time: 5 minutes
Cooking time: 10 minutes
Servings: 1
Ingredients:
- 2 tsp. coconut flour
- 4 tsp. Swerve/monk fruit
- ¼ tsp. baking powder
- 1 egg
- 1 oz. cream cheese
- ½ tsp. vanilla extract

Directions:
Turn on the waffle maker to heat and oil it with cooking spray.
Mix the Swerve/monk fruit, coconut flour, and baking powder in a small mixing bowl.
Add the cream cheese, egg, vanilla extract, and whisk until well-combined.
Pour half of the mixture into the waffle maker and cook for 3 minutes, until golden brown.
Serve with your favorite toppings.
Per serving: Calories: 240Kcal; Fat: 19g; Carbs: 4g; Protein: 20g

436. Raspberries Chaffles

Preparation time: 5 minutes
Cooking time: 5 minutes
Servings: 5
Ingredients:
- 4 tbsp. almond flour
- 4 large eggs
- 2⅓ cup shredded mozzarella cheese
- 1 tsp. vanilla extract
- 1 tbsp. erythritol sweetener
- 1½ tsp. baking powder
- ½ cup raspberries

Directions:
Turn on the waffle maker to heat and oil it with cooking spray.
Mix the almond flour, sweetener, and baking powder in a bowl.
Add the cheese, eggs, and vanilla extract and mix until well-combined.
Add 1 portion of the batter to the waffle maker and spread it evenly.
Close and cook for 3 minutes, or until golden.
Repeat until the remaining batter is used.
Serve them with raspberries.
Per serving: Calories: 248Kcal; Fat: 14g; Carbs: 1g; Protein: 22g

437. Chocolate Chips and Heavy Cream Chaffles

Preparation time: 8 minutes
Cooking time: 6 minutes
Servings: 1
Ingredients:
- 1 egg
- 1 tsp. coconut flour

- 1 tsp. sweetener
- ½ tsp. vanilla extract
- ¼ cup heavy whipping cream, for serving
- ½ cup almond milk ricotta, finely shredded
- 2 tbsp. sugar-free chocolate chips

Directions:
Preheat your mini waffle iron.
Mix the egg, coconut flour, vanilla, and sweetener. Whisk together with a fork.
Stir in the almond milk ricotta.
Drop half of the mixture into the waffle iron and dot with a pinch of chocolate chips.
Cook for 6 minutes.
Repeat with the remaining batter.
Serve it hot with whipped cream.
Per serving: Calories: 362Kcal; Fat: 18g; Carbs: 2g; Protein: 12g

438. Protein Pumpkin and Psyllium Husk Chaffles

Preparation time: 8 minutes
Cooking time: 16 minutes
Servings: 2
Ingredients:
- 2 organic eggs
- ½ cup cheddar cheese, shredded
- 1 tbsp. homemade pumpkin puree
- 2 tsp. erythritol
- ½ tsp. psyllium husk powder
- ½ tsp. organic vanilla extract

Directions:
Turn on the waffle maker to heat and oil it with cooking spray.
Beat the eggs in a bowl and place all the ingredients. Mix well.
Place ¼ of the mixture into the preheated waffle iron and cook for about 4 minutes.
Remove the chaffle and add the other half of the batter.
Serve them warm.
Per serving: Calories: 332Kcal; Fat: 16g; Carbs: 1g; Protein: 14g

439. Cinnamon, Vanilla, and Blackberries Chaffles

Preparation time: 5 minutes
Cooking time: 8 minutes
Servings: 1
Ingredients:
- 1 organic egg, beaten
- 1/3 cup mozzarella cheese, shredded
- 1 tsp. cream cheese, softened
- 1 tsp. coconut flour
- ¼ tsp. organic baking powder
- ¾ tsp. powdered erythritol
- ¼ tsp. ground cinnamon
- ¼ tsp. organic vanilla extract
- a pinch of salt
- 1 tbsp. fresh blackberries

Directions:
Preheat a mini waffle maker and then grease it.
In a medium-sized bowl, place all the ingredients except for the blackberries and beat until well combined.
Fold in the blackberries.
Drop half of the mixture into the preheated waffle maker and cook for about 4 minutes or until golden brown.
Repeat with the remaining mixture.
Per serving: Calories: 318Kcal; Fat: 18g; Carbs: 3g; Protein: 12g

440. Pumpkin Puree and Heavy Cream Chaffles

Preparation time: 5 minutes
Cooking time: 10 minutes
Servings: 1
Ingredients:
- 1 organic egg, beaten
- ½ cup cheddar cheese, shredded
- 1½ tbsp. sugar-free pumpkin puree
- 3 tsp. heavy cream
- 1 tbsp. almond flour
- 1 tbsp. erythritol
- ½ tsp. organic baking powder
- 1 tsp. organic vanilla extract

Directions:
Turn on the waffle maker to heat and oil it with cooking spray.
In a medium bowl, place all the ingredients, and with a fork, mix until properly mixed.
Drop half of the mixture into the waffle maker and cook for about 5 minutes or until golden brown.
Repeat with the remaining mixture.
Serve them warm.
Per serving: Calories: 286Kcal; Fat: 14g; Carbs: 2g; Protein: 15g

441. Pecan Cinnamon Chaffles

Preparation time: 5 minutes
Cooking time: 40 minutes
Servings: 1
Ingredients:
- 1 tbsp. butter
- 1 egg
- ½ tsp. vanilla
- 2 tbsp. almond flour
- 1 tbsp. coconut flour
- ⅛ tsp. baking powder
- 1 tbsp. monk fruit sweetener

Crumble:
- ½ tsp. cinnamon
- 1 tbsp. melted butter
- 1 tsp. monk fruit
- 1 tbsp. chopped pecans

Directions:
Turn on the waffle maker to heat and oil it with cooking spray.
Melt the butter in a bowl, then mix in the egg and vanilla.
Mix in the remaining chaffle ingredients.
Combine the crumble ingredients in a separate bowl.
Pour half of the chaffle mix into the waffle maker. Top with half of the crumble mixture.
Cook for 5 minutes, or until done.
Repeat with the other half of the batter.
Per serving: Calories: 253Kcal; Fat: 26g; Carbs: 2g; Protein: 20g

442. Simple Donuts Chaffle

Preparation time: 5 minutes
Cooking time: 5 minutes
Servings: 1
Ingredients:
Donut Chaffles:
- 1 egg
- ¼ cup cheddar cheese, shredded
- 2 tsp. cream cheese, softened
- 1 tsp. sweetener
- ½ tsp. coconut flour

- ½ tsp. baking powder
- 20 drops glazed donut flavoring

Donut Glaze:
- 1 tsp. powdered sweetener
- heavy whipping cream

Directions:
Spray your waffle maker with cooking oil and add the batter into the waffle maker.
Cook for 4 minutes and set aside.
Donut Glaze:
Stir together the ingredients
Assembling:
Lay your chaffles on a plate and drizzle the glaze on top.
Per serving: Calories: 350Kcal; Fat: 16g; Carbs: 2g; Protein: 12g

443. Cinnamon-and Vanilla Chaffles

Preparation time: 5 minutes
Cooking time: 12 minutes
Servings: 2
Ingredients:
Chaffles:
- 2 eggs
- 1 cup mozzarella cheese, shredded
- 2 tbsp. blanched almond flour
- ½ tbsp. butter, melted
- 2 tbsp. erythritol
- ½ tsp. cinnamon
- ½ tsp. vanilla extract
- ½ tsp. psyllium husk powder
- ¼ tsp. baking powder

Toppings:
- 1 tbsp. melted butter
- ¾ tsp. cinnamon

Directions:
Plug in your mini waffle maker to preheat it.
In a medium-sized bowl, add all the chaffle ingredients, and stir them until smooth
Pour a quarter of the batter into the waffle maker. Cook for about 4 minutes.
Repeat the same steps to create more chaffles.
For the topping: Brush your chaffles with the melted butter and then sprinkle with cinnamon.
Per serving: Calories: 388Kcal; Fat: 29g; Carbs: 1g; Protein: 22g

444. Sweet Cream Cheese Chaffle

Preparation time: 5 minutes
Cooking time: 8 minutes
Servings: 2
Ingredients:
- 2 tsp. coconut flour
- 3 tsp. erythritol
- ¼ tsp. organic baking powder
- 1 organic egg, beaten
- 1 oz. cream cheese, softened
- ½ tsp. organic vanilla extract

Directions:
Preheat the mini waffle iron and then grease it.
In a bowl, place the flour, erythritol, and baking powder and mix well.
Add the egg, cream cheese, and vanilla extract and beat until properly blended.
Drop half of the mixture into the waffle iron and cook for about 3 minutes or until golden brown.
Repeat with the remaining mixture.
Per serving: Calories: 245Kcal; Fat: 16g; Carbs: 5g; Protein: 8g

445. Mozzarella and Butter Chaffles

Preparation time: 5 minutes
Cooking time: 8 minutes
Servings: 1
Ingredients:
- 1 large organic egg, beaten
- ¾ cup mozzarella cheese, shredded
- ½ tbsp. unsalted butter, melted
- 2 tbsp. blanched almond flour
- 2 tbsp. erythritol
- ½ tsp. ground cinnamon
- ½ tsp. psyllium husk powder
- ¼ tsp. organic baking powder
- ½ tsp. organic vanilla extract

Directions:
Preheat your mini waffle iron and then grease it.
Mix all the ingredients with a fork until well combined.
Fill the waffle maker with half of the batter and cook for about 5 minutes or until golden brown.
Repeat with the remaining mixture.
Per serving: Calories: 375Kcal; Fat: 28g; Carbs: 2g; Protein: 12g

446. Chocolate and Cream Chaffles

Preparation time: 5 minutes
Cooking time: 10 minutes
Servings: 1
Ingredients:
- 1 organic egg
- 1½ tbsp. cacao powder
- 2 tbsp. erythritol
- 1 tbsp. heavy cream
- 1 tsp. coconut flour
- ½ tsp. organic baking powder
- ½ tsp. organic vanilla extract
- ½ tsp. powdered erythritol

Directions:
Preheat the mini waffle iron and then grease it.
In a mixing bowl, place all the ingredients except the powdered erythritol and beat until properly combined.
Pour half of the mixture into the preheated waffle iron and cook for about 5 minutes or until golden brown.
Repeat with the remaining mixture.
Serve them warm with the sprinkling of powdered erythritol.
Per serving: Calories: 344Kcal; Fat: 15g; Carbs: 2g; Protein: 8g

447. Gingerbread Chaffles with Heavy Cream

Preparation time: 5 minutes
Cooking time: 5 minutes
Servings: 1
Ingredients:
- ½ cup mozzarella cheese grated
- 1 medium egg
- ½ tsp. baking powder
- 1 tsp. erythritol powdered
- ½ tsp. ground ginger
- ¼ tsp. ground nutmeg
- ½ tsp. ground cinnamon
- ground cloves
- 2 tbsp. almond flour
- 1 cup heavy whipped cream
- ¼ cup keto-friendly maple syrup

Directions:

Turn on the waffle maker to heat and oil it with cooking spray.

Beat the egg in a bowl.

Add the flour, mozzarella, spices, baking powder, and erythritol. Mix well.

Spoon one-half of the batter into the waffle maker and spread out evenly.

Close and cook for 2-3 minutes.

Remove the cooked chaffle and repeat with the remaining batter.

Serve the chaffles with whipped cream and maple syrup.

Per serving: Calories: 215Kcal; Fat: 18g; Carbs: 1g; Protein: 20g

448. Chocolate Whipping Cream Chaffle

Preparation time: 5 minutes
Cooking time: 8 minutes
Servings: 1
Ingredients:

- 1 tbsp. almond flour
- 2 tbsp. cacao powder
- 2 tbsp. granulated erythritol
- ¼ tsp. organic baking powder
- 1 organic egg
- 1 tbsp. heavy whipping cream
- ¼ tsp. organic vanilla extract
- ⅛ tsp. organic almond extract

Directions:

Preheat the mini waffle iron and then grease it.

In a mixing bowl, place all the ingredients and beat until well combined.

Drop half of the mixture into the waffle maker and cook for about 4 minutes or until golden brown.

Repeat with the remaining mixture.

Per serving: Calories: 223Kcal; Fat: 19g; Carbs: 1g; Protein: 15g

449. Almond Flour Chaffle

Preparation time: 5 minutes
Cooking time: 20 minutes
Servings: 1
Ingredients:

- 1 large egg
- 1 tbsp. blanched almond flour
- ¼ tsp. baking powder
- ½ cup shredded mozzarella cheese

Directions:

Whisk the egg, almond flour, and baking powder together.

Stir in the mozzarella and set the batter aside.

Turn on the waffle maker to heat and oil it with cooking spray.

Spoon half of the batter onto the waffle maker and spread it evenly with a spoon.

Cook for about 4 minutes, or until it reaches the desired doneness.

Transfer to a plate and repeat with the remaining batter.

Let the chaffles cool for 2-3 minutes to crisp up.

Per serving: Calories: 220Kcal; Fat: 18g; Carbs: 1g; Protein: 20g

450. Strawberry Cake Chaffle

Preparation time: 5 minutes
Servings: 1
Cooking time: 25 minutes
Ingredients:

Batter:

- 1 egg
- ¼ cup mozzarella cheese
- 1 tbsp. cream cheese
- ¼ tsp. baking powder
- 2 strawberries, sliced
- 1 tsp. strawberry extract

Glaze:

- 1 tbsp. cream cheese
- ¼ tsp. strawberry extract
- 1 tbsp. monk fruit confectioners' sugar

Whipped Cream:

- 1 cup heavy whipping cream
- 1 tsp. vanilla
- 1 tbsp. monk fruit

Directions:

Turn on the waffle maker to heat and oil it with cooking spray.

Beat the egg in a small bowl.

Add the remaining batter components.

Divide the mixture in half.

Cook one-half of the batter in a waffle maker for 4 minutes, or until golden brown.

Repeat with the remaining batter.

Mix all the glaze ingredients and spread over each warm chaffle.

Mix all the whipped cream ingredients and whip until it starts to form peaks.

Top each waffle with whipped cream and strawberries.

Per serving: Calories: 420Kcal; Fat: 22g; Carbs: 1g; Protein: 21g

451. Cream Cheese and Butter Chaffles

Preparation time: 8 minutes
Cooking time: 16 minutes
Servings: 2
Ingredients:

- 2 tbsp. butter, melted and cooled
- 2 large organic eggs
- 2 oz. cream cheese, softened
- ¼ cup powdered erythritol
- 1½ tsp. organic vanilla extract
- a pinch of salt
- ¼ cup almond flour
- 2 tbsp. coconut flour
- 1 tsp. organic baking powder

Directions:

Preheat the mini waffle iron and then grease it.

In a bowl, place the butter and eggs and beat until creamy.

Add the cream cheese, erythritol, vanilla extract, and salt and beat until well combined.

Add the flours and baking powder and beat until well combined.

Place ¼ of the mixture into the preheated waffle iron and cook for about 4 minutes or until golden brown.

Repeat with the remaining mixture.

Per serving: Calories: 453Kcal; Fat: 36g; Carbs: 6g; Protein: 16g

452. Chocolate Cherry Chaffles

Preparation time: 5 minutes
Cooking time: 5 minutes
Servings: 1
Ingredients:

- 1 tbsp. almond flour
- 1 tbsp. cocoa powder
- 1 tbsp. sugar-free sweetener
- ½ tsp. baking powder
- 1 whole egg
- ½ cup mozzarella cheese shredded
- 2 tbsp. heavy whipping cream whipped
- 2 tbsp. sugar-free cherry pie filling
- 1 tbsp. chocolate chips

Directions:
Turn on the waffle maker to heat and oil it with cooking spray.
Mix all the dry components in a bowl.
Add the egg and mix well.
Add the cheese and stir again.
Fill the waffle maker with half of the batter and close the lid.
Cook for 5 minutes, until done.
Top with whipping cream, cherries, and chocolate chips.
Per serving: Calories: 323Kcal; Fat: 44g; Carbs: 4g; Protein: 20g

453. Coconut and Walnut Chaffles

Preparation time: 5 minutes
Cooking time: 24 minutes
Servings: 8
Ingredients:

- 4 organic eggs, beaten
- 4 oz. cream cheese, softened
- 1 tbsp. butter, melted
- 4 tbsp. coconut flour
- 1 tbsp. almond flour
- 2 tbsp. erythritol
- 1½ tsp. organic baking powder
- 1 tsp. organic vanilla extract
- ½ tsp. ground cinnamon
- 1 tbsp. unsweetened coconut, shredded
- 1 tbsp. walnuts, chopped

Directions:
Preheat your mini waffle iron and then grease it.
In a blender, place all the ingredients and pulse until creamy and smooth.
Divide the mixture into 8 portions.
Place 1 portion of the mixture into the preheated waffle iron and cook for about 2-3 minutes or until golden brown.
Repeat with the remaining mixture.
Per serving: Calories: 338Kcal; Fat: 19g; Carbs: 2g; Protein: 14g

454. Coconut Chaffles with Chocolate Chips

Preparation time: 5 minutes
Cooking time: 8 minutes
Servings: 1
Ingredients:

- 1 organic egg
- 1 tbsp. heavy whipping cream
- ½ tsp. coconut flour
- 1¾ tsp. monk fruit sweetener
- ¼ tsp. organic baking powder
- 1 tbsp. blackberries
- a pinch of salt
- 1 tbsp. 70% dark chocolate chips

Directions:
Preheat a mini waffle maker and then grease it.
In a mixing bowl, place all the ingredients except for chocolate chips, and beat until well combined.
Fold in the blackberries.
Drop half of the mixture into the waffle maker and top with half of the chocolate chips.
Cook for about 3-4 minutes or until golden brown.
Repeat with the remaining mixture and chocolate chips.
Per serving: Calories: 260Kcal; Fat: 18g; Carbs: 2g; Protein: 14g

455. Spiced Ginger and Nutmeg Chaffles

Preparation time: 5 minutes
Cooking time: 8 minutes
Servings: 2
Ingredients:

- 1 organic egg, beaten
- ½ cup mozzarella cheese, shredded
- 1 tbsp. sugar-free canned solid pumpkin
- ¼ tsp. ground cinnamon
- a pinch ground ginger
- a pinch ground nutmeg
- a pinch ground cloves

Directions:
Preheat the mini waffle iron and then grease it.
In a medium-sized bowl, place all the ingredients, and with a fork, mix until properly combined.
Pour half of the mixture into the preheated waffle iron and cook for about 4 minutes or until golden brown.
Repeat with the remaining mixture.
Per serving: Calories: 234Kcal; Fat: 16g; Carbs: 3g; Protein: 20g

456. Vanilla and Butter Chaffles

Preparation time: 5 minutes
Cooking time: 8 minutes
Servings: 2
Ingredients:

- 2 tbsp. butter, softened
- 2 oz. cream cheese, softened
- 2 eggs
- ¼ cup almond flour
- 2 tbsp. coconut flour
- 1 tsp. baking powder
- 1 tsp. vanilla extract
- ¼ cup Swerve confectioners' sugar
- a pinch of pink salt

Directions:
Preheat the waffle maker and spray with non-stick cooking spray.
Melt the butter and set it aside for a minute to cool.
Add the eggs into the melted butter and whisk until creamy.
Pour in the sweetener, vanilla, extract, and salt. Blend properly.
Next, add the coconut flour, almond flour, and baking powder. Mix well.
Fill the waffle maker with half of the mixture and cook for 4 minutes.
Repeat the process with the remaining batter.
Remove and set aside to cool before serving.
Per serving: Calories: 328Kcal; Fat: 16g; Carbs: 3g; Protein: 12g

457. Walnuts and Banana Chaffles

Preparation time: 5 minutes
Cooking time: 10 minutes
Servings: 1
Ingredients:

- 1 egg
- 1 tbsp. cream cheese, softened and room temp
- 1 tbsp. sugar-free cheesecake pudding
- ½ cup mozzarella cheese
- 1 tbsp. sweetener
- ¼ tsp. banana extract

Toppings:

- chopped walnuts

Directions:
Turn on the waffle maker to heat and grease it with cooking spray.
Beat the egg in a small bowl.

Add the remaining ingredients and mix until well incorporated.
Add one-half of the batter to the waffle maker and cook for 5 minutes, until golden brown.
Remove the chaffle and add the other half of the batter.
Top with chopped walnuts and serve it warm!
Per serving: Calories: 246Kcal; Fat: 18g; Carbs: 4g; Protein: 20g

458. Chocolaty Chips and Pumpkin Chaffles

Preparation time: 5 minutes
Cooking time: 12 minutes
Servings: 1
Ingredients:

- 1 organic egg
- 4 tsp. homemade pumpkin puree
- ½ cup mozzarella cheese, shredded
- 1 tbsp. almond flour
- 2 tbsp. granulated erythritol
- ¼ tsp. pumpkin pie spice
- 2 tsp. 70% dark chocolate chips

Directions:
In a bowl, place the egg and pumpkin puree and mix well.
Add the remaining ingredients, except for chocolate chips, and mix until well combined.
Gently, fold in the chocolate chips.
Drop half of the mixture into the waffle iron and cook for about 4 minutes or until golden brown.
Repeat with the remaining mixture.
Per serving: Calories: 329Kcal; Fat: 19g; Carbs: 2g; Protein: 22g

459. Finely Knit Chaffles

Preparation time: 5 minutes
Cooking time: 5 minutes
Servings: 2
Ingredients:
Chocolate Chaffle:

- 2 eggs
- 2 tbsp. cocoa, unsweetened
- 2 tbsp. heavy cream
- 2 tsp. almond flour
- ½ tsp. baking powder
- 1 tsp. vanilla

Topping:

- keto maple syrup

Directions:
Plug in your mini waffle maker to preheat it and grease it.
In a medium-sized bowl, add all the chaffles ingredients, and stir until smooth.
Pour a quarter of the mixture into the waffle maker.
Cook for 5 minutes, and then carefully remove. Set aside to cool
Repeat with the remaining chaffle mixture.
Once they have cooled, add the keto maple syrup on top and enjoy!
(a sprinkling of keto powdered sugar is also fine, just in case you don't like maple syrup)
Per serving: Calories: 293Kcal; Fat: 30g; Carbs: 3g; Protein: 12g

460. Whipping Cream and Pumpkin Chaffles

Preparation time: 8 minutes
Cooking time: 12 minutes
Servings: 2

Ingredients:

- 2 organic eggs
- 2 tbsp. homemade pumpkin puree
- 2 tbsp. heavy whipping cream
- 1 tbsp. coconut flour
- 1 tbsp. erythritol
- 1 tsp. pumpkin pie spice
- ½ tsp. organic baking powder
- ½ tsp. organic vanilla extract
- a pinch of salt
- ½ cup mozzarella cheese, shredded

Directions:
Preheat the mini waffle iron and then grease it.
In a medium-sized mixing bowl, place all the ingredients, except mozzarella cheese, and beat until well combined.
Add the mozzarella cheese and mix until homogeneous.
Fill the waffle maker with half of the mixture and cook for about 6 minutes or until golden brown.
Repeat with the remaining mixture.
Serve them warm.
Per serving: Calories: 336Kcal; Fat: 18g; Carbs: 3g; Protein: 20g

461. Chocolate Vanilla Chaffles

Preparation time: 5 minutes
Cooking time: 5 minutes
Servings: 1
Ingredients:

- ½ cup shredded mozzarella cheese
- 1 egg
- 1 tbsp. granulated sweetener
- 1 tsp. vanilla extract
- 1 tbsp. sugar-free chocolate chips
- 2 tbsp. almond meal/flour

Directions:
Turn on the waffle maker to heat and oil it with cooking spray.
Mix all the components in a bowl until combined.
Drop half of the mixture into the waffle maker.
Cook for 2 minutes, then remove and repeat with the remaining batter.
Top with more chips and favorite toppings.
Per serving: Calories: 230Kcal; Fat: 17g; Carbs: 2g; Protein: 21g

462. Churro Styled Chaffle

Preparation time: 5 minutes
Cooking time: 10 minutes
Servings: 1
Ingredients:
Chaffles:

- 1 tbsp. coconut cream
- 1 egg
- 4 tbsp. almond flour
- ¼ tsp. xanthan gum
- ½ tsp. cinnamon
- 2 tbsp. keto brown sugar

Coating:

- 2 tbsp. butter, melt
- 1 tbsp. keto brown sugar

Directions:
Warm up your mini waffle maker.
Combine all the chaffles ingredients in a mixing bowl. Stir until homogeneous.
Pour half of the batter into the mini waffle maker.
Cook for about 4 minutes to achieve the desired crunch.

Carefully remove the cooked waffle and repeat the steps with the remaining batter.

Allow the chaffles to cool and spread with the melted butter and top with brown sugar.

Per serving: Calories: 247Kcal; Fat: 14g; Carbs: 3g; Protein: 8g

463. Chocolate Coconut Chaffles

Preparation time: 8 minutes
Cooking time: 8 minutes
Servings: 2
Ingredients:
- 2 organic eggs
- ½ cup cheddar cheese, shredded
- ½ tsp. organic vanilla extract
- 2 tsp. erythritol
- ½ tsp. psyllium husk powder
- 1 tbsp. cocoa powder
- a pinch of salt
  Other:
- 1 tbsp. 70% dark chocolate chips
- 1 tbsp. grated coconut

Directions:
Preheat the mini waffle iron and then grease it.

Combine all the chaffles ingredients in a mixing bowl. Beat until well combined.

Gently, fold in the chocolate chips and grated coconut.

Place a quarter of the mixture into the preheated waffle iron and cook for about 4 minutes or until golden brown.

Repeat with the remaining mixture.

Per serving: Calories: 278Kcal; Fat: 18g; Carbs: 1g; Protein: 21g

464. Mocha Chaffles

Preparation time: 8 minutes
Cooking time: 9 minutes
Servings: 1
Ingredients:
- 1 organic egg, beaten
- 1 tbsp. cacao powder
- 1 tbsp. erythritol
- ¼ tsp. organic baking powder
- 2 tbsp. cream cheese, softened
- 1 tbsp. mayonnaise
- ¼ tsp. instant coffee powder
- a pinch of salt
- 1 tsp. organic vanilla extract

Directions:
Preheat your mini waffle iron and then grease it.

In a medium bowl, place all the ingredients, and with a fork, mix until well combined.

Place ½ of the mixture into the preheated waffle iron and cook for about 2½-3 minutes or until golden brown.

Repeat with the remaining mixture.

Per serving: Calories: 242Kcal; Fat: 16g; Carbs: 1g; Protein: 14g

465. Carrot Bread Chaffle

Preparation time: 8 minutes
Cooking time: 18 minutes
Servings: 2
Ingredients:
- ¾ cup almond flour
- 1 tbsp. walnuts, chopped
- 2 tbsp. powdered erythritol
- 1 tsp. organic baking powder
- ½ tsp. ground cinnamon
- ½ tsp. pumpkin pie spice
- 1 organic egg, beaten
- 2 tbsp. heavy whipping cream
- 2 tbsp. butter, melted
- ½ cup carrot, peeled and shredded

Directions:
Preheat the mini waffle iron and then grease it.

In a bowl, place the flour, walnut, erythritol, cinnamon, baking powder, and spices and mix well.

Add the egg, heavy whipping cream, and butter and mix until well combined.

Gently, fold in the carrot.

Fill the waffle maker with 3 tbsp. of the mixture.

Cook for about 2-3 minutes or until golden brown.

Repeat with the remaining mixture, and serve the chaffles warm.

Per serving: Calories: 188Kcal; Fat: 14g; Carbs: 2g; Protein: 8g

466. Yogurt Chaffle

Preparation time: 8 minutes
Cooking time: 10 minutes
Servings: 1
Ingredients:
- ½ cup shredded mozzarella
- 1 egg
- 2 tbsp. ground almonds
- ½ tsp. psyllium husk
- ¼ tsp. baking powder
- 1 tbsp. yogurt

Directions:
Turn on the waffle maker to heat and oil it with cooking spray.

Whisk the eggs in a bowl.

Add in the remaining ingredients, except mozzarella, and mix well.

Add the mozzarella and mix once again. Let it sit for 5 minutes.

Add the batter into each waffle mold.

Close and cook for 4-5 minutes.

Repeat with the remaining batter.

Per serving: Calories: 304Kcal; Fat: 18g; Carbs: 1g; Protein: 21g

467. Ube Chaffles and Ice Cream

Preparation time: 5 minutes
Cooking time: 10 minutes
Servings: 1
Ingredients:
- 1/3 cup mozzarella cheese, shredded
- 1 tbsp. whipped cream cheese
- 2 tbsp. sweetener
- 1 egg
- 2-3 drops ube or pandan extract
- ½ tsp. baking powder
- keto ice cream

Directions:
Add in 2 or 3 drops of ube extract, mix until creamy and smooth.

Pour half of the batter mixture into the mini waffle maker and cook for about 5 minutes. Repeat with the remaining batter mixture.

Top with keto ice cream and enjoy.

Per serving: Calories: 386Kcal; Fat: 16g; Carbs: 2g; Protein: 20g

468. Orange Cake Chaffle

Preparation time: 10 minutes
Cooking time: 28 minutes
Servings: 2

Ingredients:
  Chaffles:
- 2 eggs, beaten
- ½ cup finely grated Swiss cheese
- 2 oz. cream cheese, softened
- ½ tsp. orange extract
- 20 drops cake batter extract

  Frosting:
- 5 tbsp butter (softened)
- 5 tbsp orange juice
- sweetener
- 1 tsp. vanilla
- 3 tbsp orange zest

Directions:
Chaffles:
Preheat the waffle iron.
In a medium bowl, mix all the ingredients for the chaffles.
Open the iron and add a quarter of the mixture. Close and cook until crispy, 7 minutes.
Transfer the chaffle to a plate and make 3 more chaffles with the remaining batter.
Frosting:
In a medium bowl, using a hand mixer, beat the frosting ingredients until creamy.
Assemble the chaffles with the frosting to make the cake.
Slice and serve them.
Per serving: Calories: 2866Kcal; Fat: 14g; Carbs: 1g; Protein: 8g

469. Butter Frosting Almond Chaffles

Preparation time: 20 minutes
Cooking time: 28 minutes
Servings: 2
Ingredients:
  Chaffles:
- 2 eggs, beaten
- finely grated mozzarella cheese
- 1 tbsp. almond flour
- 2 tbsp. almond butter
- 1 tbsp. Swerve confectioners' sugar
- ½ tsp. vanilla extract

  Chocolate Butter Frosting:
- 1½ cup butter, room temperature
- 1 cup unsweetened cocoa powder
- ½ cup almond milk
- 5 cup Swerve confectioners' sugar
- 2 tsp. vanilla extract

Directions:
Chaffles:
Preheat the waffle iron.
In a medium bowl, mix the egg, mozzarella cheese, almond flour, almond butter, Swerve confectioners' sugar, and vanilla extract.
Open the iron and add a quarter of the mixture. Close and cook until crispy, 7 minutes.
Transfer the chaffle to a plate and make 3 more chaffles with the remaining batter.
Frosting:
In a medium bowl, cream the butter and cocoa powder until smooth.
Gradually, whisk in the almond milk and Swerve confectioners' sugar until smooth.
Add the vanilla extract and mix well.
Assemble the chaffles with the frosting to make the cake.
Slice and serve them.
Per serving: Calories: 326Kcal; Fat: 20g; Carbs: 1g; Protein: 22g

470. Coconut Chaffles with Mint Frosting

Preparation time: 15 minutes
Cooking time: 28 minutes
Servings: 2
Ingredients:
  Chaffles:
- 2 eggs, beaten
- 2 tbsp. cream cheese, softened
- 1 cup finely grated Monterey Jack cheese
- 2 tbsp. coconut flour
- ¼ tsp. baking powder
- 1 tbsp. unsweetened shredded coconut
- 1 tbsp. walnuts, chopped

  Frosting:
- ¼ cup unsalted butter, room temperature
- 3 tbsp. almond milk
- 1 tsp. mint extract
- 2 drops green food coloring
- 3 cup Swerve confectioners' sugar

Directions:
Chaffles:
Preheat the waffle iron.
In a medium bowl, mix all the ingredients for the chaffles.
Open the iron and add a quarter of the mixture. Close and cook until crispy, 7 minutes.
Transfer the chaffle to a plate and make 3 more with the remaining batter.
Frosting:
In a medium bowl, cream the butter using an electric hand mixer until smooth.
Gradually, mix in the almond milk until smooth.
Add the mint extract and green food coloring; whisk until well combined.
Finally, mix in the Swerve confectioners' sugar a cup at a time until smooth.
Layer the chaffles with the frosting.
Slice and serve afterward.
Per serving: Calories: 184Kcal; Fat: 23g; Carbs: 3g; Protein: 16g

471. Whipping Cream Chaffles

Preparation time: 10 minutes
Cooking time: 8 minutes
Servings: 1
Ingredients:
- 1 organic egg, beaten
- 1 tbsp. heavy whipping cream
- 2 tbsp. sugar-free peanut butter powder
- 2 tbsp. erythritol
- ¼ tsp. organic baking powder
- ¼ tsp. peanut butter extract

Directions:
Preheat your mini waffle iron and then grease it.
Combine all the ingredients in a mixing bowl and stir until homogeneous.
Drop half of the mixture into the waffle iron and cook for about 3-4 minutes or until golden brown.
Repeat with the remaining mixture.
Serve them warm.
Per serving: Calories: 180Kcal; Fat: 12g; Carbs: 1g; Protein: 6g

472. Blueberry Cream Chaffles

Preparation time: 10 minutes
Cooking time: 8 minutes
Servings: 1
Ingredients:

- 1 organic egg, beaten
- 1 tbsp. cream cheese, softened
- 3 tbsp. almond flour
- ¼ tsp. organic baking powder
- 1 tsp. organic blueberry extract
- 5-6 fresh blueberries

Directions:
Preheat the mini waffle iron and then grease it.
In a mixing bowl, place all the ingredients except blueberries and beat until well combined.
Fold in the blueberries.
Divide the mixture into 5 portions.
Drop half of the mixture into the waffle maker. Let it cook for about 3-4 minutes or until golden brown.
Repeat with the remaining mixture.
Serve them warm.
Per serving: Calories: 180Kcal; Fat: 14g; Carbs: 2g; Protein: 8g

473. Super Strawberry Chaffles

Preparation time: 10 minutes
Cooking time: 8 minutes
Servings: 1
Ingredients:

- 1 organic egg, beaten
- ¼ cup mozzarella cheese, shredded
- 1 tbsp. cream cheese, softened
- ¼ tsp. organic baking powder
- 1 tsp. organic strawberry extract
- 2 fresh strawberries, hulled and sliced

Directions:
Preheat a mini waffle maker and then grease it.
In a bowl, place all the ingredients except strawberry slices, and beat until well combined.
Fold in the strawberry slices.
Drop half of the mixture into the waffle maker and cook for about 4 minutes or until golden brown.
Repeat with the remaining mixture.
Per serving: Calories: 238Kcal; Fat: 17g; Carbs: 1g; Protein: 23g

474. Berries Chaffles

Preparation time: 10 minutes
Cooking time: 10 minutes
Servings: 1
Ingredients:

- 1 organic egg
- 1 tsp. organic vanilla extract
- 1 tbsp. of almond flour
- 1 tsp. organic baking powder
- a pinch of ground cinnamon
- 1 cup mozzarella cheese, shredded
- 2 tbsp. fresh blueberries
- 2 tbsp. fresh blackberries

Directions:
Preheat your waffle iron and then grease it.
In a bowl, place the egg and vanilla extract and beat well.
Add the flour, baking powder, and cinnamon and mix well.
Add the mozzarella cheese and mix until just combined.
Gently, fold in the berries.

Fill the waffle maker with half of the batter and close the lid. Cook for about 4-5 minutes or until golden brown.
Repeat with the remaining mixture.
Per serving: Calories: 223Kcal; Fat: 16g; Carbs: 1g; Protein: 22g

475. Vanilla Raspberry Chaffles

Preparation time: 5 minutes
Cooking time: 8 minutes
Servings: 1
Ingredients:

- ½ cup cream cheese, soft
- 1 tsp. vanilla extract
- 1 tbsp. almond flour
- ¼ cup raspberries, pureed
- 1 egg, whisked
- 1 tbsp. monk fruit

Directions:
Heat up the waffle iron over high heat
In a bowl, mix the cream cheese with the other ingredients and whisk well.
Pour half of the batter, close the waffle maker, and cook for 8 minutes or until golden brown.
Repeat with the remaining batter and serve the chaffles warm.
Per serving: Calories: 160Kcal; Fat: 12g; Carbs: 1g; Protein: 7g

476. Pumpkin and Psyllium Husk Chaffles

Preparation time: 8 minutes
Cooking time: 16 minutes
Servings: 2
Ingredients:

- 2 organic eggs
- 1 cup mozzarella cheese, shredded
- 1 tbsp. homemade pumpkin puree
- 2 tsp. erythritol
- ½ tsp. psyllium husk powder
- 1/3 tsp. ground cinnamon
- a pinch of salt
- ½ tsp. organic vanilla extract

Directions:
Preheat your mini waffle iron and then grease it.
In a bowl, place all the ingredients and beat until well combined.
Place ¼ of the mixture into the preheated waffle iron and cook for about 4 minutes or until golden brown.
Repeat with the remaining mixture.
Serve them warm.
Per serving: Calories: 225Kcal; Fat: 16g; Carbs: 1g; Protein: 20g

477. Blackberry Chaffles

Preparation time: 5 minutes
Cooking time: 8 minutes
Servings: 1
Ingredients:

- 1 organic egg, beaten
- 1/3 cup mozzarella cheese, shredded
- 1 tsp. cream cheese, softened
- 1 tsp. coconut flour
- ¼ tsp. organic baking powder
- ¾ tsp. powdered erythritol
- ¼ tsp. ground cinnamon
- ¼ tsp. organic vanilla extract
- a pinch of salt
- 1 tbsp. fresh blackberries

Directions:
Preheat the mini waffle iron and then grease it.
In a medium-sized bowl, place all the ingredients except for blackberries, and beat until well combined.
Fold in the blackberries.
Fill the waffle maker with half of the batter and close the lid. Cook for about 4 minutes or until golden brown.
Repeat the process with the remaining mixture.
Per serving: Calories: 260Kcal; Fat: 15g; Carbs: 1g; Protein: 22g

478. Raspberry with Glazed Chaffle

Preparation time: 5 minutes
Cooking time: 5 minutes
Servings: 1
Ingredients:

Donut Chaffle:
- 1 egg
- ¼ cup mozzarella cheese, shredded
- 2 tsp. cream cheese, softened
- 1 tsp. sweetener
- 1tsp. almond flour
- ½ tsp. baking powder
- 20 drops glazed donut flavoring

Raspberry Jelly Filling:
- ¼ cup raspberries
- 1 tsp. chia seeds
- 1 tsp. confectioners' sugar

Donut Glaze:
- 1 tsp. powdered sweetener
- heavy whipping cream

Directions:
Spray your waffle maker with cooking oil and add the butter mixture into the waffle maker.
Cook for 3 minutes and set aside.
Raspberry Jelly Filling:
Place in a pot and heat on medium.
Gently mash the raspberries and set them aside to cool.
Donut Glaze:
Stir together the ingredients
Assembling:
Lay your chaffles on a plate and add the filling mixture between the layers.
Drizzle the glaze on top and enjoy.
Per serving: Calories: 230Kcal; Fat: 12g; Carbs: 2g; Protein: 16g

479. Vanilla Oreo Chaffle

Preparation time: 5 minutes
Cooking time: 5 minutes
Servings: 2
Ingredients:

- 1 egg
- 1½ tbsp. unsweetened cocoa
- 2 tbsp. Lakanto monk fruit, or choice of sweetener
- 1 tbsp. heavy cream
- 1 tsp. coconut flour
- ½ tsp. baking powder
- ½ tsp. vanilla

Cheese Cream:
- 1 tbsp. Lakanto powdered sweetener
- 2 tbsp. softened cream cheese
- ¼ tsp. vanilla

Directions:
Turn on the waffle maker to heat and oil it with cooking spray.
Combine all the chaffle ingredients in a small bowl.

Pour one-half of the chaffle mixture into the waffle maker and cook for 5 minutes.
Remove and repeat with the second half of the mixture. Let chaffles sit for 2-3 to crisp up.
Combine all the cream ingredients and spread them on the chaffle when they have cooled to room temperature.
Per serving: Calories: 190Kcal; Fat: 16g; Carbs: 1g; Protein: 7g

480. Cream Cheese and Vanilla Chaffles

Preparation time: 5 minutes
Cooking time: 8 minutes
Servings: 2
Ingredients:

- 2 tsp. coconut flour
- 3 tsp. erythritol
- ¼ tsp. organic baking powder
- 1 organic egg, beaten
- 1 oz. cream cheese, softened
- ½ tsp. organic vanilla extract

Directions:
Preheat the mini waffle iron and then grease it.
In a bowl, place flour, erythritol, and baking powder and mix well.
Add the egg, cream cheese, and vanilla extract and beat until well combined.
Drop half of the mixture into the waffle maker and cook for about 3 minutes or until golden brown.
Repeat with the remaining mixture.
Per serving: Calories: 108Kcal; Fat: 12g; Carbs: 5g; Protein: 6g

481. Pumpkin Pecan Chaffles

Preparation time: 5 minutes
Cooking time: 10 minutes
Servings: 1
Ingredients:

- 1 egg
- ½ cup mozzarella cheese grated
- 1 tbsp. pumpkin puree
- ½ tsp. pumpkin spice
- 1 tsp. erythritol low carb sweetener
- 2 tbsp. almond flour
- 2 tbsp. pecans, toasted chopped
- 1 cup heavy whipped cream
- ¼ cup low carb caramel sauce

Directions:
Turn on the waffle maker to heat and oil it with cooking spray.
In a bowl, beat the egg.
Mix in mozzarella, pumpkin, flour, pumpkin spice, and erythritol.
Stir in the pecan pieces.
Spoon one-half of the batter into the waffle maker and spread evenly.
Close and cook for 5 minutes.
Remove the cooked waffles to a plate.
Repeat with the remaining batter.
Serve with pecans, whipped cream, and low-carb caramel sauce.
Per serving: Calories: 273Kcal; Fat: 18g; Carbs: 4g; Protein: 22g

482. Chocolate Cream Chaffles

Preparation time: 5 minutes
Cooking time: 10 minutes
Servings: 1
Ingredients:

- 1 organic egg
- 1½ tbsp. cacao powder
- 2 tbsp. erythritol

- 1 tsp. coconut flour
- ½ tsp. organic baking powder
- ½ tsp. organic vanilla extract
- ½ tsp. powdered erythritol

Directions:
Preheat the mini waffle iron and then grease it.
In a mixing bowl, add all the ingredients except the powdered erythritol, and stir until well combined.
Drop half of the mixture into the waffle maker. Let it cook for about 5 minutes or until golden brown.
Repeat with the remaining mixture.
Serve them warm with the sprinkling of powdered erythritol.
Per serving: Calories: 180Kcal; Fat: 12g; Carbs: 4g; Protein: 6g

483. Blueberry Cinnamon Chaffles

Preparation time: 5 minutes
Cooking time: 10 minutes
Servings: 2
Ingredients:
- 1 cup shredded mozzarella cheese
- 3 tbsp. almond flour
- 2 eggs
- 2 tsp. Swerve or granulated sweetener of choice
- 1 tsp. cinnamon
- ½ tsp. baking powder
- ½ cup fresh blueberries
- ½ tsp. of powdered Swerve

Directions:
Turn on the waffle maker to heat and oil it with cooking spray.
Mix the eggs, flour, mozzarella, cinnamon, vanilla extract, sweetener, and baking powder in a bowl until well combined.
Add in the blueberries.
Pour ¼ of the batter into each waffle mold.
Close and cook for 8 minutes.
If it's crispy and the waffle maker opens without pulling the chaffles apart, the chaffle is ready. If not, close and cook for 1-2 more minutes.
Serve it with your favorite topping and more blueberries.
Per serving: Calories: 244Kcal; Fat: 20g; Carbs: 3g; Protein: 22g

484. Chocolate and Butter Chaffles

Preparation time: 5 minutes
Cooking time: 10 minutes
Servings: 1
Ingredients:
- ¾ cup shredded mozzarella
- 1 large egg
- 2 tbsp. almond flour
- 2 tbsp. allulose
- ½ tbsp. melted butter
- 1½ tbsp. cocoa powder
- ½ tsp. vanilla extract
- ½ tsp. psyllium husk powder
- ¼ tsp. baking powder

Directions:
Turn on the waffle maker to heat and oil it with cooking spray.
Mix all the ingredients in a small bowl.
Pour ¼ cup of the batter into a 4-inch waffle maker.
Cook for 2-3 minutes or until crispy.
Transfer the chaffle to a plate and set it aside.
Repeat with the remaining batter
Per serving: Calories: 274Kcal; Fat: 14g; Carbs: 2g; Protein: 168g

485. Oreo Chaffles

Preparation time: 5 minutes
Cooking time: 5 minutes
Servings: 2
Ingredients:
Chocolate Chaffles:
- 2 eggs
- 2 tbsp. cocoa, unsweetened
- 2 tbsp. sweetener
- 2 tbsp. heavy cream
- 2 tsp. coconut flour
- ½ tsp. baking powder
- 1 tsp. vanilla
Filling:
- ½ tsp. whipped cream

Directions:
Plug in your waffle maker to preheat it and grease it.
In a medium-sized bowl, mix all the chaffles ingredients until smooth.
Fill the waffle maker with half of the batter and close the lid. Cook for 5 minutes.
Once ready, carefully remove and repeat with the remaining chaffle mixture.
Allow the cooked chaffles to sit for 3 minutes.
Once they have cooled, spread the whipped cream on the chaffles and stack them cream side facing down to form a sandwich.
Slice into halves and enjoy
Per serving: Calories: 180Kcal; Fat: 31g; Carbs: 5g; Protein: 6g

486. Chocolate and Vanilla Chaffles

Preparation time: 5 minutes
Cooking time: 5 minutes
Servings: 1
Ingredients:
- ½ cup shredded mozzarella cheese
- 1 egg
- 1 tbsp. granulated sweetener
- 1 tsp. vanilla extract
- 1 tbsp. sugar-free chocolate chips
- 2 tbsp. almond meal/flour

Directions:
Turn on the waffle maker to heat and oil it with cooking spray.
Mix all the components in a bowl until combined.
Drop half of the mixture into the waffle maker and let it cook for 4 minutes, then remove and repeat with the remaining batter.
Top with more chips and favorite toppings
Per serving: Calories: 244Kcal; Fat: 17g; Carbs: 1g; Protein: 23g

487. Coconut Cream Churro Chaffles

Preparation time: 5 minutes
Cooking time: 10 minutes
Servings: 2
Ingredients:
- 1 tbsp. coconut cream
- 1 egg
- 1 tbsp. almond flour
- ¼ tsp. xanthan gum
- ½ tsp. cinnamon
- 2 tbsp. keto brown sugar
Coating:
- 2 tbsp. butter, melt
- 1 tbsp. keto brown sugar
- warm up your waffle maker

Directions:
Drop half of the mixture into the waffle maker and cook for 5 minutes. Carefully remove the cooked waffle and repeat the steps with the remaining batter.
Allow the chaffles to cool and spread with the melted butter and top with brown sugar.
Per serving: Calories: 112Kcal; Fat: 8g; Carbs: 28g; Protein: 4g

488. Chocolate Chips Lemon Chaffle

Preparation time: 8 minutes
Cooking time: 8 minutes
Servings: 1
Ingredients:
- 1 organic egg
- ½ cup mozzarella cheese, shredded
- ¾ tsp. organic lemon extract
- ½ tsp. organic vanilla extract
- 2 tsp. erythritol
- ½ tsp. psyllium husk powder
- a pinch of salt
- 1 tbsp. 70% dark chocolate chips
- ¼ tsp. lemon zest, grated finely

Directions:
Preheat the mini waffle iron and then grease it.
In a mixing bowl, add all the ingredients except chocolate chips and lemon zest, then beat until well combined.
Gently, fold in the chocolate chips and lemon zest.
Spoon half of the prepared mixture into the waffle iron and cook for about 4 minutes or until golden brown.
Repeat with the remaining mixture.
Per serving: Calories: 240Kcal; Fat: 21g; Carbs: 1g; Protein: 20g

489. Peanut Butter Chaffles with Dark Chocolate

Preparation time: 5 minutes
Cooking time: 8 minutes
Servings: 1
Ingredients:
- 1 organic egg, beaten
- ¼ cup mozzarella cheese, shredded
- 2 tbsp. creamy peanut butter
- 1 tbsp. almond flour
- 1 tbsp. granulated erythritol
- 1 tsp. organic vanilla extract
- 1 tbsp. 70% dark chocolate chips

Directions:
Preheat a mini waffle iron and then grease it.
In a bowl, add all the ingredients except chocolate, and beat until well combined. Gently, fold in the chocolate chips.
Drop half of the mixture into the waffle maker and cook for about 4 minutes.
Repeat with the remaining mixture and serve them warm
Per serving: Calories: 190Kcal; Fat: 18g; Carbs: 2g; Protein: 22g

490. Double Berries Chaffles

Preparation time: 5 minutes
Cooking time: 10 minutes
Servings: 1
Ingredients:
- 1 organic egg
- 1 tsp. organic vanilla extract
- 1 tbsp. almond flour
- 1 tsp. organic baking powder

- a pinch of ground cinnamon
- 1 cup mozzarella cheese, shredded
- 2 tbsp. fresh blueberries
- 2 tbsp. fresh blackberries

Directions:
Preheat the waffle iron and then grease it.
In a bowl, place the egg and vanilla extract and beat well.
Add the flour, baking powder, and cinnamon and mix well.
Add the mozzarella cheese and mix until just combined.
Gently, fold in the berries.
Cook for around 4 minutes half of the mixture into the mini waffle iron. Repeat with the remaining mixture.
Serve them warm.
Per serving: Calories: 225Kcal; Fat: 16g; Carbs: 2g; Protein: 22g

491. Easy Cinnamon Swirl Chaffle

Preparation time: 8 minutes
Cooking time: 12 minutes
Servings: 1
Ingredients:
Chaffles:
- 1 organic egg
- ½ cup mozzarella cheese, shredded
- 1 tbsp. almond flour
- ¼ tsp. organic baking powder
- 1 tsp. granulated erythritol
- 1 tsp. ground cinnamon

Toppings:
- 1 tbsp. butter
- 1 tsp. ground cinnamon
- 2 tsp. powdered erythritol

Directions:
Preheat the waffle iron and then grease it.
For chaffles: in a bowl, place all the ingredients and mix until well combined.
For the topping: In a small microwave-safe bowl, place all the ingredients and microwave for about 15 seconds.
Remove from the microwave and mix well.
Place 1/3 of the chaffles mixture into the preheated waffle iron.
Top with 1/3 of the butter mixture, and with a skewer, gently swirl into the chaffles mixture.
Cook for about 3-4 minutes or until golden brown.
Repeat with the remaining chaffles and topping mixture.
Serve them warm.
Per serving: Calories: 220Kcal; Fat: 16g; Carbs:2; Protein: 21g

492. Chocolate Cream Cheese Chaffles

Preparation time: 5 minutes
Cooking time: 8 minutes
Servings: 1
Ingredients:
- 1 large organic egg, beaten
- 1 oz. cream cheese, softened
- 1 tbsp. sugar-free chocolate syrup
- 1 tbsp. erythritol
- ½ tbsp. cacao powder
- ¼ tsp. organic baking powder
- ½ tsp. organic vanilla extract

Directions:
Preheat the mini waffle iron and then grease it.
Combine all the ingredients in a mixing bowl, and stir until homogeneous.

Drop half of the mixture into the waffle maker and let it cook for about 4 minutes or until golden brown.
Repeat with the remaining mixture.
Per serving: Calories: 207Kcal; Fat: 16g; Carbs: 1g; Protein: 6g

493. Colby Jack Chaffles

Preparation time: 8 minutes
Cooking time: 6 minutes
Servings: 1
Ingredients:
- 2 oz. Colby Jack cheese, sliced thinly in triangles
- 1 large organic egg, beaten

Directions:
Preheat your waffle iron and then grease it.
Arrange 1 thin layer of cheese slices in the bottom of the preheated waffle iron.
Place the beaten egg on top of the cheese.
Now, arrange another layer of cheese slices on top to cover evenly.
Cook for about 6 minutes.
Per serving: Calories: 254 Kcal; Fat: 21g; Carbs: 4g; Protein: 19g

494. Easy Birthday Cake Chaffle

Preparation time: 8 minutes
Cooking time: 16 minutes
Servings: 4
Ingredients:
- buttercream icing
- 3 tbsp. cream cheese
- 1 tbsp. almond flour
- 5 tbsp. coconut flour
- 1 tsp. baking powder
- 6 eggs
- 2 tbsp. birthday cake syrup

Directions:
Scoop 3 tbsp of the mixture into your waffle maker. Cook for 4 minutes and set it aside.
Repeat the process until you have 4 cake chaffles.
Just like a normal cake, start assembling your cake by placing one chaffle at the bottom as the base and adding a buttercream icing layer. Repeat the same process.
Pipe your cake edges with the icing and pile colorful shredded coconut at the center.
Once all the layers are completed, top with more icing and shredded coconut sprinkles.
Per serving: Calories: 188 Kcal; Fat: 8g; Carbs: 8g; Protein: 12g

495. Butter Churros Chaffles

Preparation time: 5 minutes
Cooking time: 5 minutes
Servings: 1
Ingredients:
- 1 egg
- 1 tbsp. almond flour
- ½ tsp. vanilla extract
- 1 tsp. cinnamon, divided
- ¼ tsp. baking powder
- ½ cup shredded mozzarella
- 1 tbsp. Swerve confectioners' sugar substitute
- 1 tbsp. Swerve brown sugar substitute
- 1 tbsp. butter, melted

Directions:
Turn on the waffle maker to heat and oil it with cooking spray.
Mix the egg, flour, vanilla extract, ½ tsp. of cinnamon, baking powder, mozzarella, and sugar substitute in a bowl.

Place half of the mixture into the waffle maker and cook for 5 minutes or until the desired doneness.
Remove and place the second half of the batter into the maker.
Cut the chaffles into strips.
Place the strips in a bowl and cover with melted butter.
Mix brown sugar substitute and the remaining cinnamon in a bowl.
Pour the sugar mixture over the strips and toss to coat them well.
Per serving: Calories: 280Kcal; Fat: 18g; Carbs: 2g; Protein: 20g

496. Glazed Chaffles

Preparation time: 5 minutes
Cooking time: 5 minutes
Servings: 2
Ingredients:
- ½ cup mozzarella shredded cheese
- ⅛ cup cream cheese
- 2 tbsp. unflavored whey protein isolate
- 2 tbsp. Swerve confectioners' sugar substitute
- ½ tsp. baking powder
- ½ tsp. vanilla extract
- 1 egg

Glaze Topping:
- 2 tbsp. heavy whipping cream
- 3-4 tbsp. Swerve confectioners' sugar substitute
- ½ tsp. vanilla extract

Directions:
Turn on the waffle maker to heat and oil it with cooking spray.
In a microwave-safe bowl, mix the mozzarella and cream cheese. Heat at 30-second intervals until melted and fully combined.
Add protein, 2 tbsp of sweetener, baking powder to cheese. Knead with your hands until well incorporated.
Place the dough into a mixing bowl and beat in the egg and vanilla until a smooth and creamy batter.
Put 1/3 of the batter into the waffle maker and cook for 3 minutes, until golden brown.
Repeat until all 3 chaffles are made.
Beat the glaze ingredients in a bowl and pour over chaffles before serving.
Per serving: Calories: 226Kcal; Fat: 18g; Carbs: 1g; Protein: 22g

497. Banana Nut Muffin Chaffle

Preparation time: 6 minutes
Cooking time: 12 minutes
Servings: 2
Ingredients:
- 1 egg
- 1 oz. cream cheese
- ¼ cup mozzarella cheese, shredded
- 1 tsp. banana extract
- 2 tbsp. sweetener
- 1 tsp. baking powder
- 4 tbsp. almond flour
- 2 tbsp. walnuts, chopped

Directions:
Combine all the ingredients in a bowl.
Turn on the waffle maker.
Add the batter to the waffle maker.
Seal and cook for 6 minutes.
Open and transfer the waffle to a plate. Let cool for 2 minutes.
Do the same steps with the remaining mixture.
Per serving: Calories: 234Kcal; Fat: 12g; Carbs: 2g; Protein: 12g

498. Cinnamon Rolls Cheddar Chaffles

Preparation time: 10 minutes
Cooking time: 5 minutes
Servings: 1
Ingredients:

- 1 tbsp. almond flour
- 1 tsp. cinnamon powder
- ½ cup cheddar cheese
- 1 tbsp. cocoa powder
- ½ tsp. baking powder
- 1 large egg
- 2 tbsp. peanut oil for topping

Directions:
Preheat the waffle maker and mix together all the ingredients in a bowl.
Pour the chaffle mixture into the center of the greased waffle maker.
Close the waffle maker.
Cook the chaffles for about 5 minutes until cooked and crispy.
Once the chaffles are cooked, remove them.
Pour melted butter oil on top.
Per serving: Calories: 320 Kcal; Fat: 26g; Carbs: 2g; Protein: 20g

499. Choco Chips Lemon Chaffles

Preparation time: 10 minutes
Cooking time: 15 minutes
Servings: 1
Ingredients:

- 1 egg, lightly beaten
- 1 tbsp. unsweetened chocolate chips
- 2 tsp. Swerve
- ½ tsp. vanilla
- ½ tsp. lemon extract
- ½ cup mozzarella cheese, shredded
- 2 tsp. almond flour

Directions:
Preheat your waffle maker.
In a bowl, whisk the eggs, Swerve, vanilla, lemon extract, cheese, and almond flour.
Add chocolate chips and stir well.
Spray waffle maker with cooking spray.
Pour ½ of the batter in the hot waffle maker and cook for 4 minutes or until golden brown.
Repeat with the remaining batter.
Serve them and enjoy.
Per serving: Calories: 146Kcal; Fat: 12g; Carbs: 2g; Protein: 17g

CHAPTER 8:

Savory Chaffles

500. Mayonnaise Chaffles

Preparation time: 5 minutes
Cooking time: 10 minutes
Servings: 1
Ingredients:

- 1 large organic egg, beaten
- 1 tbsp. mayonnaise
- 2 tbsp. almond flour
- ⅛ tsp. organic baking powder
- 1 tsp. water 2-4 drops liquid stevia

Directions:
Preheat the mini waffle iron and then grease it.
In a small-sized bowl, stir all the ingredients until well mixed.
Add half of the mixture into the preheated waffle iron and cook for about 4-5 minutes.
Repeat with the remaining mixture.
Per serving: Calories: 105 Kcal; Fat: 7g; Carbs: 2g; Protein: 6g

501. Basic Black Pepper Chaffles

Preparation time: 6 minutes
Cooking time: 8 minutes
Servings: 1
Ingredients:

- 1 large organic egg, beaten
- ½ cup cheddar cheese, shredded
- a pinch of salt
- ¼ tsp. freshly ground black pepper

Directions:
Preheat the mini waffle iron and then grease it.
In a small-sized bowl, stir all the ingredients and beat until properly combined.
Pour half of the mixture into the waffle maker. Let it cook for about 3-4 minutes or until golden brown.
Repeat with the remaining mixture, and serve the chaffles warm.
Per serving: Calories: 300 Kcal; Fat: 20g; Carbs: 1g; Protein: 20g

502. Parmesan and Cream Cheese Garlic Chaffles

Preparation time: 6 minutes
Cooking time: 5 minutes
Servings: 2
Ingredients:

- 1 tbsp. fresh garlic minced
- 2 tbsp. butter
- 1 oz. cream cheese, cubed
- 2 tbsp. almond flour
- 1 tsp. baking soda
- 2 large eggs
- 1 tsp. dried chives
- ½ cup parmesan cheese, shredded
- ¾ cup mozzarella cheese, shredded

Directions:
Heat the cream cheese and butter in a saucepan over medium-low until melted.
Add garlic and cook, stirring, for 2-3 minutes.
Turn on the waffle maker to heat and oil it with cooking spray.
In a small mixing bowl, whisk together the flour and baking soda, then set aside.
In a separate bowl, beat the eggs for 1 minute 30 seconds on high, then add in the cream cheese mixture and beat for 60 seconds more.
Add the flour mixture, chives, and cheeses to the bowl and stir well.
Add ¼ cup of batter to the waffle maker.
Close and cook for 4 minutes, until golden brown.
Repeat for the remaining batter.
Add your favorite toppings and serve.
Per serving: Calories: 346Kcal; Fat: 23g; Carbs: 2g; Protein: 6g

503. Chicken and Veggies Chaffles

Preparation time: 10 minutes
Cooking time: 15 minutes
Servings: 1
Ingredients:

- 1/3 cup cooked grass-fed chicken, chopped
- 1/3 cup cooked spinach, chopped
- 1/3 cup marinated artichokes, chopped
- 1 organic egg, beaten
- 1/3 cup mozzarella cheese, shredded
- 1 oz. cream cheese, softened
- ¼ tsp. garlic powder

Directions:
Preheat your mini waffle iron and then grease it.
In a medium bowl, place all the ingredients and mix until well combined.
Place ½ of the mixture into the preheated waffle iron and cook for about 4-5 minutes or until golden brown.
Repeat with the remaining mixture.
Per serving: Calories: 227 Kcal; Fat: 16g; Carbs: 1g; Protein: 22g

504. Turkey Chaffles

Preparation time: 10 minutes
Cooking time: 16 minutes
Servings: 2
Ingredients:

- ½ cup cooked turkey meat, chopped
- 2 organic eggs, beaten
- ½ cup parmesan cheese, grated
- ½ cup mozzarella, shredded
- ¼ tsp. poultry seasoning
- ¼ tsp. onion powder

Directions:
Preheat the mini waffle iron and then grease it.
In a medium bowl, place all the ingredients and mix until well combined.

Place ¼ of the mixture into the preheated waffle iron and cook for about 4 minutes or until golden brown.
Repeat with the remaining mixture.
Per serving: Calories: 330Kcal; Fat: 16g; Carbs: 2g; Protein: 22g

505. Chicken and Zucchini Chaffles

Preparation time: 10 minutes
Cooking time: 5 minutes
Servings: 2
Ingredients:

- 4 oz. cooked grass-fed chicken, chopped
- 2 cup zucchini, shredded and squeezed
- ¼ cup scallion, chopped
- 2 large organic eggs
- ½ cup mozzarella cheese, shredded
- ½ cup cheddar cheese, shredded
- ½ cup blanched almond flour
- 1 tsp. organic baking powder
- ½ tsp. garlic salt
- ½ tsp. onion powder

Directions:
Preheat the waffle iron and then grease it.
In a bowl, place all the ingredients and mix until well combined.
Divide the mixture into 9 portions.
Place 1 portion of the mixture into the preheated waffle iron and cook for about 2-3 minutes or until golden brown.
Repeat with the remaining mixture.
Per serving: Calories: 122Kcal; Fat: 16g; Carbs: 2g; Protein: 14g

506. Pepperoni Chaffles

Preparation time: 5 minutes
Cooking time: 5 minutes
Servings: 1
Ingredients:

- 1 organic egg, beaten
- ½ cup mozzarella cheese, shredded
- 2 tbsp. pepperoni slice, chopped
- 1 tbsp. sugar-free pizza sauce
- ¼ tsp. Italian seasoning

Directions:
Preheat the mini waffle iron and then grease it.
Combine all the ingredients in a bowl and mix well.
Let cook half of the mixture into the waffle iron.
Repeat the process to create the second chaffle.
Per serving: Calories: 245Kcal; Fat: 16g; Carbs: 1g; Protein: 20g

507. Hot Sauce and Jalapeño Chaffles

Preparation time: 6 minutes
Cooking time: 8 minutes
Servings: 1
Ingredients:

- ½ cup cheddar cheese, shredded and divided
- 1 organic egg, beaten
- 6 jalapeño pepper slices
- ¼ tsp. hot sauce
- a pinch of salt

Directions:
Preheat your mini waffle iron and then grease it.
In a bowl, place ½ cup of cheese and the remaining ingredients and mix until well combined.
Place about 1 tsp. of cheese in the bottom of the waffle maker for about 30 seconds before adding the mixture.

Drop half of the mixture into the preheated waffle maker and cook for about 3 minutes or until golden brown.
Repeat with the remaining cheese and mixture.
Per serving: Calories: 310Kcal; Fat: 27g; Carbs: 1g; Protein: 20g

508. Chicken Chaffles with Zucchini

Preparation time: 10 minutes
Cooking time: 15 minutes
Servings: 2
Ingredients:

- 2 oz. chicken breasts, cooked, shredded
- ½ cup mozzarella cheese, finely shredded
- 2 eggs
- 6 tbsp. parmesan cheese, finely shredded
- 1 cup zucchini, grated
- ½ cup almond flour
- 1tsp. baking powder
- ¼ tsp. garlic powder
- ¼ tsp. black pepper, ground
- ½ tsp. Italian seasoning
- ¼ tsp. salt

Directions:
Sprinkle the zucchini with a pinch of salt and set it aside for a few minutes. Squeeze out the excess water.
Warm up your mini waffle maker.
Mix the chicken, almond flour, baking powder, cheeses, garlic powder, salt, pepper, and seasonings in a bowl.
Use another small bow to beat the eggs. Add them to squeezed zucchini, mix well.
Combine the chicken and egg mixture, and mix.
For a crispy crust, add 1 tsp. of shredded cheese to the waffle maker and cook for 30 seconds.
Drop a quarter of the mixture into the waffle maker and cook for 5 minutes or until crispy.
Repeat with the remaining batter the same steps.
Per serving: Calories: 261Kcal; Fat: 14g; Carbs: 2g; Protein: 21g

509. Garlicky Chicken Chaffles

Preparation time: 6 minutes
Cooking time: 12 minutes
Servings: 1
Ingredients:

- 1 organic egg, beaten
- 1/3 cup grass-fed cooked chicken, chopped
- 1/3 cup mozzarella cheese, shredded
- ¼ tsp. garlic, minced
- ¼ tsp. dried basil, crushed

Directions:
Preheat your mini waffle iron and then grease it.
In a bowl, place all the ingredients and mix until properly combined.
Spoon half of the prepared batter into the preheated waffle iron and cook for about 4-6 minutes or until golden brown.
Repeat with the remaining mixture.
Per serving: Calories: 238Kcal; Fat: 17g; Carbs: 2g; Protein: 22g

510. Low Carb Honey Mustard Chaffles

Preparation time: 5 minutes
Cooking time: 10 minutes
Servings: 1
Ingredients:

- 1 organic egg, beaten and divided
- ½ cup cheddar cheese, shredded and divided
- 3 tbsp. low carb honey mustard

Directions:
Preheat a mini waffle iron and then grease it.
Place about ⅛ cup of cheese in the bottom of the waffle iron and top with half of the beaten egg.
Now, place ⅛ cup of cheese on top and cook for about 4-5 minutes.
Repeat with the remaining batter.
Serve them warm with the honey mustard beside
Per serving: Calories: 315Kcal; Fat: 26g; Carbs: 1g; Protein: 20g

511. Herb Blend Seasoning Chaffles

Preparation time: 6 minutes
Cooking time: 8 minutes
Servings: 1
Ingredients:
- 1 large organic egg, beaten
- ¼ cup parmesan cheese, shredded
- ¼ cup mozzarella cheese, shredded
- ½ tbsp. butter, melted
- 1 tsp. garlic herb blend seasoning
- salt, to taste

Directions:
Preheat the mini waffle iron and then grease it.
In a bowl, place all the ingredients and beat until properly stirred.
Fill the waffle maker with half of the batter and close the lid. Cook for about 4 minutes or until golden brown.
Repeat the process with the remaining mixture.
Per serving: Calories: 269Kcal; Fat: 16g; Carbs: 2g; Protein: 22g

512. Salmon Chaffles

Preparation time: 6 minutes
Cooking time: 10 minutes
Servings: 1
Ingredients:
- 1 large egg
- ½ cup shredded mozzarella
- 1 tbsp. cream cheese
- 2 slices salmon
- 1 tbsp. everything bagel seasoning

Directions:
Turn on the waffle maker to heat and oil it with cooking spray.
Beat the egg in a bowl, then add ½ cup of mozzarella.
Drop half of the mixture into the preheated waffle maker and cook for 4 minutes.
Remove and repeat with the remaining mixture.
Let the chaffles cool, then spread the cream cheese, sprinkle with seasoning, and top with the salmon.
Per serving: Calories: 225Kcal; Fat: 16g; Carbs: 5g; Protein: 24g

513. Katsu Sandwich

Preparation time: 10 minutes
Cooking time: 00 minutes
Servings: 2
Ingredients:
 Chicken:
- ¼ lb. boneless and skinless chicken thigh
- ⅛ tsp. salt
- ⅛ tsp. black pepper
- ½ cup almond flour
- 1 egg
- 2 cup vegetable oil for deep frying
 Brine:
- 2 cups of water
- 1 tbsp. salt

 Sauce:
- 2 tbsp. sugar-free ketchup
- 1½ tbsp. Worcestershire Sauce
- 1 tbsp. oyster sauce
- 1 tsp. Swerve/monk fruit
 Chaffles:
- 2 eggs
- 1 cup shredded mozzarella cheese

Directions:
Add the brine ingredients to a large mixing bowl.
Add the chicken and brine for 1 hour.
Pat the chicken dry with a paper towel. Sprinkle with salt and pepper. Set it aside.
Mix the ketchup, oyster sauce, Worcestershire sauce, and Swerve in a small mixing bowl.
Pulse the pork rinds in a food processor, making fine crumbs.
Fill one bowl with flour, a second bowl with beaten eggs, and a third with the crushed pork rinds.
Dip and coat each thigh in flour, eggs, and crushed pork rinds. Transfer to a plate.
Add the oil to cover ½ inch of the frying pan. Heat to 375°F.
Once the oil is hot, reduce the heat to medium and add the chicken. Cook time depends on the chicken thickness.
Transfer it to a drying rack.
Turn on the waffle maker to heat and oil it with cooking spray.
Beat the egg in a small bowl.
Place ⅛ cup of cheese on the waffle maker, then add ¼ of the egg mixture and top with ⅛ cup of cheese.
Cook for 3-4 minutes.
Repeat for the remaining batter.
Top the chaffles with chicken katsu, 1 tbsp. of sauce, and another piece of chaffle.
Per serving: Calories:376Kcal; Fat: 32g; Carbs: 4g; Protein: 26g

514. Pork Rind Chaffles

Preparation time: 6 minutes
Cooking time: 10 minutes
Servings: 1
Ingredients:
- 1 organic egg, beaten
- ½ cup ground pork rinds
- 1/3 cup mozzarella cheese, shredded
- a pinch of salt

Directions:
Preheat the mini waffle iron and then grease it.
In a bowl, place all the ingredients and beat until properly mixed.
Fill the waffle maker with half of the batter. Cook for about 4-5 minutes or until it reaches the desired doneness.
Repeat with the remaining mixture.
Per serving: Calories: 280Kcal; Fat: 26g; Carbs: 1g; Protein: 20g

515. Parmesan Bruschetta Chaffles

Preparation time: 5 minutes
Cooking time: 5 minutes
Servings: 1
Ingredients:
- ½ cup shredded mozzarella cheese
- 1 whole egg beaten
- ¼ cup grated parmesan cheese
- 1 tsp. Italian Seasoning
- ¼ tsp. garlic powder
Toppings:
- 3-4 cherry tomatoes, chopped
- 1 tsp. fresh basil, chopped

- splash of olive oil
- a pinch of salt

Directions:
Turn on the waffle maker to heat and oil it with cooking spray.
Whisk all the chaffle ingredients, except mozzarella, in a bowl.
Add in the cheese and mix.
Fill the waffle maker with half of the batter and close the lid. Cook for 5 minutes.
Mix tomatoes, basil, olive oil, and salt. Serve over the top of the chaffles.
Per serving: Calories: 250Kcal; Fat: 16g; Carbs: 1g; Protein: 22g

516. Protein Cheddar Chaffles

Preparation time: 10 minutes
Cooking time: 40 minutes
Servings: 2
Ingredients:
- ½ cup golden flax seeds meal
- ½ cup coconut flour
- 2 tbsp. unsweetened whey protein powder
- 1 tsp. organic baking powder
- salt and freshly ground black pepper, to taste
- ¾ cup cheddar cheese, shredded
- 1/3 cup unsweetened almond milk
- 2 tbsp. unsalted butter, melted
- 2 large organic eggs, beaten

Directions:
Preheat the mini waffle iron and then grease it.
In a large bowl, place flax seeds meal, flour, protein powder, and baking powder and mix well.
Stir in the cheddar cheese.
In another bowl, place the remaining ingredients and beat until well combined.
Add the egg mixture into the bowl with flax seeds meal mixture and mix until well combined.
Place the desired amount of the mixture into the preheated waffle iron and cook for about 4-5 minutes or until golden brown.
Repeat with the remaining mixture.
Per serving: Calories: 325Kcal; Fat: 24g; Carbs: 3g; Protein: 22g

517. Chicken and Ham Chaffles

Preparation time: 10 minutes
Cooking time: 16 minutes
Servings: 1
Ingredients:
- ¼ cup grass-fed cooked chicken, chopped
- 1 oz. sugar-free ham, chopped
- 1 organic egg, beaten
- ¼ cup Swiss cheese, shredded
- ¼ cup mozzarella cheese, shredded

Directions:
Preheat the mini waffle iron and then grease it.
In a medium bowl, place all the ingredients and mix until well combined.
Place ¼ of the mixture into the preheated waffle iron and cook for about 4 minutes or until golden brown.
Repeat with the remaining mixture.
Per serving: Calories: 437Kcal; Fat: 28g; Carbs: 3g; Protein: 26g

518. Herb, Garlic and Onions Chaffles

Preparation time: 10 minutes
Cooking time: 12 minutes
Servings: 2
Ingredients:
- 4 tbsp. almond flour
- 1 tbsp. coconut flour
- 1 tsp. mixed dried herbs
- ½ tsp. organic baking powder
- ¼ tsp. garlic powder
- ¼ tsp. onion powder
- salt and ground black pepper, to taste
- ¼ cup cream cheese, softened
- 2 large organic eggs
- ½ cup cheddar cheese, grated
- 1/3 cup parmesan cheese, grated

Directions:
Preheat the waffle iron and then grease it.
In a bowl, mix together the flours, dried herbs, baking powder, and seasoning, and mix well.
In a separate bowl, put the cream cheese and eggs and beat until well combined.
Add the flour mixture, cheddar, and parmesan cheese and mix until well combined.
Place the desired amount of the mixture into the preheated waffle iron and cook for about 2-3 minutes.
Repeat with the remaining mixture.
Per serving: Calories: 352Kcal; Fat: 28g; Carbs: 4g; Protein: 23g

519. Scallion Chaffles

Preparation time: 6 minutes
Cooking time: 8 minutes
Servings: 1
Ingredients:
- 1 organic egg, beaten
- ½ cup mozzarella cheese, shredded
- 1 tbsp. scallion, chopped
- ½ tsp. Italian seasoning

Directions:
Preheat the mini waffle iron and then grease it.
Combine all the ingredients in a mixing bowl. Stir until homogeneous.
Spoon half of the prepared batter into the preheated waffle iron and cook for about 4 minutes or until golden brown.
Repeat the process to create the second chaffle.
Per serving: Calories: 224Kcal; Fat: 16g; Carbs: 3g; Protein: 20g

520. Broccoli and Parmesan Chaffles

Preparation time: 5 minutes
Cooking time: 5 minutes
Servings: 2
Ingredients:
- 1 cup broccoli, processed
- 1 cup shredded cheddar cheese
- 1/3 cup grated parmesan cheese
- 2 eggs

Directions:
Turn on the waffle maker to heat and grease it with cooking spray.
Use a powerful blender or food processor to process the broccoli until rice consistency.
Beat the eggs and mix them with all the ingredients in a medium bowl.
Add 1/3 of the mixture to the waffle iron and cook for 4-5 minutes until golden.
Per serving: Calories: 319Kcal; Fat: 24g; Carbs: 1g; Protein: 19g

521. Eggs Benedict Chaffle

Preparation time: 6 minutes
Cooking time: 10 minutes
Servings: 2
Ingredients:
Chaffles:
- 2 egg whites
- 2 tbsp. almond flour
- 1 tbsp. sour cream
- ½ cup mozzarella cheese
Hollandaise Sauce:
- ½ cup salted butter
- 4 egg yolks
- 2 tbsp. lemon juice
Poached Eggs:
- 2 eggs
- 1 tbsp. white vinegar
- 3 oz. deli ham

Directions:
Whip the egg white until frothy, then mix in the remaining ingredients.
Turn on the waffle maker to heat and oil it with cooking spray.
Cook for 7 minutes until golden brown.
Remove the chaffle and repeat with the remaining batter.
Fill half of the pot with water and bring to a boil.
Place a heat-safe bowl on top of the pot, ensuring the bottom doesn't touch the boiling water.
Heat the butter to a boil in a microwave.
Add the yolks to a double boiler bowl and bring to a boil.
Add the hot butter to the bowl and whisk briskly. Cook until the egg yolk mixture has thickened.
Remove the bowl from the pot and add in lemon juice. Set it aside.
Add more water to the pot if needed to make the poached eggs (the water should completely cover the eggs). Bring to a simmer. Add white vinegar to the water.
Crack the eggs into simmering water and cook for 1 minute 30 seconds. Remove using a slotted spoon.
Warm the chaffles in a toaster for 2-3 minutes. Top with ham, poached eggs, and hollandaise sauce.
Per serving: Calories: 367Kcal; Fat: 20g; Carbs: 4g; Protein: 25g

522. Chicken Bacon Chaffles

Preparation time: 6 minutes
Cooking time: 5 minutes
Servings: 1
Ingredients:
- 1 egg
- 1/3 cup cooked chicken, diced
- 1 piece of bacon, cooked and crumbled
- 1/3 cup shredded cheddar Jack cheese
- 1 tsp. powdered ranch dressing

Directions:
Turn on the waffle maker to heat and oil it with cooking spray.
Mix the egg, dressing, and Monterey cheese in a small bowl.
Add the bacon and chicken.
Spoon half of the prepared batter into the waffle maker and cook for 3-minutes.
Remove and cook the remaining batter to make a second chaffle.
Let the chaffles sit for 2 minutes before serving.
Per serving: Calories: 375Kcal; Fat: 28g; Carbs: 2g; Protein: 20g

523. Bacon with Veggies Chaffles

Preparation time: 6 minutes
Cooking time: 24 minutes
Servings: 2

Ingredients:
- 2 cooked bacon slices, crumbled
- ½ cup frozen chopped spinach, thawed and squeezed
- ½ cup cauliflower rice
- 2 organic eggs
- ½ cup cheddar cheese, shredded
- ½ cup mozzarella cheese, shredded
- ¼ cup parmesan cheese, grated
- 1 tbsp. butter, melted
- 1 tsp. garlic powder
- 1 tsp. onion powder

Directions:
Preheat the mini waffle iron and then grease it.
In a bowl, place all the ingredients, except blueberries, and beat until well combined.
Fold in the blueberries.
Divide the mixture into 6 portions.
Place 1 portion of the mixture into the preheated waffle iron and cook for about 3-4 minutes or until golden brown.
Repeat with the remaining mixture.
Serve them warm.
Per serving: Calories: 358Kcal; Fat: 18g; Carbs: 2g; Protein: 20g

524. Vegan Nutmeg Chaffles

Preparation time: 5 minutes
Cooking time: 25 minutes
Servings: 1
Ingredients:
- 1 tbsp. flaxseed meal
- ¼ tsp. nutmeg
- 2½ tbsp. water
- ¼ cup low carb vegan cheese
- 2 tbsp. almond flour
- 1 tbsp. low carb vegan cream cheese, softened
- a pinch of salt

Directions:
Turn on the waffle maker to heat and oil it with cooking spray.
Mix the flaxseed and water in a bowl. Leave for 5 minutes, until thickened and gooey.
Whisk the remaining ingredients for the chaffle.
Pour one-half of the batter into the center of the waffle maker. Close and cook for 3-5 minutes.
Remove the chaffle and serve them.
Per serving: Calories: 80Kcal; Fat: 5g; Carbs: 1g; Protein: 1g

525. Lemony Fresh Herbs Chaffles

Preparation time: 10 minutes
Cooking time: 24 minutes
Servings: 2
Ingredients:
- ½ cup ground flaxseed
- 2 organic eggs
- ½ cup goat cheddar cheese, grated
- 2-4 tbsp. plain Greek yogurt
- 1 tbsp. avocado oil
- ½ tsp. baking soda
- 1 tsp. fresh lemon juice
- 2 tbsp. fresh chives, minced
- 1 tbsp. fresh basil, minced
- ½ tbsp. fresh mint, minced
- ¼ tbsp. fresh thyme, minced
- ¼ tbsp. fresh oregano, minced
- salt, and freshly ground black pepper, to taste

Directions:
Preheat the waffle iron and then grease it.
In a medium-sized bowl, place all the ingredients, and with a fork, mix until well combined.
Divide the mixture into 6 portions.
Place a quarter of the mixture into the preheated waffle iron and cook for about 4 minutes or until golden brown.
Repeat with the remaining mixture.
Serve them warm.
Per serving: Calories: 180Kcal; Fat: 15g; Carbs: 1g; Protein: 12g

526. Italian Seasoning Chaffles

Preparation time: 6 minutes
Cooking time: 8 minutes
Servings: 1
Ingredients:
- ½ cup mozzarella cheese, shredded
- 1 tbsp. parmesan cheese, shredded
- 1 organic egg
- ¾ tsp. coconut flour
- ¼ tsp. organic baking powder
- ⅛ tsp. Italian seasoning
- a pinch of salt

Directions:
Preheat your mini waffle iron and then grease it.
In a medium bowl, place all the ingredients, and with a fork, mix until well combined.
Drop half of the mixture into the waffle iron and cook for about 4 minutes or until golden brown.
Repeat with the remaining mixture.
Per serving: Calories: 263 Kcal; Fat: 18g; Carbs: 3g; Protein: 14g

527. Basil Chaffles

Preparation time: 10 minutes
Cooking time: 16 minutes
Servings: 2
Ingredients:
- 2 organic eggs, beaten
- 1 cup mozzarella cheese, shredded
- 1 tbsp. parmesan cheese, grated
- 1 tsp. dried basil, crushed
- a pinch of salt

Directions:
Preheat your mini waffle iron and then grease it.
In a medium bowl, place all the ingredients and mix.
Place ½ of the mixture into the preheated waffle iron and cook for about 3-4 minutes or until golden brown.
Repeat with the remaining mixture.
Per serving: Calories: 225Kcal; Fat: 18g; Carbs: 9g; Protein: 22g

528. Almond Flour Chaffles with Bacon

Preparation time: 6 minutes
Cooking time: 5 minutes
Servings: 2
Ingredients:
- 2 eggs
- ½ cup cheddar cheese
- ½ cup mozzarella cheese
- ¼ tsp. baking powder
- ½ tbsp. almond flour
- 1 tbsp. butter, for the waffle maker

Filling:
- ¼ cup bacon, chopped
- 2 tbsp. green onions, chopped

Directions:
Turn on the waffle maker to heat and oil it with butter.
Add the eggs, mozzarella, cheddar, almond flour, and baking powder to a blender and pulse 10 times, so the cheese is still chunky.
Add the bacon and green onions. Pulse 2 times to combine.
Add one-half of the batter to the waffle maker and cook for 3 minutes, until golden brown.
Repeat with the remaining batter.
Add your toppings and serve hot.
Per serving: Calories: 312Kcal; Fat: 18g; Carbs: 2g; Protein: 20g

529. Spinach and Cheeses Mix Chaffles

Preparation time: 10 minutes
Cooking time: 20 minutes
Servings: 2
Ingredients:
- 2 large organic eggs, beaten
- 1 cup ricotta cheese, crumbled
- ½ cup mozzarella cheese, shredded
- ¼ cup parmesan cheese, grated
- 4 oz. frozen spinach, thawed and squeezed
- 1 garlic clove, minced
- salt and freshly ground black pepper, to taste

Directions:
Preheat the mini waffle iron and then grease it.
In a medium bowl, place all the ingredients and mix until well combined.
Place ¼ of the mixture into the preheated waffle iron and cook for about 4-5 minutes or until golden brown.
Repeat with the remaining mixture.
Per serving: Calories: 346Kcal; Fat: 22g; Carbs: 6g; Protein: 30g

530. Zucchini and Mozzarella Chaffles

Preparation time: 10 minutes
Cooking time: 20 minutes
Servings: 1
Ingredients:
- 1 cup grated zucchini
- 1 beaten egg
- ½ cup mozzarella cheese, shredded
- 1 tsp. dried basil
- ¾ tsp. divided Kosher salt
- ½ tsp. ground black pepper

Directions:
Sprinkle on the zucchini approximately ¼ tsp. of salt, and then let it sit whilst collecting your ingredients. In a paper towel, wrap the zucchini before just using it, then to force all the extra water out, squeeze it.
Beat the egg in a little bowl. Combine the grated zucchini, basil, mozzarella, ½ tsp. of salt, and pepper.
Scatter 1-2 spoonsful of chopped parmesan to coat the waffle iron base.
Scatter ¼ of the mixture. Use about 1-2 tsp of chopped parmesan to cover and shut the lid. Use enough for surface covering.
Let it cook for about 4-8 minutes. Usually, it is pretty much done when the processor has stopped the steam cloud emits. Let it cook till it's golden brown for great results.
Remove it and repeat the same with the next waffle.
Make one full-size chaffle or two smaller chaffles if you are using a mini chaffle maker.

These chaffles freeze well if you intend to consume them another day. Warm them up again in the toaster or in your fryer to gain back crispness. Warm them up again in the toaster or in your fryer to gain back crispness.
Per serving: Calories: 188Kcal; Fat: 16g; Carbs: 8g; Protein: 12g

531. Cauliflower Chaffles

Preparation time: 10 minutes
Cooking time: 5 minutes
Servings: 1
Ingredients:

- 1 cup cauliflower, riced
- ¼ tsp. garlic powder
- ¼ tsp. black pepper, ground
- ½ tsp. Italian Seasoning
- ¼ tsp. kosher salt
- ½ cup mozzarella cheese shredded
- 1 egg
- ½ cup of parmesan cheese, shredded

Directions:
Warm up your waffle maker.
Combine all the ingredients and put them into a blender.
In waffle maker, scatter ⅛ cup of parmesan cheese. Ensure the waffle iron bottom is covered.
Pour the cauliflower batter into the waffle machine.
Put another bit of parmesan cheese on the mixture's top.
Ensure the top of the waffle iron is covered by the batter.
Cook it for 4 to 5 minutes, or till it's crispy.
Make four mini chaffles or two full-size chaffles.
Per serving: Calories: 265Kcal; Fat: 17g; Carbs: 3g; Protein: 20g

532. Parmesan and Garlic Bruschetta Chaffles

Preparation time: 10 minutes
Cooking time: 5 minutes
Servings: 1
Ingredients:

- ½ cup mozzarella cheese, shredded
- 1 beaten egg
- ¼ cup parmesan cheese, grated
- 1 tsp. Italian Seasoning
- ¼ tsp. garlic powder

Directions:
Switch on your mini waffle maker.
Bring in all the products, with the exception of the mozzarella cheese, to a bowl and mix. Put in the cheese and blend till it's mixed well.
Spray non-stick spray on your waffle plates, then add half of the batter in the center. Shut the cover and cook for 3 to 5 minutes; it depends entirely on how crisp you want in your chaffles.
Start preparing the base mixture with grated parmesan cheese, a drizzle of olive oil, and chopped fresh parsley or basil.
Add 3 to 4 chopped cherry tomatoes, sliced, ½ tsp. of chopped fresh basil and olive oil spray, and a sprinkle of salt.
Put over the upper part of the chaffles and serve.
Per serving: Calories: 246Kcal; Fat: 17g; Carbs: 1g; Protein: 20g

533. Easy Pizza Chaffle

Preparation time: 10 minutes
Cooking time: 20 minutes
Servings: 1
Ingredients:

- 1 egg
- ½ cup crushed mozzarella cheese

- a pinch of seasoning, Italian
- 1 tbsp. pizza sauce (sugar-free)
- topping with more crushed cheese pepperoni

Directions:
Preheat the waffle machine.
In the mixing bowl, beat the egg as well as seasonings together.
Combine it with the crushed cheese and mix.
To the hot waffle maker, insert a tbsp. of shredded cheese and then let it for around 30 seconds. That will help produce a crispier crust.
Apply half of the batter to the machine, then cook till it is golden brown and mildly crispy for around 4 minutes.
To the second chaffle, put the waffle out and insert the leftover mixture into the maker.
Top it with pizza sauce, pepperoni, and crushed cheese. Microwave it for around 20 seconds on high, and serve them.
Per serving: Calories: 267Kcal; Fat: 28g; Carbs: 3g; Protein: 22g

534. Taco Chaffles

Preparation time: 10 minutes
Cooking time: 5 minutes
Servings: 2
Ingredients:

- 2 egg white
- ¼ cup shredded Monterey Jack cheese, (packed firmly)
- ¼ cup shredded sharp cheddar cheese, (packed firmly)
- ¾ tsp. water
- 1 tsp. coconut flour
- ¼ tsp. baking powder
- ⅛ tsp. chili powder
- 1 a pinch salt

Directions:
Plug in the Dash Mini Waffle Maker to the wall and lightly grease it once it is warm.
Incorporate all the components in a bowl and mix well to combine them.
Pour half of the mixture on the maker and then shut the lid.
Setup a 4-minute timer, and thus do not remove the cover till the cooking duration is finished.
If you do so, the taco chaffle will appear like it is not set up completely, but it would.
Before you open the lid, you get to just let it the whole 4 minutes
Put the taco shell out from the iron as well as set it aside. Repeat the same procedure for the remaining portion of the chaffle batter.
Switch a muffin pan over and place the taco chaffle between cups to create a taco shell. Let it sit for a couple of minutes.
Per serving: Calories: 392Kcal; Fat: 28g; Carbs: 4g; Protein: 31g

535. Garlic Cheesy Chaffle Bread Sticks

Preparation time: 10 minutes
Cooking time: 5 minutes
Servings: 2
Ingredients:

- 2 medium-sized egg
- ½ cup grated mozzarella cheese
- 2 tbsp. almond flour
- ½ tsp. garlic powder
- ½ tsp. oregano
- ½ tsp. salt

Toppings:

- 2 tbsp. unsalted softened butter
- ½ tsp. garlic powder
- ¼ cup grated mozzarella cheese

Directions:

Turn the waffle maker on and grease it gently by using olive oil.

In a mixing bowl, whisk the egg.

Insert the almond flour, mozzarella, oregano, garlic powder as well as salt and combine properly.

Pour the mixture into the waffle maker.

Shut the cover and cook for about 5 minutes.

Use tongs, pick the prepared waffles, and then slice each waffle into 4 pieces.

Put these sticks on a tray and heat the grill before that.

Combine the garlic powder and butter together and scatter on the sticks.

Spray the mozzarella over all the sticks and put for 2 to 3 minutes, under the grill till the cheese melts and makes bubbles.

Per serving: Calories: 282Kcal; Fat: 20g; Carbs: 2g; Protein: 23g

536. Chaffles Benedict

Preparation time: 10 minutes
Cooking time: 20 minutes
Servings: 2
Ingredients:
Chaffles:
- 2 egg whites
- 2 tbsp. almond flour
- 1 tbsp. sour cream
- ½ cup mozzarella cheese

Hollandaise Sauce
- ½ cup butter, salted
- 4 yolks eggs
- 2 tbsp. Lemon juice

Poached Eggs
- 2 whole eggs
- 1 tbsp. white vinegar
- 3 oz. deli ham

Directions:
Chaffle:

Beat the egg white till frothy, now add in the rest of the ingredients, and blend.

Preheat the Mini Waffle Machine, then insert half of the batter of the chaffle into that. Sprinkle non-stick spray onto the chaffle maker.

Cook till it becomes golden brown, for around 7 minutes. Pull the chaffle out and repeat.

Hollandaise sauce:

Organize a dual boiler (a pot that best fits on top with such a heat-safe bowl). Add sufficient water to boil in the pot, but do not contact the bowl's bottom.

In the microwave, heat up the butter to a boil. Place the egg yolks in the double boiler bowl and put the pot to boil. Transfer the heated butter into the bowl when boiling the pot.

Beat nimbly, heating the batter with the water under the bowl. Keep cooking till the pot water boils, the yolk-butter combination has thickened, as well as very extremely hot. Take the bowl out of the pot and insert the lemon juice. Set it aside.

To poach the eggs:

If required, add a little more water in the pot (you have sufficient to completely cover the egg) and take it to simmer. Put two tbsp. of white vinegar into the water. Drop an egg cautiously into the boiling water and cook it for 90 seconds. Put it out using a slotted spoon.

To assemble:

Heat up the chaffle for some minutes in a toaster. Top the crispy, crunchy chaffle with a poached egg, two tbsp of hollandaise sauce, and half of the ham pieces.

Per serving: Calories: 367Kcal; Fat: 35g; Carbs: 4g; Protein: 32g

537. Chicken Feta Chaffles

Preparation time: 10 minutes
Cooking time: 15 minutes
Servings: 2
Ingredients:
- ¼ cup almond flour
- 1 tsp. baking powder
- 2 large eggs
- 1/2 cup shredded chicken
- ¼ cup mozzarella cheese, crushed
- ¼ cup Frank's red-hot sauce plus 1 tbsp. (optional) for topping
- ¾ cup shredded cheddar cheese, sharp
- ¼ cup crushed feta cheese
- ¼ cup diced celery

Directions:

Mix and beat the baking powder into the almond flour in a medium mixing bowl, then put aside.

Preheat your waffle maker on medium-high heat, then brush with low-carb non-stick spray generously.

Put the eggs in a mixing bowl and whisk till foamy.

First, add in the hot sauce and mix till well integrated.

Transfer the flour batter to the eggs and blend till well mixed.

Lastly, put in the crumbled cheeses, and then mix well till combined. Mix in the shredded chicken.

Transfer the chaffle mixture to the preheated maker, then cook till the outside browns. Approximately four minutes.

Take it out from the waffle maker and repeat step 7 till all the batter has been used up.

Plate the chaffles and top with celery, hot sauce, or feta and serve them.

Per serving: Calories: 330Kcal; Fat: 22g; Carbs: 3g; Protein: 25g

538. BLT Regular Sandwich Chaffle

Preparation time: 10 minutes
Cooking time: 5 minutes
Servings: 2
Ingredients
Chaffles
- 1 egg
- ½ cup shredded cheddar cheese

Sandwich:
- 2 bacon strips
- 1-2 tomato slices
- 2-3 lettuce pieces
- 1 tbsp. mayonnaise

Directions:

Preheat your waffle maker as instructed by the manufacturer.

Mix the shredded cheese and egg together in a little mixing bowl. Mix until you have integrated well.

Pour half of the mixture into the maker. Cook for 3 to 4 minutes, or till it's light brown. Do the same with the batter's second half.

Cook the bacon in a large saucepan at medium heat till it's crispy and switch as required. Remove onto paper towels to drain.

Organize the sandwich with tomato, lettuce, and mayonnaise.

Note: If you're using a waffle maker of large size, you might be able to cook the entire batter amount in one waffle. That would vary with your machine's size.

Per serving: Calories: 397Kcal; Fat: 28g; Carbs: 5g; Protein: 20g

539. Garlic Bread Chaffle

Preparation time: 10 minutes
Cooking time: 5 minutes
Servings: 2

Ingredients:

- 2 eggs
- ½ cup mozzarella, finely shredded
- 1 tsp. coconut flour
- ¼ tsp. baking powder
- ½ tsp. garlic powder
- 1 tbsp. melted butter
- ¼ tsp. garlic salt
- 2 tbsp. parmesan
- 1 tsp. finely chopped parsley

Directions:

Plug in your waffle maker to preheat it. Set the oven temperature at 375°F and preheat.

In a mixing bowl, add the mozzarella, egg, coconut flour, garlic powder, and baking powder and stir well to blend.

Put half of the batter in the waffle iron, then cook for about 3 minutes or till the steam is gone. On a baking sheet, put the prepared chaffle.

With the leftover batter of the chaffle, repeat the same steps.

Mix garlic salt and butter together, and then over the chaffles, brush it.

Sprinkle the parmesan on the chaffles.

Put the pan for 5 minutes in the oven to melt the cheese.

Scatter the parsley over it prior to serving.

Note: The garlic salt could be mildly salty—if you're watching salt, feel free to add in freshly chopped garlic or even garlic powder.

Per serving: Calories: 362Kcal; Fat: 17g; Carbs: 4g; Protein: 22g

540. Hot Ham and Cheese Chaffles

Preparation time: 10 minutes
Cooking time: 5 minutes
Servings: 1
Ingredients:

- 1 large egg
- ½ cup crushed Swiss cheese
- ¼ cup deli ham, chopped
- ¼ tsp. garlic salt
- 1 tbsp. mayonnaise
- 2 tsp. Dijon mustard

Directions:

Plug the waffle iron in to preheat it.

Beat the egg into a bowl. And add and combine in the ham, cheese, and garlic salt.

In the heated waffle iron, put half of the batter, cover it and cook for 3-4 minutes or till the waffle iron finishes steaming as well as the waffle is prepared completely.

Transfer the waffle to a tray and continue with the remaining batter.

Mix the mustard and mayo together to use as a sauce.

Break the waffles into half or quarters, then serve with sauce.

Per serving: Calories: 363Kcal; Fat: 24g; Carbs: 4g; Protein: 23g

541. Big Mac Chaffle

Preparation time: 10 minutes
Cooking time: 10 minutes
Servings: 1
Ingredients:

Cheeseburger:

- 1/3 lb. ground beef
- ½ tsp. garlic salt
- 2 pieces American cheese

Chaffles:

- 1 big egg
- ½ cup of mozzarella finely shredded
- ¼ tsp. garlic salt

Big Mac Sauce:

- 2 tsp. mayonnaise
- 1 tsp. ketchup
- 1 tsp. dill pickle relish
- Splash vinegar as per your taste

To Assemble:

- 2 tbsp. chopped lettuce
- 3 to 4 dill pickles
- 2 tsp. finely chopped onion

Directions:

Burgers:

Put the griddle over a medium-high heat

Split the beef into two spheres of similar size and put each, at about 6 inches away, on the griddle.

Let them cook for around 1 minute.

Use a tiny salad plate to push the beef balls tightly, to straight down to flatten. Scatter the garlic salt.

Cook for 2 minutes, or when cooked half completely.

Carefully turn the burgers, then spray lightly with the remaining garlic salt.

Keep cooking for 2 minutes or till cooked completely.

Put one cheese slice on each patty, then pile the patties onto a plate and set aside. Wrap in foil.

Chaffles:

Heat and spray the waffle iron with non-stick cooking oil spray.

Mix the cheese, egg, and garlic salt together until well mixed.

In the waffle iron, add half of the egg mixture, and then cook for 2 to 3 minutes. Place aside and replicate the step with the remaining batter.

Big Mac Sauce:

Mix all the items together

To Organize the Burgers:

With stacked patties, chopped lettuce, onions, and pickle, top one chaffle.

Scatter the Big Mac sauce on the other chaffle, then put the sauce on the sandwich face down.

Per serving: Calories: 353Kcal; Fat: 36g; Carbs: 2g; Protein: 22g

542. Japanese Style Pizza Chaffle

Preparation time: 12 minutes
Cooking time: 6 minutes
Servings: 2
Ingredients:

Crust:

- 1 cup mozzarella cheese (shredded)
- 2 eggs

Toppings:

- 4 tbsp. pizza sauce
- 2 whole Japanese sausages
- 2 stalks asparagus
- 2 tbsp. mozzarella cheese (shredded)
- 2 tbsp. kewpie mayo
- 2 tsp. dried seaweed

Directions:

Quickly, preheat a mini-sized waffle and grease it.

Using a mixing bowl, add beaten eggs with mozzarella cheese, mix evenly and pour into the lower side of the waffle maker.

With the lid closed, heat for 5 minutes to a crunch.

Preheat an oven to 500F, with the chaffle on a baking tray, pizza topping by adding the Asparagus and Japanese sausage into ¼ inch.

Spread the sliced asparagus, Japanese sausage, and kewpie mayo on the pizza sauce on the chaffle.

Bake in the oven for 4 minutes at 500F until the cheese melts.

Garnish on the top with shredded dried seaweed and enjoy.

Per serving: Calories: 414Kcal; Fat: 35g; Carbs: 3g; Protein: 20g

543. Pepperoni Pizza Chaffle

Preparation time: 18 minutes
Cooking time: 12 minutes
Servings: 2
Ingredients:
> **Toppings:**
> - 2 tsp. tomato sauce (sugar-free)
> - 8 pepperoni slices
> - ½ cup shredded mozzarella cheese
>
> **Pizza Chaffle:**
> - 2 eggs
> - ¼ tsp. Italian season
> - ½ cup cheddar cheese
> - 2 tbsp. parmesan cheese

Directions:
Preheat and grease a waffle maker. Make a combined mixture of all the Pizza chaffles ingredients, evenly mixed and pour into the base of the waffle maker evenly and spread.

With the lid closed, cook for 4 minutes till the chaffles turn crispy and then set aside.

Transfer the chaffle into a parchment paper-lined plate.

Pour some tomato sauce with pepperoni sauce on each chaffle and sprinkle with shredded mozzarella.

Bake the chaffle in the oven for 2 minutes until the cheese turns light brown.

Per serving: Calories: 346Kcal; Fat: 36g; Carbs: 1g; Protein: 18g

544. Cauliflower and Onion Pizza Chaffle

Preparation time: 18 minutes
Cooking time: 12 minutes
Servings: 2
Ingredients:
> **Toppings:**
> - 2 tsp. tomato sauce (sugar-free)
> - 1 tbsp. butter
> - 4 tbsp. cauliflower (diced)
> - ½ cup shredded mozzarella cheese
> - 4 tbsp. onion (diced)
> - a pinch salt
>
> **Pizza Chaffle:**
> - 2 eggs
> - ¼ tsp. Italian season
> - ½ cup cheddar cheeses
> - 2 tbsp. parmesan cheese

Directions:
Heat some butter in a saucepan with cauliflower, heat, and stir for 4 minutes.

Add in the onions and stir for 3 minutes more, then keep aside. Preheat and grease a waffle maker.

Combine all the Pizza chaffles ingredients, evenly mixed and pour into the base of the waffle maker evenly and spread.

With closed lids, cook for 7 minutes till the chaffles turn crispy, and then set it aside.

Transfer the chaffle into a parchment paper-lined plate.

Pour some tomato sauce with the onion and diced cauliflower on each chaffle and sprinkle with shredded mozzarella cheese.

Bake the chaffle in the oven for 2 minutes until the cheese turns light brown.

Per serving: Calories: 158Kcal; Fat: 16g; Carbs: 1g; Protein: 12g

545. BBQ Chicken Pizza Chaffle

Preparation time: 18 minutes
Cooking time: 12 minutes
Servings: 2

Ingredients:
> **Toppings:**
> - 2 tsp. tomato sauce (sugar-free)
> - ½ cup shredded mozzarella cheese
>
> **Pizza Chaffle:**
> - 2 eggs
> - ¼ tsp. Italian season
> - ½ cup cheddar cheese
> - 2 tbsp. parmesan cheese
>
> **BBQ Chicken:**
> - 1 tbsp. butter
> - ½ cup chicken
> - 1 tbsp. BBQ sauce (sugar-free)

Directions:
Heat some butter in a saucepan with diced chicken, heat using medium-low heat, and stir for 9 minutes.

Add BBQ sauce, and then keep aside.

Preheat and grease a waffle maker. Make a combined mixture of all the Pizza chaffles ingredients, evenly mixed and pour into the base of the waffle maker evenly and spread.

With closed lids, cook for 7 minutes till the chaffles turn crispy, and then set them aside.

Transfer the chaffle into a parchment paper-lined plate.

Pour some tomato sauce with 5-6 chicken cubes on each chaffle and sprinkle with shredded mozzarella cheese.

Bake the chaffle in the oven for 2 minutes until the cheese turns light brown.

Per serving: Calories: 253Kcal; Fat: 28g; Carbs: 1g; Protein: 32g

546. Vegetable Pizza Chaffle

Preparation time: 28 minutes
Cooking time: 18 minutes
Servings: 2
Ingredients:
> **Toppings:**
> - 2 tsp. tomato sauce (sugar-free)
> - 4 tbsp. cauliflower (diced)
> - ½ cup shredded mozzarella cheese
> - 4 tbsp. onion (diced)
> - 4 tbsp. olives (diced)
> - 4 tbsp. red pepper (diced)
> - 4 tbsp. tomatoes (diced)
> - 1 tbsp. butter
> - a pinch salt
>
> **Pizza Chaffle:**
> - 2 eggs
> - ¼ tsp. Italian season
> - ½ cup cheddar cheese
> - 2 tbsp. parmesan cheese

Directions:
Heat some butter in a saucepan with the vegetables (onion, tomatoes, cauliflower, red pepper) and salt for 3 minutes and keep aside.

Preheat and grease a waffle maker. Make a combined mixture of all the Pizza chaffles ingredients, evenly mixed and pour into the base of the waffle maker evenly and spread.

With closed lids, cook for 4 minutes till the chaffles turn crispy, and then set them aside.

Transfer the chaffle into a parchment paper-lined plate.

Pour some tomato sauce with the vegetable mixture on each chaffle and sprinkle with shredded mozzarella cheese.

Bake the chaffle in the oven for 2 minutes until the cheese turns light brown.

Per serving: Calories: 338Kcal; Fat: 18g; Carbs: 1g; Protein: 22g

547. Thyme Chaffles

Preparation time: 5 minutes
Cooking time: 8 minutes
Servings: 2
Ingredients:
- 1 large organic egg, beaten
- ½ cup cheddar cheese, shredded
- a pinch of salt and freshly ground black pepper
- a pinch of thyme

Directions:
Preheat a mini waffle iron and then grease it.
Place all the ingredients in a bowl and beat until properly mixed.
Fill the waffle maker with half of the batter and close the lid.
Cook for about 3-4 minutes. Repeat with the remaining mixture.
Per serving: Calories: 300Kcal; Fat: 25g; Carbs: 1g; Protein: 20g

548. Hot Pork Chaffles

Preparation time: 10 minutes
Cooking time: 10 minutes
Servings: 4
Ingredients:
- 1 cup pulled pork, cooked
- 2 tbsp. parmesan, grated
- 2 eggs, whisked
- 2 red chilies, minced
- 1 cup almond milk
- 1 cup almond flour
- 2 tbsp. coconut oil, melted
- 1 tsp. baking powder

Directions:
In a bowl, mix the pulled pork with the eggs, parmesan, and the other ingredients and whisk well.
Heat up the waffle maker, pour ¼ of the chaffle mix, cook for 8 minutes and transfer to a plate.
Repeat with the rest of the mix and serve them.
Per serving: Calories: 310 Kcal; Fat: 18g; Carbs: 1g; Protein: 14g

549. Spicy Chicken Chaffles

Preparation time: 10 minutes
Cooking time: 10 minutes
Servings: 2
Ingredients:
- 2 eggs, whisked
- 1 cup rotisserie chicken, skinless, boneless, and shredded
- 1 cup mozzarella, shredded
- ½ cup milk
- 2 tsp. chili powder
- 1 tsp. sriracha sauce
- 1 tbsp. chives, chopped
- ½ tsp. baking powder

Directions:
Combine all the chaffles ingredients in a mixing bowl. Stir until homogeneous.
Preheat the waffle maker, pour a quarter of the batter, cook for 10 minutes, and transfer to a plate.
Cook more chaffles using the remaining batter.
Per serving: Calories: 263Kcal; Fat: 21g; Carbs: 3g; Protein: 13g

550. Spicy Ricotta Chaffles

Preparation time: 10 minutes
Cooking time: 10 minutes
Servings: 2
Ingredients:
- 2 cup coconut flour
- 1½ cup coconut milk
- 2 tbsp. olive oil
- a pinch of salt and black pepper
- ½ cup ricotta cheese
- 1 tsp. baking powder
- 2 eggs, whisked
- ½ cup chives, chopped
- 1 red chili pepper, minced
- 1 jalapeño, chopped

Directions:
In a bowl, mix the flour with the milk, oil, and the other ingredients and whisk well.
Heat up the waffle iron, pour ¼ of the batter and cook for 10 minutes.
Repeat with the rest of the chaffle mix and serve them.
Per serving: Calories: 373Kcal; Fat: 32g; Carbs: 6g; Protein: 26g

551. Spicy Black Sesame Chaffles

Preparation time: 10 minutes
Cooking time: 10 minutes
Servings: 2
Ingredients:
- 1 cup almond flour
- 1 cup almond milk
- juice of ½ lemon
- 1/3 cup black sesame seeds
- a pinch of salt and black pepper
- 2 eggs, whisked
- 1 tsp. chili powder
- 1 tsp. hot paprika

Directions:
In a bowl, mix the almond flour with the almond milk and the other ingredients and whisk well.
Heat up the waffle iron, pour ¼ of the batter and cook for 5 minutes.
Repeat with the rest of the mix and serve them.
Per serving: Calories: 169Kcal; Fat: 14g; Carbs: 3g; Protein: 8g

552. Spicy Zucchini Chaffles

Preparation time: 10 minutes
Cooking time: 8 minutes
Servings: 2
Ingredients:
- 1½ cup almond flour
- 2 tsp. baking powder
- 2 eggs, whisked
- 1½ cup coconut milk
- 2 zucchinis, grated
- 1 tsp. chili powder
- 1 tsp. cayenne pepper
- 1 cup cheddar cheese, shredded

Directions:
In a medium-sized bowl, add all the chaffle ingredients, and stir them well.
Preheat the waffle iron, pour 1/6 of the batter, cook the chaffle for 6 minutes and set it aside.
Repeat the process with the rest of the batter to create more chaffles.
Per serving: Calories: 180Kcal; Fat: 28g; Carbs: 3g; Protein: 12g

553. Tabasco Chaffles

Preparation time: 5 minutes
Cooking time: 8 minutes
Servings: 2

Ingredients:
- 1 cup coconut milk
- 1 cup coconut flour
- 2 tsp. Tabasco sauce
- 2 eggs, whisked
- 2 tbsp. ghee, melted
- ½ cup mozzarella, shredded
- 1 tsp. cayenne pepper
- 1 tbsp. chives, chopped
- 1 tbsp. baking powder
- a pinch of salt and black pepper

Directions:
Turn on the waffle maker to heat and grease it with cooking spray.
In a bowl, mix the milk with the flour, and then add Tabasco sauce and the other ingredients and whisk well.
Pour a quarter of the batter, cook for 5 minutes and set it aside.
Repeat with the rest of the batter and serve them.
Per serving: Calories: 210Kcal; Fat: 10g; Carbs: 4g; Protein: 8g

554. Green Cayenne Chaffles

Preparation time: 10 minutes
Cooking time: 10 minutes
Servings: 3
Ingredients:
- 1 cup coconut flour
- ½ cup cream cheese, soft
- ½ cup coconut milk
- 1 tbsp. chives, chopped
- 1 tbsp. parsley, chopped
- 1 green chili pepper, minced
- ½ tsp. cayenne pepper
- 1 tsp. baking soda
- 3 eggs

Directions:
In a bowl, mix the eggs with the cream cheese, milk, and the other ingredients and whisk well.
Preheat the waffle iron, pour ¼ of the batter, close the waffle maker, cook for 10 minutes and transfer to a plate.
Repeat with the rest of the batter and serve them.
Per serving: Calories: 184Kcal; Fat: 12g; Carbs: 11g; Protein: 8g

555. Pesto Chaffles

Preparation time: 10 minutes
Cooking time: 7 minutes
Servings: 2
Ingredients:
- 1 cup almond milk
- 1 cup mozzarella, shredded
- ½ cup coconut flour
- 3 tbsp. basil pesto
- 1 tsp. hot paprika
- 1 tsp. chili powder
- 2 eggs, whisked
- 1 tbsp. ghee, melted
- 1 tsp. baking soda

Directions:
In a bowl, mix the milk with the cheese, pesto, and the other ingredients and whisk.
Heat up the waffle maker, pour ¼ of the mix, cook for 7 minutes and transfer to a plate.
Repeat with the rest of the mix and serve them.
Per serving: Calories: 141Kcal; Fat: 12g; Carbs: 10g; Protein: 18g

556. Katsu Sandwich Chaffle with Pork Rinds

Preparation time: 90 minutes
Cooking time: 40 minutes
Servings: 2
Ingredients:
Sauce:
- 2 tbsp. ketchup (sugar-free)
- 1 tsp. Swerve/monk fruit
- 2 tbsp. Worcestershire sauce
- 1 tbsp. oyster sauce

Chaffles:
- 2 green lettuce leaves (optional)
- 2 eggs
- 1 cup mozzarella cheese (shredded)

Chicken:
- 2 pieces chicken thigh boneless or ¼ lb. (boneless)
- 1 egg
- ¼ tsp. black pepper, or as per your taste
- 2 cup vegetable oil (deep frying)
- 1 cup almond flour
- ¼ tsp. salt, or as per your taste
- 3 oz. unflavored pork rinds

Brine:
- 2 cup water
- 1 tbsp. salt

Directions:
Using a skillet, boil the chicken with salt and 2 cups of water.
With the lid closed, boil for 28 minutes.
Once done, dry the chicken using a small towel to pat, and then add salt and dried pepper on its sides.
Using a mixing bowl, a mixture containing the oyster sauce, monk fruit, sugar-free ketchup, and Worcestershire and set it aside.
Using a food processor or blender, grind the pork rinds to fine crumbs.
Using 3 mixing bowls containing the ingredients respectively (almond flour, beaten eggs in another, and the crushed pork in the last), coat the chicken using the ingredients in these bowls in this order (Flour-Eggs-Pork).
Deep fry the chicken pieces in a frying pan to a golden brown, then place in a rack for excess oil to drip out.
Use another bowl to mix shredded mozzarella cheese with beaten eggs.
With a closed lid, mix evenly and heat the waffle for 5 minutes to a crunch.
Once timed out, remove the chaffle from the waffle maker.
Repeat for the remaining chaffles mixture.
Slice the avocados with the green leaf lettuce washed and dried.
With one chaffle, spread sauce on it, the green lettuce, chicken katsu, and close with another chaffle. Serve the dish and savor the taste.
Per serving: Calories: 383Kcal; Fat: 35g; Carbs: 5g; Protein: 28g

557. Bread Sandwich Chaffle

Preparation time: 18 minutes
Cooking time: 12 minutes
Servings: 2
Ingredients:
- 1 tbsp. almond flour
- 2 tbsp. mayo
- ½ tsp. garlic powder
- 2 eggs
- 2 tsp. water
- ⅛ tsp. baking powder

Directions:
Preheat and grease the waffle maker, and combine all the ingredients in a mixing bowl.
Drop half of the mixture into the waffle maker and spread evenly.

Heat the mixture to a crispy form (about 4 minutes).
Repeat the process with the remaining batter.
Per serving: Calories: 75 Kcal; Fat: 7g; Carbs: 1g; Protein: 4g

558. Eggs and Bacon Sandwich Chaffle

Preparation time: 12 minutes
Cooking time: 6 minutes
Servings: 2
Ingredients:
   Sandwich:
   - 4 bacon strips
   - 2 eggs
   - 2 slices American cheese
   Chaffles:
   - 2 eggs
   - 1 cup cheddar cheese(shredded)

Directions:
Preheat and grease the waffle maker.
Mix the shredded cheddar with beaten eggs.
Blend to a froth,
Mix evenly and pour into the lower side of the waffle maker.
With a closed lid, heat the waffle for 5 minutes to a crunch, and then remove the chaffle.
Heat the sliced bacon to a crispy form using medium heat in a large non-stick pan; drain the fried bacon, then fry the eggs.
Put off the heat on the chaffle. Repeat for the remaining chaffles mixture to make more batter.
Serve egg and cheese with slices of bacon in between two chaffles and enjoy.
Per serving: Calories: 348Kcal; Fat: 32g; Carbs: 2g; Protein: 20g

559. BBQ Chicken Sandwich Chaffle

Preparation time: 1 hr.
Cooking time: 30 minutes
Servings: 2
Ingredients:
   - 2 pieces boneless chicken breast
   - BBQ sauce (sugar-free)
   - ¼ tsp. paprika
   - 1 tbsp. lime juice
   - ¼ tsp. salt
   - ¼ tsp. pepper
   - 1 piece coal
   - ½ cup cheddar cheese
   - 2 eggs
   - ½ tbsp. Italian herbs
   - 1 slice cheese
   - ½ tomato (sliced)
   - 2 slices lettuce
   - ½ tbsp. oil

Directions:
To make your BBQ chicken chaffle sandwich, start with the preparation of your chicken. Take the boneless chicken pieces and cut them into cubes.
Marinate the cubes with Italian herbs, paprika, lime juice, oil, salt, and pepper. Then, mix them thoroughly. Let the marinade set on the chicken for around 20 minutes.
Next, melt the butter in a pan and cook your chicken.
Take the piece of coal and burn it. Use a tong to pick it up and place it in an aluminum foil. Put the coal on the chicken and cover it with a lid.
Let the chicken cook with the smoky flavor for around 7 to 10 minutes.

Then, remove the chicken and place it in a dish. Then, start preparing your chaffle bread. Preparing the chaffle bread is easy and requires only two ingredients. Whisk together egg and cheddar cheese.
You can add some Italian seasonings to give some taste to the bread.
Then, preheat your waffle maker to medium heat and pour the mixture into the machine.
Cook it well for about 3 to 5 minutes. Repeat the process to get another chaffle.
Then, assemble your sandwich. Put the chicken into the chaffle bread and add tomatoes, lettuce, BBQ sauce, and a cheese slice to your sandwich. Voila! Your keto sandwich is ready.
Per serving: Calories: 388 Kcal; Fat: 29g; Carbs: 1g; Protein: 25g

560. Cajun Shrimp and Avocado Chaffle

Preparation time: 45 minutes
Cooking time: 30 minutes
Servings: 1
Ingredients:
   - 1 egg
   - ½ cup shredded cheddar cheese
   - 1 tbsp. almond flour
   - 2 tsp. Cajun seasoning
   - 1 lb. raw shrimps
   - 1 tbsp. avocado oil
   - 2 slices bacon
   - ⅓ cup sliced red onions

Directions:
This sandwich is full of nutrients and contains a lot of ingredients. So, let's start by preparing the ingredients. To begin with, heat a pan to medium heat with avocado oil. Then, add the bacon strips to the pan and let each side cook until crispy and brown.
Remove the bacon strips and dry them on a paper towel. This will help absorb excess oil.
Then, the shrimps. Put them in a bowl and add 1 tsp. of Cajun seasoning. Add a small amount of avocado oil and salt and pepper. Leave them for 15 minutes.
Next, put the shrimps in the pan and fry them in the same bacon grease. Fry each side for a small amount of time. Once they are fried, dry them on kitchen paper. Scoop out the avocado in a bowl.
Now, your chaffle bread. For the chaffle bread, add an egg with shredded cheddar cheese, almond flour, 1 tsp. of Cajun seasoning and cook in the waffle machine that is preheated to medium heat for around 3 to 4 minutes.
Assemble your Cajun Shrimp and Avocado chaffle sandwich. Add the shrimps, onions, bacon slices, and avocado.
Per serving: Calories: 329Kcal; Fat: 28g; Carbs: 1g; Protein: 22g

561. Pork Rinds Chaffle Sandwich

Preparation time: 45 minutes
Cooking time: 15 minutes
Servings: 2
Ingredients:
   - 1 chicken breast
   - 4 tbsp. pickle juice
   - 2½ tbsp. cheddar cheese (powdered)
   - 2½ tbsp. pork rinds
   - 1 tbsp. flaxseed
   - 2 tbsp. butter, melted
   - ¼ tsp. salt
   - ¼ tsp. pepper
   - ½ tsp. paprika
   - 2 eggs
   - ½ cup cheddar cheese (shredded)
   - 2 slices pickle

Directions:

For this recipe, you need to focus on preparing the chicken. Therefore, first of all, get your chicken and cut it into two pieces.

Keep these pieces in a zip lock bag with pickle juice. Make sure you let your chicken absorb the pickle juice for at least 2 hours for better taste. Ensure that you keep the chicken in the refrigerator.

In a bowl, add the dry ingredients such as pork rinds, flaxseed, powdered cheese, paprika, salt, and pepper.

Mix these ingredients. Turn on your air fryer. Preheat it at around 400°F.

Then, take out the chicken and drain the pickle water. Dip the chicken in the unsalted butter and then into the mixture. Then, let it cook in the air fryer for around 7 to 9 minutes.

Now your chaffle keto bread. For the preparation of this low-carb bread, add an egg and shredded cheddar cheese to a bowl. Then, beat the mixture and place it in a waffle machine that is preheated to medium heat for around 3 to 4 minutes.

After making your chaffle bread, assemble the sandwich. Add the chicken to the chaffle bread and top it off with cheese and pickle slices.

Per serving: Calories: 329Kcal; Fat: 28g; Carbs: 1g; Protein: 22g

562. Salami Sandwich Chaffle

Preparation time: 45 minutes
Cooking time: 15 minutes
Servings: 1
Ingredients:

- 2 salami patties
- 2 tbsp. coconut oil
- ¼ tsp. salt
- 1 slice cheddar cheese
- 2 slices lettuce
- 2 slices tomato
- 1 egg
- ½ cup mozzarella cheese (shredded)
- 1 tsp. Italian seasoning

Directions:

Start with the preparation of the salami patties. Take a pan and heat it to medium heat. Put 2 tbsp of coconut oil in the pan and let it melt.

Then, add your salami patties to the oil and let them fry.

Once they are fried, keep them on kitchen paper to absorb any excess oil.

Now, you can make your chaffle bread. This bread can be prepared by adding an egg and shredded mozzarella cheese to a bowl.

Whisk these ingredients together and add Italian seasoning to give a spicy taste, and pour the mixture in a waffle machine that is preheated to medium heat for around 3 to 4 minutes until the chaffle turns golden brown.

Now comes the part of the assembly of the sandwich. Add the salami, cheese slice, lettuce, and tomato to the chaffle bread.

Per serving: Calories: 287Kcal; Fat: 24g; Carbs: 3g; Protein: 26g

563. Reuben Chaffle Sandwich

Preparation time: 15 minutes
Cooking time: 5 minutes
Servings: 1
Ingredients:

- 1 egg
- ½ cup shredded cheddar cheese
- 1 tbsp. almond flour
- 1 tbsp. low carb thousand island sauce
- a pinch of baking powder
- 2 slices corned beef
- 1 slice mozzarella cheese
- 1 tbsp. sauerkraut

Directions:

Start by preparing your chaffle bread. The chaffle bread is a great low-carb bread alternative.

All you need for this bread is an egg and shredded mozzarella cheese. Add the items along with baking powder, coconut flour, 1 tbsp. of thousand islands sauce in a bowl.

Whisk these ingredients together. Then, preheat your waffle machine to around 450°F.

When it is warm enough, you should pour the mixture into the waffle machine. Let the chaffle cook for around 3 to 4 minutes until you see the golden-brown color.

Once your chaffle bread is prepared, then start preparing your meat. Take a microwave-friendly plate and add the beef slice to it.

Top it off with the cheese slice and microwave it until the cheese melts. Add the thousand island sauce and sauerkraut to the chaffle bread. Place your meat in the sandwich and enjoy.

Per serving: Calories: 290Kcal; Fat: 27g; Carbs: 3g; Protein: 22g

564. Italian Herbs Breakfast Sandwich Chaffle

Preparation time: 30 minutes
Cooking time: 5 minutes
Servings: 1
Ingredients:

- 1 egg
- ½ cup shredded mozzarella cheese
- 2 tbsp. coconut flour
- ½ tsp. baking powder
- 1 tsp. Italian herbs
- 2 tbsp. almond oil
- 2 slices tomato
- 2 slices lettuce

Directions:

This is a simple breakfast chaffle that is very easy to cook and does not require a lot of ingredients. Begin by preparing the base of the chaffle. You can do so by taking the shredded mozzarella, egg, baking powder, and Italian herbs together in a bowl. Mix them well.

Then, turn on your waffle machine to medium heat. Pour the batter into the waffle machine.

Don't open the machine before 3 minutes and let it cook until it is golden brown.

Now, you can take a pan and turn on the heat to medium. Then, add the unsalted butter to the pan and let it melt.

Once the butter melts, add the chaffle and cook it in the butter until it becomes crispy.

Make sure you cook both sides well. Then, assemble your sandwich. Add your vegetables to the sandwich and enjoy your healthy and nutritious breakfast.

Per serving: Calories: 195Kcal; Fat: 18g; Carbs: 3g; Protein: 21g

565. Bacon and Cheese Sandwich Chaffle

Preparation time: 30 minutes
Cooking time: 5 minutes
Servings: 1
Ingredients:

- 1 egg
- ½ cup shredded mozzarella cheese
- 2 tbsp. coconut flour
- ½ tsp. baking powder
- 1 tsp. Italian herbs
- 2 tbsp. almond oil
- 1 slice cheddar cheese
- 2 bacon strips

Directions:

Start with a simple chaffle base. Mix in a bowl the shredded mozzarella cheese, coconut flour, baking powder, Italian herbs, and an egg. Whisk this mixture well. Then, take a waffle machine and preheat it to around medium heat.

Once it is preheated, sprinkle some cheese on the waffle machine. Add the mixture on top of the cheese base and top it off with more cheese. Let this cook in the machine for 4 minutes until the color changes to a golden brown.

Then, turn the heat below a pan. Then, add almond oil to the pan, cook the bacon strips in the oil. Take them out once they are fried.

Now, it is time for the assembly of the sandwich. Add your bacon and cheese to the sandwich and enjoy it.

Per serving: Calories: 297Kcal; Fat: 24g; Carbs: 3g; Protein: 20g

566. Grilled Cheese Chaffle Sandwich

Preparation time: 45 minutes
Cooking time: 10 minutes
Servings: 1
Ingredients:

- 1 egg
- ½ cup cheddar cheese (shredded)
- ¼ tsp. baking powder
- 2 slices American cheese
- 1½ tbsp. butter

Directions:

To make the chaffle bread. Begin your preparation by mixing in a bowl shredded the cheddar cheese, baking powder, and the egg.

Once you have mixed them thoroughly, turn your waffle machine and preheat it to around medium heat. Once it is preheated, pour the mixture on the machine and close the lid.

The chaffle should cook for at least 3 to 4 minutes until the color changes to a golden brown. Repeat the process to have two chaffles.

Then, take a pan and turn the heat below it to medium. During that time, place two slices of your favorite cheese (in this case, American cheese) in between two chaffles. Put butter on the pan and allow it to melt.

Remove the sandwich from the pan and enjoy your hot and tasty keto sandwich.

Per serving: Calories: 376Kcal; Fat: 32g; Carbs: 1g; Protein: 26g

567. Mini Eggy Sandwich Chaffle

Preparation time: 5 minutes
Cooking time: 10 minutes
Servings: 1
Ingredients:

- 2 mini keto chaffle
- 2 slice cheddar cheese
- 1 egg, simple omelet

Directions:

Preheat your oven to 400°F.

Arrange the egg omelet and cheese slice between chaffles.

Bake in the preheated oven for about 4-5 minutes until the cheese is melted.

Once the cheese is melted, remove it from the oven.

Per serving: Calories: 324Kcal; Fat: 28g; Carbs: 2g; Protein: 25g

568. Chicken, Spinach, and Artichoke Chaffle

Preparation time: 10 minutes
Cooking time: 8 minutes
Servings: 1

Ingredients:

- 1/3 cup cooked diced chicken
- 1/3 cup cooked spinach chopped
- 1/3 cup marinated artichokes chopped
- 1/3 cup shredded mozzarella cheese
- 1 oz. softened cream cheese
- ¼ tsp. garlic powder
- 1 egg

Directions:

Turn on the waffle maker to heat and grease it with cooking spray.

In a small-sized bowl, beat the egg, and add mozzarella cheese, garlic powder, and cream cheese.

Add spinach, artichoke, and chicken. Mix well until homogeneous.

Drop 1/3 of the mixture into the waffle maker. Cook for 2-3 minutes.

Repeat the steps to create as many chaffle as the batter allow.

Before serving, let sit the chaffle for about 2-3 minutes.

Enjoy the chaffles with ranch dressing, sour cream, or enjoy alone.

Per serving: Calories: 188Kcal; Fat: 13g; Carbs: 9g; Protein: 13g

569. Chicken Bacon Ranch Chaffle

Preparation time: 10 minutes
Cooking time: 8 minutes
Servings: 1
Ingredients:

- 1 egg
- 1/3 cup cooked chicken diced
- 1 piece bacon cooked and crumbled
- 1/3 cup shredded cheddar Jack cheese
- 1 tsp. powdered ranch dressing

Directions:

Turn on the waffle maker to heat and grease it with cooking spray.

Combine the ranch dressing, egg, and Monterey Jack Cheese into a small-sized bowl. Add the chicken and bacon. Mix well until homogeneous.

Drop half of the mixture into the waffle maker and spread evenly. Cook for 5 minutes and then let it sit for 2 minutes.

Use the remaining mixture for cooking a second chaffle with the same process.

Dip in ranch dressing, sour cream, or enjoy alone.

Per serving: Calories: 185Kcal; Fat: 17g; Carbs: 1g; Protein: 14g

570. Beef Chaffle, the Classic

Preparation time: 10 minutes
Cooking time: 15 minutes
Servings: 4
Ingredients:
Batter:

- 4 eggs
- 2 cup grated mozzarella cheese
- 3 tbsp. coconut flour
- 3 tbsp. almond flour
- 2 tsp. baking powder
- salt and pepper to taste
- 1 tbsp. freshly chopped parsley

Seasoned Beef:

- 1 lb. beef tenderloin
- salt and pepper to taste
- 2 tbsp. olive oil
- 2 tbsp. olive oil to brush the waffle maker

Directions:

Preheat the waffle maker.

Add the eggs, grated mozzarella cheese, coconut flour, almond flour, baking powder, salt and pepper, and freshly chopped parsley to a bowl.

Mix until you have a creamy batter.

Brush the heated waffle maker with olive oil and add a few tbsp. of the batter.

Close the lid and cook for about 7 minutes, depending on your waffle maker.

Meanwhile, heat the olive oil in a non-stick pan over medium heat.

Season the beef tenderloin with oil, salt, and pepper

Cook on each side for about 4-5 minutes.

Serve each chaffle with beef tenderloin.

Per serving: Calories: 247Kcal; Fat: 19g; Carbs: 5g; Protein: 23g

571. Turkey BBQ Sauce Chaffle

Preparation time: 10 minutes
Cooking time: 10 minutes
Servings: 2
Ingredients:
- ½ lb. ground turkey meat
- 2 eggs
- 1 cup grated Swiss cheese
- ¼ cup cream cheese
- ¼ cup BBQ sauce
- 1 tsp. dried oregano
- salt and pepper to taste
- 2 garlic cloves, minced
- 2 tbsp. butter to brush the waffle maker
- ¼ cup BBQ sauce for serving
- 2 tbsp. freshly chopped parsley for garnish

Directions:
Preheat the waffle maker.

Add the ground turkey, eggs, grated Swiss cheese, cream cheese, BBQ sauce, dried oregano, salt and pepper, and minced garlic to a bowl.

Mix everything until combined and a creamy batter.

Brush the heated waffle maker with butter and add a few tbsp. of the batter.

Close the lid and cook for about 8-10 minutes, depending on your waffle maker.

Serve each chaffle with a tbsp. of BBQ sauce and a sprinkle of freshly chopped parsley.

Per serving: Calories: 280Kcal; Fat: 12g; Carbs: 4g; Protein: 25g

572. Chicken Sandwich Chaffle

Preparation time: 10 minutes
Cooking time: 8 minutes
Servings: 1

Ingredients:
Chaffles:
- 1 large organic egg, beaten
- ½ cup cheddar cheese, shredded
- a pinch of salt and ground black pepper

Filling:
- 1 (6 oz.) cooked chicken breast, halved
- 2 lettuce leaves
- ¼ of a small onion, sliced
- 1 small tomato, sliced

Directions:
Preheat your mini waffle iron and then grease it.

For chaffles: In a medium bowl, put all the ingredients and, with a fork, mix until well combined.

Cook for around 4 minutes half of the mixture on the mini waffle iron.

Repeat with the remaining mixture.

Serve each chaffle with the filling ingredients.

Per serving: Calories: 369Kcal; Fat: 34g; Carbs: 1g; Protein: 27g

573. Cuban-Style Pork Sandwich Chaffle

Preparation time: 10 minutes
Cooking time: 16 minutes
Servings: 2
Ingredients:
Chaffles:
- 2 large organic eggs
- ¼ cup superfine blanched almond flour
- ¾ tsp. organic baking powder
- ½ tsp. garlic powder
- 1 cup cheddar cheese, shredded

Filling:
- 12 oz. cooked pork, cut into slices
- 2 tsp. unsalted butter
- 3 cup yellow mustard
- 12 large dill pickles, thinly sliced crosswise
- 8 Swiss cheese slices
- Kosher salt, to taste

Directions:
Preheat your mini waffle iron and then grease it.

For chaffles: in a bowl, add the eggs, almond flour, baking powder, and garlic powder, and beat until well combined.

Add the cheese and stir to combine.

Place ¼ of the mixture into the preheated waffle iron and cook for about 3-minutes.

Repeat with the remaining mixture.

Serve each chaffle with the filling ingredients.

Per serving: Calories: 479Kcal; Fat: 34g; Carbs: 1g; Protein: 29g

CHAPTER 9:

Snack and Appetizer

574. Hot Beef Taco Chaffles

Preparation time: 30 minutes
Cooking time: 25minutes
Servings: 1
Ingredients:

- 1 tsp. chili powder
- 1 tsp. ground cumin
- ½ tsp. garlic powder
- ½ tsp. cocoa powder
- ¼ tsp. onion powder
- ¼ tsp. salt
- 1/12 tsp. smoked paprika
- 1 tbsp. olive oil
- ¼ lb. ground beef or ground turkey
- ½ cup cheddar cheese, shredded
- 1 large egg
- ½ an onion
- 1 handful cilantro, chopped
- 1 lime, cut into wedges
- hot sauce of your choice

Directions:
Take all of the taco seasonings and mix them together.
Take the olive oil and put it on the medium-sized pan, and add your ground beef or turkey. Put it on medium heat.
Add all of the taco meat seasonings to the meat.
Continue stirring until the meat has browned.
Dice the cilantro, onions, and limes.
Shred the cheese in a bowl.
Take the meat off the heat once it is done. Set it aside.
Follow the classic chaffle recipe.
Once the chaffles are done, put them in a taco stand to help them take shape.
Fill the chaffles with the meat, cheese, cilantro, lettuce, onions, and limes.
Per serving: Calories: 427Kcal; Fat: 36g; Carbs: 1g; Protein: 22g

575. Classic Pizza Chaffle

Preparation time: 30 minutes
Cooking time: 40 minutes
Servings: 1
Ingredients:

- 2 classic chaffles
  Toppings:
- 1 oz. mozzarella, thinly sliced
- 1 tsp. Italian seasoning
- 1 tbsp. sugar-free pizza sauce
- 4-6 pepperoni slices

Directions:
Preheat the oven to 350°F and take out a baking pan.
Follow the classic chaffle recipe.
Once the chaffles are done, lay them on the baking pan.

Spread the tomato sauce on one, then layer the mozzarella cheese and pepperoni slices.
Bake in the oven for 5-10 minutes or until the cheese is melting.
Per serving: Calories: 260 Kcal; Fat: 24g; Carbs: 1g; Protein: 14g

576. Hamburger Chaffle

Preparation time: 30 minutes
Cooking time: 40 minutes
Servings: 1
Ingredients:

- 2 classic chaffles
  Hamburger:
- 1/3 lb. ground beef
- 2-3 dill pickles
- 1 slice red onion
- 1 handful of lettuce, shredded
- 1 slice of an heirloom tomato

Directions:
Slice the onions, shred the lettuce and slice the tomatoes.
Take a medium-sized pan and put it on medium heat.
Take the ground meat and form it into patties roughly the same size as your chaffle maker. Fry the ground meat on the pan until cooked through. Set it aside when done.
Follow the classic chaffle recipe.
Once the chaffles are done, lay two chaffles side by side.
Layer on the lettuce, meat, tomatoes, onions, pickles, and any sauces of your choosing.
Per serving: Calories: 383Kcal; Fat: 28g; Carbs: 1g; Protein: 25g

577. Easy BLT Chaffle Sandwich

Preparation time: 30 minutes
Cooking time: 40 minutes
Servings: 1
Ingredients:

- 2 classic chaffles
  BLT:
- 1 tbsp. mayonnaise
- 1 handful of lettuce, shredded
- 1 slice of an heirloom tomato
- 2 slices bacon

Directions:
Clean the lettuce and slice the tomatoes.
Take a medium-sized pan and put it on medium heat.
Take the bacon and cook until the desired texture, chewy or crunchy. Set it aside when done.
Follow the classic chaffle recipe.
Once the chaffles are done, lay two chaffles side by side.
Layer on the mayonnaise, bacon, lettuce, and tomatoes.
Per serving: Calories: 366Kcal; Fat: 20g; Carbs: 1g; Protein: 23g

578. Fried Chicken Chaffles

Preparation time: 30 minutes
Cooking time: 40 minutes
Servings: 1
Ingredients:

- 2 classic chaffles

Fried Chicken

- 2 boneless skinless chicken thighs
- oil for frying

Egg Wash

- 2 large eggs, whole
- 2 tbsp. heavy whipping cream

Keto Breading

- 2/3 cup blanched almond flour
- 2/3 cup grated parmesan cheese
- 1 tsp. salt
- ½ tsp. black pepper
- ½ tsp. paprika
- ½ tsp. cayenne

Directions:

Pour 1-3 inches of oil into a pot on high heat.
Have the oil heat up to 350°F.
While the oil is heating, take a bowl and mix the eggs and heavy cream until well mixed. Set aside.
In another bowl, mix together the breading ingredients. Set it aside.
Take each thawed chicken thigh and cut into 3-4 evenly-sized pieces.
Dip each chicken slice in the breading, followed by dipping the slice in the egg wash and then back in the breading again.
Make sure each side is evenly coated with breading.
Then, dip the chicken slices slowly and carefully into the hot oil.
Keep the chicken slices in the oil until the slices are a deep brown and cooked through. About 5-7 minutes.
Do only a few slices at a time to avoid overcrowding the pot.
Follow the classic chaffle recipe.
Serve the chaffles and chicken on a plate and add some sugar-free pancake syrup or hot sauce to taste.
Per serving: Calories: 373Kcal; Fat: 26g; Carbs: 2g; Protein: 22g

579. Chicken Sandwich Chaffle

Preparation time: 30 minutes
Cooking time: 40 minutes
Servings: 1
Ingredients:

- 2 classic chaffles

Chicken Salad

- 1-½ cup chicken, cooked and sliced apart
- 3 tbsp. red onion, finely chopped
- ¼ cup celery, finely chopped
- 1 large hard-boiled egg, chopped
- 1 tbsp. dill pickle relish
- ½ cup mayonnaise
- ¼ tsp. salt
- 1-2 cracks of freshly ground black pepper

Directions:

Slice the onions, celery, and hard-boiled egg until finely chopped.
Cut the chicken into small pieces and add to the mixing bowl.
Mix the onions, celery, hard-boiled egg, and chicken together until well combined.
Add the mayonnaise, dill relish, salt, and pepper to the mixing bowl and mix together until well combined. Set aside.
Follow the classic chaffle recipe.
Lay two chaffles side by side and layer on the chicken salad.
Sandwich together.
Per serving: Calories: 397Kcal; Fat: 34g; Carbs: 2g; Protein: 22g

580. Tuna Melt Chaffle

Preparation time: 30 minutes
Cooking time: 40 minutes
Servings: 1
Ingredients:

- 2 classic chaffles

Tuna Salad:

- 1 can white meat tuna
- 3 tbsp. red onion, finely chopped
- ¼ cup celery, finely chopped
- ½ cup mayonnaise
- ¼ tsp. salt
- 1-2 cracks freshly ground black pepper
- 1-2 slices cheddar cheese

Directions:

Preheat your oven to 350°F.
Slice the onions and celery until finely chopped. Set aside in a mixing bowl.
Add the tuna to the mixing bowl.
Mix the onions, celery, and tuna together until well combined.
Add the mayonnaise, salt, and pepper to the mixing bowl and mix together until well combined. Set aside.
Follow the classic chaffle recipe.
Lay the chaffles side by side on a baking sheet and layer on the tuna salad.
Add 1-2 slices of cheese per chaffle.
Place in the oven until the cheese is melted.
Take out and enjoy immediately.
Per serving: Calories: 309Kcal; Fat: 26g; Carbs: 1g; Protein: 23g

581. Italian Herbs Sandwich Chaffle with Deli Ham

Preparation time: 5 minutes
Cooking time: 10 minutes
Servings: 1
Ingredients:

- 2 slices deli ham
- 1 egg
- 1 slice cheddar cheese
- ½ cup mozzarella cheese (shredded)
- ½ tsp. baking powder
- 2 tbsp. almond flour
- 1 tsp. Italian herbs
- 1 tbs mayonnaise

Directions:

In a medium-sized bowl, combine the almond flour, egg, mozzarella cheese, Italian herbs, and baking powder. Mix thoroughly.
Preheat the waffle machine, sprinkle some cheese, and leave for a few seconds. Pour the mixture and sprinkle more cheese.
Cook for 3-4 minutes or until it turns golden brown.
Assemble the sandwich with deli ham, cheese, and mayonnaise
Per serving: Calories: 230Kcal; Fat: 24; Carbs: 4g; Protein: 20g

582. Corn Bread with Hot Dog Chaffle

Preparation time: 5 minutes
Cooking time: 20 minutes
Servings: 1
Ingredients:

- 2 tsp. almond flour
- ½ cup cheddar cheese (shredded)
- 1 sausage
- 2 tbsp. unsalted butter
- 1 tbsp. diced jalapeño

- 1 egg
- cornbread flavoring
- 1 small onion (diced)
- ¼ tsp. baking powder
- tomato ketchup (unsweetened)
- mustard sauce

Directions:

To prepare the cornbread, preheat the waffle maker. In a bowl, add the egg, ½ tbsp. of jalapeños, almond flour, baking powder, and cheddar cheese. Mix.

Pour the mixture into the machine and cook for 3-4 minutes or until it turns golden brown. Set aside.

Fill a pot with water, place over high-medium heat and allow it to boil. Add the sausage and boil for 3-5 minutes.

Place a pan over medium heat, add unsalted butter and fry your sausage. Place the fried sausage inside the cornbread; add onions, cheddar cheese, jalapeño, ketchup, and mustard sauce. Serve it.

Per serving: Calories: 383Kcal; Fat: 25g; Carbs: 2g; Protein: 24g

583. Coconut Flour Sandwich Chaffle with Bacon

Preparation time: 5 minutes
Cooking time: 25 minutes
Servings: 1
Ingredients:

- ½ cup mozzarella cheese
- 2 strips bacon (either pork or beef)
- 1 tbsp. coconut flour
- 2 tbsp. coconut oil
- 2 slice cheddar cheese
- 1 egg

Directions:

In a bowl, add egg, mozzarella, and flour. Mix the ingredients.

Preheat the waffle machine, sprinkle cheese, and allow it to melt. Pour the mixture and cook for 3-4 minutes.

In a pan, heat coconut oil, add your bacon, and fry for 2-3 minutes per side, or until it is crispy.

Arrange the bacon and cheese on your chaffle, enjoy.

Per serving: Calories: 345Kcal; Fat: 27g; Carbs: 5g; Protein: 24g

584. Sausage Ball Chaffle

Preparation time: 5 minutes
Cooking time: 20 minutes
Servings: 1
Ingredients:

- 1 egg
- ½ lb. Italian sausage
- ¼ cup parmesan cheese
- 2 tbsp. almond flour
- 1 tsp. baking powder

Directions:

In a bowl, combine the egg, flour, baking powder, and Italian sausage. Mix well.

Preheat the waffle-maker, sprinkle parmesan cheese, and allow it to cook for about 30 seconds.

Pour in the sausage mixture, close, and allow to cook for 3-4 minutes or until it turns golden brown.

Per serving: Calories: 165Kcal; Fat: 12g; Carbs: 2g; Protein: 7g

585. Chicken Pizza Chaffle

Preparation time: 5 minutes
Cooking time: 15 minutes
Servings: 1

Ingredients:

- 2 slices parmesan cheese
- ½ cup chicken breast (shredded)
- ¼ cup parmesan cheese
- 1 tbsp. pizza sauce
- 1 egg
- ¼ cup mozzarella cheese
- 1 tsp. thick cream cheese
- ¼ tsp. garlic powder
- ¼ tsp. Italian seasoning

Directions:

In a bowl, combine the shredded chicken, garlic powder, Italian seasoning, mozzarella, parmesan, cream cheese, egg, and mix until smooth.

Preheat your waffle maker, sprinkle some cheese on top. Leave for seconds, pour the chicken mixture and sprinkle some cheese. Close the waffle maker.

Cook the chaffle for 3-5 minutes or until it turns golden brown. Remove and spread pizza sauce on top, add the parmesan cheese slice (make sure the chaffle is still hot when adding the cheese to allow it to melt).

Per serving: Calories: 223Kcal; Fat: 12g; Carbs: 2g; Protein: 15g

586. Grated Zucchini Chaffle

Preparation time: 5 minutes
Cooking time: 25 minutes
Servings: 1
Ingredients:

- 1 zucchini (grated)
- 1 egg
- ½ cup cheddar cheese (shredded)
- 1 garlic clove (mashed)
- ¼ cup diced onion

Directions:

In a bowl, add the egg, grated zucchini, onions, and garlic. Mix well.

Preheat the waffle maker, add cheese, and allow it to melt. Add the mixture, sprinkle more cheese, and allow to cook for 3-5 minutes or until it turns golden brown.

Per serving: Calories: 307Kcal; Fat: 25g; Carbs: 1g; Protein: 20g

587. Chocolate Vanilla Chaffle

Preparation time: 5 minutes
Cooking time: 15 minutes
Servings: 1
Ingredients:

- 1 tsp. vanilla extract
- 1 egg
- 1 tsp. cocoa powder
- ¾ oz. cream cheese
- 1½ tbsp. coconut flour

Directions:

In a bowl, add all the ingredients and mix thoroughly.

Preheat the waffle maker, pour the mixture and allow to cook for 3-4 minutes or until it turns golden brown.

Per serving: Calories: 174Kcal; Fat: 14g; Carbs: 3g; Protein: 6g

588. Jalapeño Chicken Popper Chaffle

Preparation time: 5 minutes
Cooking time: 15 minutes
Servings: 2

Ingredients:

- ½ cup chicken (shredded)
- ¼ cup mozzarella cheese
- ¼ tsp. garlic powder
- ¼ cup parmesan cheese
- ¼ tsp. onion powder
- 1 fresh jalapeño (diced)
- 1 egg
- 1 tsp. cream cheese

Directions:

Preheat the waffle-maker.

In a bowl, add all the ingredients and mix thoroughly.

Sprinkle cheese on the waffle maker and heat for 20 seconds. Pour the mixture on top and allow it to cook for 3-4 minutes.

Serve with any sauce or toppings of choice

Per serving: Calories: 310cal; Fat: 32g; Carbs: 1g; Protein: 27g

589. Cauliflower and Chicken Chaffles

Preparation time: 5 minutes
Cooking time: 25 minutes
Servings: 1
Ingredients:

- ¼ cup diced chicken thigh (into cubes)
- 1 garlic clove (mashed)
- 1 cup cauliflower (shredded and pre-cooked)
- ½ cup mozzarella cheese (shredded)
- ½ tsp. black pepper (grounded)
- ½ cup parmesan cheese
- ½ tsp. soy sauce
- 1 egg

Directions:

In a blender, add the cauliflower, egg, mozzarella cheese, garlic, and pepper.

Blend the ingredients and pour the mixture into a bowl.

Preheat the waffle maker, sprinkle parmesan cheese.

Add soy sauce and diced chicken to the cauliflower mixture, then mix well.

Pour the mixture over the melted cheese, sprinkle parmesan cheese and cook for 4-5 minutes.

Per serving: Calories: 233Kcal; Fat: 15.6g; Carbs: 1g; Protein: 21g

590. Classic Sloppy Joe Chaffle

Preparation time: 5 minutes
Cooking time: 20 minutes
Servings: 1
Ingredients:

- ¼ lb. ground beef
- 1 egg
- 2 tbsp. tomato paste
- ½ cup cheddar cheese
- 1 tsp. garlic paste
- ½ tsp. pepper
- ½ cup broth
- ½ tsp. salt
- 2 tsp. soy sauce
- ½ tsp. paprika
- 2 tsp. coconut oil
- ½ tsp. mustard sauce
- ½ tsp. cocoa powder

Directions:

Place a pot over medium heat, add coconut oil and garlic paste. Sauté for 1 minute, then add the grounded beef, salt, and pepper. Allow it to cook for 2-3 minutes.

Add the tomato paste, paprika, soy sauce, cocoa powder, mustard sauce, and broth. Cook for 1 minute, then simmer the mixture.

Preheat the waffle maker. In a bowl, whisk the egg and cheese.

Sprinkle cheese on the waffle maker, pour the mixture and allow to cook for 3-4 minutes.

Arrange the beef mixture on your chaffle and serve them.

Per serving: Calories: 338Kcal; Fat: 28g; Carbs: 1g; Protein: 16g

591. Jamaican Jerk Chicken Chaffle

Preparation time: 15 minutes
Cooking time: 30 minutes
Servings: 2
Ingredients:
Chaffles:

- 2 eggs
- 1 cup mozzarella cheese (shredded)
- 1 tbsp. butter
- 2 tbsp. almond flour
- ¼ tsp. turmeric
- ¼ tsp. baking powder
- a pinch xanthan gum
- a pinch onion powder
- a pinch garlic powder
- a pinch salt

Jamaican Jerk Chicken:

- 1 lb. organic ground chicken
- 1 tsp. dried thyme
- 1 tsp. garlic (granulated)
- 2 tbsp. butter
- 2 tsp. dried parsley
- ⅛ tsp. black pepper
- 1 tsp. salt
- ½ cup chicken broth
- 2 tbsp. Jerk seasoning
- ½ medium chopped Onion

Directions:

In a pan, melt butter and sauté the onion.

Add all the remaining ingredients of Jamaican jerk chicken and sauté.

Now, add the chicken and chicken broth and stir.

Cook on medium-low heat for 10 minutes.

Then, cook on high heat and dry all the liquid.

For the chaffles, preheat a mini waffle maker if needed and grease it.

In a mixing bowl, beat all the chaffle ingredients.

Pour the mixture into the lower plate of the waffle maker and spread it evenly to cover the plate properly, and close the lid.

Cook for about 4-5 minutes or until it reaches the desired doneness.

Repeat the steps to create as many chaffle as the mixture allow.

Add the chicken in between a chaffle and fold and enjoy.

Per serving: Calories: 272Kcal; Fat: 29g; Carbs: 1g; Protein: 23g

592. Chicken and Cabbage Chaffles

Preparation time: 10 minutes
Cooking time: 15 minutes
Servings: 2
Ingredients:
Chaffles:

- 1/3 cup chicken, boiled and shredded
- 1/3 cup cabbage
- 2 eggs
- 1 cup mozzarella cheese (shredded)
- 1 tbsp. butter
- 2 tbsp. almond flour

- ¼ tsp. baking powder
- a pinch salt

Directions:

In a deep saucepan, boil the cabbage for five minutes or till it tenders, strain it, and blend it.

Mix all the remaining ingredients well together.

Pour a thin layer on a preheated waffle iron.

Add a layer of the blended cabbage to the mixture.

Again, add more mixture over the top.

Cook the chaffle for around 5 minutes.

Serve with your favorite sauce.

Per serving: Calories: 283Kcal; Fat: 28g; Carbs: 2g; Protein: 24g

593. Chicken Halloumi Burger Chaffle

Preparation time: 15 minutes
Cooking time: 20 minutes
Servings: 2
Ingredients:

Chaffle:
- 2 eggs
- 1 cup mozzarella cheese (shredded)
- 1 tbsp. butter
- 2 tbsp. almond flour
- ¼ tsp. baking powder
- a pinch onion powder
- a pinch garlic powder
- a pinch salt

Chicken Patty:
- 1 lb. ground chicken
- ½ tbsp. onion powder
- ½ tbsp. garlic powder
- 1 cup halloumi cheese
- ¼ tsp. salt, or as per your taste
- ¼ tsp. black pepper, or as per your taste

To Serve:
- 2 lettuce leaves
- 2 slices American cheese

Directions:

Turn on the waffle maker to heat and grease it with cooking spray.

Mix all the chicken patty ingredients in a bowl.

Make equal-sized patties; either grill them or fry them.

Combine all the chaffles ingredients in a mixing bowl. Stir until homogeneous.

Pour the batter into the waffle maker and spread it evenly to cover the plate properly, and close the lid. Cook for about 4 minutes to achieve the desired crunch.

Repeat the process with the remaining batter to create more chaffles.

Serve with the chicken patties, lettuce, and a cheese slice in between two chaffles.

Per serving: Calories: 318Kcal; Fat: 23g; Carbs: 3g; Protein: 23g

594. Chicken Eggplant Chaffle

Preparation time: 15 minutes
Cooking time: 25 minutes
Servings: 2
Ingredients:
- 2 eggs
- 1 cup cheddar cheese
- 2 tbsp. parmesan cheese
- ¼ tsp. Italian season
- 1 cup chicken

- 1 big eggplant
- a pinch salt
- a pinch black pepper

Directions:

Boil the chicken in water for 15 minutes and strain.

Shred the chicken into small pieces and set aside.

Cut the eggplant into slices and boil in water, and strain.

Add a pinch of salt and pepper.

Add all the chaffle ingredients to a bowl and mix well to make a mixture. Add the boiled chicken as well.

Warm your waffle maker and grease it if needed.

Pour the mixture into the lower plate of the waffle maker and spread it evenly to cover the plate properly.

Add the eggplant over two slices on the mixture and cover the lid.

Cook it for 4 to 5 minutes, or till it's crispy.

Make as many chaffles as your mixture allow.

Serve hot with your favorite sauce.

Per serving: Calories: 303Kcal; Fat: 25g; Carbs: 1g; Protein: 28g

595. Chicken Garlic Roll Chaffle

Preparation time: 20 minutes
Cooking time: 30 minutes
Servings: 2
Ingredients:
- 1 cup chicken mince
- ¼ tsp. salt
- ¼ tsp. black pepper, or as per your taste
- 2 eggs
- 1 tbsp. lemon juice
- 1 cup mozzarella cheese (shredded)
- 2 tbsp. butter
- 1½ tsp. garlic powder
- ½ tsp. bay seasoning
- parsley for garnishing

Directions:

Grease your waffle maker and preheat it.

In a frying pan, melt the butter and add the chicken mince.

When done, add salt, pepper, 1 tbsp. of garlic powder, lemon juice, and set aside.

In a mixing bowl, beat the eggs and add mozzarella cheese to them with ½ garlic powder and bay seasoning.

Mix them all well and pour the mixture into the mini waffle maker.

Let it cook for at least 4 minutes to get the desired crunch.

Remove the chaffle from the heat, add the chicken mixture in between and fold.

Repeat the steps to create as many chaffle as the batter allow.

Top with parsley.

Per serving: Calories: 293Kcal; Fat: 22g; Carbs: 1g; Protein: 27g

596. Bacon, Egg and Cheese Chaffle

Preparation time: 3 minutes
Cooking time: 7 minutes
Servings: 1
Ingredients:
- 1 egg
- ½ cup cheddar cheese
- 2 slices thin bacon
- a pinch of salt
- ¼ tsp. pepper

Directions:

Cut small pieces of bacon. Scramble the egg in a medium-sized bowl and mix salt and pepper in the cheese, then add the pieces of bacon and mix them all together.

Preheat your waffle iron when it is open at the proper cooking temperature, and pour the mixture into the center of the iron to ensure that it is distributed evenly.

Close your waffle iron and set the timer for 4 minutes, and do not open too quickly. No matter how good it begins to smell, let it cook. A good rule to follow is that if the waffle machine stops steaming, the chaffle will be done.

When the time is up, gently open the waffle iron and make sure not all of it sticks to the top. If so, use a Teflon or other non-metallic spatula to pry the chaffle softly away from the top and then gently pull the chaffle from the bottom and onto the plate after you have fully opened the unit.

Per serving: Calories: 370Kcal; Fat: 29g; Carbs: 1g; Protein: 21g

597. Easy Cinnamon Chaffles

Preparation time: 5 minutes
Cooking time: 10 minutes
Servings: 1
Ingredients:
- 1 tbsp. almond flour
- 1 egg
- 1 tsp. vanilla
- cinnamon 1 shake
- 1 tsp. baking powder
- ½ cup mozzarella cheese

Directions:
Mix the egg and vanilla extract in a bowl.
Mix almond flour and cinnamon with baking powder.
Finally, add the cheese to the mozzarella and coat with the mixture evenly.
Spray oil on your waffle maker and let it heat up to its maximum setting.
Cook the waffle; test it every 5 minutes until it becomes golden and crunchy. A tip: Make sure you put half of the batter in it. It can overflow the waffle maker, rendering it a sloppy operation. I suggest you put down a Silpat mat to make it easy to clean.
With butter and your favorite low-carb syrup, take it out carefully.

Per serving: Calories: 270Kcal; Fat: 16g; Carbs: 3g; Protein: 20g

598. Sweet Burger Bun Chaffle

Preparation time: 5 minutes
Cooking time: 14 minutes
Servings: 1
Ingredients:
- 1 egg
- ½ cup mozzarella cheese shredded
- ¼ tsp. baking powder
- ¼ tsp. glucomannan powder
- ¼ tsp. allulose or another sweetener
- ¼ tsp. caraway seed or another seasoning

Directions:
In a pot, add all the ingredients and blend together with a fork.
Spoon part of the mixture into the waffle maker; depending on whether you want them soft or crispy, cook for 5 to 7 minutes.
Prepare as you usually do your burger. Usually, I cook a bacon strip in a cast iron pan and then fry a burger over medium-low heat with salt and pepper in the bacon fat. After frying, I add the cheese for a couple of minutes, pour in a ¼ cup of water, and place a metal bowl over the burger to steam the cheese.
I love to serve my burgers with tomato, lettuce, onion, a bit of ranch dressing, salt, and pepper.
Pop it in the toaster oven when the first chaffle comes out to keep it warm while the second chaffle is being made, again for 5 to 7 minutes.

Per serving: Calories: 222Kcal; Fat: 17g; Carbs: 3g; Protein: 21g

599. Vegan Chaffle

Preparation time: 5 minutes
Cooking time: 5 minutes
Servings: 1
Ingredients:
- 1 tbsp. flax seed
- 2 glasses water
- ¼ cup low-carb vegan cheese
- 2 tbsp. coconut powder
- 1 tbsp. low-carb vegan cream cheese
- a pinch of salt

Directions:
Preheat the waffle maker to medium-high heat.
In a small-sized bowl, mix the flaxseed meal and water. Leave for 5 minutes until thick and sticky.
Make the flax eggs.
Whisk all the vegan chaffle ingredients together.
Pour half of the vegan waffle dough into the center of the waffle iron.
Cook it for 4 to 5 minutes, till it's golden and firm.
Remove the vegan chaffle from the waffle maker and enjoy.

Per serving: Calories: 128Kcal; Fat: 6g; Carbs: 5g; Protein: 1g

600. Maple Syrup Birthday Cake Chaffle

Preparation time: 15 minutes
Cooking time: 28 minutes
Servings: 2
Ingredients:
Chaffles:
- 2 eggs, beaten
- 1 cup finely grated Swiss cheese

Toppings:
- ½ cup heavy cream
- 2 tbsp. sugar-free maple syrup
- ½ tsp. vanilla extract
- 3 tbsp. funfetti

Directions:
Chaffles:
Preheat the waffle iron.
In a medium bowl, mix the egg and Swiss cheese.
Open the iron and add a quarter of the mixture. Close and cook until crispy, 7 minutes.
Transfer the chaffle to a plate and make 3 more chaffles with the remaining batter.
Frosting and Topping:
Add the heavy cream, maple syrup, and vanilla extract to a medium bowl and whisk using an electric mixer until smooth and fluffy.
Layer the chaffles one on another but with some frosting spread between the layers.
Top with the remaining bit of frosting and garnish with the funfetti.

Per serving: Calories: 194Kcal; Fat: 18g; Carbs: 3g; Protein: 17g

601. Red Velvet Chaffle Cake

Preparation time: 15 minutes
Cooking time: 28 minutes
Servings: 2
Ingredients:
Chaffles:
- 2 eggs, beaten
- ½ cup finely grated parmesan cheese
- 2 oz. cream cheese, softened
- 2 drops red food coloring
- 1 tsp. vanilla extract

Frosting:
- 3 tbsp. cream cheese, softened
- 1 tbsp. sugar-free maple syrup
- ¼ tsp. vanilla extract

Directions:
Chaffles:
Preheat the waffle iron.
In a medium bowl, mix all the ingredients for the chaffles.
Open the iron and add a quarter of the mixture. Close and cook until crispy, 7 minutes.
Transfer the chaffle to a plate and make 3 more chaffles with the remaining batter.
Frosting:
In a medium bowl, using a hand mixer, whisk the cream cheese, maple syrup, and vanilla extract until smooth.
Assemble the chaffles with the frosting to make the cake.
Per serving: Calories: 215Kcal; Fat: 18g; Carbs: 1g; Protein: 7g

602. Basic Chaffles

Preparation time: 5 minutes
Cooking time: 8 minutes
Servings: 1
Ingredients:
- 1 large organic egg, beaten
- ½ cup cheddar cheese, shredded
- a pinch of salt and freshly ground black pepper

Directions:
Preheat the mini waffle iron and then grease it.
In a bowl, place all the ingredients and beat until well combined.
Drop half of the mixture into the waffle maker and cook for about 3-4 minutes or until golden brown.
Repeat with the remaining mixture.
Per serving: Calories: 300Kcal; Fat: 25g; Carbs: 1g; Protein: 20g

603. Two Cheese Chaffles

Preparation time: 10 minutes
Cooking time: 8 minutes
Servings: 1
Ingredients:
- 1 organic egg white
- ¼ cup sharp cheddar cheese, shredded
- ¼ cup Monterey Jack cheese, shredded
- ¾ tsp. water
- ½ tsp. coconut flour
- ¼ tsp. organic baking powder
- ⅛ tsp. red chili powder
- a pinch of salt

Directions:
Preheat the mini waffle iron and then grease it.
In a bowl, place all the ingredients and beat until well combined.
Spoon half of the prepared batter into the preheated waffle iron and cook for about 4 minutes or until golden brown.
Repeat with the remaining mixture and serve the chaffles warm.
Per serving: Calories: 380Kcal; Fat: 29g; Carbs: 3g; Protein: 24g

604. Cheddar and Sour Cream Chaffles

Preparation time: 10 minutes
Cooking time: 32 minutes
Servings: 1
Ingredients:
- 1 organic egg
- 1 cup cheddar cheese, shredded
- ¼ cup sour cream
- ¼ cup unflavored whey protein powder

- ½ tsp. organic baking powder
- a pinch of salt

Directions:
Preheat the mini waffle iron and then grease it.
In a bowl, place all the ingredients and beat until well combined.
Divide the mixture into 8 portions.
Place 1 portion of the mixture into the preheated waffle iron and cook for about 4 minutes or until golden brown.
Repeat with the remaining mixture.
Per serving: Calories: 346Kcal; Fat: 27g; Carbs: 1g; Protein: 20g

605. Cheddar and Psyllium Husk Chaffles

Preparation time: 10 minutes
Cooking time: 8 minutes
Servings: 1
Ingredients:
- 1 medium organic egg
- ¾ cup cheddar cheese, shredded
- 1 tsp. psyllium husk
- dash of hot sauce
- a pinch of salt and freshly ground black pepper

Directions:
Preheat your mini waffle iron and then grease it.
In a bowl, place all the ingredients and beat until well combined.
Fill the waffle maker with half of the batter and close the lid. Cook for about 4 minutes or until golden brown.
Repeat with the remaining mixture.
Per serving: Calories: 300Kcal; Fat: 25g; Carbs: 1g; Protein: 20g

606. Heavy Cream Chaffles

Preparation time: 5 minutes
Cooking time: 16 minutes
Servings: 1
Ingredients:
- 1 organic egg
- 1 tbsp. heavy cream
- ¼ tsp. organic baking powder
- ¼ tbsp. coconut flour
- a pinch of salt and freshly ground black pepper

Directions:
Preheat your mini waffle iron and then grease it.
In a bowl, place all the ingredients and beat until well combined.
Place ¼ of the mixture into the preheated waffle iron and cook for about 4 minutes or until golden brown.
Repeat with the remaining mixture.
Per serving: Calories: 132Kcal; Fat: 8g; Carbs: 3g; Protein: 6g

607. Mayonnaise and Gelatin Chaffles

Preparation time: 10 minutes
Cooking time: 6 minutes
Servings: 2
Ingredients:
- 2 large organic eggs
- 1 tbsp. mayonnaise
- 1 tbsp. coconut flour
- 1 tbsp. grass-fed beef gelatin powder
- a pinch of salt

Directions:
Preheat your mini waffle iron and then grease it.
In a bowl, place all the ingredients and beat until well combined.
Place 1/3 of the mixture into the preheated waffle iron and cook for about 2 minutes or until golden brown.
Repeat with the remaining mixture.
Per serving: Calories: 301Kcal; Fat: 27g; Carbs: 4g; Protein: 20g

608. Jack Cheese Garlic Chaffles

Preparation time: 5 minutes
Cooking time: 8 minutes
Servings: 1
Ingredients:

- 1 organic egg, beaten
- ½ cup Monterrey Jack cheese, shredded
- 1 tsp. coconut flour
- a pinch of garlic powder

Directions:
Preheat your mini waffle iron and then grease it.
In a bowl, place all the ingredients and beat until well combined.
Add about half of the mixture into the preheated waffle iron and cook for about 3-4 minutes or until golden brown.
Repeat with the remaining mixture.
Serve them warm.
Per serving: Calories: 260Kcal; Fat: 22g; Carbs: 5g; Protein: 22g

609. Garlic and Onion Powder Chaffles

Preparation time: 5 minutes
Cooking time: 5 minutes
Servings: 1
Ingredients:

- 1 organic egg, beaten
- ¼ cup cheddar cheese, shredded
- 2 tbsp. almond flour
- ½ tsp. organic baking powder
- ¼ tsp. garlic powder
- ¼ tsp. onion powder
- a pinch of salt

Directions:
Preheat the waffle iron and then grease it.
In a bowl, place all the ingredients and beat until well combined.
Place the mixture into the preheated waffle iron and cook for about 3-5 minutes or until golden brown.
Per serving: Calories: 374Kcal; Fat: 24g; Carbs: 2g; Protein: 20g

610. Garlic Powder and Oregano Chaffles

Preparation time: 5 minutes
Cooking time: 10 minutes
Servings: 1
Ingredients:

- ½ cup mozzarella cheese, grated
- 1 medium organic egg, beaten
- 2 tbsp. almond flour
- ½ tsp. dried oregano, crushed
- ½ tsp. garlic powder
- salt, to taste

Directions:
Preheat the mini waffle iron and then grease it.
In a medium bowl, place all the ingredients and mix until well combined.
Fill the waffle maker with half of the batter and let it cook for about 4-5 minutes or until golden brown.
Repeat with the remaining mixture.
Per serving: Calories: 240Kcal; Fat: 17g; Carbs: 3g; Protein: 23g

611. Garlic Powder and Italian Seasoning Chaffles

Preparation time: 10 minutes
Cooking time: 20 minutes
Servings: 1

Ingredients:

- 1 large organic egg, beaten
- ½ cup mozzarella cheese, shredded
- ¼ cup parmesan cheese, grated
- 1 tsp. Italian seasoning
- ¼ tsp. garlic powder

Directions:
Preheat your mini waffle iron and then grease it.
In a medium bowl, place all the ingredients and mix until well combined.
Place ¼ of the mixture into the preheated waffle iron and cook for about 3-5 minutes or until golden brown.
Repeat with the remaining mixture.
Per serving: Calories: 280Kcal; Fat: 18g; Carbs: 3g; Protein: 21g

612. Caraway Seed Chaffles

Preparation time: 10 minutes
Cooking time: 6 minutes
Servings: 1
Ingredients:

- 2 Swiss cheese slices, chopped finely
- 1 tsp. caraway seeds
- 1 large organic egg, beaten

Directions:
Preheat your mini waffle iron and then grease it.
In the bottom of the preheated waffle iron, place ¼ of the cheese and sprinkle with ¼ tsp. of caraway seeds.
Place half of the beaten egg over the cheese and caraway.
Top with ¼ of the cheese and sprinkle with ¼ tsp. of caraway seeds.
Cook for about 3 minutes or until golden brown.
Repeat with the remaining cheese, caraway seeds, and egg.
Per serving: Calories: 260Kcal; Fat: 20g; Carbs: 4g; Protein: 20g

613. Sour Cream Protein Chaffles

Preparation time: 10 minutes
Cooking time: 16 minutes
Servings: 2
Ingredients:

- 2 organic eggs
- 1 cup cheddar cheese, shredded
- ½ cup sour cream
- ½ cup unsweetened whey protein powder
- 1 tsp. organic baking powder
- ½ tsp. salt

Directions:
Preheat the waffle iron and then grease it.
In a medium bowl, place all the ingredients and mix until well combined.
Place ¼ of the mixture into the preheated waffle iron and cook for about 3-4 minutes or until golden brown.
Repeat with the remaining mixture.
Per serving: Calories: 360Kcal; Fat: 27g; Carbs: 1g; Protein: 22g

614. Pulled Pork Chaffle

Preparation time: 20 minutes
Cooking time: 28 minutes
Servings: 2
Ingredients:

- 2 eggs, beaten
- 1 cup finely grated cheddar cheese
- ¼ tsp. baking powder
- 2 cups cooked and shredded pork
- 1 tbsp. sugar-free BBQ sauce

- 2 cup shredded coleslaw mix
- 2 tbsp. apple cider vinegar
- ½ tsp. salt
- ¼ cup ranch dressing

Directions:

Preheat the waffle iron.

In a medium bowl, mix the eggs, cheddar cheese, and baking powder.

Open the iron and add a quarter of the mixture. Close and cook until crispy, 7 minutes.

Transfer the chaffle to a plate and make 3 more chaffles in the same manner.

Meanwhile, in another medium bowl, mix the pulled pork with the BBQ sauce until well combined. Set aside.

Also, mix the coleslaw mix, apple cider vinegar, salt, and ranch dressing in another medium bowl.

When the chaffles are ready, on two pieces, divide the pork and then top with the ranch coleslaw. Cover with the remaining chaffles and insert mini skewers to secure the sandwiches.

Per serving: Calories: 454Kcal; Fat: 36g; Carbs: 8g; Protein: 23g

615. Italian Sausage Chaffle

Preparation time: 5 minutes
Cooking time: 8 minutes
Servings: 2
Ingredients:

- 1 egg, beaten
- 1 cup cheddar cheese, shredded
- ¼ cup parmesan cheese, grated
- 1 lb. Italian sausage, crumbled

- 2 tsp. baking powder
- 1 cup almond flour

Directions:

Preheat your waffle maker.

Mix all the ingredients in a bowl.

Fill in half of the batter into the waffle maker.

Cover and cook for 4 minutes.

Transfer to a plate and let it cool to make it crispy.

Do the same steps to make the next chaffle.

Per serving: Calories: 352Kcal; Fat: 27g; Carbs: 2g; Protein: 22g

616. Lt Sandwich Chaffle

Preparation time: 10 minutes
Cooking time: 15 minutes
Servings: 2
Ingredients:

- cooking spray
- 4 slices bacon
- 1 tbsp. mayonnaise
- 4 basic chaffles
- 2 lettuce leaves
- 2 tomato slices

Directions:

Coat your pan with foil and place it over medium heat.

Cook the bacon until golden and crispy.

Spread the mayo on top of the chaffle.

Top with lettuce, bacon, and tomato.

Top with another chaffle.

Per serving: Calories: 360Kcal; Fat: 29g; Carbs: 7g; Protein: 24g

CHAPTER 10:

Vegetarian Chaffles

617. Almond Flour Bagel Chaffle
Preparation time: 5 minutes
Cooking time: 30 minutes
Servings: 2
Ingredients:
- 2 eggs
- ½ cup parmesan cheese
- ½ tsp. bagel seasoning
- 1 cup mozzarella cheese
- 1 tsp. almond flour

Directions:
Turn on the waffle maker to heat and oil it with cooking spray.
Evenly sprinkle half of the cheeses to a griddle and let them melt.
Then, toast for 30 seconds and leave them to wait for the batter.
Whisk eggs, the other half of cheeses, almond flour, and bagel seasoning in a small bowl.
Pour the batter into the waffle maker. Cook for 5 minutes.
Let cool for 2-3 minutes before serving.
Per serving: Calories: 320Kcal; Fat: 26g; Carbs: 4g; Protein: 28

618. Glazed Cinnamon Rolls Chaffles
Preparation time: 7 minutes
Cooking time: 10 minutes
Servings: 1
Ingredients:
- ½ cup mozzarella cheese
- 1 tbsp. almond flour
- 1 egg
- 1 tsp. cinnamon
- 1 tsp. stevia

Cinnamon Roll Glaze:
- 1 tbsp. butter
- 1 tbsp. cream cheese
- 1 tsp. cinnamon
- ¼ tsp. vanilla extract
- 1 tbsp. coconut flour

Directions:
Switch on a round waffle maker and let it heat up.
In a small-sized bowl, mix together the cheese, egg, flour, cinnamon powder, and stevia in a bowl.
Spray the round waffle maker with non-stick spray.
Pour the batter into a waffle maker and close the lid. Cook for about 3-4 minutes.
Once the chaffles are cooked, remove them from the maker.
Mix together butter, cream cheese, cinnamon, vanilla, and coconut flour in a bowl.
Spread this glaze over the chaffle and roll it up.
Per serving: Calories: 340Kcal; Fat: 26g; Carbs: 4g; Protein: 21g

619. Fresh Broccoli and Almond Flour Chaffles
Preparation time: 6 minutes
Cooking time: 8 minutes
Servings: 1
Ingredients:
- 1 organic egg, beaten
- ½ cup cheddar cheese, shredded
- ¼ cup fresh broccoli, chopped
- 1 tbsp. almond flour
- ¼ tsp. garlic powder

Directions:
Preheat the mini waffle iron and then grease it.
Combine all the ingredients in a mixing bowl, and stir until homogeneous.
Fill the waffle maker with half of the batter and close the lid. Cook for about 4 minutes or until golden brown.
Repeat with the remaining mixture to create the second chaffle.
Per serving: Calories: 300Kcal; Fat: 25g; Carbs: 2g; Protein: 20g

620. Jalapeño and Cream Cheese Chaffles
Preparation time: 6 minutes
Cooking time: 5 minutes
Servings: 2
Ingredients:
- 2 large eggs
- ½ cup shredded mozzarella
- ¼ cup almond flour
- ½ tsp. baking powder
- ¼ cup shredded cheddar cheese
- 2 tbsp. diced jalapeños jarred or canned

Toppings:
- ½ cooked bacon, chopped
- 2 tbsp. cream cheese
- ¼ jalapeño slices

Directions:
Turn on the waffle maker to heat and oil it with cooking spray.
Mix the mozzarella, eggs, baking powder, almond flour, and garlic powder in a bowl.
Sprinkle 2 tbsp of cheddar cheese in a thin layer on the waffle maker and ½ of jalapeño.
Ladle half of the egg mixture on top of the cheese and jalapeños.
Cook for 2-3 minutes, or until done.
Repeat for the second chaffle.
Top with cream cheese, bacon, and jalapeño slices.
Per serving: Calories: 320Kcal; Fat: 28g; Carbs: 3g; Protein: 23g

621. Spinach and Cauliflower Chaffles

Preparation time: 6 minutes
Cooking time: 10 minutes
Servings: 2
Ingredients:

- ½ cup frozen chopped spinach, thawed and squeezed
- ½ cup cauliflower, chopped finely
- ½ cup cheddar cheese, shredded
- ½ cup mozzarella cheese, shredded
- 1/3 cup parmesan cheese, shredded
- 2 organic eggs
- 1 tbsp. butter, melted
- 1 tsp. garlic powder
- 1 tsp. onion powder
- salt and freshly ground black pepper, to taste

Directions:
Preheat your waffle iron and then grease it.
Combine all the chaffles ingredients in a medium-sized mixing bowl. Stir until homogeneous.
Drop half of the mixture into the waffle maker. Let it cook for about 3-4 minutes or until golden brown.
Repeat with the remaining mixture.
Serve them warm.
Per serving: Calories: 3870Kcal; Fat: 32g; Carbs: 1g; Protein: 21g

622. Rosemary in Chaffles

Preparation time: 6 minutes
Cooking time: 8 minutes
Servings: 1
Ingredients:

- 1 organic egg, beaten
- ½ cup cheddar cheese, shredded
- 1 tbsp. almond flour
- 1 tbsp. fresh rosemary, chopped
- a pinch salt
- a pinch freshly ground black pepper

Directions:
Preheat the mini waffle iron and then grease it.
For chaffles: In a medium bowl, place all the ingredients, and with a fork, mix until well combined.
Cook for around 4 minutes half of the mixture on the mini waffle iron.
Repeat with the remaining mixture to create the second chaffle.
Serve them warm.
Per serving: Calories: 180Kcal; Fat: 25g; Carbs: 2g; Protein: 20

623. Zucchini Chaffles with Peanut Butter

Preparation time: 5 minutes
Cooking time: 5 minutes
Servings: 2
Ingredients:

- 1 cup zucchini grated
- 2 eggs beaten
- ½ cup shredded parmesan cheese
- ¼ cup shredded mozzarella cheese
- 1 tsp. dried basil
- ½ tsp. salt
- ½ tsp. black pepper
- 2 tbsp. peanut butter for topping

Directions:
Sprinkle salt over the zucchini and let it sit for minutes.
Squeeze out the water from the zucchini.
Beat the egg with the zucchini, basil salt, mozzarella cheese, and pepper.

Sprinkle ½ of the parmesan cheese over the preheated waffle maker and pour the zucchini batter over it.
Sprinkle the remaining cheese over it.
Close the lid.
Cook the zucchini chaffles for about 4-8 minutes.
Remove the chaffles from the maker and repeat with the remaining batter.
Serve them with peanut butter on top and enjoy!
Per serving: Calories: 330Kcal; Fat: 27g; Carbs: 4g; Protein: 29g

624. Zucchini and Pepper Flakes Chaffles

Preparation time: 10 minutes
Cooking time: 18 minutes
Servings: 2
Ingredients:

- 2 large zucchinis, grated and squeezed
- 2 large organic eggs
- 2/3 cup cheddar cheese, shredded
- 2 tbsp. coconut flour
- ½ tsp. garlic powder
- ½ tsp. red pepper flakes, crushed
- salt, to taste

Directions:
Preheat the waffle iron and then grease it.
In a medium bowl, place all the ingredients and mix until well combined.
Place ¼ of the mixture into the preheated waffle iron and cook for about 4-4½ minutes or until golden brown.
Repeat with the remaining mixture.
Per serving: Calories: 310Kcal; Fat: 25g; Carbs: 5g; Protein: 20g

625. 3-Cheese Broccoli Chaffles

Preparation time: 10 minutes
Cooking time: 16 minutes
Servings: 2
Ingredients:

- ½ cup cooked broccoli, chopped finely
- 2 organic eggs, beaten
- ½ cup cheddar cheese, shredded
- ½ cup mozzarella cheese, shredded
- 2 tbsp. parmesan cheese, grated
- ½ tsp. onion powder

Directions:
Preheat your waffle iron and then grease it.
In a medium-sized bowl, place all the ingredients and mix until properly combined.
Spoon half of the batter into the preheated waffle iron and cook for about 4-5 minutes or until it reaches the desired doneness.
Repeat the steps to create as many chaffle as the batter allow.
Per serving: Calories: 364Kcal; Fat: 28g; Carbs: 3g; Protein: 25g

626. Bagel Seasoning Chaffle

Preparation time: 10 minutes
Cooking time: 5 minutes
Servings: 2
Ingredients:

- 2 tbsp. everything bagel seasoning
- 2 eggs
- 1 cup mozzarella cheese
- ½ cup grated parmesan

Directions:
Preheat the square waffle maker and grease with cooking spray.
Mix together the eggs, mozzarella cheese, and grated cheese in a bowl.
Fill the waffle maker with half of the batter.

Sprinkle 1 tbsp. of the everything bagel seasoning over batter.
Cook the chaffles for about 3-4 minutes.
Repeat with the remaining batter.
Per serving: Calories: 320Kcal; Fat: 20g; Carbs: 1g; Protein: 28g

627. Dried Herbs Chaffle

Preparation time: 6 minutes
Cooking time: 8 minutes
Servings: 1
Ingredients:
- 1 organic egg, beaten
- ½ cup cheddar cheese, shredded
- 1 tbsp. almond flour
- a pinch of dried thyme, crushed
- a pinch of dried rosemary, crushed

Directions:
Preheat the mini waffle iron and then grease it.
In a bowl, place all the ingredients and beat until properly mixed.
Spoon half of the prepared batter into the preheated waffle iron and cook for about 4 minutes or until golden brown.
Repeat with the remaining mixture to cook the second chaffle.
Per serving: Calories: 300Kcal; Fat: 25g; Carbs: 2g; Protein: 20g

628. Zucchini and Basil Chaffles

Preparation time: 6 minutes
Cooking time: 10 minutes
Servings: 1
Ingredients:
- 1 organic egg, beaten
- ¼ cup mozzarella cheese, shredded
- 2 tbsp. parmesan cheese, grated
- ½ small zucchini, grated and squeezed
- ¼ tsp. dried basil, crushed
- freshly ground black pepper, as required

Directions:
Preheat the mini waffle iron and then grease it.
In a medium bowl, add all the ingredients and mix until well combined.
Drop half of the mixture into the waffle maker and spread evenly.
Cook for about 4-5 minutes or until golden brown.
Repeat with the remaining mixture.
Per serving: Calories: 310Kcal; Fat: 20g; Carbs: 1g; Protein: 27g

629. Hash Brown Chaffles

Preparation time: 6 minutes
Cooking time: 10 minutes
Servings: 2
Ingredients:
- 1 large jicama root, peeled and shredded
- ½ medium onion, minced
- 2 garlic cloves, pressed
- 1 cup cheddar shredded cheese
- 2 eggs
- salt and pepper, to taste

Directions:
Place jicama in a colander, sprinkle with 2 tsp. of salt and let drain.
Squeeze out all the excess liquid.
Microwave jicama for 5-8 minutes.
Mix ¾ of cheese and all the other ingredients in a bowl.
Sprinkle 1-2 tsp. of cheese on the waffle maker, add 3 tbsp. of the mixture, and top with 1-2 tsp. the cheese.
Close the lid and let it cook for about 4 minutes or until golden and crunchy. Remove and repeat for the remaining batter.
Serve while hot with preferred toppings.
Per serving: Calories: 305Kcal; Fat: 25g; Carbs: 1g; Protein: 20g

630. Cheese Garlic Chaffles

Preparation time: 10 minutes
Cooking time: 8 minutes
Servings: 1
Ingredients:
Chaffle:
- 1 egg
- 1 tsp. cream cheese
- ½ cup mozzarella cheese, shredded
- ½ tsp. garlic powder
- 1 tsp. Italian seasoning

Toppings:
- 1 tbsp. butter
- ½ tsp. garlic powder
- ½ tsp. Italian seasoning
- 2 tbsp. mozzarella cheese, shredded

Directions:
Preheat your waffle maker and the oven to 350°F.
In a bowl, combine all the chaffle ingredients.
Fill the waffle maker with half of the batter. Cook for about 4 minutes.
Transfer to a baking pan.
Spread the butter on top of each chaffle.
Sprinkle garlic powder and Italian seasoning on top.
Top with mozzarella cheese.
Bake until the cheese has melted.
Per serving: Calories: 340Kcal; Fat: 22g; Carbs: 3g; Protein:24g

631. Cinnamon Cream Cheese Chaffle

Preparation time: 10 minutes
Cooking time: 15 minutes
Servings: 2
Ingredients:
- 2 eggs, lightly beaten
- 1 tsp. collagen
- ¼ tsp. baking powder, gluten-free
- 1 tsp. monk fruit sweetener
- ½ tsp. cinnamon
- ¼ cup cream cheese, softened
- a pinch of salt

Directions:
Preheat your waffle maker.
Add all the ingredients into the bowl and beat using a hand mixer until well combined.
Spray the waffle maker with cooking spray.
Pour ½ of batter in the hot waffle maker and cook for 3 minutes or until golden brown. Repeat with the remaining batter.
Per serving: Calories: 160Kcal; Fat: 15g; Carbs: 2g; Protein: 7g

632. Apple Cinnamon Chaffles

Preparation time: 6 minutes
Cooking time: 20 minutes
Servings: 2
Ingredients:
- 2 eggs, lightly beaten
- 1 cup mozzarella cheese, shredded
- ¼ cup apple, chopped
- ½ tsp. monk fruit sweetener
- 1½ tsp. cinnamon
- ¼ tsp. baking powder, gluten-free
- 2 tbsp. coconut flour

Directions:
Preheat your waffle maker.
Add the remaining ingredients and stir until well combined.

Spray the waffle maker with cooking spray.

Pour 1/3 of the batter in the hot waffle maker and cook for 6-7 minutes or until golden brown. Repeat with the remaining batter.

Per serving: Calories: 167Kcal; Fat: 14g; Carbs: 2g; Protein: 16g

633. Pumpkin Cheesecake Chaffle

Preparation time: 10 minutes
Cooking time: 15 minutes
Servings: 1
Ingredients:

Chaffles:

- 1 egg
- ½ tsp. vanilla
- ½ tsp. baking powder, gluten-free
- ¼ tsp. pumpkin spice
- 1 tsp. cream cheese, softened
- 2 tsp. heavy cream
- 1 tbsp. Swerve
- 1 tbsp. almond flour
- 2 tsp. pumpkin puree
- ½ cup mozzarella cheese, shredded

Filling:

- ¼ tsp. vanilla
- 1 tbsp. Swerve
- 2 tbsp. cream cheese

Directions:

Preheat your mini waffle maker.

In a small bowl, mix all the chaffle ingredients.

Spray the waffle maker with cooking spray.

Pour half of the batter into the hot waffle maker and cook for 3-5 minutes. Repeat with the remaining batter.

In a small bowl, combine all the filling ingredients.

Spread the filling mixture between two chaffles and place in the fridge for 10 minutes.

Per serving: Calories: 282Kcal; Fat: 26g; Carbs: 2g; Protein: 22g

CHAPTER 11:

Special and Festive

634. Christmas Smoothie with Chaffles
Preparation time: 10 minutes
Cooking time: 0 minutes
Servings: 2
Ingredients:
- 4 classics sweet chaffles
- 1 cup coconut milk
- 2 tbsp. almonds chopped
- ¼ cup cherries
- 1 a pinch sea salt
- ¼ cup ice cubes

Toppings:
- 2 oz. keto chocolate chips
- 2 oz. cherries
- 2 mini chaffles
- 2 scoop heavy cream, frozen

Directions:
Add the almond milk, almonds, cherries, salt, and ice in a blender, blend for 2 minutes until smooth and fluffy.
Pour the smoothie into glasses.
Top with one scoop of heavy cream, chocolate chips, cherries, and chaffle in each glass.
Per serving: Calories: 365Kcal; Fat: 25g; Carbs: 2g; Protein: 23g

635. Raspberry and Chocolate Chaffles
Preparation time: 5 minutes
Cooking time: 7-9 minutes
Servings: 2
Ingredients:
Batter:
- 2 eggs
- 2 oz. cream cheese, softened
- 2 oz. sour cream
- 1 tsp. vanilla extract
- 5 tbsp. almond flour
- ¼ cup cocoa powder
- 1½ tsp. baking powder
- 2 oz. fresh or frozen raspberries

Other:
- 2 tbsp. butter to brush the waffle maker
- fresh sprigs of mint to garnish

Directions:
Preheat the waffle maker.
Add the eggs, cream cheese, and sour cream to a bowl and stir with a wire whisk until just combined.
Add the vanilla extract and mix until combined.
Stir in the almond flour, cocoa powder, and baking powder and mix until combined.
Add the raspberries and stir until combined.
Brush the heated waffle maker with butter and add a few tbsp. of the batter.

Close the lid and cook for about 8 minutes, depending on your waffle maker.
Serve them with fresh sprigs of mint.
Per serving: Calories: 296Kcal; Fat: 23g; Carbs: 2g; Protein: 28g

636. Belgian Sugar Chaffles
Preparation time: 8 minutes
Cooking time: 24 minutes
Servings: 1
Ingredients:
- 1 egg, beaten
- 2 tbsp. Swerve brown sugar
- ½ tbsp. butter, melted
- 1 tsp. vanilla extract
- 1 cup finely grated parmesan cheese

Directions:
Preheat the waffle iron.
Mix all the ingredients in a medium bowl.
Open the iron and pour in a quarter of the mixture. Close and cook until crispy, 6 minutes.
Remove the chaffle onto a plate and make 3 more with the remaining ingredients.
Cut each chaffle into wedges, plate, allow cooling, and serve them.
Per serving: Calories: 280Kcal; Fat: 23g; Carbs: 2g; Protein: 20g

637. Pumpkin Chaffles with Maple Syrup
Preparation time: 10 minutes
Cooking time: 16 minutes
Servings: 2
Ingredients:
- 2 eggs, beaten
- ½ cup mozzarella cheese, shredded
- 1 tsp. coconut flour
- ¾ tsp. baking powder
- ¾ tsp. pumpkin pie spice
- 2 tsp. pureed pumpkin
- 4 tsp. heavy whipping cream
- ½ tsp. vanilla
- a pinch salt
- 2 tsp. maple syrup (sugar-free)

Directions:
Turn your waffle maker on.
Mix all the ingredients, except maple syrup, in a large bowl.
Pour half of the batter into the waffle maker.
Close and cook for 8 minutes.
Transfer to a plate to cool for 2 minutes.
Repeat the steps with the remaining mixture.
Drizzle the maple syrup on top of the chaffles before serving.
Per serving: Calories: 323Kcal; Fat: 24g; Carbs: 4g; Protein: 26g

638. Sweet Vanilla Chocolate Chaffle

Preparation time: 10 minutes
Cooking time: 10 minutes
Servings: 1
Ingredients:

- 1 egg, lightly beaten
- ¼ tsp. cinnamon
- ½ tsp. vanilla
- 1 tbsp. Swerve
- 2 tsp. unsweetened cocoa powder
- 1 tbsp. coconut flour
- 2 oz. cream cheese, softened

Directions:
Add all the ingredients into a bowl and mix until well combined.
Spray the waffle maker with cooking spray.
Drop half of the mixture into the waffle maker and cook until golden brown.
Per serving: Calories: 210Kcal; Fat: 16g; Carbs: 5g; Protein: 7g

639. Thanksgiving Keto Chaffles

Preparation time: 10 minutes
Cooking time: 15minutes
Servings: 2
Ingredients:

- 4 eggs
- 1 tsp. stevia
- 1 tsp. baking powder
- 2 tsp. vanilla extract
- ¼ cup almond butter, melted
- 3 tbsp. almond milk
- 1 tsp. avocado oil for greasing
- ¼ cup almond flour

Directions:
Beat the eggs in a mixing bowl, and add almond flour, stevia, and baking powder. Stir well.
Slowly add the melted butter to the previous mixture, mix well to ensure a smooth consistency.
Add the almond milk and vanilla to the flour and butter mixture, be sure to mix well.
Preheat the waffles maker according to the manufacturer's instructions and grease it with avocado oil.
A little at a time, cook the mixture into the waffle maker until golden brown. The mixture should cover the waffle maker plate evenly
Dust coconut flour on the chaffles and serve with coconut cream on the top.
Per serving: Calories: 360Kcal; Fat: 32; Carbs: 3g; Protein: 22g

640. Garlic Cauliflower Chaffles

Preparation time: 10 minutes
Cooking time: 8 minutes
Servings: 1
Ingredients:

- 1 egg, beaten
- 1 cup cauliflower rice
- ½ cup cheddar cheese, shredded
- 1 tsp. garlic powder

Directions:
Plug in your waffle maker.
Mix all the ingredients in a bowl.
Transfer half of the mixture to the waffle maker.
Close the device and cook for 4 minutes.
Put the chaffle on a plate to cool for 2 minutes.
Repeat the procedure to make the next chaffle.
Per serving: Calories: 305Kcal; Fat: 25g; Carbs: 1g; Protein: 21g

641. Blueberry Coconut Chaffle

Preparation time: 10 minutes
Cooking time: 15 minutes
Servings: 1
Ingredients:

- 1 egg, lightly beaten
- ¼ cup blueberries
- ½ tsp. vanilla
- 1 oz. cream cheese
- ¼ tsp. baking powder, gluten-free
- 4 tsp. Swerve
- 1 tbsp. coconut flour

Directions:
Preheat your waffle maker.
In a small bowl, mix the coconut flour, baking powder, and Swerve until well combined.
Add the vanilla, cream cheese, egg, and vanilla, and whisk until combined.
Spray the waffle maker with cooking spray.
Pour half of the batter into the hot waffle maker and top with 4 blueberries and cook for 4-5 minutes until golden brown. Repeat with the remaining batter.
Per serving: Calories: 110 Kcal; Fat: 16g; Carbs: 3g; Protein: 7g

642. Raspberries Fluffy Chaffle

Preparation time: 10 minutes
Cooking time: 8 minutes
Servings: 1
Ingredients:

- 1 egg, beaten
- ½ cup mozzarella cheese, shredded
- 1 tsp. baking powder
- 2 tbsp. almond flour
- 2 tsp. sweetener
- ¼ cup raspberries, chopped

Directions:
Heat up your waffle maker.
Combine all the ingredients in a bowl. Mix well to ensure a smooth consistency.
Pour half of the mixture into the maker and cook for 4 minutes.
Open the waffle maker and transfer it to a plate.
Let cool it for 2 minutes.
Repeat the process to create the second chaffle.
Per serving: Calories: 221Kcal; Fat: 16g; Carbs: 4g; Protein: 21g

643. Festive Sandwich Chaffle

Preparation time: 10 minutes
Cooking time: 10 minutes
Servings: 1
Ingredients:

- 2 basic chaffles
- cooking spray
- 2 slices bacon
- 1 egg

Directions:
Spray your pan with oil and warm it over medium heat.
Cook the bacon until golden and crispy.
Put the bacon on top of one chaffle.
In the same pan, cook the egg without mixing until the yolk is set.
Add the egg on top of the bacon.
Top with another chaffle.
Per serving: Calories: 380Kcal; Fat: 29g; Carbs: 1g; Protein: 24g

644. Cookie Dough Chaffle

Preparation time: 5 minutes
Cooking time: 7-9 minutes
Servings: 4
Ingredients:
Batter:
- 4 eggs
- ¼ cup heavy cream
- 1 tsp. vanilla extract
- ¼ cup stevia
- 6 tbsp. coconut flour
- 1 tsp. baking powder
- a pinch of salt
- ¼ cup unsweetened chocolate chips
Other:
- 2 tbsp. cooking spray to brush the waffle maker
- ¼ cup heavy cream, whipped

Directions:
Preheat the waffle maker and grease it with cooking spray.
Beat the eggs in a bowl, and add heavy cream, vanilla extract, stevia, coconut flour, baking powder, and salt. Mix until properly combined.
Stir in the chocolate chips and combine.
Let cook a few tbsp. of the mixture into the waffle maker. It should cover the plate evenly.
Let it cook for about 7-8 minutes, depending on your waffle maker.
Serve with whipped cream on top.
Per serving: Calories: 347Kcal; Fat: 26g; Carbs: 6g; Protein: 22g

645. Thanksgiving Pumpkin Spice Chaffle

Preparation time: 5 minutes
Cooking time: 5 minutes
Servings: 2
Ingredients:
- 1 cup egg whites
- ¼ cup pumpkin puree
- 2 tsp. pumpkin pie spice
- 2 tsp. coconut flour
- 1 tsp. baking powder
- 1 tsp. baking soda
- ⅛ tsp. cinnamon powder
- 1 cup mozzarella cheese, grated
- ½ tsp. garlic powder

Directions:
Switch on your square waffle maker. Spray with non-stick spray.
Beat the egg whites with the beater until fluffy and white.
Add the pumpkin puree, pumpkin pie spice, coconut flour in egg whites and beat again.
Stir in the cheese, cinnamon powder, garlic powder, baking soda, and powder.
Close the maker and cook for about 3 minutes.
Repeat with the remaining batter.
Remove the chaffles from the maker and serve hot.
Per serving: Calories: 225Kcal; Fat: 18g; Carbs: 6g; Protein: 22g

646. Pumpkin Spiced Cake Chaffle

Preparation time: 10 minutes
Cooking time: 14 minutes
Servings: 4
Ingredients:
- 4 eggs, beaten
- 4 cup finely grated mozzarella cheese
- ½ cup pumpkin, canned, mashed
- 1 ½ tbsp coconut Flour
- 1 tbsp. sugar-free pumpkin puree
- 1 spy baking powder
- ¼ cup butter, unsalted
- a pinch of salt
- ¾ cup erythritol
Frosting:
- 4 oz cream cheese (room temperature)
- ¼ cup butter, unsalted
- ½ tsp. vanilla extract
- ¾ cup sweetener

Directions:
Preheat the waffle iron.
In a medium bowl, mix all the ingredients.
Open the iron, pour in half of the batter, close and cook until crispy, 5 to 6 minutes.
Repeat until you have all the chaffles and set them aside.
Frosting:
Make the frosting. In a medium bowl, mix the cream cheese and butter until properly blended and fluffy. While mixing slowly, add vanilla extract, sweeteners (a bit at a time), and salt, until properly combined with a fluffy texture.
Assembling:
Place one waffle on a cake plate to assemble. Layer 1/3 cup of icing, another waffle, 1/3 cup of frosting, and the top waffle.
Cover the top waffle with the remaining icing.
Per serving: Calories: 280Kcal; Fat: 24g; Carbs: 3g; Protein: 20g

647. Fruit Snacks Chaffles

Preparation time: 10 minutes
Cooking time: 14 minutes
Servings: 1
Ingredients:
- 1 egg, beaten
- ½ cup finely grated cheddar cheese
- ½ cup Greek yogurt for topping
- 8 raspberries and blackberries for topping

Directions:
Preheat the waffle iron.
Mix the egg and cheddar cheese in a medium bowl.
Open the iron and add half of the mixture. Close and cook until crispy, 7 minutes.
Remove the chaffle onto a plate and make another with the remaining mixture.
Cut each chaffle into wedges and arrange them on a plate.
Top each waffle with a tbsp. of yogurt and then two berries.
Per serving: Calories: 400Kcal; Fat: 35g; Carbs: 7g; Protein: 24g

648. Ham and Green Bell Pepper Sandwich Chaffle

Preparation time: 10 minutes
Cooking time: 10 minutes
Servings: 2
Ingredients:
- 2 slices ham
- cooking spray
- 1 green bell pepper, sliced into strips
- 2 slices cheese
- 1 tbsp. black olives, pitted and sliced
- 2 basic chaffles

Directions:
Cook the ham in a pan coated with oil over medium heat.
Next, cook the bell pepper.

Assemble the open-faced sandwich by topping each chaffle with ham and cheese, bell pepper, and olives.

Toast in the oven until the cheese has melted a little.

Per serving: Calories: 360Kcal; Fat: 28g; Carbs: 1g; Protein: 20g

649. Taco Chaffle with Cabbage

Preparation time: 8 minutes
Cooking time: 20 minutes
Servings: 2
Ingredients:

- 1 tbsp. olive oil
- 1 lb. ground beef
- 1 tsp. ground cumin
- 1 tsp. chili powder
- ¼ tsp. onion powder
- ½ tsp. garlic powder
- salt to taste
- 4 basic chaffles
- 1 cup cabbage, chopped
- 4 tbsp. salsa (sugar-free)

Directions:

Pour the olive oil into a pan over medium heat.

Add the ground beef and season with salt and spices.

Cook until brown and crumbly.

Fold the chaffle to create a "taco shell."

Stuff each chaffle taco with cabbage.

Top with the ground beef and salsa.

Per serving: Calories: 387Kcal; Fat: 32g; Carbs: 1g; Protein: 23g

650. Christmas Morning Choco Cake Chaffle

Preparation time: 5 minutes
Cooking time: 5 minutes
Servings: 8
Ingredients:

- 8 keto chocolate square chaffles
- 1 cup peanut butter
- 16 oz. raspberries

Directions:

Assemble the chaffles in layers.

Spread peanut butter in each layer and top with raspberries.

Enjoy cake on Christmas morning with keto coffee!

Per serving: Calories: 500Kcal; Fat: 36g; Carbs: 8g; Protein: 26g

651. Orange Marmalade Chaffles

Preparation time: 10 minutes
Cooking time: 15 minutes
Servings: 1
Ingredients:

- 1 egg, lightly beaten
- 2 tbsp. peanut butter
- 2 tbsp. low carb orange marmalade
- ½ cup Swiss cheese, shredded

Directions:

Preheat your waffle maker.

In a bowl, mix the egg, cheese, and peanut butter until well combined.

Spray the waffle maker with cooking spray.

Pour half of the batter into the hot waffle maker and cook for 7-8 minutes or until golden brown. Repeat with the remaining batter.

Top chaffles with the orange marmalade them and serve.

Per serving: Calories: 310Kcal; Fat: 21g; Carbs: 8g; Protein: 17g

652. Keto Ice Cream Chaffle

Preparation time: 15 minutes
Cooking time: 30 minutes
Servings: 1
Ingredients:

- 1 egg
- 2 tbsp. Swerve/monk fruit
- 1 tbsp. baking powder
- 1 tbsp. heavy whipping cream
- keto ice cream: as per your choice

Directions:

Take a small bowl and whisk the egg and add all the ingredients.

Beat until the mixture becomes creamy.

Pour the mixture into the lower plate of the waffle maker and spread it evenly to cover the plate properly.

Close the lid and cook for about 4-5 minutes or until it reaches the desired doneness.

Take the chaffle off the maker and keep it aside to cool it down.

Repeat the steps to create the second chaffle.

Top with your favorite ice cream and enjoy!

Per serving: Calories: 145Kcal; Fat: 14g; Carbs: 2g; Protein: 5g

653. Double Chocolate Chaffle

Preparation time: 5 minutes
Cooking time: 10 minutes
Servings: 2
Ingredients:

- 2 eggs
- 2 tbsp. coconut flour
- 2 tbsp. cocoa powder
- 2 oz. cream cheese
- ½ tsp. baking powder
- 2 tbsp. chocolate chips (unsweetened)
- 1 tsp. vanilla extract
- 4 tbsp. Swerve/monk fruit

Directions:

Grease your waffle maker and preheat it.

In a small-sized bowl, beat the eggs.

In a separate mixing bowl, add the coconut flour, cocoa powder, Swerve/monk fruit, and baking powder; then combine. Pour in eggs with cream cheese and vanilla extract.

Mix them all well to give them uniform consistency and pour the mixture into the lower plate of the waffle maker.

On top of the mixture, sprinkle around ½ tsp. of unsweetened chocolate chips and close the lid.

Let it cook for about 3-4 minutes or until golden brown.

Repeat the steps to create as many chaffle as the batter allow.

Serve with your favorite whipped cream or berries.

Per serving: Calories: 290Kcal; Fat: 18g; Carbs: 5g; Protein: 8g

654. Mini Cream Cheese Coconut Chaffles

Preparation time: 5 minutes
Cooking time: 10 minutes
Servings: 2
Ingredients:

- 2 eggs
- 2 tbsp. coconut flour
- 1 oz. cream cheese
- ¼ tsp. baking powder
- ½ tsp. vanilla extract
- 4 tsp. Swerve/monk fruit

Directions:

Preheat a waffle maker if needed and grease it.

In a mixing bowl, mix coconut flour, Swerve/monk fruit, and baking powder.

Now, add an egg to the mixture with cream cheese and vanilla extract.

Mix them all well and pour the mixture into the lower plate of the waffle maker.

Close the lid.

Cook for at least 4 minutes to get the desired crunch.

Remove the chaffle from the heat.

Cook the other chaffles with the same procedure, using the remaining mixture.

Enjoy the chaffles with your favorite toppings.

Per serving: Calories: 160Kcal; Fat: 9g; Carbs: 3g; Protein: 6g

655. Blackberries Chaffles

Preparation time: 15 minutes
Cooking time: 20 minutes
Servings: 1
Ingredients:

- 1/3 cup cheddar cheese
- 1 egg
- ½ cup blackberries
- 2 tbsp. almond flour
- ¼ tsp. baking powder
- 2 tbsp. ground almonds
- 1/3 cup mozzarella cheese

Directions:

Mix the cheddar cheese, egg, blackberries, almond flour, almond ground, and baking powder together in a bowl.

Preheat your waffle iron and grease it.

In your mini waffle iron, shred half of the mozzarella cheese.

Add the mixture to your mini waffle iron.

Again, shred the remaining mozzarella cheese on the mixture.

Cook till the desired crisp is achieved.

Repeat the process to create the next chaffle.

Per serving: Calories: 243Kcal; Fat: 34g; Carbs: 2g; Protein: 27g

656. Choco Chips Cannoli Chaffle

Preparation time: 10 minutes
Cooking time: 20 minutes
Servings: 2
Ingredients:

Chaffles:

- 1 egg yolk
- 1 tbsp. Swerve/monk fruit
- ⅛ tbsp. baking powder
- ⅛ tsp. vanilla extract
- 3 tbsp. almond flour
- 1 tbsp. chocolate chips

Toppings:

- 4 tbsp. cream cheese
- 6 tbsp. ricotta
- 2 tbsp. sweetener
- ¼ tbsp. vanilla extract
- 5 drops lemon extract

Directions:

Grease your waffle maker and preheat it.

Combine all the chaffles ingredients in a mixing bowl, and stir until homogeneous.

Spoon the chaffles batter into the waffle maker and spread it evenly to cover the plate properly, and close the lid.

Cook for at least 4 minutes to get the desired crunch.

In the meanwhile, make the cannoli topping by adding all the ingredients to the blender to give the creamy texture.

Take the chaffle off the maker and keep it aside to cool them down.

Repeat the steps to create as many chaffle as the mixture allow.

Serve with the cannoli toppings and enjoy.

Per serving: Calories: 410Kcal; Fat: 30g; Carbs: 2g; Protein: 14g

657. Tomatoes and Onions Chaffles

Preparation time: 10 minutes
Cooking time: 20 minutes
Servings: 2
Ingredients:

Chaffles:

- 2 eggs
- ½ cup mozzarella cheese (shredded)
- ½ cup chopped onion
- ½ tsp. garlic powder
- ½ tsp. dried basil

For Baking:

- 1 large thickly sliced tomato
- ½ cup mozzarella cheese (shredded)
- ½ tsp. oregano

Directions:

Plug in your waffle maker to preheat it and grease it.

Combine all the chaffles ingredients in a mixing bowl, and stir until homogeneous.

Pour the mixture into the waffle maker.

Cook for at least 4 minutes to get the desired crunch, and make as many chaffles as your batter allows.

Preheat the oven.

Spread the chaffles on the baking sheet and top one tomato slice.

Sprinkle cheese on top and put the baking sheet into the oven.

Heat for 5 minutes to melt the cheese.

Spread oregano on top and serve hot.

Per serving: Calories: 225Kcal; Fat: 16g; Carbs: 3g; Protein: 20g

658. Cream Cheese Pumpkin Chaffle

Preparation time: 5 minutes
Cooking time: 10 minutes
Servings: 2
Ingredients:

- 2 eggs
- 2 oz. cream cheese
- 2 tsp. coconut flour
- 4 tsp. Swerve/monk fruit
- ½ tsp. baking powder:
- 1 tsp. vanilla extract
- 2 tbsp. canned pumpkin
- ½ tsp. pumpkin spice

Directions:

Take a small mixing bowl and add Swerve/monk fruit, coconut flour, and baking powder and mix them all well.

Now, add the egg, vanilla extract, pumpkin, and cream cheese and beat them all together till uniform consistency is achieved.

Preheat a mini waffle maker if needed.

Pour the mixture into the greasy waffle maker.

Cook for at least 4 minutes to get the desired crunch.

Remove the chaffle from the heat.

Cook the other chaffles with the same procedure, using the remaining mixture.

Serve with butter or whipped cream that you like!

Per serving: Calories: 160Kcal; Fat: 15g; Carbs: 1g; Protein: 7g

659. Berries-Coco Chaffles

Preparation time: 5 minutes
Cooking time: 20 minutes
Servings: 2
Ingredients:
- 1/3 cup cheddar cheese
- 2 eggs
- ½ cup blackberries
- 2 tbsp. coconut flour
- ¼ tsp. baking powder
- 2 tbsp. coconut flakes
- 1/3 cup mozzarella cheese

Directions:
Mix the cheddar cheese, egg, coconut flour, coconut flakes, blackberries, and baking powder together in a bowl.
Preheat your waffle iron and grease it.
In your mini waffle iron, shred half of the mozzarella cheese.
Add the mixture to your mini waffle iron.
Again, shred the remaining mozzarella cheese on the mixture.
Cook till the desired crisp is achieved.
Repeat the process with the remaining batter to create more chaffles.
Per serving: Calories: 280Kcal; Fat: 16g; Carbs: 5g; Protein: 17g

660. Plum Almonds Chaffle

Preparation time: 15 minutes
Cooking time: 20 minutes
Servings: 2
Ingredients:
- 1/3 cup cheddar cheese
- 2 eggs
- 1 tbsp. lemon juice
- ½ cup puree plum
- 2 tbsp. almond flour
- ¼ tsp. baking powder
- 2 tbsp. ground almonds
- 1/3 cup mozzarella cheese

Directions:
Mix the cheddar cheese, egg, lemon juice, almond flour, plum, almond ground, and baking powder together in a bowl.
Preheat your waffle iron and grease it.
In your mini waffle iron, shred half of the mozzarella cheese.
Add the mixture to your mini waffle iron.
Again, shred the remaining mozzarella cheese on the mixture.
Cook till the desired crisp is achieved.
Make as many chaffles as your mixture allow.
Per serving: Calories: 235Kcal; Fat: 26g; Carbs: 3g; Protein: 16g

661. Easy Blueberry Chaffles

Preparation time: 5 minutes
Cooking time: 10 minutes
Servings: 2
Ingredients:
- 2 eggs
- 2 oz. cream cheese
- 2 tbsp. coconut flour
- 4 tsp. Swerve/monk fruit
- ½ tsp. baking powder
- 1 tsp. vanilla extract
- ½ cup blueberries

Directions:
Turn on the waffle maker to heat and grease it with cooking spray.
Take a small mixing bowl and add the Swerve/monk fruit, baking powder, and coconut flour and mix them all well.

Now, add the eggs, vanilla extract, and cream cheese, and beat them all together till a uniform consistency is achieved.
Pour the mixture into the lower plate of the waffle maker.
Add 3-4 fresh blueberries above the mixture and close the lid.
Cook for at least 4 minutes to get the desired crunch.
Remove the chaffle from the heat.
Repeat the steps to create as many chaffle as the batter allow.
Serve with butter or whipped cream that you like!
Per serving: Calories: 300Kcal; Fat: 14g; Carbs: 5g; Protein: 7g

662. Sweet and Sour Coconut Chaffles

Preparation time: 5 minutes
Cooking time: 20 minutes
Servings: 2
Ingredients:
- 1/3 cup cheddar cheese
- 2 eggs
- 2 tsp. sweetener
- 2 tbsp. lemon juice
- 2 tbsp. coconut flour
- ¼ tsp. baking powder
- 2 tbsp. coconut flakes
- 1/3 cup mozzarella cheese

Directions:
Mix the cheddar cheese, egg, coconut flour, coconut flakes, sweetener, lemon juice, and baking powder together in a bowl.
Preheat your waffle iron and grease it.
In your mini waffle iron, shred half of the mozzarella cheese.
Add the mixture to your mini waffle iron.
Again, shred the remaining mozzarella cheese on the mixture.
Cook till the desired crisp is achieved.
Use the remaining mixture for cooking more chaffles.
Sprinkle cinnamon powder on top.
Per serving: Calories: 340Kcal; Fat: 16g; Carbs: 3g; Protein: 12g

663. Plum Coconut Chaffles

Preparation time: 5 minutes
Cooking time: 20 minutes
Servings: 2
Ingredients:
- 1/3 cup cheddar cheese
- 2 eggs
- ½ cup pureed plum
- 2 tbsp. coconut flour
- ¼ tsp. baking powder
- 2 tbsp. coconut flakes
- 1/3 cup mozzarella cheese

Directions:
Mix the cheddar cheese, egg, coconut flour, coconut flakes, plum puree, and baking powder together in a bowl.
Preheat your waffle iron and grease it.
In your mini waffle iron, shred half of the mozzarella cheese.
Add the mixture to your mini waffle iron.
Again, shred the remaining mozzarella cheese on the mixture.
Cook till the desired crisp is achieved.
Repeat the process to create more chaffles with the remaining batter.
Per serving: Calories: 375Kcal; Fat: 14g; Carbs: 3g; Protein: 13g

664. Apple Pie Chayote Tacos Chaffle

Preparation time: 15 minutes
Cooking time: 50 minutes
Servings: 2

Ingredients:
  Chaffles:
- 2 eggs
- ½ cup cream cheese
- 1 tsp. baking powder
- ½ tsp. vanilla extract
- 2 tbsp. powdered sweetener

  Apple Pie Chayote Filling:
- 1 chayote squash
- 1 tbsp. butter
- ¼ cup Swerve
- 2 tsp. cinnamon powder
- 2 tbsp. lemon
- ⅛ tsp. cream of tartar
- ⅛ tsp. nutmeg
- ⅛ tsp. ginger powder

Directions:
For around 25 minutes, boil the whole chayote; when it cools, peel it and slice.
Add all the remaining filling ingredients to it.
Bake the chayote for 20 minutes covered with foil.
Pour ¼ of the mixtures into the blender to make it a sauce.
Add to chayote slices and mix.
For the chaffles: Plug in your waffle maker to preheat it and grease it.
Stir well all the chaffles ingredients in a bowl, till a uniform consistency is achieved.
Drop the mixture into the waffle maker and spread it evenly to cover the plate properly, and close the lid.
Cook for at least 4 minutes to get the desired crunch.
Repeat the steps to create as many chaffle as the batter allow.
Fold the chaffles and serve with the chayote sauce in between.
Per serving: Calories: 387Kcal; Fat: 26g; Carbs: 1g; Protein: 7g

665. Kiwi with Almonds Chaffles
Preparation time: 15 minutes
Cooking time: 20 minutes
Servings: 2
Ingredients:
- 1/3 cup cheddar cheese
- 2 eggs
- ½ cup mashed kiwi
- 2 tbsp. almond flour
- ¼ tsp. baking powder
- 2 tbsp. ground almonds
- 1/3 cup mozzarella cheese

Directions:
Mix the cheddar cheese, egg, lemon juice, almond flour, kiwi, almond ground, and baking powder together in a bowl.
Preheat your waffle iron and grease it.
In your mini waffle iron, shred half of the mozzarella cheese.
Add the mixture to your mini waffle iron.
Again, shred the remaining mozzarella cheese on the mixture.
Cook till the desired crisp is achieved.
Cook as many chaffles as your batter allow.
Per serving: Calories: 360Kcal; Fat: 14g; Carbs: 2g; Protein: 162g

666. Easy Marshmallow Frosting Chaffles
Preparation time: 15 minutes
Cooking time: 25 minutes
Servings: 2

Ingredients:
  Chaffles:
- 2 eggs
- 6 tbsp. cream cheese
- 2 tsp. baking powder
- ½ tsp. vanilla extract
- 3 tbsp. powdered sweetener
- 6 tbsp. pork rinds (crushed)

  Marshmallow Frosting:
- ½ cup organic unsalted butter (room temperature)
- ¼ cup erythritol crystals
- 20 drops vanilla stevia
- 1 tsp. gelatin
- 3 egg whites from extra-large organic eggs

Directions:
Warm up your waffle maker and grease it with cooking spray.
Mix all of the chaffles ingredients in a bowl and stir until homogeneous.
Pour the mixture into the lower plate of the waffle maker and spread it evenly to cover the plate properly, and close the lid.
Let it cook for about 5 minutes, or till it's crispy.
Once the chaffle is done, set it aside for around one minute.
Repeat the process to create more chaffles.
For the marshmallow frosting, add all the frosting ingredients, and whip to form a thick consistency.
Top the chaffles with the frosting and enjoy!
Per serving: Calories: 628Kcal; Fat: 65g; Carbs: 3g; Protein: 12g

667. Peppermint Mocha Chaffles
Preparation time: 10 minutes
Cooking time: 20 minutes
Servings: 2
Ingredients:
  Chaffles:
- 2 eggs
- 2 tbsp. powdered sweetener
- 2 tbsp. cream cheese
- 2 tbsp. butter (melted)
- 2 tsp. coconut flour
- 1 tsp. almond flour
- ¼ tsp. baking powder
- ¼ tsp. vanilla extract
- 1 tbsp. cocoa powder (unsweetened)
- a pinch salt

  For the Filling:
- 2 tbsp. butter
- ½ cup Heavy cream
- 2 tbsp. powdered sweetener
- ¼ tsp. vanilla extract
- ⅛ tsp. peppermint extract
- Starlight mints for garnishing

Directions:
Turn on the waffle maker to heat and grease it with cooking spray.
Put all the chaffle ingredients in a medium-sized bowl.
Mix them all well.
Pour the mixture into the lower plate of the waffle maker and spread it evenly to cover the plate properly, and close the lid.
Cook for about 4-5 minutes, or until golden and crunchy.
Take the chaffle off the maker and keep it aside for a few minutes.
Use the remaining mixture for cooking the rest of the chaffles.
For the filling:
Combine all the filling ingredients into a bowl and beat using the hand blender.

On each chaffle, spread the filling and top with starlight mint.
Per serving: Calories: 395Kcal; Fat: 34g; Carbs: 5g; Protein: 10g

668. Coco-Kiwi Chaffles

Preparation time: 5 minutes
Cooking time: 20 minutes
Servings: 2
Ingredients:

- 1/3 cup cheddar cheese
- 2 eggs
- ½ cup finely grated kiwi
- 2 tbsp. coconut flour
- ¼ tsp. baking powder
- 2 tbsp. coconut flakes
- 1/3 cup mozzarella cheese

Directions:
Mix the cheddar cheese, egg, coconut flour, coconut flakes, kiwi, and baking powder together in a bowl.
Preheat your waffle iron and grease it.
In your mini waffle iron, shred half of the mozzarella cheese.
Add the mixture to your mini waffle iron.
Again, shred the remaining mozzarella cheese on the mixture.
Cook till the desired crisp is achieved.
Make as many chaffles as your mixture allow.
Per serving: Calories: 320Kcal; Fat: 24g; Carbs: 6g; Protein: 18g

669. Rhubarb Almonds Chaffle

Preparation time: 15 minutes
Cooking time: 20 minutes
Servings: 2
Ingredients:

- 1/3 cup cheddar cheese
- 2 eggs
- ¼ cup rhubarb puree
- 2 tbsp. almond flour
- ¼ tsp. baking powder
- 2 tbsp. ground almonds
- 1/3 cup mozzarella cheese

Directions:
Mix the cheddar cheese, egg, rhubarb puree, almond flour, almond ground, and baking powder together in a bowl.
Preheat your waffle iron and grease it.
In your mini waffle iron, shred half of the mozzarella cheese.
Add the mixture to your mini waffle iron.
Again, shred the remaining mozzarella cheese on the mixture.
Cook till the desired crisp is achieved.
Make as many chaffles as your mixture allow.
Per serving: Calories: 328Kcal; Fat: 23g; Carbs: 5g; Protein: 16g

670. Strawberry Coconut Chaffles

Preparation time: 5 minutes
Cooking time: 20 minutes
Servings: 2
Ingredients:

- 1/3 cup cheddar cheese
- 2 eggs
- ½ cup strawberry, finely chopped or mashed
- 2 tbsp. coconut flour
- ¼ tsp. baking powder
- 2 tbsp. coconut flakes
- 1/3 cup mozzarella cheese

Directions:
Mix the cheddar cheese, egg, coconut flour, coconut flakes, strawberry, and baking powder together in a bowl.
Preheat your waffle iron and grease it.
In your mini waffle iron, shred half of the mozzarella cheese.
Add the mixture to your mini waffle iron.
Again, shred the remaining mozzarella cheese on the mixture.
Cook till the desired crisp is achieved.
Cook as many chaffles as your batter allow.
Per serving: Calories: 308Kcal; Fat: 28g; Carbs: 6g; Protein: 19g

671. Raspberries Almonds Chaffles

Preparation time: 15 minutes
Cooking time: 20 minutes
Servings: 2
Ingredients:

- 1/3 cup cheddar cheese
- 2 eggs
- ½ cup raspberries
- 2 tbsp. almond flour
- ¼ tsp. baking powder
- 2 tbsp. ground almonds
- 1/3 cup mozzarella cheese

Directions:
Mix the cheddar cheese, egg, raspberries, almond flour, almond ground, and baking powder together in a bowl.
Preheat your waffle iron and grease it.
In your mini waffle iron, shred half of the mozzarella cheese.
Add the mixture to your mini waffle iron.
Again, shred the remaining mozzarella cheese on the mixture.
Cook till the desired crisp is achieved.
Cook as many chaffles as your batter allow.
Per serving: Calories: 302Kcal; Fat: 21g; Carbs: 6g; Protein: 20g

672. S'mores Dark Chocolate Chaffles

Preparation time: 15 minutes
Cooking time: 25 minutes
Servings: 2
Ingredients:

- 2 eggs
- ½ cup mozzarella cheese (shredded)
- ¼ tsp. baking powder
- ½ tsp. vanilla extract
- 2 tbsp. Swerve
- a pinch pink salt
- ½ tbsp. Psyllium husk powder
- ¼ dark chocolate bar
- 2 tbsp. keto marshmallow crème fluff

Directions:
Create the keto marshmallow crème fluff.
Beat the egg that much that it will become creamy, and then add the Swerve brown and vanilla to it and mix well.
Now, add cheese to the mixture with Psyllium husk powder, salt, and baking powder, and leave chocolate and marshmallow.
Mix them all well and allow the batter to sit for 3-4 minutes.
Warm your waffle maker and grease it if needed.
Pour the mixture into the lower plate of the waffle maker and spread it evenly to cover the plate properly.
Close the lid.
Cook for at least 4 minutes to get the desired crunch.
Take the chaffle off the maker and keep it aside to cool them down.
Repeat the process to cook more chaffles using the remaining mixture.
Now, serve the chaffle with 2 tbsp of marshmallow and chocolate bar.
Per serving: Calories: 240Kcal; Fat: 19g; Carbs: 5g; Protein: 20g

673. Rhubarb and Coconut Chaffles

Preparation time: 5 minutes
Cooking time: 20 minutes
Servings: 2
Ingredients:

- 1/3 cup cheddar cheese
- 2 eggs
- ½ cup rhubarb puree
- 2 tbsp. coconut flour
- ¼ tsp. baking powder
- 2 tbsp. coconut flakes
- 1/3 cup mozzarella cheese

Directions:
Mix the cheddar cheese, egg, coconut flour, coconut flakes, rhubarb puree, and baking powder together in a bowl.
Preheat your waffle iron and grease it.
In your mini waffle iron, shred half of the mozzarella cheese.
Add the mixture to your mini waffle iron.
Again, shred the remaining mozzarella cheese on the mixture.
Cook till the desired crisp is achieved.
Repeat the process with the remaining batter to create more chaffles.
Per serving: Calories: 322Kcal; Fat: 26g; Carbs: 5g; Protein: 16g

674. Strawberry Almonds Chaffle

Preparation time: 15 minutes
Cooking time: 20 minutes
Servings: 2
Ingredients:

- 1/3 cup cheddar cheese
- 2 eggs
- ½ cup strawberry, mashed with a fork
- 2 tbsp. almond flour
- ¼ tsp. baking powder
- 2 tbsp. ground almonds
- 1/3 cup mozzarella cheese

Directions:
Mix the cheddar cheese, egg, strawberry, almond flour, almond ground, and baking powder together in a bowl.
Preheat your waffle iron and grease it.
In your mini waffle iron, shred half of the mozzarella cheese.
Add the mixture to your mini waffle iron.
Again, shred the remaining mozzarella cheese on the mixture.
Cook till the desired crisp is achieved.
Make as many chaffles as your mixture allow.
Per serving: Calories: 320Kcal; Fat: 24g; Carbs: 4g; Protein: 18g

675. Lemony Sweet Chaffles

Preparation time: 5 minutes
Cooking time: 17 minutes
Servings: 2
Ingredients:

- 2 eggs
- 1 cup shredded mozzarella
- 2 tbsp. lemon juice
- 2 tsp. any keto sweetener
- 2 tsp. coconut flour

Directions:
Turn on the waffle maker to heat and grease it with cooking spray.
Mix all the ingredients in a bowl and whisk.
Cook your mixture in the mini waffle iron for at least 4 minutes.
Serve hot and make as many chaffles as your mixture and waffle maker allow.
Per serving: Calories: 260Kcal; Fat: 16g; Carbs: 3g; Protein: 20g

676. Chocolate Chips Walnut Chaffles

Preparation time: 5 minutes
Cooking time: 10 minutes
Servings: 2
Ingredients:

- 2 eggs
- ½ cup shredded mozzarella cheese
- 1 tsp. Swerve/monk fruit
- ½ tsp. vanilla extract
- ¼ cup chopped walnut
- 1 tbsp. coconut flour
- 2 tbsp. chocolate chips

Directions:
Plug in your waffle maker to preheat it and grease it if needed.
Add all the chaffle ingredients to a bowl and stir well.
Cook your mixture in the mini waffle iron for at least 4 minutes.
Make as many chaffles as you can and spread cream or low-carb ice cream on top.
Per serving: Calories: 240Kcal; Fat: 24g; Carbs: 56g; Protein: 20g

677. Italian Cream Sandwich-Cake Chaffle

Preparation time: 8 minutes
Cooking time: 20 minutes
Servings: 4
Ingredients:

- 4 oz. cream cheese, softened, at room temperature
- 4 eggs
- 1 tbsp. melted butter
- 1 tsp. vanilla extract
- 1 tbsp. sweetener
- 4 tbsp. coconut flour
- 1 tbsp. almond flour
- 1½ tsp. baking powder
- 1 tbsp. coconut, shredded, and unsweetened
- 1 tbsp. walnuts, chopped

Italian cream Frosting:

- 2 oz. cream cheese, softened, at room temperature
- 2 tbsp. butter room temp
- 2 tbsp. monk fruit sweetener
- ½ tsp. vanilla

Directions:
Combine the cream cheese, eggs, melted butter, vanilla, sweetener, flours, and baking powder in a blender.
Add walnuts and coconut to the mixture.
Blend to get a creamy mixture.
Turn on the waffle maker to heat and oil it with cooking spray.
Add enough batter to fill the waffle maker. Cook for 2-3 minutes, until the chaffles are done.
Remove and let them cool.
Mix all the frosting ingredients in another bowl. Stir until smooth and creamy.
Frost the chaffles once they have cooled.
Top with cream and more nuts.
Per serving: Calories: 412Kcal; Fat: 28g; Carbs: 10g; Protein: 18g

678. Cinnamon Pumpkin Chaffles

Preparation time: 8 minutes
Cooking time: 16 minutes
Servings: 2
Ingredients:

- 2 organic eggs
- 2/3 cup mozzarella cheese, shredded
- 3 tbsp. sugar-free pumpkin puree

- 3 tsp. almond flour
- 2 tsp. granulated erythritol
- 2 tsp. ground cinnamon

Directions:

Preheat the mini waffle iron and then grease it.

In a medium-sized bowl, place all the ingredients, and with a fork, mix until properly stirred.

Drop half of the mixture into the waffle iron and cook for about 4 minutes or until golden brown.

Repeat with the remaining mixture.

Per serving: Calories: 228Kcal; Fat: 17g; Carbs: 3g; Protein: 20g

679. Chocolate Peanut Butter Chaffle

Preparation time: 5 minutes
Cooking time: 10 minutes
Servings: 2
Ingredients:

- ½ cup shredded mozzarella cheese
- 1 tbsp. cocoa powder
- 2 tbsp. powdered sweetener
- 2 tbsp. peanut butter
- ½ tsp. vanilla
- 2 eggs
- 2 tbsp. crushed peanuts
- 2 tbsp. whipped cream
- ¼ cup sugar-free chocolate syrup

Directions:

Combine the mozzarella, egg, vanilla, peanut butter, cocoa powder, and sweetener in a bowl.

Add in the peanuts and mix well.

Turn on the waffle maker and oil it with cooking spray.

Pour one-half of the batter into the waffle maker and cook for 5 minutes, then transfer it to a plate.

Top with whipped cream, peanuts, and sugar-free chocolate syrup.

Per serving: Calories: 328Kcal; Fat: 28g; Carbs: 6g; Protein: 25g

680. Protein Mozzarella Chaffles

Preparation time: 8 minutes
Cooking time: 20 minutes
Servings: 2
Ingredients:

- ½ scoop unsweetened protein powder
- 2 large organic eggs
- ½ cup mozzarella cheese, shredded
- 1 tbsp. erythritol
- ¼ tsp. organic vanilla extract

Directions:

Preheat your mini waffle iron and then grease it.

In a medium bowl, place all the ingredients, and with a fork, mix until well combined.

Place ¼ of the mixture into the preheated waffle iron and cook for about 4-5 minutes or until golden brown.

Repeat with the remaining mixture.

Serve them warm.

Per serving: Calories: 224Kcal; Fat: 17g; Carbs: 3g; Protein: 20g

681. Peanut Butter and Chocolate Chips Chaffles

Preparation time: 5 minutes
Cooking time: 8 minutes
Servings: 2

Ingredients:

- 2 organic eggs, beaten
- ¼ cup mozzarella cheese, shredded
- 2 tbsp. creamy peanut butter
- 1 tbsp. almond flour
- 1 tbsp. granulated erythritol
- 1 tsp. organic vanilla extract
- 1 tbsp. chocolate chips

Directions:

Preheat your mini waffle iron and then grease it.

In a mixing bowl, place all the ingredients except chocolate chips, and beat until well combined.

Gently, fold in the chocolate chips.

Spoon half of the prepared batter into the preheated waffle iron and let it cook for about 2 minutes or until it reaches the desired doneness.

Repeat with the remaining mixture to create more chaffles.

Serve them warm.

Per serving: Calories: 338Kcal; Fat: 24g; Carbs: 7g; Protein: 22g

682. Dessert Pumpkin Chaffles

Preparation time: 5 minutes
Cooking time: 12 minutes
Servings: 1
Ingredients:

- 1 organic egg, beaten
- ½ cup mozzarella cheese, shredded
- 1½ tbsp. homemade pumpkin puree
- ½ tsp. erythritol
- ½ tsp. organic vanilla extract
- ¼ tsp. pumpkin pie spice

Directions:

Preheat the mini waffle iron and then grease it.

In a bowl, place all the ingredients and beat until well combined.

Place ¼ of the mixture into the preheated waffle iron and cook for about 4-6 minutes or until golden brown.

Repeat with the remaining mixture.

Per serving: Calories: 220Kcal; Fat: 16g; Carbs: 3g; Protein: 20g

683. Mozzarella Chaffles with Dark Chocolate Chips

Preparation time: 5 minutes
Cooking time: 8 minutes
Servings: 1
Ingredients:

- 1 large organic egg
- 1 tsp. coconut flour
- 1 tsp. erythritol
- ½ tsp. organic vanilla extract
- ½ cup mozzarella cheese, shredded finely
- 2 tbsp. 70% dark chocolate chips

Directions:

Preheat mini waffle iron and then grease it.

In a bowl, place the egg, coconut flour, sweetener, and vanilla extract and beat until well combined.

Add the cheese and stir to combine.

Drop half of the mixture into the waffle maker and spread evenly. Top with half of the chocolate chips.

Place a little of the egg mixture over each chocolate chip.

Cook for about 3-4 minutes or until golden brown.

Repeat the process with the remaining mixture and chocolate chips.

Serve them warm.

Per serving: Calories: 254Kcal; Fat: 18g; Carbs: 5g; Protein: 21g

684. Cream Mini Almond Chaffles

Preparation time: 5 minutes
Cooking time: 10 minutes
Servings: 1
Ingredients:

- 2 tsp. almond flour
- 4 tsp. sweetener
- ¼ tsp. baking powder
- 1 egg
- 1 oz. cream cheese

Directions:
Preheat your mini waffle iron and then grease it.
Mix the sweetener, coconut flour, and baking powder in a small mixing bowl.
Add the cream cheese, egg, vanilla extract, and whisk until well-combined.
Place the mixture into the preheated mini waffle iron.
Serve with your favorite toppings.
Per serving: Calories: 105Kcal; Fat: 9g; Carbs: 2g; Protein: 6g

685. Lemon Chaffles

Preparation time: 5 minutes
Cooking time: 10 minutes
Servings: 1
Ingredients:

- 1 organic egg, beaten
- 1 oz. cream cheese, softened
- 2 tbsp. almond flour
- 1 tbsp. fresh lemon juice
- 2 tsp. erythritol
- ½ tsp. fresh lemon zest, grated
- ¼ tsp. organic baking powder
- a pinch of salt
- ½ tsp. powdered erythritol

Directions:
Preheat the mini waffle iron and then grease it.
In a bowl, combine all the ingredients except the powdered erythritol, and beat until properly combined.
Fill the waffle maker with half of the mixture and cook for about 5 minutes or until golden brown.
Repeat with the remaining mixture.
Serve warm with the sprinkling of powdered erythritol.
Per serving: Calories: 112Kcal; Fat: 10g; Carbs: 2g; Protein: 6g

686. Strawberry Pistachios Chaffles

Preparation time: 5 minutes
Cooking time: 20 minutes
Servings: 2
Ingredients:

- 1/3 cup cheddar cheese
- 2 eggs
- ½ cup strawberry, finely chopped or mashed
- 2 tbsp. coconut flour
- ¼ tsp. baking powder
- ¼ cup pistachios
- 1/3 cup mozzarella cheese

Directions:
Mix the cheddar cheese, egg, coconut flour, pistachios, strawberry, and baking powder together in a bowl.
Preheat your waffle iron and grease it.
In your mini waffle iron, shred half of the mozzarella cheese.
Add the mixture to your mini waffle iron.
Again, shred the remaining mozzarella cheese on the mixture.

Cook till the desired crisp is achieved.
Cook as many chaffle as you can with the remaining batter.
Per serving: Calories: 393Kcal; Fat: 28g; Carbs: 9g; Protein: 22g

687. Maple Iced Soft Chaffles

Preparation time: 20 minutes
Cooking time: 45 minutes
Servings: 2
Ingredients:
Chaffles:

- 1 egg yolk
- ⅛ tsp. cake batter extract
- 3 tbsp. almond flour
- ⅛ tsp. baking powder
- ⅛ tsp. vanilla extract
- 1 tbsp. sweetener
- 1 tbsp. butter

Garnishing:

- Nutmeg for garnishing
- 1 tbsp. Cinnamon powder

Icing:

- 1 tbsp. powdered sweetener
- ½ tsp. Heavy cream
- ⅛ tsp. maple extract
- ½ tsp. water

Directions:
Turn on the waffle maker to heat and grease it with cooking spray.
In a medium-sized mixing bowl, add all the chaffle ingredients and stir well until homogeneous.
Pour the mixture into the lower plate of the waffle maker and spread it evenly to cover the plate properly and cover the lid.
Cook it for 4 to 5 minutes, or till it's crispy.
Take the chaffle off the maker and keep it aside to cool them down.
Cook as many chaffles as your mixture allow.
For the maple icing: Add all the icing ingredients and whisk well.
Spread the icing on the chaffle and sprinkle nutmeg and cinnamon on top.
Per serving: Calories: 295Kcal; Fat: 26g; Carbs: 9g; Protein: 14g

688. Lemony Coco Chaffles

Preparation time: 5 minutes
Cooking time: 20 minutes
Servings: 1
Ingredients:

- 1/3 cup cheddar cheese
- 1 egg
- 2 tbsp. lemon juice
- 2 tbsp. coconut flour
- ¼ tsp. baking powder
- 2 tbsp. coconut flakes
- 1/3 cup mozzarella cheese

Directions:
Mix the cheddar cheese, egg, coconut flour, coconut flakes, lemon juice, and baking powder together in a bowl.
Preheat your waffle iron and grease it.
In your mini waffle iron, shred half of the mozzarella cheese.
Add the mixture to your mini waffle iron.
Again, shred the remaining mozzarella cheese on the mixture.
Cook till the desired crisp is achieved.
Make as many chaffles as your mixture allow.
Per serving: Calories: 320Kcal; Fat: 24g; Carbs: 6g; Protein: 18g

689. Choco Bagel Chaffle

Preparation time: 5 minutes
Cooking time: 10 minutes
Servings: 1
Ingredients:

- 1 egg
- ½ cup shredded mozzarella cheese
- 1 tsp. coconut flour
- 1 tsp. everything bagel seasoning
- 2 tbsp. cocoa powder
- 2 tbsp. cream cheese, for serving

Directions:
Turn on the waffle maker to heat and grease it with cooking spray.
Add all the chaffle ingredients to a bowl and stir well.
Cook your mixture in the mini waffle iron for at least 4 minutes.
Make as many chaffles as you can and spread cream cheese on top.
Per serving: Calories: 1870Kcal; Fat: 12g; Carbs: 6g; Protein: 8g

690. Pumpkin Chaffle with Vanilla Icing

Preparation time: 20 minutes
Cooking time: 45 minutes
Servings: 2
Ingredients:
Chaffles:

- 2 egg yolk
- ⅛ tsp. cake batter extract
- 3 tbsp. almond flour
- ⅛ tsp. baking powder
- ⅛ tsp. vanilla extract
- 1 tbsp. sweetener
- 1 tbsp. butter

Icing:

- 1 tbsp. powdered sweetener
- ¼ tsp. vanilla extract
- ½ tsp. water

Sprinkles:

- 1 tbsp. granular sweetener
- 1 drop food coloring

Directions:
Preheat a pumpkin waffle maker if needed and grease it.
In a mixing bowl, combine all the chaffle ingredients and mix well.
Pour the mixture into the lower plate of the pumpkin waffle maker and spread it evenly to cover the plate properly.
Close the lid and let it cook for about 4 minutes or until golden and crunchy.
Take the chaffle off the maker and keep it aside to cool it down.
Use the remaining mixture for cooking more chaffles.
For the icing: Whisk all the ingredients.
Do the same as above for sprinkles.
Add these toppings to the chaffles and enjoy.
Per serving: Calories: 162Kcal; Fat: 8g; Carbs: 2g; Protein: 7g

691. Apple Fritter Keto Chaffle

Preparation time: 20 minutes
Cooking time: 45 minutes
Servings: 2
Ingredients:
Chaffle:

- 2 eggs
- ½ cup mozzarella cheese (grated)
- 1 tbsp. almond flour
- 1 tsp. coconut flour
- ½ tsp. baking powder

Apple Fritter Filling:

- 2 cup jicama (diced)
- ¼ cup and 1 tbsp. Swerve
- 1 tsp. cinnamon powder
- 4 tbsp. butter
- ½ tbsp. cloves (grounded)
- ⅛ tsp. nutmeg
- ½ tsp. vanilla
- 20 drops apple flavoring

For the Glaze:

- 1 tbsp. butter
- 3 tbsp. powdered sweetener
- ¼ tsp. vanilla extract
- 2 tsp. heavy cream

Directions:
Take a small saucepan and melt butter on it on medium-low heat.
Add the peeled and cut jicama and allow it to simmer for 20 minutes while stirring in between.
It will thicken over time.
When the jicama becomes soft, add the other filling ingredients and remove them from the heat and keep it aside.
Warm your waffle maker and grease it if necessary.
In a mixing bowl, beat the eggs and the other chaffle ingredients, except cheese.
Now, add the prepared jicama paste to it.
Mix them all well.
Put around 1 tbsp. of grated cheese on the waffle maker's lower plate.
Pour the chaffle mixture above the cheese spread it evenly to cover the plate properly.
Add 1 tbsp. of cheese again on top of the mixture and close the lid.
Cook for about 4-5 minutes or until it reaches the desired crunch.
Once the chaffle is done, keep it aside for a few minutes.
Cook as many chaffle as you can with the remaining batter.
For the apple fritter icing, melt butter in a small skillet and add the heavy cream, and Swerve.
Simmer the mixture for 4-5 minutes on medium-low heat.
When it starts to thicken, add the vanilla.
Pour this hot icing on top of the prepared chaffles; it will become hard when it cools down.
Per serving: Calories: 227Kcal; Fat: 24g; Carbs: 4g; Protein: 13g

692. Avocado Chaffles

Preparation time: 5 minutes
Cooking time: 17 minutes
Servings: 2
Ingredients:

- 2 eggs
- 1 cup shredded mozzarella
- 1 cup avocado, peeled and mashed
- 2 tsp. any keto sweetener
- 1 tsp. coconut flour
- ½ tsp. vanilla

Directions:
Turn on the waffle maker to heat and grease it with cooking spray.
Combine all the ingredients in a mixing bowl and stir until homogeneous.
Cook your mixture in the mini waffle iron for at least 4 minutes.
Serve hot and make as many chaffles as your mixture and waffle maker allow.
Per serving: Calories: 235Kcal; Fat: 17g; Carbs: 4g; Protein: 20g

693. Mashed Strawberries Chaffles

Preparation time: 5 minutes
Cooking time: 17 minutes
Servings: 2
Ingredients:

- 2 eggs
- 1 cup shredded mozzarella
- 1 cup strawberries, mashed
- 2 tsp. any keto sweetener
- 2 tsp. coconut flour
- ½ tsp. vanilla

Directions:
Preheat and grease your mini waffle iron if needed.
Put all the ingredients in a bowl and mix until homogeneous.
Cook your mixture in the mini waffle iron for at least 4 minutes.
Serve cold and make as many chaffles as your mixture and waffle maker allow.
Per serving: Calories: 220Kcal; Fat: 16g; Carbs: 5g; Protein: 20g

694. Banana and Pistachios Chaffles

Preparation time: 5 minutes
Cooking time: 10 minutes
Servings: 2
Ingredients:

- 2 eggs
- ½ cup shredded mozzarella cheese
- 1 tsp. sweetener
- ½ tsp. vanilla extract
- 1 tbsp. banana extract
- ½ cup chopped pistachios

Directions:
Turn on the waffle maker to heat and grease it with cooking spray.
Add all the chaffle ingredients to a bowl and stir well.
Cook your mixture in the mini waffle iron for at least 4 minutes.
Make as many chaffles as you can and spread cream or low-carb ice cream on top.
Per serving: Calories: 326Kcal; Fat: 23g; Carbs: 8g; Protein: 16g

695. Cranberry Swirl Chaffles with Orange Cream Cheese

Preparation time: 20 minutes
Cooking time: 45 minutes
Servings: 2
Ingredients:
Chaffles:

- 2 eggs
- 1 tbsp. cream cheese
- 1 tbsp. Swerve blend
- 1 tsp. coconut flour
- ½ tsp. vanilla extract
- ¼ tsp. baking powder

Cranberry Sauce:

- ½ cup cranberries
- 2 tbsp. erythritol (granulated)
- ½ tsp. vanilla extract
- ½ cup water

Frosting:

- 2 tbsp. cream cheese
- 1 tbsp. butter
- 1 tbsp. sweetener
- 2 tbsp. orange zest (grated)
- ⅛ tsp. orange extract

Directions:
Mix the cranberries with erythritol and water in a saucepan and boil on medium-low heat.
Simmer the mixture for 15 minutes till the sauce thickens.
Remove the mixture from the stove and add vanilla extract.
Use a spoon to mash cranberries and heat again for a bit.
Heat up your waffle maker and grease it if needed.
In a mixing bowl, add all the chaffles ingredients and blend.
Pour the mixture into the lower plate of the waffle maker and spread it evenly to cover the plate properly.
Add the cranberry sauce on the top of the mixture in a way that it covers it all, and close the lid.
Cook for at least 5 minutes or till it's crispy.
Take the chaffle off the maker and set it aside for a few minutes to allow it to cool.
Cook as many chaffles as your batter allow.
Combine all the ingredients for the frosting, excluding orange zest, and spread over the chaffle.
Add orange zest on top at the end before serving.
Per serving: Calories: 284Kcal; Fat: 22g; Carbs: 7g; Protein: 19g

696. Cantaloupe Walnut Chaffles

Preparation time: 5 minutes
Cooking time: 10 minutes
Servings: 1
Ingredients:

- 1 egg
- ½ cup shredded mozzarella cheese
- 1 tsp. Swerve/monk fruit
- ½ tsp. vanilla extract
- ¼ cup walnut, finely chopped
- 1 tbsp. coconut flour
- ½ cup cantaloupe

Directions:
Add all the chaffle ingredients to a bowl and mix well.
Plug in your waffle maker to preheat it and grease it.
Cook half of your mixture in the mini waffle iron for at least 4 minutes or until golden and crispy.
Make as many chaffles as you can and spread cream or low-carb ice cream on top.
Per serving: Calories: 244Kcal; Fat: 16g; Carbs: 5g; Protein: 20g

697. Sandwich Swerve Chaffles

Preparation time: 10 minutes
Cooking time: 15 minutes
Servings: 2
Ingredients:
Chaffles:

- 2 eggs
- ½ cup butter
- ½ cup chocolate chips (sugar-free)
- ¼ cup sweetener
- 1 tsp. vanilla extract

Cream Cheese Frosting:

- ½ cup butter (room temperature)
- ½ cup cream cheese (room temperature)
- ½ cup powdered Swerve
- ¼ cup heavy whipping cream
- 1 tsp. vanilla extract

Directions:
In a bowl, add the butter and chocolate chips and microwave for one minute only.
Remove from the microwave and stir to melt the chocolate using the butter's heat and set aside.

Warm up your waffle maker; grease it if needed.
In a mixing bowl, beat the eggs, and add sweetener and vanilla. Stir until smooth.
Now, add chocolate and butter to the mixture.
Mix them all well and pour the mixture into the lower plate of the waffle maker.
Close the lid.
Cook for at least 5 minutes to get the desired crunch.
Now, make the frosting by adding all the ingredients to the food processor and making a smooth cream.
Take the chaffle off the heat and keep it aside for around 1 minute.
In between the two chaffles, put frosting generously to make the sandwich Chaffle.
Repeat the steps to create as many chaffle as the mixture allow.
Serve them hot.
Per serving: Calories: 875Kcal; Fat: 95g; Carbs: 7g; Protein: 7g

698. Orange Pistachios Chaffles

Preparation time: 5 minutes
Cooking time: 10 minutes
Servings: 2
Ingredients:
- 2 eggs
- ½ cup shredded mozzarella cheese
- 1 tsp. Swerve/monk fruit
- ½ tsp. vanilla extract
- 1 tbsp. orange extract
- ½ cup chopped pistachios

Directions:
Add all the chaffle ingredients to a mixing bowl and whisk.
Warm your waffle maker and grease it if needed.
Cook your mixture in the mini waffle iron for at least 4 minutes.
Make as many chaffles as you can and spread cream or low-carb ice cream on top.
Per serving: Calories: 306Kcal; Fat: 22g; Carbs: 6g; Protein: 23g

699. Banana Walnut Chaffles

Preparation time: 5 minutes
Cooking time: 10 minutes
Servings: 1
Ingredients:
- 1 egg
- ½ cup shredded mozzarella cheese
- 1 tsp. sweetener
- ½ tsp. vanilla extract
- ¼ cup finely chopped walnut
- 1 tbsp. coconut flour
- 1 tbsp. banana extract

Directions:
Add all the chaffle ingredients to a bowl and mix well.
Turn on the waffle maker to heat and grease it with cooking spray.
Cook your mixture in the mini waffle iron for at least 4 minutes.
Make as many chaffles as you can and spread cream or low-carb ice cream on top.
Per serving: Calories: 285Kcal; Fat: 19g; Carbs: 6g; Protein: 20g

700. Peachy Walnut Chaffles

Preparation time: 5 minutes
Cooking time: 10 minutes
Servings: 1
Ingredients:
- 1 egg
- ½ cup shredded mozzarella cheese
- 1 tsp. sweetener

- ½ tsp. vanilla extract
- ¼ cup walnut, finely chopped
- 1 tbsp. coconut flour
- ½ cup pulp peach

Directions:
Add all the chaffle ingredients to a bowl and stir.
Heat up your waffle iron if needed and grease it.
Cook your mixture for at least 4 minutes.
Make as many chaffles as you can and spread cream or low-carb ice cream on top.
Per serving: Calories: 282Kcal; Fat: 17g; Carbs: 6g; Protein: 21g

701. Banana Cheddar Chaffle

Preparation time: 5 minutes
Cooking time: 10 minutes
Servings: 1
Ingredients:
- 1 egg
- 1 tbsp. cream cheese
- ½ cup cheddar cheese
- ¼ tbsp. banana extract
- ½ tsp. vanilla extract
- 1 tbsp. sweetener
- 2 tbsp. caramel sauce (sugar-free)

Directions:
Grease your waffle maker and warm it up.
In a mixing bowl, beat the eggs and add all the chaffle ingredients, except caramel sauce.
Mix them all well.
Pour the mixture into the lower plate of the waffle maker and spread it evenly to cover the plate properly.
Close the lid.
Cook half of your mixture in the mini waffle iron for at least 4 minutes or until golden and crispy.
Take the chaffle off the maker and keep it aside for around one minute.
Cook the other chaffles with the same procedure, using the remaining mixture.
Serve them with caramel sauce.
Per serving: Calories: 385Kcal; Fat: 30g; Carbs: 1g; Protein: 21g

702. Cantaloupe Chaffles

Preparation time: 5 minutes
Cooking time: 17 minutes
Servings: 1
Ingredients:
- 1 egg
- 1 cup shredded cheddar cheese
- 1 cup mashed cantaloupe
- 2 tsp. coconut flour
- ½ tsp. vanilla

Directions:
Warm your waffle maker and grease it if needed.
Mix all the ingredients in a bowl and mix well.
Cook your mixture for at least 4 minutes.
Cook as many chaffles as your batter allow.
Per serving: Calories: 280Kcal; Fat: 16g; Carbs: 6g; Protein: 20g

703. Creamy Pistachios Chaffles

Preparation time: 5 minutes
Cooking time: 10 minutes
Servings: 1
Ingredients:
- 1 egg
- ½ cup shredded mozzarella cheese

- 1 tsp. Swerve/monk fruit
- ½ tsp. vanilla extract
- 1 tbsp. coconut flour
- ¼ cup cream
- ½ cup chopped pistachios

Directions:

Add all the chaffle ingredients to a bowl and whisk well.

Turn on the waffle maker to heat and grease it with cooking spray. Cook your mixture for at least 4 minutes.

Make as many chaffles as you can and spread cream or low-carb ice cream on top.

Per serving: Calories: 380Kcal; Fat: 28g; Carbs: 7g; Protein: 26g

704. Chocolate Keto Chaffle

Preparation time: 5 minutes
Cooking time: 10 minutes
Servings: 2
Ingredients:

- 2 eggs
- ½ cup butter
- ½ cup chocolate chips
- ¼ cup sweetener
- 1 tsp. vanilla extract

Directions:

In a bowl, add the butter and chocolate chips and microwave for only 1 minute.

Remove from the microwave and stir to melt the chocolate using the butter's heat and set aside.

Plug in your waffle maker to preheat it and grease it.

In a mixing bowl, beat the eggs, and add Truvia and vanilla and blend to froth.

Now, add the chocolate and butter to the mixture.

Mix them all well and pour the mixture into the lower plate of the waffle maker.

Close the lid.

Cook for at least 5 minutes to get the desired crunch.

Remove the chaffle from the heat.

Make as many chaffles as your mixture allow.

Serve with your favorite toppings and enjoy!

Per serving: Calories: 448Kcal; Fat: 50g; Carbs: 1g; Protein: 5g

705. Raspberries Nutty Chaffles

Preparation time: 5 minutes
Cooking time: 10 minutes
Servings: 1
Ingredients:

- 1 egg
- ½ cup shredded mozzarella cheese
- 1 tsp. Swerve
- ½ tsp. vanilla extract
- ¼ cup walnut, finely chopped
- 1 tbsp. coconut flour
- ½ cup raspberries

Directions:

Turn on the waffle maker to heat and grease it with cooking spray.

Add all the chaffle ingredients to a mixing bowl and whisk well.

Cook your mixture in the mini waffle iron for at least 4 minutes.

Make as many chaffles as you can and spread cream or low-carb ice cream on top.

Per serving: Calories: 526Kcal; Fat: 34g; Carbs: 8g; Protein: 26g

706. Nutty Crispy Chaffles

Preparation time: 5 minutes
Cooking time: 10 minutes
Servings: 2
Ingredients:

- 2 eggs
- ½ cup shredded mozzarella cheese
- 1 tsp. sweetener
- ½ tsp. vanilla extract
- 1 tbsp. coconut flour
- ¼ cup chopped peanut
- ¼ cup chopped walnut

Directions:

Add all the chaffle ingredients to a bowl and whisk.

Cook your mixture in the mini waffle iron for at least 4 minutes.

Make as many chaffles as you can and spread cream or low-carb ice cream on top.

Per serving: Calories: 530Kcal; Fat: 35g; Carbs: 8g; Protein: 28g

707. Fresh Strawberries Chaffle

Preparation time: 5 minutes
Cooking time: 10 minutes
Servings: 1
Ingredients:

- 1 egg
- ½ cup mozzarella cheese
- 1 tbsp. almond flour
- 1½ tbsp. Swerve
- ¼ tsp. vanilla extract
- 2 tbsp. whipped cream
- 4 strawberries

Directions:

Preheat a mini waffle maker if needed.

Chop fresh strawberries and mix with half tbsp. of granulated Swerve and keep it aside.

In a medium-sized mixing bowl, beat the eggs and add mozzarella cheese, almond flour, granulated Swerve, and vanilla extract.

Mix them all well and pour the mixture into the lower plate of the waffle maker.

Close the lid.

Cook for 4-5 minutes, or until golden and crunchy.

Take the chaffle off the heat and keep it aside for around two minutes.

Cook as many chaffle as you can with the remaining batter.

Serve with the fresh strawberries mixture you made with the whipped cream on top.

Per serving: Calories: 314Kcal; Fat: 26g; Carbs: 5g; Protein: 20g

708. Cinnamon Peach Chaffles

Preparation time: 5 minutes
Cooking time: 20 minutes
Servings: 2
Ingredients:

- 1/3 cup cheddar cheese
- 2 eggs
- ¼ cup peach puree
- 1 tsp. favorite sweetener
- 2 tbsp. cinnamon powder
- ¼ tsp. baking powder
- 1/3 cup mozzarella cheese

Directions:

Mix the cheddar cheese, egg, peach puree, sweetener, and baking powder together in a bowl.

Preheat your waffle iron and grease it.

In your mini waffle iron, shred half of the mozzarella cheese.
Add the mixture to your mini waffle iron.
Again, shred the remaining mozzarella cheese on the mixture.
Cook till the desired crisp is achieved.
Repeat the process with the remaining batter to create more chaffles.
Sprinkle cinnamon on top before serving.
Per serving: Calories: 265Kcal; Fat: 22g; Carbs: 3g; Protein: 18g

709. Lemon and Peach Chaffles

Preparation time: 5 minutes
Cooking time: 17 minutes
Servings: 2
Ingredients:

- 2 eggs
- 1 cup shredded cheddar cheese
- 1 cup peach, peeled and mashed
- 2 tbsp. lemon juice
- 2 tsp. coconut flour

Directions:
Heat up your waffle maker.
Mix all the ingredients in a bowl and whisk.
Cook your mixture in the mini waffle iron for at least 4 minutes.
Repeat the steps to create as many chaffle as the batter allow.
Per serving: Calories: 300Kcal; Fat: 25g; Carbs: 5g; Protein: 20g

710. Creamy Strawberry Chaffles

Preparation time: 5 minutes
Cooking time: 10 minutes
Servings: 1
Ingredients:

- 1 egg
- ½ cup shredded mozzarella cheese
- 1 tsp. sweetener
- ½ tsp. vanilla extract
- ¼ cup finely chopped walnuts
- 1 tbsp. coconut flour
- ½ cup pulp strawberry

Directions:
Turn on the waffle maker to heat and grease it with cooking spray.
Add all the chaffle ingredients to a bowl and whisk well.
Cook your mixture in the mini waffle iron for at least 4 minutes.
Make as many chaffles as you can and spread cream or low-carb ice cream on top.
Per serving: Calories: 228Kcal; Fat: 18g; Carbs: 3g; Protein: 2g

711. Kiwi Cheddar Chaffles

Preparation time: 5 minutes
Cooking time: 20 minutes
Servings: 2
Ingredients:

- 1/3 cup cheddar cheese
- 2 eggs
- ¼ cup mashed kiwi
- 1 tsp. favorite sweetener
- 2 tbsp. cinnamon powder
- ¼ tsp. baking powder
- 1/3 cup mozzarella cheese

Directions:
Mix the cheddar cheese, egg, kiwi, sweetener, and baking powder together in a bowl and preheat your waffle iron, and grease it.
In your mini waffle iron, shred half of the mozzarella cheese.
Add the mixture to your mini waffle iron.
Again, shred the remaining mozzarella cheese on the mixture.

Cook till the desired crisp is achieved.
Re-do the process again with the remaining batter to create more chaffles. Sprinkle cinnamon on top before serving.
Per serving: Calories: 290Kcal; Fat: 18g; Carbs: 3g; Protein: 23g

712. Peach and Pistachios Chaffles

Preparation time: 5 minutes
Cooking time: 10 minutes
Servings: 1
Ingredients:

- 1 egg
- ½ cup shredded mozzarella cheese
- 1 tsp. Swerve/monk fruit
- ½ tsp. vanilla extract
- 1 tbsp. coconut flour
- 1 cup peach puree
- ¼ cup cream
- ½ cup chopped pistachios

Directions:
Add all the chaffle ingredients to a bowl and stir well.
Grease your waffle maker and preheat it.
Cook your mixture in the mini waffle iron for at least 4 minutes.
Make as many chaffles as you can and spread cream or low-carb ice cream on top.
Per serving: Calories: 423Kcal; Fat: 32g; Carbs: 7g; Protein: 25g

713. Raspberries Coconut Chaffles

Preparation time: 5 minutes
Cooking time: 20 minutes
Servings: 1
Ingredients:

- 1/3 cup cheddar cheese
- 1 egg
- ½ cup raspberries
- 2 tbsp. coconut flour
- ¼ tsp. baking powder
- 2 tbsp. coconut flakes
- 1/3 cup mozzarella cheese

Directions:
Mix cheddar cheese, egg, coconut flour, coconut flakes, raspberries, and baking powder together in a bowl.
Preheat your waffle iron and grease it.
In your mini waffle iron, shred half of the mozzarella cheese.
Add the mixture to your mini waffle iron.
Again, shred the remaining mozzarella cheese on the mixture.
Cook till the desired crisp is achieved.
Cook the second chaffle using the remaining batter.
Per serving: Calories: 294Kcal; Fat: 17g; Carbs: 3g; Protein: 22g

714. Orange Walnuts Chaffles

Preparation time: 5 minutes
Cooking time: 10 minutes
Servings: 1
Ingredients:

- 1 egg
- ½ cup shredded mozzarella cheese
- 1 tsp. sweetener
- ½ tsp. vanilla extract
- 1 tbsp. orange extract

Directions:
Warm your waffle maker and grease it if needed.
Add all the chaffle ingredients to a bowl and mix well.
Cook your mixture in the mini waffle iron for at least 4 minutes.

Make as many chaffles as you can and spread cream or low-carb ice cream on top.

Per serving: Calories: 220Kcal; Fat: 16g; Carbs: 8g; Protein: 20g

715. Dark Chocolate Chaffles

Preparation time: 5 minutes
Cooking time: 10 minutes
Servings: 1
Ingredients:

- 1 large egg
- ½ cup mozzarella cheese shredded
- ½ tsp. vanilla extract
- 2 tbsp. sweetener
- ½ tbsp. Psyllium Husk Powder optional
- ¼ tsp. baking powder
- a pinch of pink salt
- ¼ Lily's original dark chocolate bar
- 2 tbsp. keto marshmallow creme

Directions:
Make the batch of Keto Marshmallow Creme Fluff.
Whisk the egg until creamy.
Add the vanilla and Swerve Brown; mix well.
Mix in the shredded cheese and blend.
Then add the Psyllium Husk Powder, baking powder, and salt.
Mix well and let the batter rest for 3-4 minutes.
Plug in your waffle maker to preheat.
Spread half of the batter on the waffle maker and cook for 3-4 minutes.
Remove and set on a cooling rack.
Cook the second half of the batter, and then remove to cool.
Once cool, assemble the chaffles with the marshmallow fluff and chocolate. Use two tbsp. of marshmallow creme and ¼ bar of Lily's Chocolate.
Eat as it is, or toast it!

Per serving: Calories: 230Kcal; Fat: 22g; Carbs: 5g; Protein: 23g

716. Granulated Strawberry Cake Chaffle

Preparation time: 5 minutes
Cooking time: 8 minutes
Servings: 1
Ingredients:

- ½ tsp. cinnamon
- ½ cup shredded mozzarella cheese
- 1 tsp. sugar-free maple syrup
- 2 tsp. granulated Swerve
- 1 egg (beaten)
- 1 tbsp. almond flour

Toppings:

- 3 fresh strawberries (sliced)
- 2 tsp. granulated Swerve
- 1 tbsp. heavy cream
- ¼ tsp. vanilla extract
- 2 tbsp. cream cheese (softened)

Directions:
Plug the waffle maker to preheat it and spray it with a non-stick cooking spray.
In a mixing bowl, combine the cinnamon, Swerve, cheese, and almond flour. Add the egg and maple syrup. Mix until the ingredients are well combined.
Pour half of the batter into the waffle maker and cook for about 4 minutes or according to your waffle maker's settings.
After the cooking cycle, remove the chaffle from the waffle maker with a plastic or silicone utensil.
Repeat the process until you have cooked all the batter into chaffles.

For the topping, combine the cream cheese, Swerve, vanilla, and heavy cream in a mixing bowl. Whisk until the mixture is smooth and fluffy.
Top the chaffles with cream and sliced strawberries.

Per serving: Calories: 343Kcal; Fat: 32g; Carbs: 8g; Protein: 22g

717. Carrot Cake Chaffle

Preparation time: 10 minutes
Cooking time: 18 minutes
Servings: 10 (6 mini chaffles)
Ingredients:

- 1 tbsp. toasted pecans (chopped)
- 2 tbsp. granulated Swerve
- 1 tsp. pumpkin spice
- ½ shredded carrots
- 2 tbsp. butter (melted)
- 1 tsp. cinnamon
- 1 tsp. vanilla extract (optional)
- 2 tbsp. heavy whipping cream
- ¾ cup almond flour
- 1 egg (beaten)

Buttercream Cheese Frosting:

- ½ cup cream cheese (softened)
- ¼ cup butter (softened)
- ½ tsp. vanilla extract
- ¼ cup granulated Swerve

Directions:
Plug the chaffle maker to preheat it and. Apply non-stick cooking spray.
In a mixing bowl, combine the almond flour, cinnamon, carrot, pumpkin spice, and Swerve.
In another mixing bowl, whisk together the egg, butter, heavy whipping cream, and vanilla extract.
Pour the flour mixture into the egg mixture and mix until you form a smooth batter.
Fold in the chopped pecans.
Fill the waffle maker with some of the batter and spread it evenly to cover the plate properly, and close the lid.
Let it cook for about 3 minutes or according to your waffle maker's settings.
After the cooking cycle, use a plastic or silicone utensil to remove the chaffle from the waffle maker.
Repeat until you have cooked all the batter into chaffles.
For the frosting, combine the cream cheese and butter in a mixer and mix until well combined.
Add the Swerve and vanilla extract and slowly until the sweetener is well incorporated. Mix on high until the frosting is fluffy.
Place one chaffle on a flat surface and spread some cream frosting over it. Layer another chaffle over the first one a spread some cream over it, too.
Repeat step 11 until you have assembled all the chaffles into a cake.
Cut and serve.

Per serving: Calories: 308Kcal; Fat: 24g; Carbs: 2g; Protein: 4g

718. Chaffles with Ice Cream

Preparation time: 10 minutes
Cooking time: 14 minutes
Servings: 1
Ingredients:

- 1 egg, beaten
- ½ cup finely grated mozzarella cheese
- ¼ cup almond flour
- 2 tbsp. sweeteners
- ⅛ tsp. xanthan gum
- low-carb ice cream for serving

Directions:

Preheat the waffle iron.

In a medium bowl, mix all the ingredients, except the ice cream.

Open the iron and add half of the mixture. Close and cook until crispy, 7 minutes.

Transfer the chaffle to a plate and make the second one with the remaining batter.

On each chaffle, add a scoop of low-carb ice cream, fold into half-moons and enjoy.

Per serving: Calories: 288Kcal; Fat: 24g; Carbs: 3g; Protein: 20g

719. Chocolatey Chaffles

Preparation time: 5 minutes
Cooking time: 4 minutes
Servings: 1
Ingredients:

- 1 large egg
- 1 oz. cream cheese, softened
- 1 tbsp. sugar-free chocolate syrup
- ½ tsp. vanilla
- 1 tbsp. stevia sweetener
- ½ tbsp. cacao powder
- ¼ tsp. baking powder

Directions:

Preheat mini waffle maker until hot.

Whisk egg in a bowl, add cheese, and then mix well.

Stir in the remaining ingredients (except toppings, if any).

Scoop ½ of the batter onto the waffle maker, spread across evenly.

Cook until a bit browned and crispy, about 4 minutes.

Gently remove from the waffle maker and let it cool.

Repeat with the remaining batter.

Per serving: Calories: 225Kcal; Fat: 18g; Carbs: 1g; Protein: 7g

720. Chocolate Chip Chaffle

Preparation time: 5 minutes
Cooking time: 8 minutes
Servings: 1
Ingredients:

- 1 egg
- ¼ tsp. baking powder
- a pinch of salt
- 1 tbsp. heavy whipping cream
- ½ tsp. coconut flour
- 1 tbsp. chocolate chips

Directions:

Preheat your mini waffle maker until hot.

Whisk the egg in a bowl, add cheese, then mix well.

Stir in the remaining ingredients (except toppings, if any).

Grease the preheated waffle maker with cooking oil. This will help to create a crisper crust.

Scoop ½ of the batter onto the waffle maker, spread across evenly.

Sprinkle chocolate chips on top.

Cook until a bit browned and crispy, about 4 minutes.

Gently remove from the waffle maker and let it cool.

Repeat with the remaining batter.

Top with whipping cream.

Per serving: Calories: 180Kcal; Fat: 12g; Carbs: 3g; Protein: 6g

721. Chocolate Chips Cannoli Chaffle

Preparation time: 15 minutes
Cooking time: 5 minutes
Servings: 4

Ingredients:

Chocolate Chips Chaffle:

- 1 tbsp. butter, melted
- 1 tbsp. monk fruit
- 1 egg yolk
- ⅛ tsp. vanilla extract
- 3 tbsp. almond flour
- ⅛ tsp. baking powder
- 1 tbsp. chocolate chips, sugar-free

Toppings:

- 2 oz. cream cheese
- 2 tbsp. confectioners' sugar
- 6 tbsp. ricotta cheese, full-fat
- ¼ tsp. vanilla extract
- 5 drops lemon extract

Directions:

Preheat the mini waffle maker.

Mix all the ingredients for the chocolate chip chaffle in a mixing bowl. Combine well to make a batter.

Place half of the batter on the waffle maker. Allow it to cook for 3-4 minutes.

While waiting for the chaffles to cook, start making your cannoli topping by combining all the ingredients until the consistency is creamy and smooth.

Place the cannoli topping on the cooked chaffles before serving.

Per serving: Calories: 340Kcal; Fat: 24g; Carbs: 2g; Protein: 12g

722. Heavy Cream Biscuits Chaffle

Preparation time: 10 minutes
Cooking time: 20 minutes
Servings: 2
Ingredients:

- 2 tsp. almond flour
- 3 tbsp. dark chocolate powder
- 1 tsp. baking powder
- 4 tbsp. sweetener
- 1 tsp. vanilla extract, unsweetened
- 2 tbsp. heavy cream
- 2 eggs, at room temperature
- 2 tbsp. whipped cream

Directions:

Take a non-stick waffle iron; plug it in, and let it preheat.

Meanwhile, make the batter. Take a large bowl, add the flour in it along with other ingredients and mix until smooth.

Use a ladle to pour one-fourth of the prepared batter into the heated waffle iron in a spiral direction, starting from the edges, then shut the lid and cook for 5 minutes or more until solid and nicely browned; the cooked waffle will look like a cake.

When done, transfer the chaffles to a plate with a silicone spatula and repeat with the remaining batter.

When done, make a sort of biscuits sandwiches, and for this, spread 1 tbsp. of whipped cream on one side of two chaffles and then cover with the remaining chaffles.

Per serving: Calories: 215Kcal; Fat: 17g; Carbs: 1g; Protein: 7g

723. Brownie Batter Chaffle

Preparation time: 10 minutes
Cooking time: 25 minutes
Servings: 10
Ingredients:

- ½ cup almond flour
- ½ cup chopped chocolate, unsweetened
- 1 tsp. baking powder

- ¼ tsp. salt
- ¼ cup cocoa powder, unsweetened
- ¼ tsp. liquid stevia
- ½ cup sweetener
- ½ tsp. vanilla extract, unsweetened
- 12 tbsp. coconut butter
- 5 eggs, at room temperature

Directions:

Take a non-stick waffle iron; plug it in. Select the medium or medium-high heat setting and let it preheat until ready to use. It could be known with an indicator light changing its color.

Meanwhile, make the batter. Take a saucepan, place it over medium heat; add cocoa powder, chocolate, and butter. Cook for 3 to 4 minutes until the butter has melted, whisking frequently.

Then, add the sweetener, stevia, and vanilla into the pan, stir until combined, remove the pan from the heat and let it stand for 5 minutes. Take a medium bowl, add the flour in it and then stir in the baking powder and salt until mixed.

After 5 minutes, beat the eggs into the chocolate-butter mixture and stir the flour until blended.

Use a ladle to pour ¼ of the prepared batter into the heated waffle iron in a spiral direction, starting from the edges, then shut the lid and cook for 5 minutes or more until solid and nicely browned; the cooked waffle will look like a cake.

When done, transfer the chaffles to a plate with a silicone spatula and repeat with the remaining batter.

Let the chaffles stand for some time until crispy and serve straight away.

Per serving: Calories: 485Kcal; Fat: 38g; Carbs: 1g; Protein: 2g

724. Keto Cornbread Chaffle

Preparation time: 10 minutes
Cooking time: 5 minutes
Servings: 1
Ingredients:

- 1 egg
- ½ cup cheddar cheese shredded (or mozzarella)
- 5 slices jalapeño optional - picked or fresh
- 1 tsp. Frank's red-hot sauce
- ¼ tsp. corn extract
- a pinch salt

Directions:

Grease your waffle maker and preheat it.

Beat the egg in a small-sized bowl, and add the remaining ingredients. Mix well to ensure a smooth consistency.

Before adding the mixture into the waffle maker, add 1 tsp. of shredded cheese and let it melt for about 30 seconds. This will result in a nice, crunchy crust that is really delicious!

Drop half of the mixture into the waffle maker and spread evenly. Cook it for about 3-4 minutes.

The longer you cook it, the creepier it gets; be careful not to burn it.

Per serving: Calories: 335Kcal; Fat: 28g; Carbs: 1g; Protein: 21g

725. Lime Pie Chaffle

Preparation time: 10 minutes
Cooking time: 5 minutes
Servings: 1
Ingredients:

Chaffles:

- 1 egg
- ¼ cup almond flour
- 2 tsp. cream cheese room temp
- 1 tsp. powdered sweetener Swerve or monk fruit
- ½ tsp. lime extract or 1 tsp. freshly squeezed lime juice
- ½ tsp. baking powder
- ½ tsp. lime zest
- a pinch of salt to bring out the flavors

Cream Cheese Lime Frosting:

- 4 oz. cream cheese softened
- 4 tbsp. butter
- 2 tsp. powdered sweetener Swerve or monk fruit
- 1 tsp. lime extract
- ½ tsp. lime zest

Directions:

Plug the waffle maker to preheat it and spray it with a non-stick cooking spray.

Add all the chaffle ingredients in a blender, and mix on high until the mixture is smooth and creamy.

Pour the mixture into the waffle maker and spread it evenly to cover the plate properly.

Cook each chaffle for about 3 to 4 minutes until it's golden brown and crispy.

Set the chaffles aside to completely cool before frosting them.

Make the frosting: In a small-sized bowl, combine all the ingredients for the frosting and stir until smooth.

Top with the frosting and add a small amount of lime zest for an extra touch!

Per serving: Calories: 416Kcal; Fat: 34g; Carbs: 2g; Protein: 9g

CHAPTER 12:

... Many More Chaffle Recipes

726. Eggs-Free Chaffles and Raspberry Syrup
Preparation time: 10 minutes
Cooking time: 20 minutes
Servings: 2
Ingredients:
- 2 tbsp stevia
- 1 and ¼ cup coconut milk
- ¼ cup coconut oil, melted
- ½ tsp. almond extract
- 1 cup almond flour
- ½ cup coconut flour
- 1 and ½ tsp baking powder
- ¼ tsp. cinnamon powder

For the Syrup:
- 1 and 1/3 cup raspberries
- 4 tbsp lemon juice
- ½ cup water

Directions:
Use a mixing bowl to mix the stevia with the coconut oil, milk, and the other ingredients except for the ones for the syrup and whisk.
Pour ¼ of the batter in your waffle iron, cover, and cook for about 5 minutes.
Transfer to a plate and repeat with the rest of the batter.
Meanwhile, combine the raspberries with the lemon juice and the water, whisk heat up over medium heat for 10 minutes.
Drizzle the raspberry mix over your chaffles and serve
Per serving: Calories: 147Kcal; Fat: 18g; Carbs: 1g; Protein: 2g

727. Pumpkin Seeds Eggs-Free Chaffles
Preparation time: 6 minutes
Cooking time: 5 minutes
Servings: 3
Ingredients:
- 1 tbsp. coconut oil, melted
- 1 cup almond flour
- 1 egg, whisked
- 3 tbsp cream cheese, soft
- 1 ½ cups almond milk
- 3 tbsp stevia
- 2 tbsp pumpkin seeds
- 1 tsp. vanilla extract
- 1 tsp. baking soda

Directions:
In a bowl, mix the melted coconut oil with the flour and the other ingredients and whisk well.
Heat up the waffle iron, pour ¼ of the batter, and cook for 5 minutes.
Repeat with the rest of the batter and serve the chaffles cold.
Per serving: Calories: 106Kcal; Fat: 8g; Carbs: 2g; Protein: 4g

728. Peppermint Chaffles
Preparation time: 10 minutes
Cooking time: 10 minutes
Servings: 2
Ingredients:
- ¼ cup cream cheese, soft
- 2 eggs, whisked
- 1 cup coconut flour
- ½ cup coconut milk
- 3 tbsp ghee, melted
- ¼ tsp. vanilla extract
- ¼ tsp. peppermint extract

Directions:
In a medium-sized bowl, mix the cream cheese with the eggs and the other ingredients and whisk well.
Heat up the waffle iron, pour ⅛ of the batter, and cook for 6 minutes.
Repeat with the rest of the batter
Per serving: Calories: 268Kcal; Fat: 16g; Carbs: 2g; Protein: 11g

729. Blackberries + Cranberries Chaffles
Preparation time: 10 minutes
Cooking time: 10 minutes
Servings: 2
Ingredients:
- 1 and ¾ cup coconut flour
- zest from 1 lime, grated
- ¼ cup blackberries
- ¼ cup cranberries
- 2 tsp baking powder
- ¼ cup Swerve
- ¼ cup heavy cream
- ¼ cup cream cheese, warm
- 2 eggs, whisked
- 1 tsp. vanilla extract

Directions:
Mix the flour with the berries, lime zest, and the other ingredients in mixing bowls and whisk well.
Heat up the waffle iron, pour some of the batter into it, and cook for 8 minutes.
Repeat with the rest of the batter and serve.
Per serving: Calories: 290Kcal; Fat: 16g; Carbs: 6g; Protein: 12g

730. Chia and Coconut Cream Chaffles
Preparation time: 10 minutes
Cooking time: 8 minutes
Servings: 3
Ingredients:
- 1 cup almond flour
- 1 cup coconut cream
- 2 tbsp chia seeds

- ¼ cup cream cheese, soft
- ¼ tsp. almond extract
- ½ tsp. baking soda
- 1 and ½ tsp. baking powder
- 2 tbsp Swerve
- 3 eggs
- 3 tbsp coconut oil, melted

Directions:

In a bowl, combine the flour with the cream, cream cheese, and the other ingredients and whisk well.

Pour 1/6 of the batter in your waffle iron, close, and cook for 6 minutes.

Repeat this with the rest of the batter and serve.

Per serving: Calories: 228Kcal; Fat: 11g; Carbs: 3g; Protein: 6g

731. Coconut and Cheese Cream Chaffles

Preparation time: 5 minutes
Cooking time: 8 minutes
Servings: 2
Ingredients:

- 1 cup almond flour
- 3 tbsp tomato passata
- 1 cup cream cheese, soft
- 2 eggs, whisked
- 1 tbsp. stevia
- 1 tsp. avocado oil
- ½ cup coconut cream
- 1 tbsp. coconut butter, melted

Directions:

In a bowl, combine the flour with the passata and the other ingredients and whisk well.

Pour 1/6 of the batter into the heated waffle maker and cook for 8 minutes.

Repeat with the rest of the batter and serve.

Per serving: Calories: 378Kcal; Fat: 26g; Carbs: 2g; Protein: 8g

732. Sweet Cauliflower Chaffles

Preparation time: 5 minutes
Cooking time: 10 minutes
Servings: 2
Ingredients:

- 1 tbsp. coconut oil, melted
- 1 and ½ cups almond milk
- 1 cup cauliflower rice
- 3 tbsp stevia
- ½ cup almond flour
- ½ cup cream cheese, soft
- 2 eggs, whisked
- 1 tsp. vanilla extract
- 1 tsp. baking soda

Directions:

In a bowl, mix the almond milk with the cauliflower rice and the other ingredients and whisk well.

Pour ¼ of the batter into the waffle iron, cook for 8 minutes and transfer to a plate.

Re-do the process with the rest of the batter and serve the chaffles warm.

Per serving: Calories: 240Kcal; Fat: 8g; Carbs: 2g; Protein: 9g

733. Blackberry Sauce Chaffles

Preparation time: 15 minutes
Cooking time: 15 minutes
Servings: 2
Ingredients:

- cooking spray
- 2 cups almond flour
- 2 cups almond milk
- 2 eggs
- 1/3 cup vegetable oil
- 1 tbsp. baking powder
- ½ tsp. salt
- ½ cup mozzarella cheese, shredded

Blackberry Sauce:

- 2 cups fresh blackberries
- 1/3 cup white Swerve
- 1 tbsp. lemon juice

Directions:

Preheat the waffle iron and sprinkle the cooking surface with a cooking spray.

Beat the eggs in a mixing bowl, and add the milk, flour, vegetable oil, baking powder, and salt. Mix well by using an electric mixer until the batter is thoroughly stirred.

Add mozzarella cheese and stir well.

Pour about ¼ cup batter per waffle into the preheated waffle iron and cook according to manufacturers' directions.

In a saucepan over high heat, combine blackberries and cook until cooked through 3 to 4 minutes.

Decrease the heat to medium and add sugar, cornstarch, and lemon juice to blackberries; Cook and stir until the sauce thickens approximately 5 minutes.

Per serving: Calories: 260Kcal; Fat: 15g; Carbs: 1g; Protein: 22g

734. Coconut Oil Chaffles

Preparation time: 10 minutes
Cooking time: 5 minutes
Servings: 1
Ingredients:

- 1 ½ cups almond flour
- 2 tbsp Swerve
- 2 tsp baking powder
- ½ cup mozzarella cheese, shredded
- ½ tsp. salt
- 1 ½ cups almond milk, room temperature
- 1/3 cup virgin coconut oil, melted
- 1 large egg, beaten
- ½ tsp. vanilla extract

Directions:

Preheat your waffle iron.

In a medium-sized bowl, combine the flour, baking powder, sugar, and salt. Stir well until a uniform consistency is achieved.

In the middle of the flour mixture, make a well.

In another bowl, beat the egg, and add coconut oil, milk, vanilla extract, and mozzarella cheese. Mix until homogeneous.

Spoon the egg mixture into the flour mixture well and stir until a uniform consistency is achieved.

Drop some batter into preheated waffle iron and cook until golden and crisp. It will take about 2 to 5 minutes.

Enjoy.

Per serving: Calories: 290Kcal; Fat: 18g; Carbs: 3g; Protein: 21g

735. Garlic Bread Sticks Chaffle

Preparation time: 3 minutes
Cooking time: 7 minutes
Servings: 2
Ingredients:

- 2 medium eggs
- ½ cup of mozzarella cheese grated
- 2 tbsp almond flour
- ½ tsp. garlic powder
- ½ tsp. oregano
- ½ tsp. salt

Toppings:

- 2 tbsp butter, salt-free
- ½ tsp. garlic powder
- ¼ cup mozzarella cheese grated

Directions:
Turn on your waffle maker and graze it slightly.
Beat the egg in a bowl and add the almond flour, garlic powder, mozzarella, oregano, and salt. Mix thoroughly.
Drop the mixture into the waffle maker. Use half of the mixture for a mini waffle maker.
I usually pour my mixture into the center of my waffle maker and sprinkle it gently on the bottom.
Close the lid and cook for about 5 minutes.
Use tongs to remove the cooked waffles and cut each waffle into 4 strips.
Place the sticks on a tray and fire the grill beforehand.
Mix the butter with the paste of garlic and scatter over the ends.
Sprinkle the mozzarella over the sticks chaffles and place them 2-3 minutes under the grill until the cheese melts and bubbles.
Per serving: Calories: 342Kcal; Fat: 26g; Carbs: 3g; Protein: 20g

736. Cream Cheese Mini Chaffles

Preparation time: 5 minutes
Cooking time: 8 minutes
Servings: 4
Ingredients:

- 4 oz. cream cheese
- 4 eggs
- 1 tbsp. butter
- 1 tsp. of vanilla essence
- 1 tbsp. powdered stevia
- 4 tbsp coconut powder
- 1 ½ cup baking powder

Directions:
Add all ingredients to the blender and mix until all ingredients are smooth and smooth for up to about 1 minute. If you don't have a mixer, you need to mix in a small bowl at medium speed for 1-2 minutes.
Make sure that all cream cheese is creamed together so that there are no lumps.
Optional: Add cinnamon flavor.
Preheat iron from waffles.
Oil non-stick cooking spray on the waffle iron
Pour ⅛ into ¼ cup dough for each waffle. Please note that the batter will stretch slightly more than the amount placed on the waffle iron.
Unlike regular waffle recipes with carbohydrates, iron a small amount and drip to the edge after a few minutes.
These are full, so don't be surprised to eat only two of the four waffle squares.
Optional: No sugar in butter top and syrup.
Per serving: Calories: 160Kcal; Fat: 16g; Carbs: 9g; Protein: 7g

737. Jelly Donut Chaffle

Preparation time: 5 minutes
Cooking time: 8 minutes
Servings: 2
Ingredients:

- 2 eggs
- ¼ cup mozzarella cheese shredded
- 2 tsp. cream cheese softening
- 1 tsp. sweetener
- 1 tsp. almond powder
- ½ tsp. baking powder
- 20 drops of glazed donut flavor

Raspberry jelly filling:

- ¼ raspberry cup
- 1 tsp. chia seed
- 1 tsp. confectioners' sugar

Donut Glaze Ingredients:

- 1 tsp. of powdered sweetener
- a few drops of water or cream

Directions:
Create a chaffle.
Mix everything and make the chaffle first.
Cooking for about 2 ½ minutes.
Make a raspberry jelly filling:
Stir in a small pan over medium heat.
Gently mash the raspberry.
Let cool.
Add between layers of chaffle.
Make Donut Glaze:
Stir together in a small dish.
Chaffle drizzle on top.
Per serving: Calories: 310Kcal; Fat: 25g; Carbs: 2g; Protein: 22g

738. Jicama Hash Brown Chaffles

Preparation time: 5 minutes
Cooking time: 8 minutes
Servings: 2
Ingredients:

- 1 large jicama root
- ½ onion chopped
- 2 garlic
- 1 cup halloumi
- 2 eggs
- salt and pepper

Toppings:

- sunny-side-up egg

Directions:
Peel the jicama and shred it with a food processor or a manual vegetable chopper.
Put the shredded jicama in a large colander and sprinkle a couple of tsp. of salt. Mix well, and let it drain for a few minutes.
Squeeze out as much liquid as possible (vital step).
Warm it for about 5-8 minutes into the microwave oven.
Meanwhile, turn on the waffle maker to heat and grease it with cooking spray.
Mix all ingredients together in a medium-sized mixing bowl.
Sprinkle a little cheese on the waffle maker.
Add a quarter of the mixture into the mini waffle maker and sprinkle a little more cheese on the mixture.
Cook for about 4 minutes to achieve the desired crunch.
Top with a sunny-side-up egg and enjoy.
Per serving: Calories: 225Kcal; Fat: 12g; Carbs: 1g; Protein: 17g

739. Chocolate Chips Cake Chaffle

Preparation time: 10 minutes
Cooking time: 5 minutes
Servings: 2
Ingredients:

Cake Layer:
- 1 tsp. butter melted
- 1 tsp. sweetener
- 1 egg yolk
- ⅛ tsp. vanilla essence
- ⅛ tsp. cake batter extract
- 3 tsp. almond flour
- ⅛ tsp. baking powder
- 1 tsp. chocolate chip sugar-free

Whipping Cream Frosting:
- 1 tsp. unflavored gelatin
- 4 tsp. cold water
- 1 cup heavy whipping cream
- 2 tsp. sweetener

Directions:
Mix everything and cook on a mini waffle iron for 4 minutes. Repeat for each layer. I decided to make three.
Whipping cream frosting procedure
Place the beater and mixing bowl in the freezer for about 15 minutes to cool.
Sprinkle gelatin on cold water in a microwave-compatible bowl. Stir and "bloom." This takes about 5 minutes.
Microwave the gelatin mixture for 10 seconds. It becomes liquid. Stir to make sure everything is melted.
In a chilled mixing bowl, start whipping the cream at low speed. Add the confectioners' sugar.
Move faster and observe that good peaks begin to form.
When the whipped cream has peaked, switch to low speed and squirt the melted liquid gelatin mixture slowly. Once in, switch to high speed and continue tapping until a hard peak is reached.
Put it in a piping bag and pipe the cake.
Per serving: Calories: 422Kcal; Fat: 28g; Carbs: 1g; Protein: 2g

740. Colored Chaffle Cake

Preparation time: 10 minutes
Cooking time: 5 minutes
Servings: 2
Ingredients:

- 2 tsp. Dutch-processed cocoa
- 2 tsp. monk fruit confectioners' sugar
- 2 eggs
- 2 drops of optional super drop food coloring
- ¼ tsp. baking powder
- 1 tsp. heavy whipped cream
- 2 tsp. monk fruit confectioners' sugar
- 2 tsp. cream cheese softens, room temperature
- ¼ tsp. transparent vanilla

Directions:
Put the eggs in a small bowl.
Add the remaining ingredients and mix well until smooth and creamy. Put half of the butter in a mini waffle pan and cook for 2 ½ to 3 minutes until completely cooked.
Put the sweetener, cream cheese, and vanilla in separate small pots. Mix the frosting until everything mixes well.
When the waffle cake has completely cooled to room temperature, spread the frosting.
Per serving: Calories: 288Kcal; Fat: 18g; Carbs: 9g; Protein: 7g

741. Marshmallow Chaffles

Preparation time: 5 minutes
Cooking time: 8 minutes
Servings: 1
Ingredients:

- 1 large egg
- ½c. mozzarella shredded
- ½ tsp. of vanilla essence
- 2 tbs swab brown
- ½tbs plantain shell powder
- ¼ tsp. baking powder
- a pinch of pink salt
- 2 tbs keto marshmallow cream fluff recipe

Directions:
Make a batch of keto marshmallow cream fluff.
Whisk the eggs until creamy.
Add vanilla and swirl brown and mix well.
Mix the shredded cheese and mix.
Next, add psyllium husk powder, baking powder, and salt.
Mix until well mixed and let the dough rest for 3-4 minutes; connect the waffle maker to preheat.
Spread ½ batter into the waffle maker and cook for 3-4 minutes
Remove and install the cooling rack.
Cooking the other half of the dough in the same way, remove and let cool.
Once cool, assemble the chaffle with marshmallow fluff and chocolate. Use 2 tbsp marshmallow and bar release chocolate.
Eat as it is, or toast the melted and sticky small sandwich!
Per serving: Calories: 311Kcal; Fat: 16g; Carbs: 12g; Protein: 21g

742. Cap'n Crunch Cereal Cake Chaffle

Preparation time: 5 minutes
Cooking time: 5 minutes
Servings: 1
Ingredients:

- 1 egg
- 2 tbsp almond flour
- ½ tsp. coconut flower
- 1 tbsp. butter
- 1 tbsp. cream cheese
- 20 drop Captain Cereal flavoring
- ¼ tsp. vanilla essence
- ¼ tsp. baking powder
- 1 tbsp. confectionery sweetener
- ⅛ tsp. xanthan gum

Directions:
Preheat mini waffle maker.
Mix or blend all ingredients until smooth and creamy. Let the dough rest for a few minutes until the flour has absorbed the liquid.
Add 2-3 tbsp of batter to the waffle maker and cook for about 2 ½ minutes.
Optional: you can top your chaffles with whipped cream.
Per serving: Calories: 375Kcal; Fat: 31g; Carbs: 4g; Protein: 5g

743. Fried Pickle Chaffle Sticks

Preparation time: 5 minutes
Cooking time: 5 minutes
Servings: 1
Ingredients:

- 1 egg
- ¼ cup pork punk
- ½ cup mozzarella cheese

- 1 tbsp. of pickled juice
- 6-8 thin pickled slices

Directions:
Mix together.
Add a thin layer to the waffle iron.
Suction excess juice from pickles.
Add the pickle slices and then mix another thin layer.
Cook for 4 minutes.
Per serving: Calories: 287Kcal; Fat: 23g; Carbs: 3g; Protein: 22g

744. Tofu and Espresso Chaffles
Preparation time: 10 minutes
Cooking time: 20 minutes
Servings: 4
Ingredients:
- 2 cups almond flour
- 2 tsp cinnamon powder
- 1 tbsp. baking soda
- ½ tsp. vanilla extract
- 11 ounces soft tofu
- ½ cup butter, melted
- 4 tbsp stevia
- 1 tbsp. espresso

Directions:
Mix the flour with baking soda and cinnamon and stir.
In your blender, mix tofu with espresso and the other ingredients, pulse well, add to the flour mix and stir until you obtain a batter.
Heat up the waffle iron, pour 1/4 of the batter, and cook for 6 minutes.
Repeat with the rest of the batter and serve the chaffles cold.
Per serving: Calories: 371Kcal; Fat: 38g; Carbs: 6g; Protein: 21g

745. Cranberry Chaffle
Preparation time: 10 minutes
Cooking time: 10 minutes
Servings: 2
Ingredients:
- 2 cup almond flour
- 2 tsp baking powder
- ¼ cup Swerve
- ¼ cup fat-free Greek yogurt
- ¼ cup coconut butter
- 2 eggs, whisked
- 2 tbsp cream cheese, soft
- ½ cup cranberries
- 1 tsp. vanilla extract

Directions:
In a bowl, combine the flour with the baking powder and the other ingredients and whisk.
Heat up the waffle iron, pour ⅛ of the batter, and cook for 5 minutes.
Repeat with the rest of the batter and serve the chaffles cold.
Per serving: Calories: 134Kcal; Fat: 12g; Carbs: 2g; Protein: 8g

746. Avocado and Fat-Free Yogurt Chaffles
Preparation time: 5 minutes
Cooking time: 5 minutes
Servings: 2
Ingredients:
- 2 cups almond flour
- ½ cup cream cheese, soft
- ½ cup fat-free yogurt
- ½ tsp. baking soda
- 1 tsp. baking powder
- 2 tbsp stevia

- 2 eggs, whisked
- 3 tbsp coconut oil, melted

Directions:
In a bowl, mix the flour with the yogurt and the other ingredients and whisk well.
Pour ¼ of the batter in your waffle iron, close, and cook for 5 minutes.
Repeat this with the rest of the batter and serve your chaffles right away.
Per serving: Calories: 258Kcal; Fat: 26g; Carbs: 3g; Protein: 7g

747. Coconut Oil Chaffles Version 2
Preparation time: 6 minutes
Cooking time: 5 minutes
Servings: 1
Ingredients:
- 1 tbsp. coconut oil, melted
- 1 cup almond flour
- 1 egg, whisked
- 3 tbsp cream cheese, soft
- 1 and ½ cups almond milk
- 3 tbsp stevia
- 2 tbsp pumpkin seeds
- 1 tsp. vanilla extract
- 1 tsp. baking soda

Directions:
In a bowl, mix the melted coconut oil with the flour and the other ingredients and whisk well.
Heat up the waffle iron, pour ¼ of the batter, and cook for 5 minutes.
Repeat with the rest of the batter and serve the chaffles cold.
Per serving: Calories: 102Kcal; Fat: 9g; Carbs: 1g; Protein: 3g

748. Nutmeg Almond Chaffles
Preparation time: 10 minutes
Cooking time: 10 minutes
Servings: 3
Ingredients:
- 1 cup coconut flour
- ½ cup cream cheese, soft
- ½ tsp. nutmeg, ground
- 1 cup almond flour
- 3 eggs, whisked
- ¼ cup almond butter, melted

Directions:
In a bowl, combine the flour with the cream cheese and the other ingredients and whisk.
Heat up the waffle iron, pour 1/6 of the batter, and cook for 7 minutes.
Repeat with the rest of the batter and serve.
Per serving: Calories: 350Kcal; Fat: 16g; Carbs: 9g; Protein: 13g

749. Lime Chaffles
Preparation time: 10 minutes
Cooking time: 10 minutes
Servings: 2
Ingredients:
- 1/3 cup almond butter, melted
- juice and zest of 1 lime
- 1 cup almond flour
- ½ cup almond milk
- 3 tbsp cream cheese, soft
- 1 egg, whisked
- 1 tbsp. stevia
- 1 and ½ tbsp coconut oil

Directions:

In a bowl, combine the almond butter with the lime juice, zest, and the other ingredients, and whisk well.

Heat up the waffle iron, pour 1/6 of the batter inside and cook for 7 minutes.

Repeat with the rest of the batter and serve the chaffles cold.

Per serving: Calories: 283Kcal; Fat: 12g; Carbs: 3g; Protein: 6g

750. Blackberry and Cream Chaffles

Preparation time: 10 minutes
Cooking time: 10 minutes
Servings: 2
Ingredients:

- 1 and ¾ cup almond flour
- zest from 1 lime, grated
- ¼ cup blackberries
- ¼ cup cranberries
- 2 tsp baking powder
- ¼ cup Swerve
- ¼ cup heavy cream
- ¼ cup cream cheese, warm
- 2 eggs, whisked
- 1 tsp. vanilla extract

Directions:

In a bowl, mix the flour with the berries, lime zest, and the other ingredients and whisk well.

Heat up the waffle iron, pour 1/6 of the batter, and cook for 8 minutes.

Repeat the process to create more chaffles and serve.

Per serving: Calories: 264Kcal; Fat: 18g; Carbs: 7g; Protein: 9g

751. Fruity Chaffles

Preparation time: 10 minutes
Cooking time: 10 minutes
Servings: 2
Ingredients:

- ½ cup almond flour
- ½ cup almond milk
- ½ cup coconut flour
- ½ cup cream cheese, soft
- 2 eggs, whisked
- 1 plum, pitted and chopped
- 1 avocado, peeled, pitted, and chopped
- 1 mango, peeled, pitted, and chopped
- ¼ tsp. cinnamon, ground
- ½ tsp. baking powder

Directions:

In your food processor, combine the flour with the milk, cream cheese, and the other ingredients and pulse well.

Heat up the waffle iron over medium-high heat, pour 1/6 of the batter, and cook for 8 minutes.

Repeat with the rest of the batter and serve the chaffles cold.

Per serving: Calories: 168Kcal; Fat: 13g; Carbs: 9g; Protein: 8g

752. Sweet Tomato Chaffles

Preparation time: 5 minutes
Cooking time: 8 minutes
Servings: 2
Ingredients:

- 1 cup almond flour
- 3 tbsp tomato passata
- 1 cup cream cheese, soft
- 2 eggs, whisked
- 1 tbsp. stevia

- 1 tsp. avocado oil
- ½ cup coconut cream
- 1 tbsp. coconut butter, melted

Directions:

In a bowl, combine the flour with the passata and the other ingredients and whisk well.

Pour 1/6 of the batter into the heated waffle maker and cook for 8 minutes.

Repeat with the rest of the batter and serve.

Per serving: Calories: 234Kcal; Fat: 12g; Carbs: 2g; Protein: 6g

753. Milked Chaffles

Preparation time: 5 minutes
Cooking time: 10 minutes
Servings: 2
Ingredients:

- 1 tbsp. coconut oil, melted
- 1 ½ cups almond milk
- 1 cup cauliflower rice
- 3 tbsp stevia
- ½ cup almond flour
- ½ cup cream cheese, soft
- 1 egg, whisked
- 1 tsp. vanilla extract
- 1 tsp. baking soda

Directions:

In a bowl, mix the almond milk with the cauliflower rice and the other ingredients and whisk well.

Pour ¼ of the batter into the waffle iron, cook for 8 minutes and transfer to a plate.

Repeat the steps to create as many chaffle as the mixture allow.

Serve the chaffles warm.

Per serving: Calories: 222Kcal; Fat: 14g; Carbs: 2g; Protein: 9g

754. Mango and Berries Chaffles

Preparation time: 10 minutes
Cooking time: 10 minutes
Servings: 2
Ingredients:

- ½ cup mango, peeled and cubed
- 1 cup blueberries
- 1 cup almond flour
- ½ cup cream cheese, soft
- 2 eggs, whisked
- 1 tbsp. heavy cream
- 1 tsp. baking powder
- 3 tbsp cashew butter

Directions:

In a bowl, combine the mango with the berries and the other ingredients and whisk well.

Pour ¼ of the batter into the waffle iron, cook for 7 minutes and transfer to a plate.

Cook more chaffles using the remaining batter and serve the chaffles warm.

Per serving: Calories: 296Kcal; Fat: 27g; Carbs: 2g; Protein: 6g

755. Spiced Chaffles

Preparation time: 10 minutes
Cooking time: 10 minutes
Servings: 2
Ingredients:

- 1 cup almond flour
- 2 tbsp ghee, melted

- 1 cup almond milk
- ½ cup cream cheese, soft
- 2 eggs, whisked
- 1 tsp. cinnamon powder
- 1 tsp. nutmeg, ground
- 1 tsp. turmeric powder
- 2 tbsp heavy cream

Directions:

In a bowl, combine the flour with the cream cheese and the other ingredients and whisk well.

Pour ¼ of the batter into the waffle iron and cook for 7 minutes.

Cook the other chaffles with the same procedure using the remaining mixture.

Per serving: Calories: 308Kcal; Fat: 12g; Carbs: 5g; Protein: 6g

756. Cashews Chaffles

Preparation time: 10 minutes
Cooking time: 10 minutes
Servings: 2
Ingredients:

- 1 cup coconut milk
- 1 cup almond flour
- ½ cup cashews, soaked for 8 hours in the water and drained
- 2 tbsp lemon juice
- 2 tbsp heavy cream
- 2 eggs, whisked
- 1 tsp. vanilla extract
- 2 tbsp cream cheese, soft
- ½ tsp. baking powder

Directions:

In your food processor, combine the flour with the cashews and the other ingredients and pulse well.

Heat up the waffle iron, pour ¼ of the batter, and cook for 7 minutes.

Repeat the process to create more chaffles and serve them warm.

Per serving: Calories: 448Kcal; Fat: 32g; Carbs: 11g; Protein: 11g

757. Berry and Seeds Chaffles

Preparation time: 10 minutes
Cooking time: 10 minutes
Servings: 2
Ingredients:

- 1 cup blueberries
- 1 cup almond flour
- 1 cup coconut cream
- 3 tbsp cream cheese, soft
- 2 tbsp stevia
- 1 egg, whisked
- 3 tbsp almond milk
- 1 tbsp. hemp seeds
- 1 tbsp. chia seeds

Directions:

In your blender, combine the berries with the cream, flour, and the other ingredients and pulse well.

Heat up the waffle iron, pour half of the batter, and cook for 8 minutes.

Use the remaining mixture for cooking more chaffles and serve them chaffles cold.

Per serving: Calories: 128Kcal; Fat: 8g; Carbs: 1g; Protein: 2g

758. Cinnamon and Macadamia Nuts Chaffles

Preparation time: 10 minutes
Cooking time: 10 minutes
Servings: 1
Ingredients:

- 1 tsp. cinnamon powder
- 1 cup almond flour
- 1 egg, whisked
- ¼ cup macadamia nuts, chopped
- 1 cup almond milk
- 1 tbsp. cream cheese, soft
- 2 tbsp coconut flour
- 1 tsp. almond extract
- ½ tbsp ghee, melted

Directions:

In a bowl, combine the flour with the egg, nuts, and the other ingredients and pulse well.

Heat up the waffle iron, pour ½ of the batter, and cook for 9 minutes.

Repeat with the rest of the batter and serve your chaffles warm.

Per serving: Calories: 368Kcal; Fat: 20g; Carbs: 7g; Protein: 4g

759. Boston Cream Pie Chaffle

Preparation time: 45 minutes
Cooking time: 15 minutes
Servings: 4
Ingredients:

Cake Chaffles:

- 2 eggs
- ¼ cup almond flour
- 1 tsp. coconut flour
- 2 tbsp. melted butter
- 2 tbsp. cream cheese room temp
- 20 drops Boston cream extract
- ½ tsp. vanilla extract
- ½ tsp. baking powder
- 2 tbsp. Swerve confectioners' sugar or monk fruit
- ¼ tsp. xanthan powder

Custard:

- 2 egg yolks
- ½ tbs Swerve confectioners' sugar
- ½ cup heavy whipping cream
- ½ tsp. vanilla extract
- ⅛ tsp. xanthan gum

Ganache:

- 2 tbs heavy whipping cream
- ½ tbs Swerve Confectioners Sweetener
- 2 tbs Unsweetened Baking chocolate bar chopped

Directions:

Combine all the chaffle ingredients.

Preheat and grease your waffle maker and cook your chaffles.

Mix all the cake ingredients in a blender and mix them on high until a uniform consistency of the mixture is achieved.

Bring the heavy whipping cream to a boil on the stovetop.

Meantime whisk the egg yolks in a separate small bowl.

Pour half of the boiling cream into the egg yolks. Make sure you're whisking everything together as you carefully pour in the mixture.

Put the egg and cream mixture again into the stovetop pan with the remaining cream and constantly whisk for another 2-3 minutes.

Remove the custard from the heat and mix in the vanilla and xanthan gum. Then remove it from the heat and leave it aside to cool and thicken.

In a small bowl, combine the ganache ingredients.
Microwave for 20 seconds, stirring halfway through. If necessary, repeat. Take care not to burn the ganache by overheating it. Do it for 20 seconds at a time until it's completely melted.
Assemble the cake and enjoy.
Per serving: Calories: 346Kcal; Fat: 22g; Carbs: 4g; Protein: 7g

760. Almond Joy Cake Chaffle

Preparation time: 30 minutes
Cooking time: 15 minutes
Servings: 2
Ingredients:

- 2 eggs
- 1 ounce cream cheese
- 1 tbsp. almond flour
- 1 tbsp. unsweetened cocoa powder
- 1 tbsp. erythritol sweeteners blends such as Swerve, Pyure or Lakanto
- ½ tsp. vanilla extract
- ¼ tsp. instant coffee powder

Coconut Filling:

- 1 ½ tsp coconut oil melted
- 1 tbsp. heavy cream
- ¼ cup unsweetened finely shredded coconut
- 2 ounces cream cheese
- 1 tbsp. sweetener, your favorite one
- ¼ tsp. vanilla extract
- 14 whole almonds

Directions:
For the Chaffles:
Turn on the waffle maker to heat and grease it with cooking spray.
Combine all the ingredients in a medium-sized bowl, and stir until homogeneous.
Drop half of the mixture into the waffle maker and spread evenly.
Cook it for 4 to 5 minutes, or till it's crispy.
Repeat the process to cook as many chaffles as your batter allow.
For the Filling:
Soften cream to room temperature or warm in the microwave for 10 seconds.
Add all ingredients to a bowl and mix until smooth and well-combined.
Assembly:
Spread half the filling on one chaffle and place 7 almonds evenly on top of the filling.
Repeat with the second chaffle and stack together.
Per serving: Calories: 265Kcal; Fat: 12g; Carbs: 2g; Protein: 9g

761. Vanilla Chaffle Sticks

Preparation time: 10 minutes
Cooking time: 28 minutes
Servings: 2
Ingredients:

- ½ scoop zero-carb protein powder
- 1 cup finely grated mozzarella cheese
- 2 eggs, beaten
- 1 tbsp. erythritol
- ½ tsp. vanilla extract

Directions:
Preheat the waffle iron.
In a medium bowl, mix the protein powder, mozzarella cheese, eggs, erythritol, and vanilla extract until well combined.
Open the iron and pour in a quarter of the batter.
Close the lid and let it cook for about 6 minutes or until golden and crunchy.
Remove the chaffle and set it aside.

Make three more chaffles after and transfer to a plate to cool.
Before enjoying, slice each chaffle into 4 sticks and serve.
Per serving: Calories: 225Kcal; Fat: 9g; Carbs: 3g; Protein: 20g

762. Vanilla Biscuits Chaffles

Preparation time: 13 minutes
Cooking time: 28 minutes
Servings: 2
Ingredients:

- 2 eggs, beaten
- 1 cup finely grated mozzarella cheese
- 2 tbsp. almond flour
- 1 tbsp. unsweetened dark cocoa powder
- 2 tbsp. erythritol
- 1 tbsp. cream cheese, softened
- ½ tsp. vanilla extract

For the glaze:

- 1 tbsp. Swerve confectioners' sugar
- 1 tsp. water

Directions:
Preheat the waffle iron.
In a medium bowl, combine all the ingredients until they are adequately mixed.
Open the iron and pour in a quarter of the batter. Close the iron and cook until crispy, 7 minutes.
Remove the chaffle onto a plate and set it aside.
Make 3 more chaffles with the remaining batter and transfer to a plate to cool.
For the glaze:
In a small bowl, whisk the Swerve confectioners' sugar and water until smooth.
Drizzle a little of the glaze over each chaffle and serve after.
Per serving: Calories: 240Kcal; Fat: 18g; Carbs: 3g; Protein: 20g

763. Keto Churro Sticks Chaffle

Preparation time: 10 minutes
Cooking time: 28 minutes
Servings: 1
Ingredients:

- 1 egg, beaten
- ½ cup finely grated mozzarella cheese
- 2 tbsp. Swerve brown sugar
- ½ tsp. cinnamon powder

Directions:
Preheat the waffle iron.
Combine all the ingredients in a medium-sized bowl until smooth.
Open the iron and pour in a quarter of the mixture.
Cook for about 7 minutes to get the desired crunch.
Remove the chaffle onto a plate and set it aside.
Make 3 more chaffles with the remaining ingredients.
Cut the chaffles into 4 sticks and serve after.
Per serving: Calories: 220Kcal; Fat: 161g; Carbs: 3g; Protein: 20g

764. Chocolate Chips and Butter Chaffles

Preparation time: 10 minutes
Cooking time: 28 minutes
Servings: 1
Ingredients:

- 1 tbsp. coconut butter, melted
- ⅛ tsp. vanilla extract
- 1 tbsp. sugar-free maple syrup
- 1 egg yolk
- ⅛ tsp. baking powder

- 3 tbsp. almond flour
- 1 tbsp. unsweetened chocolate chips

Directions:
Preheat the waffle iron.
Add all the ingredients to a medium bowl and mix well.
Open the iron and pour in a quarter of the mixture. Close the iron and cook until crispy, 7 minutes approximately.
Remove the chaffle onto a plate and set it aside.
Make 3 more chaffles with the remaining batter.
Cut the chaffles into sticks and serve.
Per serving: Calories: 190Kcal; Fat: 9g; Carbs: 1g; Protein: 3g

765. Oven Baked Chaffles

Preparation time: 8 minutes
Cooking time: 5 Minutes
Servings: 2
Ingredients:
- 2 eggs
- 2 cups mozzarella cheese
- ¼ cup almond flour
- 1 tsp. baking powder
- 1 tbsp. coconut oil
- 1 tsp. stevia
- 1 tbsp. coconut cream

Directions:
Preheat oven to 4000 F.
Mix together all ingredients in a bowl.
Pour batter in silicon waffle mold and set it on a baking tray.
Bake chaffles in an oven for about 10-15 minutes.
Once cooked, remove from oven.
Per serving: Calories: 275Kcal; Fat: 9g; Carbs: 3g; Protein: 23g

766. Cream Cinnamon Rolls Chaffles

Preparation time: 10 minutes
Cooking time: 9 Minutes
Servings: 1
Ingredients:
- 1 egg (beaten)
- ½ cup shredded mozzarella cheese
- 1 tsp. cinnamon
- 1 tsp. sugar-free maple syrup
- ¼ tsp. baking powder
- 1 tbsp. almond flour
- ½ tsp. vanilla extract

Toppings:
- 2 tsp. granulated Swerve
- 1 tbsp. heavy cream
- 4 tbsp. cream cheese

Directions:
Plug the waffle maker to preheat it and spray it with a non-stick spray.
In a mixing bowl, whisk together the egg, maple syrup, and vanilla extract.
In another mixing bowl, combine the cinnamon, almond flour, baking powder, and mozzarella cheese.
Pour in the egg mixture into the flour mixture and mix until the ingredients are well combined.
Pour in an appropriate amount of the batter into the waffle maker and spread out the batter to the edges to cover all the holes on the waffle maker.
Close the waffle maker and bake for about 3 minutes or according to your waffle maker's settings.
After the cooking cycle, use a silicone or plastic utensil to remove the chaffle from the waffle maker.
Repeat steps 5 to 7 until you have cooked all the batter into chaffles.

For the topping, combine the cream cheese, Swerve, and heavy cream in a microwave-safe dish. 10. Place the dish in a microwave and microwave on high until the mixture is melted and smooth.
Stir every 15 seconds.
Top the chaffles with the cream mixture and enjoy.
Per serving: Calories: 285Kcal; Fat: 18g; Carbs: 1g; Protein: 22g

767. Buffalo Chicken & Chaffles

Preparation time: 9 minutes
Cooking time: 10 Minutes
Servings: 1
Ingredients:
- 1 egg
- 5 ounces cooked chicken (diced)
- 2 tbsp. buffalo sauce
- ½ tsp. garlic powder
- ½ tsp. onion powder
- ½ tsp. dried basil
- 5 tbsp. shredded cheddar cheese
- 2 ounces cream cheese

Directions:
Plug the waffle maker and preheat it. Spray it with non-stick spray.
In a large mixing bowl, combine the onion powder, basil, garlic, buffalo sauce, cheddar cheese chicken, and cream cheese. Mix until the ingredients are well combined, and you have formed a smooth batter.
Sprinkle some shredded cheddar cheese over the waffle maker and pour in an adequate amount of the batter.
Spread out the batter to the edges of the waffle maker to cover all the holes on the waffle maker.
Close the lid and cook for about 3 to minutes or according to the waffle maker's settings.
After the cooking cycle, remove the chaffle from the waffle maker with a plastic or silicone utensil.
Repeat the process until you have cooked all the batter into chaffles.
Per serving: Calories: 328Kcal; Fat: 26g; Carbs: 1g; Protein: 35g

768. Heavy Cream Blueberry Chaffles

Preparation time: 5 minutes
Cooking time: 5 minutes
Servings: 2
Ingredients:
- ¼ cups frozen blueberries
- 1 tbsp. Swerve
- ½ cup shredded mozzarella cheese
- 1 tbsp. almond flour
- 2 eggs (beaten)
- ½ tsp. ground ginger
- ½ tsp. vanilla extract

Toppings:
- ½ cup heavy cream
- 1 tsp. cinnamon

Directions:
Plug the waffle maker to preheat it and spray it with non-stick spray.
In a large mixing bowl, combine the Swerve, almond flour, and ginger.
Add the egg, vanilla extract, and cheese. Mix until the ingredients are well combined.
Gently fold in the blueberries.
Drop half of the mixture into the waffle maker and spread it out to the edges of the waffle maker to cover all the holes on it.
Cover the lid of the waffle maker and bake for about minutes or according to the waffle maker's settings.
After the cooking cycle, remove the chaffle from the waffle maker using a plastic or silicone utensil.
Repeat the process until you have cooked all the batter into waffles.

Combine the heavy whipping cream and cinnamon in a mixing bowl. Top the chaffle with the heavy cream mixture and serve.

Per serving: Calories: 320Kcal; Fat: 22g; Carbs: 2g; Protein: 14g

769. Chia and Avocado Oil Chaffles

Preparation time: 5 minutes
Cooking time: 5 Minutes
Servings: 1
Ingredients:
- 1 tbsp. chia seeds
- 1 egg
- ½ cup cheddar cheese
- a pinch of salt
- 1 tbsp. avocado oil

Directions:
Heat your nonstick pan over medium heat.
In a small bowl, mix together chia seeds, salt, egg, and cheese together.
Grease pan with avocado oil.
Once the pan is hot, pour 2 tbsp. chaffle batter and cook for about 1-2 minutes Utes.
Flip and cook for another 1-2 minutes.
Once the chaffle is brown, remove it from the pan.
Serve with berries on top and enjoy.

Per serving: Calories: 345Kcal; Fat: 26g; Carbs: 1g; Protein: 20g

770. Bacon Chaffle with Herb Dip

Preparation time: 9 minutes
Cooking time: 10 Minutes
Servings: 1
Ingredients:
Chaffles:
- 1 organic egg, beaten
- ½ cup Swiss cheese blend, shredded
- 2 tbsp cooked bacon pieces
- 1 tbsp. jalapeño pepper, chopped

Sauce:
- ¼ cup heavy cream
- ¼ tsp. fresh dill, minced
- a pinch of ground black pepper

Directions:
Preheat your mini waffle iron and then grease it.
In a medium bowl, put all ingredients and mix well.
Drop half of the mixture into the waffle maker and cook it for about 5 minutes.
Repeat with the remaining mixture.
Meanwhile (for dip), in a bowl, mix together the cream and stevia.
Serve warm chaffles alongside the dip.

Per serving: Calories: 320Kcal; Fat: 32g; Carbs: 8g; Protein: 13g

771. Broccoli Chaffles on Pan

Preparation time: 5 minutes
Cooking time: 5 Minutes
Servings: 2
Ingredients:
- 2 eggs
- 1 cup cheddar cheese
- ½ cup broccoli chopped
- 1 tsp. baking powder
- 1 a pinch garlic powder
- 1 a pinch salt
- 1 a pinch black pepper
- 1 tbsp. coconut oil

Directions:
Heat your nonstick pan over medium heat.
Mix together all ingredients in a bowl.
Grease pan with oil.
Once the pan is hot, pour broccoli and cheese batter on greased pan
Cook for 1-2 minutes Utes.
Flip and cook for another 1-2 minutes Utes.
Once chaffles are brown, remove them from the pan.
Serve with raspberries and melted coconut oil on top.

Per serving: Calories: 300Kcal; Fat: 25g; Carbs: 7g; Protein: 21g

772. Chicken Chaffles with Tzatziki Sauce

Preparation time: 9 minutes
Cooking time: 12 Minutes
Servings: 2
Ingredients:
Chaffles:
- 2 organic eggs, beaten
- 1/3 cup grass-fed cooked chicken, chopped
- 1/3 cup mozzarella cheese, shredded
- ¼ tsp. garlic, minced
- ¼ tsp. dried basil, crushed

Tzatziki:
- ¼ cup plain Greek yogurt
- ½ of small cucumber, peeled, seeded, and chopped
- 1 tsp. olive oil
- ½ tsp. fresh lemon juice
- a pinch of ground black pepper
- ¼ tbsp. fresh dill, chopped
- ½ of garlic clove, peeled

Directions:
Preheat the mini waffle iron and then grease it.
In a medium bowl, put all ingredients, and with your hands, mix until well combined. Place half of the mixture into preheated waffle iron and cook for about 4–6 minutes.
Repeat with the remaining mixture.
Tzatziki: in a food processor, place all the ingredients and pulse until well combined.
Serve warm chaffles alongside the tzatziki.

Per serving: Calories: 395Kcal; Fat: 31g; Carbs: 2g; Protein: 27g

773. Cereal and Walnut Chaffles

Preparation time: 9 minutes
Cooking time: 6 Minutes
Servings: 2
Ingredients:
- 1 milliliter of cereal flavoring
- ¼ tsp. baking powder
- 1 tsp. granulated Swerve
- ⅛ tsp. xanthan gum
- 1 tbsp. butter (melted)
- ½ tsp. coconut flour
- 2 tbsp. toasted walnut (chopped)
- 1 tbsp. cream cheese
- 2 tbsp. almond flour
- 2 large eggs (beaten)
- ¼ tsp. cinnamon
- ⅛ tsp. nutmeg

Directions:
Plug the waffle maker to preheat it and spray it with a non-stick spray.
In a mixing bowl, whisk together the egg, cereal flavoring, cream cheese, and butter.

In another mixing bowl, combine the coconut flour, almond flour, cinnamon, nutmeg, Swerve, xanthan gum, and baking powder.

Pour the egg mixture into the flour mixture and mix until you form a smooth batter.

Fold in the chopped walnuts.

Pour in an appropriate amount of the batter into the waffle maker and spread out the batter to the edges to cover all the holes on the waffle maker.

Close the lid and let it cook for about 4 minutes or until golden and crunchy.

After the cooking cycle, use a plastic or silicone utensil to remove the chaffle from the waffle maker.

Repeat the process until you have cooked all the batter into chaffles.

Serve and top with sour cream or heavy cream.

Per serving: Calories: 215Kcal; Fat: 14g; Carbs: 2g; Protein: 7g

774. Creamy Mini Chaffles

Preparation time: 5 minutes
Cooking time: 10 minutes
Servings: 2
Ingredients:

- 2 eggs
- 1 cup shredded mozzarella
- 2 tbsp. cream cheese
- 2 tbsp. almond flour
- ¾ tbsp. baking powder
- 2 tbsp. water

Directions:
Preheat your mini waffle iron if needed.
Combine all the ingredients in a medium-sized bowl.
Grease your waffle iron lightly.
Cooking in your mini waffle iron for at least 4 minutes or till the desired crisp is achieved and serve hot.
Cook as many chaffle as you can with the remaining batter.
Per serving: Calories: 270Kcal; Fat: 21g; Carbs: 8g; Protein: 21g

775. Deli Jalapeño Cheddar Chaffles

Preparation time: 4 minutes
Cooking time: 10 minutes
Servings: 2
Ingredients:

- 2 eggs
- 1½ cup cheddar cheese
- 16 slices deli jalapeño

Directions:
Preheat a mini waffle maker if needed.
In a mixing bowl, beat eggs and add half cheddar cheese to them.
Mix them all well.
Shred some of the remaining cheddar cheese to the lower plate of the waffle maker.
Now pour the mixture into the shredded cheese.
Add the cheese again on the top with around 4 slices of jalapeño and close the lid.
Cook for at least 4 minutes to get the desired crunch and serve hot.
Make as many chaffles as your mixture allows.
Per serving: Calories: 364Kcal; Fat: 34g; Carbs: 1g; Protein: 26g

776. Coconut Crispy Chaffles

Preparation time: 5 minutes
Cooking time: 20 minutes
Servings: 2
Ingredients:

- 1/3 cup cheddar cheese
- 2 eggs
- 2 tbsp. coconut flour
- ¼ tsp. baking powder
- 2 tbsp. coconut flakes
- 1/3 cup mozzarella cheese

Directions:
Mix cheddar cheese, egg, coconut flour, coconut flakes, and baking powder together in a bowl.
Preheat your waffle iron and grease it.
In your mini waffle iron, shred half of the mozzarella cheese.
Add the mixture to your mini waffle iron.
Again, shred the remaining mozzarella cheese on the mixture.
Cooking till the desired crisp is achieved.
Make as many chaffles as your mixture allow.
Per serving: Calories: 294Kcal; Fat: 20g; Carbs: 5g; Protein: 23g

777. Simple and Crispy Parmesan Chaffles

Preparation time: 5 minutes
Cooking time: 10 minutes
Servings: 2
Ingredients:

- 1/3 cup cheddar cheese
- 2 eggs
- ¼ tsp. baking powder
- 1 tsp. flaxseed (ground)
- 1/3 cup parmesan cheese

Directions:
Mix the cheddar cheese, eggs, baking powder, and flaxseed in a bowl.
Grease your waffle iron lightly.
In your mini waffle iron, shred half of the parmesan cheese.
Add the chaffle mixture to your mini waffle iron.
Again, shred the remaining parmesan cheese on the mixture.
Cooking till the desired crisp is achieved.
Repeat the process with the remaining batter to create more chaffles.
Per serving: Calories: 294Kcal; Fat: 18g; Carbs: 1g; Protein: 21g

778. Yogurt Parmesan Chaffles

Preparation time: 5 minutes
Cooking time: 10 minutes
Servings: 2
Ingredients:

- 1/3 cup cheddar cheese
- 2 eggs
- ¼ tbsp. baking powder
- 2 tbsp. yogurt
- 1/3 cup parmesan cheese

Directions:
Mix cheddar cheese, egg, yogurt, and baking powder together.
Preheat your waffle iron and grease it.
In your mini waffle iron, shred half of the parmesan cheese.
Add the mixture to your mini waffle iron.
Again, shred the remaining parmesan cheese on the mixtures.
Cooking till the desired crisp is achieved.
Cook as many chaffles as your batter allow.
Per serving: Calories: 315Kcal; Fat: 18g; Carbs: 2g; Protein: 23g

779. Almonds and Coconut Chaffles

Preparation time: 15 minutes
Cooking time: 20 minutes
Servings: 2
Ingredients:

- 1/3 cup cheddar cheese
- 2 eggs
- 3 tbsp. almond flour
- 2 tbsp. coconut flakes

- ¼ tsp. baking powder
- 2 tbsp. ground almonds
- 1/3 cup mozzarella cheese

Directions:
Mix cheddar cheese, egg, almond flour, almond ground, coconut flakes, and baking powder together in a bowl.
Preheat your waffle iron and grease it.
In your mini waffle iron, shred half of the mozzarella cheese.
Add the mixture to your mini waffle iron.
Again, shred the remaining mozzarella cheese on the mixture.
Cooking till the desired crisp is achieved.
Repeat the process with the remaining batter to create more chaffles.
Per serving: Calories: 375Kcal; Fat: 18g; Carbs: 3g; Protein: 22g

780. Creamy Jalapeño Mini Chaffles

Preparation time: 5 minutes
Cooking time: 10 minutes
Servings: 2
Ingredients:
- 2 eggs
- 1 cup shredded mozzarella
- 16 slices deli jalapeño
- 2 tbsp. cream cheese
- 2 tbsp. almond flour
- ¾ tbsp. baking powder
- 2 tbsp. water

Directions:
Preheat your mini waffle iron if needed.
Combine all the chaffles ingredients in a mixing bowl. Stir well.
Grease your waffle iron lightly.
Adds the mixture to the waffle iron and add at least 4 jalapeños on top.
Close the lid and cook for 4-minutes.
Cook more chaffles using the remaining batter.
Per serving: Calories: 276Kcal; Fat: 21g; Carbs: 3g; Protein: 21g

781. Bacon Swiss Cheese Chaffles

Preparation time: 5 minutes
Cooking time: 10 minutes
Servings: 1
Ingredients:
- bacon bites, as per your taste
- 1 egg
- ½ cup Swiss cheese

Directions:
Preheat your waffle iron if needed.
Mix all the ingredients in a bowl.
Grease your waffle iron lightly.
Cooking for about 5 minutes or till the desired crisp is achieved.
Cook the second chaffle using the remaining batter.
Per serving: Calories: 278Kcal; Fat: 23g; Carbs: 3g; Protein: 21g

782. Double Cheddar Chaffles

Preparation time: 5 minutes
Cooking time: 20 minutes
Servings: 1
Ingredients:
- 1 egg
- ½ cup cheddar cheese
- ½ tsp. butter
- 1 cheddar cheese slices

Directions:
Preheat your waffle iron if needed.
Mix the egg and cheddar cheese. Whisk well.
Grease your waffle iron lightly.

Cooking in the waffle iron for about 5 minutes or till the desired crisp is achieved.
Cook the second chaffle with the same procedure.
Heat the pan and grease with butter.
Place one chaffle on the pan and top with the slice, and then add another chaffle.
Grill this chaffle sandwich from both sides and serve hot.
Per serving: Calories: 398Kcal; Fat: 30g; Carbs: 1g; Protein: 23g

783. Eggplant Cheddar Chaffles

Preparation time: 10 minutes
Cooking time: 30 minutes
Servings: 1
Ingredients:
- 1 medium-sized eggplant
- 1 egg
- 1½ cup cheddar cheese

Directions:
Boil eggplant in water for 15 minutes.
Remove from water and blend to make a mixture.
Preheat your waffle iron.
Mix the egg and cheddar cheese in a bowl. Add the eggplants and mix well again.
Grease your waffle iron lightly.
Cook the mixture in the waffle iron for about 5 minutes or till the desired crisp is achieved.
Cook the other chaffle with the same procedure, using the remaining mixture.
Per serving: Calories: 335Kcal; Fat: 25g; Carbs: 1g; Protein: 20g

784. Seasoned Mushrooms Chaffles

Preparation time: 5 minutes
Cooking time: 15 minutes
Servings: 2
Ingredients:
- 1 egg
- ½ cup shredded mozzarella cheese
- 1 tbsp. Chinese five-spice
- 1 cup finely sliced mushrooms
- 1 clove minced garlic
- 1 tbsp. onion powder
- salt, as you taste

Directions:
Warm your mini waffle maker and grease it if needed.
Combine all the ingredients together and whisk well.
Fill the waffle maker with half of the batter and close the lid. Cook at least for 4 minutes.
Cook the second chaffle.
Per serving: Calories: 255Kcal; Fat: 16g; Carbs: 2g; Protein: 22g

785. Spicy Chaffles with Special Sauce

Preparation time: 5 minutes
Cooking time: 10 minutes
Servings: 1
Ingredients:
- 1 egg
- ½ cup shredded mozzarella cheese
- ½ tsp. dried basil
- ½ tsp. smoked paprika
- salt, as you taste

For the Sauce:
- ¼ cup mayonnaise
- 1 tsp. vinegar

- 3 tbsp. sweet chili sauce
- 1 tbsp. hot sauce

Directions:
Add egg, dried basil, smoked paprika, salt, and cheese in a bowl and whisk well.
Warm your waffle maker and grease it if needed.
Cook your mixture in the mini waffle iron for at least 4 minutes.
Make as many chaffles as you can.
Combine the sauce ingredient well together.
Serve spicy chaffles with the sauce.
Per serving: Calories: 263Kcal; Fat: 18g; Carbs: 2g; Protein: 20g

786. Garlic Swiss Chaffles

Preparation time: 5 minutes
Cooking time: 10 minutes
Servings: 1
Ingredients:

- 1 egg
- ½ cup shredded Swiss cheese
- 2 finely chopped garlic cloves
- 1 tsp. garlic salt

Directions:
Warm up your waffle maker and grease it.
Add egg, cheese, garlic salt, and garlic in a bowl and whisk.
Cook your mixture in the mini waffle iron for at least 4 minutes.
Repeat with the second chaffle if you are using a mini waffle maker.
Per serving: Calories: 255Kcal; Fat: 20g; Carbs: 4g; Protein: 19g

787. Cheddar and Parmesan Chaffles with Bacon

Preparation time: 5 minutes
Cooking time: 10 minutes
Servings: 1
Ingredients:

- 1/3 cup cheddar cheese
- 1 egg
- ¼ tsp. baking powder
- 1 tsp. (ground) flaxseed
- 1/3 cup parmesan cheese
- 2 tbsp. bacon piece

Directions:
Cooking the bacon pieces separately in the pan.
Mix cheddar cheese, egg, baking powder, and flaxseed to it.
In your mini waffle iron, shred half of the parmesan cheese.
Grease your waffle iron lightly.
Add the mixture from step one to your mini waffle iron.
Again, shred the remaining cheddar cheese on the mixtures.
Cooking till the desired crisp is achieved.
Repeat the previous steps to cook the second chaffle.
Per serving: Calories: 315Kcal; Fat: 20g; Carbs: 1g; Protein: 21g

788. Crispy Almonds Chaffles

Preparation time: 15 minutes
Cooking time: 20 minutes
Servings: 1
Ingredients:

- 1/3 cup cheddar cheese
- 1 egg
- 2 tbsp. almond flour
- ¼ tsp. baking powder
- 2 tbsp. ground almonds
- 1/3 cup mozzarella cheese

Directions:
Mix cheddar cheese, egg, almond flour, almond ground, and baking powder together in a bowl.
Preheat your waffle iron and grease it.
In your mini waffle iron, shred half of the mozzarella cheese.
Add the mixture to your mini waffle iron.
Again, shred the remaining mozzarella cheese on the mixture.
Cooking till the desired crisp is achieved.
Make another chaffle by following the same process.
Per serving: Calories: 334Kcal; Fat: 24g; Carbs: 5g; Protein: 25g

789. Olives Layered Chaffle

Preparation time: 15 minutes
Cooking time: 20 minutes
Servings: 2
Ingredients:
Chaffles:

- 2 eggs
- 1 cup mozzarella cheese (shredded)
- ½ tsp. garlic powder
- 1 tsp. Italian seasoning

Vegetables:

- 1 cup mushrooms
- ½ tsp. garlic powder
- ½ tsp. Italian seasoning
- 1 tbsp. butter

For Layering:

- ½ cup mozzarella cheese (shredded)
- ½ cup olives
- 1 tbsp. parsley
- 1 tbsp. oregano

Directions:
Plug in your waffle maker to preheat it and grease it.
In a medium-sized bowl, add all the ingredients of the chaffle and stir well.
Pour the mixture into the waffle maker.
Cook for about 4-5 minutes or until it reaches the desired doneness.
Make as many chaffles as your batter allows.
In the meanwhile, melt butter and add all mushrooms ingredients and cooking.
Remove the chaffles from the heat and spread them on the baking sheet.
Spread the cooked mushrooms on the top and sprinkle cheese and olives.
Top again with chaffles, then mushrooms, then cheese and olives, then again chaffles, and make as many layers as you want using this layering technique.
Bake for 5 minutes in an oven at 350 degrees to melt the cheese.
Sprinkle parsley and oregano on the top and serve hot.
Per serving: Calories: 357Kcal; Fat: 27g; Carbs: 4g; Protein: 28g

790. Cin-Cheese Chaffles with Sauce

Preparation time: 5 minutes
Cooking time: 15 minutes
Servings: 1
Ingredients:
Chaffles:

- 1 egg
- ½ cup mozzarella cheese (shredded)
- ½ tsp. cinnamon

Sauce:

- ¼ cup mayonnaise
- 1 tsp. vinegar

- 3 tbsp. sweet chili sauce
- 1 tbsp. hot sauce

Directions:

Add egg, cinnamon, and cheese in a mixing bowl and whisk well.

Grease your waffle maker and preheat it.

Cook your mixture in the mini waffle iron for at least 4 minutes.

Make as many chaffles as you can.

Combine the sauce ingredient well together and serve with chaffles.

Per serving: Calories: 272Kcal; Fat: 19g; Carbs: 8g; Protein: 20g

791. Fried Pickle Chaffles

Preparation time: 5 minutes
Cooking time: 10 minutes
Servings: 1
Ingredients:
- 1 egg
- ½ cup mozzarella cheese (shredded)
- ½ cup pork panko
- 6-8 thin pickle slices
- 1 tbsp. pickle juice

Directions:

Mix all the ingredients well together.

Pour a thin layer on a preheated waffle iron.

Remove any excess juice from pickles.

Add pickle slices and pour more mixture over the top again.

Cooking the chaffle for around 5 minutes.

Make as many chaffles as your mixture allow.

Per serving: Calories: 229Kcal; Fat: 17g; Carbs: 2g; Protein: 22g

792. BBQ Crispy Chaffles

Preparation time: 5 minutes
Cooking time: 10 minutes
Servings: 1
Ingredients:
- 1/3 cup cheddar cheese
- 1 egg
- 1 tbsp. BBQ sauce
- ¼ tsp. baking powder
- 1 tsp. flaxseed (ground)
- 1/3 cup parmesan cheese

Directions:

Grease your mini waffle maker and preheat it.

Mix cheddar cheese, egg, baking powder, BBQ sauce, and flaxseed.

In your mini waffle maker, shred half of the parmesan cheese.

Grease your waffle iron lightly.

Add the cheese mixture to the mini waffle iron.

Again, shred the remaining parmesan cheese on the mixture.

Cooking till the desired crisp is achieved.

Cook the second chaffle and enjoy.

Per serving: Calories: 318Kcal; Fat: 19g; Carbs: 1g; Protein: 19g

793. Coconut Flour Bagel Chaffle

Preparation time: 5 minutes
Cooking time: 10 minutes
Servings: 1
Ingredients:
- 1 egg
- ½ cup mozzarella cheese
- 1 tsp. coconut flour
- 1 tsp. everything bagel seasoning
- 1 tbsp. cream cheese (for serving)

Directions:

Turn on your mini waffle maker to heat and grease it with cooking spray.

Combine all the ingredients in a small-sized bowl and mix well.

Fill the waffle maker with half of the batter and close the lid. Let it cook for about 4 minutes

Make the second chaffle and serve with cream cheese on top.

Per serving: Calories: 270Kcal; Fat: 21g; Carbs: 6g; Protein: 20g

794. Celery and Cottage Cheese Chaffles

Preparation time: 9 minutes
Cooking time: 15 Minutes
Servings: 4
Ingredients:

Batter:
- 4 eggs
- 2 cups grated cheddar cheese
- 1 cup fresh celery, chopped
- salt and pepper to taste
- 2 tbsp chopped almonds
- 2 tsp baking powder

Other:
- 2 tbsp cooking spray to brush the waffle maker
- ¼ cup cottage cheese for serving

Directions:

Preheat the waffle maker.

Add the eggs, grated mozzarella cheese, chopped celery, salt and pepper, almonds, and baking powder to a bowl. Mix well with a fork.

Use a cooking spray to grease the maker and add a few tbsp of the batter.

Add about 3 tbsp. of the mixture into the preheated waffle iron and close the lid.

Let it cook for about 6-7 minutes, depending on your waffle maker.

Cook as many chaffle as you can with the remaining batter.

Serve each chaffle with cottage cheese on top.

Per serving: Calories: 353Kcal; Fat: 28g; Carbs: 1g; Protein: 27g

795. Sour Cream Protein Chaffles

Preparation time: 5 minutes
Cooking time: 8 Minutes
Servings: 1
Ingredients:
- 1 egg (beaten)
- ½ cup whey protein powder
- a pinch of salt
- 1 tsp. baking powder
- 3 tbsp. sour cream
- ½ tsp. vanilla extract

Toppings:
- 1 tbsp. heavy cream
- 1 tbsp. granulated Swerve

Directions:

Plug the waffle maker to preheat it and spray it with a non-stick cooking spray.

In a mixing bowl, whisk together the egg, vanilla, and sour cream.

In another mixing bowl, combine the protein powder, baking powder, and salt.

Spoon the flour mixture into the egg mixture and mix until the ingredients are well combined, and you form a smooth batter.

Pour an appropriate amount of the batter into the waffle maker and spread the batter to the edges to cover all the holes on the waffle maker.

Close the lid and let it cook for about 4 minutes or according to your waffle maker's settings.

After the cooking cycle, use a plastic or silicone utensil to remove the chaffle from the waffle iron.

Repeat the process to transform all the batter into chaffles.

For the topping, whisk together the cream and Swerve in a mixing bowl until smooth and fluffy.

Top the chaffles with the cream and enjoy.

Per serving: Calories: 190Kcal; Fat: 11g; Carbs: 1g; Protein: 5g

796. Garlic Mayo Vegan Chaffles

Preparation time: 8 minutes
Servings: 2
Cooking time: 5minutes
Ingredients:

- 1 tbsp. chia seeds
- 2 ½ tbsp. water
- ¼ cup low carb vegan cheese
- 2 tbsp. coconut flour
- 1 cup low carb vegan cream cheese, softened
- 1 tsp. garlic powder
- a pinch of salt
- 2 tbsp. vegan garlic mayo for topping

Directions:

Preheat your square waffle maker.

In a small bowl, mix chia seeds and water, let it stand for 5 minutes Utes.

Add all ingredients to the chia seeds mixture and mix well.

Pour vegan chaffle batter in a greased waffle maker.

Close the lid and let it cook for about 4 minutes or until golden and crunchy.

Once chaffles are cooked, remove them from the maker.

Top with garlic mayo and pepper.

Per serving: Calories: 88Kcal; Fat: 7g; Carbs: 2g; Protein: 3g

797. Chili Broccoli Chaffles

Preparation time: 10 minutes
Servings: 4
Cooking time: 15 Minutes
Ingredients:

- 4 eggs
- 2 cups grated mozzarella cheese
- 1 cup steamed broccoli, chopped
- salt and pepper to taste
- 1 clove garlic, minced
- 1 tsp. chili flakes
- 2 tbsp almond flour
- 2 tsp baking powder
- 2 tbsp cooking spray to brush the waffle maker
- ¼ cup mascarpone cheese for serving

Directions:

Preheat the waffle maker.

Add the eggs, grated mozzarella, chopped broccoli, salt and pepper, minced garlic, chili flakes, almond flour, and baking powder to a bowl. Mix with a fork.

Grease the heated waffle maker with cooking spray and add a few tbsp of the batter.

Close the lid and cook for about 3 minutes, depending on your waffle maker.

Serve each chaffle with mascarpone cheese.

Per serving: Calories: 280Kcal; Fat: 23g; Carbs: 3g; Protein: 21g

798. Mozzarella and Lettuce Sandwich Chaffle

Preparation time: 9 minutes
Cooking time: 5 Minutes
Servings: 1

Ingredients:

- 1 large egg
- 1 tbsp. almond flour
- 1 tbsp. full-fat Greek yogurt
- ⅛ tsp. baking powder
- ¼ cup shredded Swiss cheese
- 4 lettuce leaves
- ¼ cup shredded mozzarella

Directions:

Switch on your waffle maker.

Grease it with cooking spray.

Mix together egg, almond flour, yogurts, baking powder, and cheese in a mixing bowl.

Pour ½ cup of the batter into the center of your waffle iron and close the lid.

Cook chaffles for about 2-3 minutes Utes until cooked through.

Repeat with remaining batter

Once cooked, carefully transfer to plate. Serve lettuce leaves between 2 chaffles.

Per serving: Calories: 292Kcal; Fat: 17g; Carbs: 3; Protein: 22g

799. Cocoa Chaffles with Coconut Cream

Preparation time: 9 minutes
Cooking time: 5 Minutes
Servings: 1
Ingredients:

- 1 egg
- ½ cup mozzarella cheese
- 1 tsp. stevia
- 1 tsp. vanilla
- 2 tbsp. almond flour
- 1 tbsp. sugar-free chocolate chips
- 2 tbsp. cocoa powder

Toppings:

- 1 scoop coconut cream
- 1 tbsp. coconut flour

Directions:

Mix together chaffle ingredients in a bowl and mix well.

Preheat your dash minutes waffle maker. Spray waffle maker with cooking spray.

Pour ½ batter into the minutes-waffle maker and close the lid.

Cook chaffles for about 2-minutes, and remove them from the maker.

Make chaffles from the rest of the batter.

Serve with a scoop of coconut cream between two chaffles.

Drizzle coconut flour on top.

Per serving: Calories: 237Kcal; Fat: 17g; Carbs: 7g; Protein: 20g

800. Almond Flour Garlic Bread Chaffle

Preparation time: 10 minutes
Cooking time: 11 minutes
Servings: 1
Ingredients:

- ½ cup shredded mozzarella cheese
- 1 egg
- ½ tsp. basil
- ⅛ tsp. garlic powder
- 1 tbsp. almond flour
- 1 tbsp. butter
- ¼ tsp. garlic powder
- ¼ cup shredded mozzarella cheese

Directions:

Heat up your Mini Dash waffle maker.

In a small bowl, mix the egg, ½ tsp. of basil, ¼ tsp. of garlic powder, 1 tbsp. of almond flour and ½ cup of mozzarella cheese.

Fill the waffle maker with half of the batter and close the lid. Let it cook for about 3-4 minutes or until golden brown.

If it is not well cooked, let it cook for another 2 minutes.

Re-do the process with the remaining batter to create the second chaffle.

In a small bowl, add 1 tbsp. of butter and ¼ tsp. of garlic powder and melt it in the microwave for about 20-30 seconds, depending on your microwave.

Place the chaffles on a baking tray and spread the butter and garlic mixture over the top.

Add ⅛ cup of cheese on top of each chaffle.

Put the chaffles in the oven or a toaster oven at 400°F and cook until the cheese is melted.

Per serving: Calories: 390Kcal; Fat: 22g; Carbs: 2g; Protein: 21g

Conclusion

The keto food plan is a low-carb diet designed to place the human frame into a heightened ketogenic state, which might inevitably result in higher-pronounced fat burn and weight loss. It is a reasonably accessible food regimen with a variety of keto-friendly meals being readily available in marketplaces at very low prices. It isn't an eating regimen reserved most effectively for the affluent and elite.

A keto diet is healthy and helpful to your wellbeing and weight reduction if you are very diligent and conscious of it. The best way to monitor your keto commitment is to use a diet-tracking app, where you will easily set the target amount of macronutrients/macro breakdown (on keto, it would most definitely be 75% fat, 5% carbohydrates, and 20% protein) and check the labels of the food you choose to consume.

Over everything, as for any transition to lifestyle, allow yourself some time to acclimate. You'll see some fast changes almost instantly, but to hold the weight off, you'll have to stay with the plan, even if improvement slows down a little. Slowing down does not mean the new diet has stopped working; it just means that the body is actually adjusting itself to meet the new diet. Weight reduction, or something like losing the unnecessary excess weight, is just a side result of a healthy, better lifestyle that can support you in the long run and not only in the short term.

Keto chaffles are a delicious alternative to traditional pancakes and waffles, and they fit perfectly with low-carb diets. These chaffles are made with egg and cheese, and the result is a fluffy waffle with a perfect texture which have nearly zero carbohydrates. They are the perfect substitutes for bread, pizza, sandwiches, burgers, and other foods, especially fast food, rich in carbohydrates, that many people love to eat.

Chaffle is a very well-established and popular technique to hold people on board, and they are more durable and better than most forms of keto bread. No matter what high-carb diet you may be desirous of, a non-stick waffle maker is something that makes life easier, and it's a trade-off that's happy to embrace for our wellbeing.

Depending on which cheese you choose, the carbs and net calorie number can shift a little bit. However, in general, whether you use real, whole milk cheese, chaffles are completely carb-free or so.

Chaffles are very simple to make even if you don't have a waffle maker; just cook the mixture like a pancake in a frying pan, or even cooler, in a fryer-pan. They won't get all the fluffy sides to achieve like you're using a waffle maker, but they're definitely going to taste great.

Finally, they are convenient for prep-ahead meals. And we know how prepping meals aids with effective keto dieting. Chaffles can be frozen for later use, and they taste excellent when warmed and enjoyed later.

Once you are hooked on chaffles, they will become a crucial part of your feeding because of the benefits that they bring.

I have been making them continuously for weeks, and I can't imagine my meals without them anymore.

Recipe Index

97566379R10109

Made in the USA
Monee, IL,
06 June 2022